Shojo Beat

Cain Saga

the seal of the red ram — Part 2

Earl Cain Series 4

Story & Art by **Kaori Yuki**

Read Kaori Yuki's entire
Earl Cain Series

Series 1:
The Cain Saga: Forgotten Juliet

Series 2:
The Cain Saga: The Sound of a Boy Hatching

Series 3:
The Cain Saga: Kafka

Series 4:
The Cain Saga: The Seal of the Red Ram, Parts 1 & 2

Series 5:
Godchild, Volumes 1-8

W hat you're holding in your angry little hands is indeed the last volume of *The Cain Saga*. But it is by no means the last you'll see of Earl Cain C. Hargreaves. *The Cain Saga* is only the beginning. Now you've got eight volumes of *Godchild* to dive into to find out what happens to Cain, Mary, Riff, Alexis and all the rest!

And, if you've already read *Godchild* – don't worry still. You've got almost twenty volumes of *Angel Sanctuary* for that necessary Kaori Yuki fix. Plus, a few new surprises coming soon! For now, turn the lights down low, cue the dark tunes, and immerse yourself in the not-so-final conclusion to "The Seal of the Red Ram."

Enjoy,
Joel Enos
Editor
Earl Cain Series

Contents

The Seal of the Red Ram, Part 2 ✻✻✻✻ 5
Elizabeth in the Mirror ✻✻✻✻✻✻✻✻✻✻✻✻✻✻✻✻✻✻✻✻✻162
Postscript ✻✻✻✻✻✻✻✻✻✻✻✻✻✻✻✻✻✻✻✻✻✻✻✻✻✻✻✻✻✻✻✻✻195

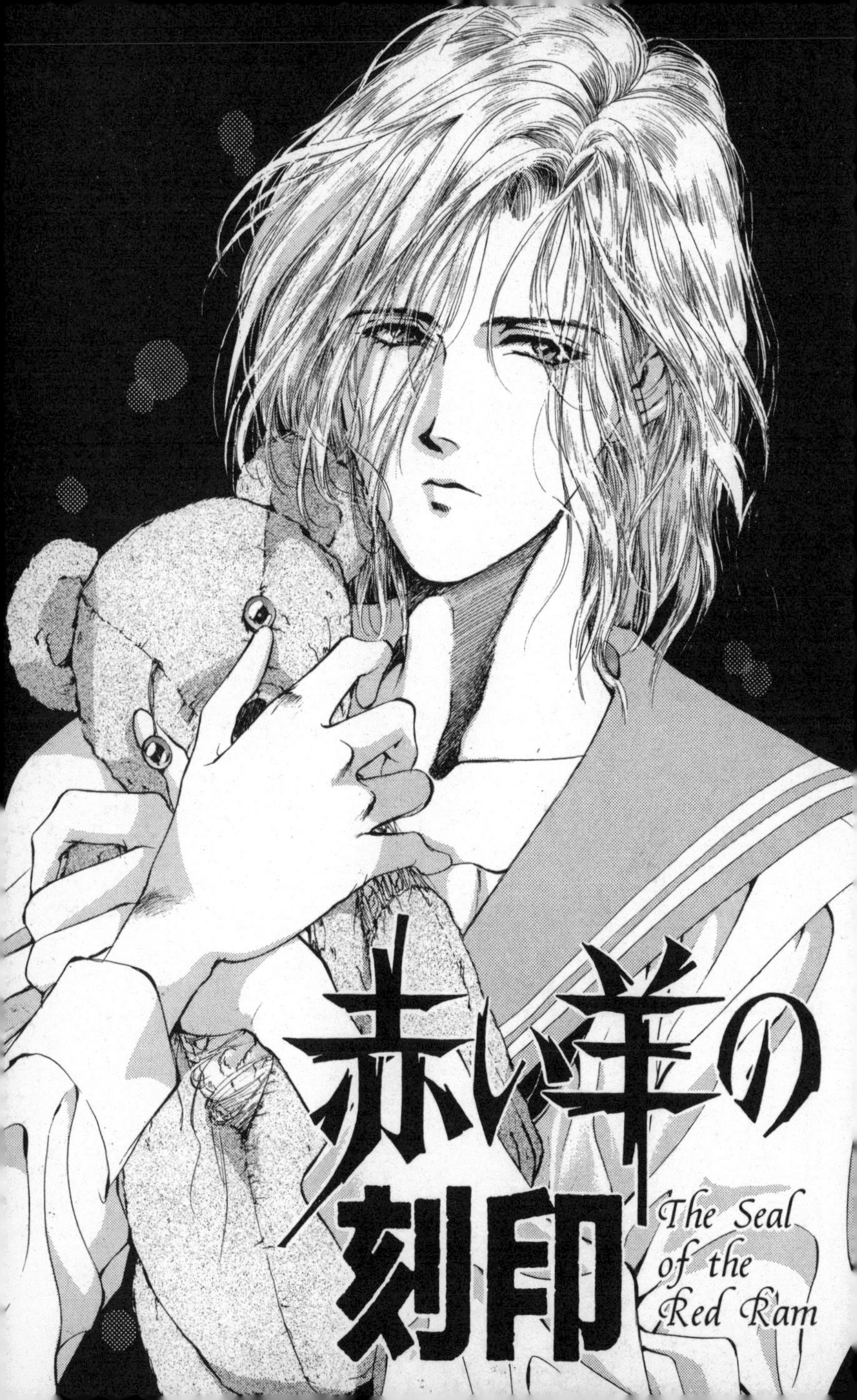
赤い羊の刻印
The Seal of the Red Ram

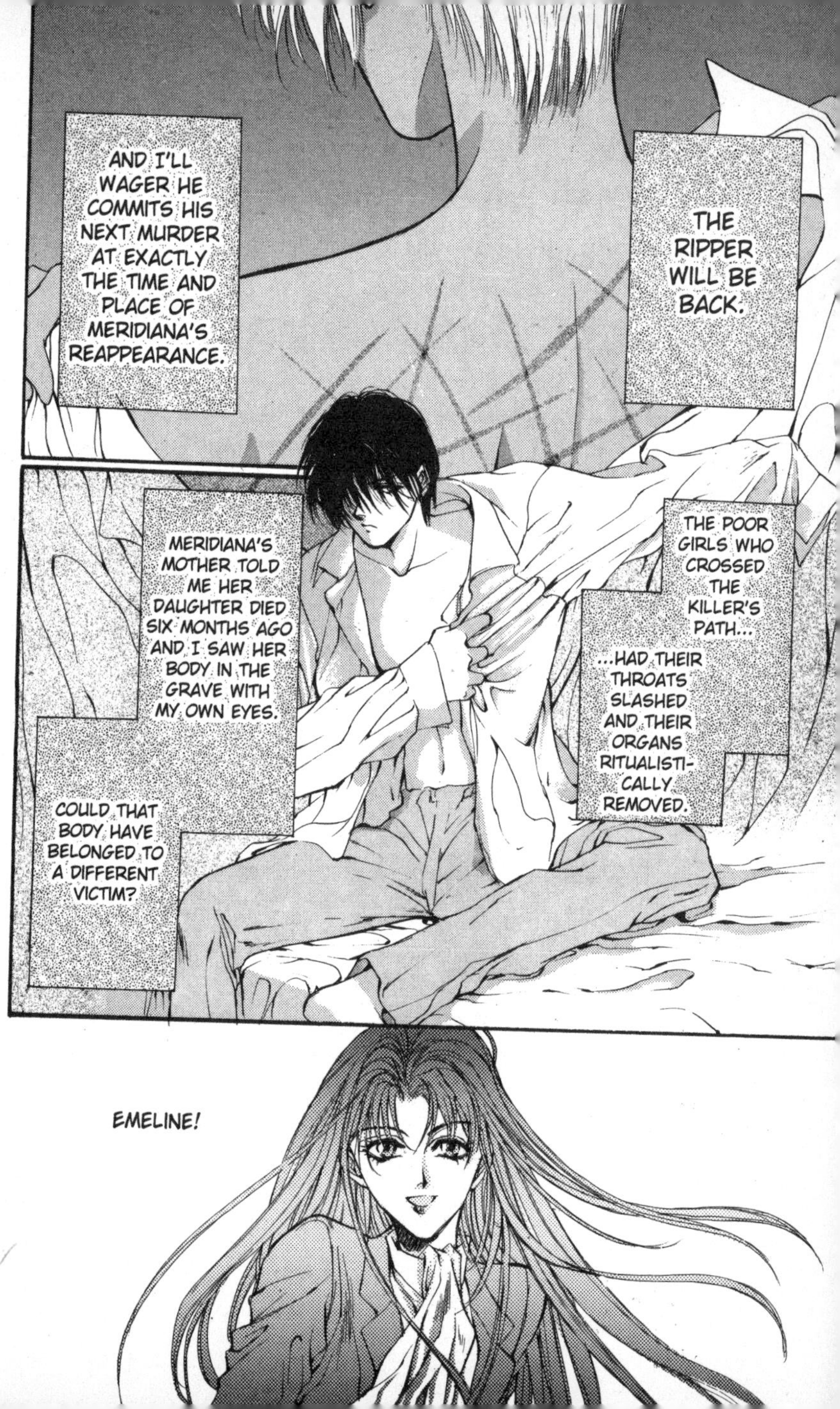
THE RIPPER WILL BE BACK.
AND I'LL WAGER HE COMMITS HIS NEXT MURDER AT EXACTLY THE TIME AND PLACE OF MERIDIANA'S REAPPEARANCE.
THE POOR GIRLS WHO CROSSED THE KILLER'S PATH...
...HAD THEIR THROATS SLASHED AND THEIR ORGANS RITUALISTI-CALLY REMOVED.
MERIDIANA'S MOTHER TOLD ME HER DAUGHTER DIED SIX MONTHS AGO AND I SAW HER BODY IN THE GRAVE WITH MY OWN EYES.
COULD THAT BODY HAVE BELONGED TO A DIFFERENT VICTIM?
EMELINE!

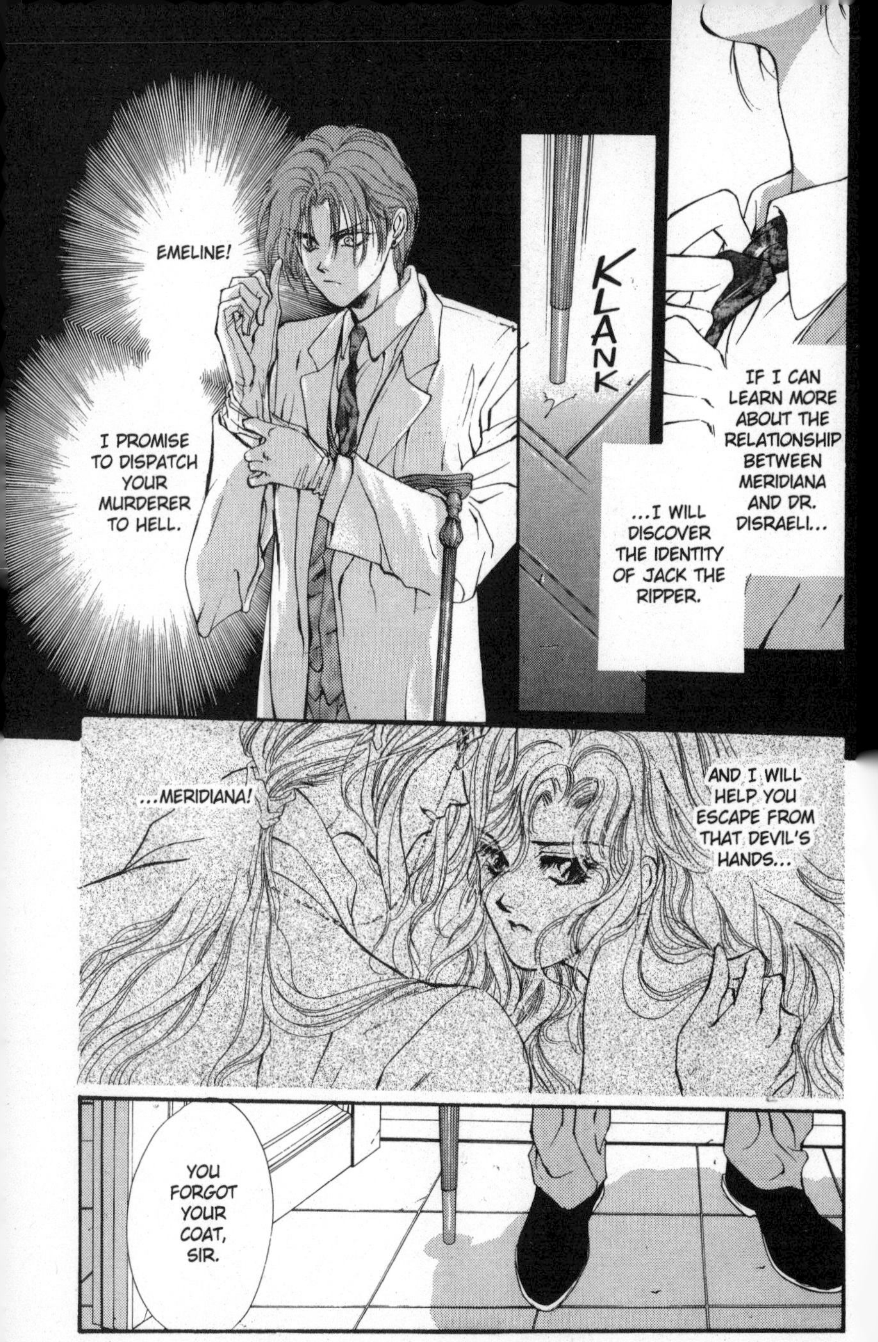
IF I CAN LEARN MORE ABOUT THE RELATIONSHIP BETWEEN MERIDIANA AND DR. DISRAELI...
...I WILL DISCOVER THE IDENTITY OF JACK THE RIPPER.
KLANK
EMELINE!
I PROMISE TO DISPATCH YOUR MURDERER TO HELL.
...MERIDIANA!
AND I WILL HELP YOU ESCAPE FROM THAT DEVIL'S HANDS...
YOU FORGOT YOUR COAT, SIR.

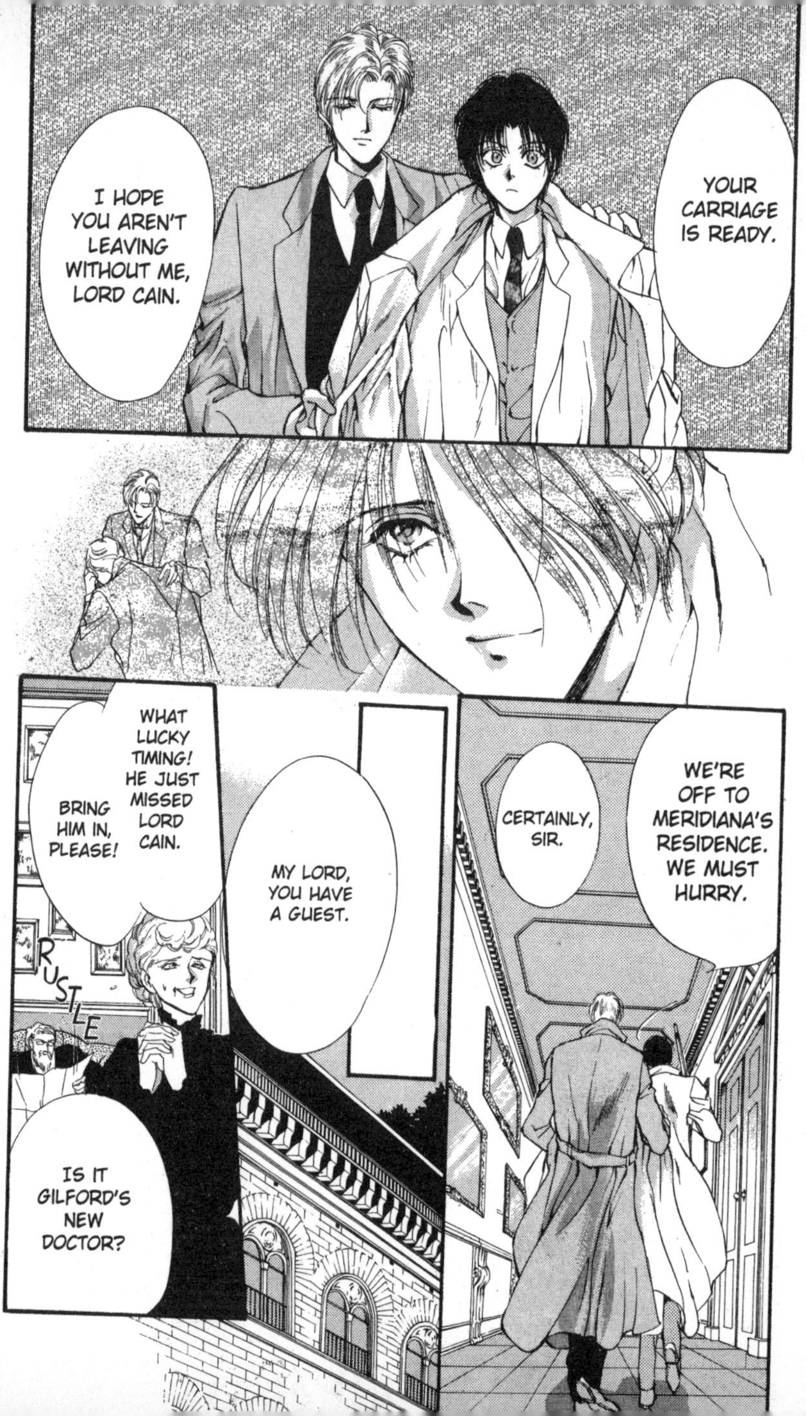
YOUR CARRIAGE IS READY.
I HOPE YOU AREN'T LEAVING WITHOUT ME, LORD CAIN.
WE'RE OFF TO MERIDIANA'S RESIDENCE. WE MUST HURRY.
CERTAINLY, SIR.
MY LORD, YOU HAVE A GUEST.
WHAT LUCKY TIMING! HE JUST MISSED LORD CAIN.
BRING HIM IN, PLEASE!
RUSTLE
IS IT GILFORD'S NEW DOCTOR?

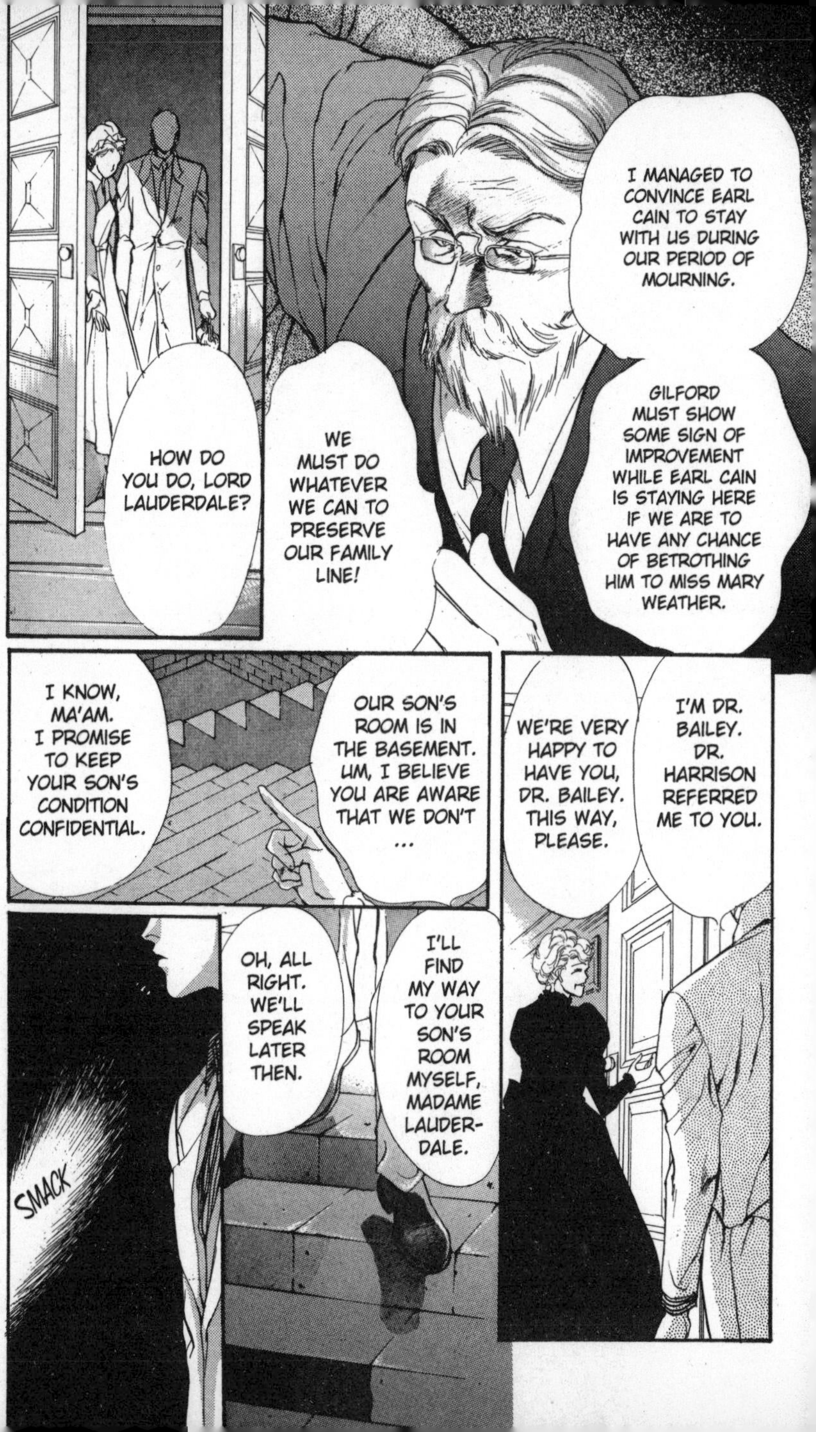
I MANAGED TO CONVINCE EARL CAIN TO STAY WITH US DURING OUR PERIOD OF MOURNING.
GILFORD MUST SHOW SOME SIGN OF IMPROVEMENT WHILE EARL CAIN IS STAYING HERE IF WE ARE TO HAVE ANY CHANCE OF BETROTHING HIM TO MISS MARY WEATHER.
WE MUST DO WHATEVER WE CAN TO PRESERVE OUR FAMILY LINE!
HOW DO YOU DO, LORD LAUDERDALE?
I'M DR. BAILEY. DR. HARRISON REFERRED ME TO YOU.
WE'RE VERY HAPPY TO HAVE YOU, DR. BAILEY. THIS WAY, PLEASE.
OUR SON'S ROOM IS IN THE BASEMENT. UM, I BELIEVE YOU ARE AWARE THAT WE DON'T ...
I KNOW, MA'AM. I PROMISE TO KEEP YOUR SON'S CONDITION CONFIDENTIAL.
I'LL FIND MY WAY TO YOUR SON'S ROOM MYSELF, MADAME LAUDER-DALE.
OH, ALL RIGHT. WE'LL SPEAK LATER THEN.
SMACK

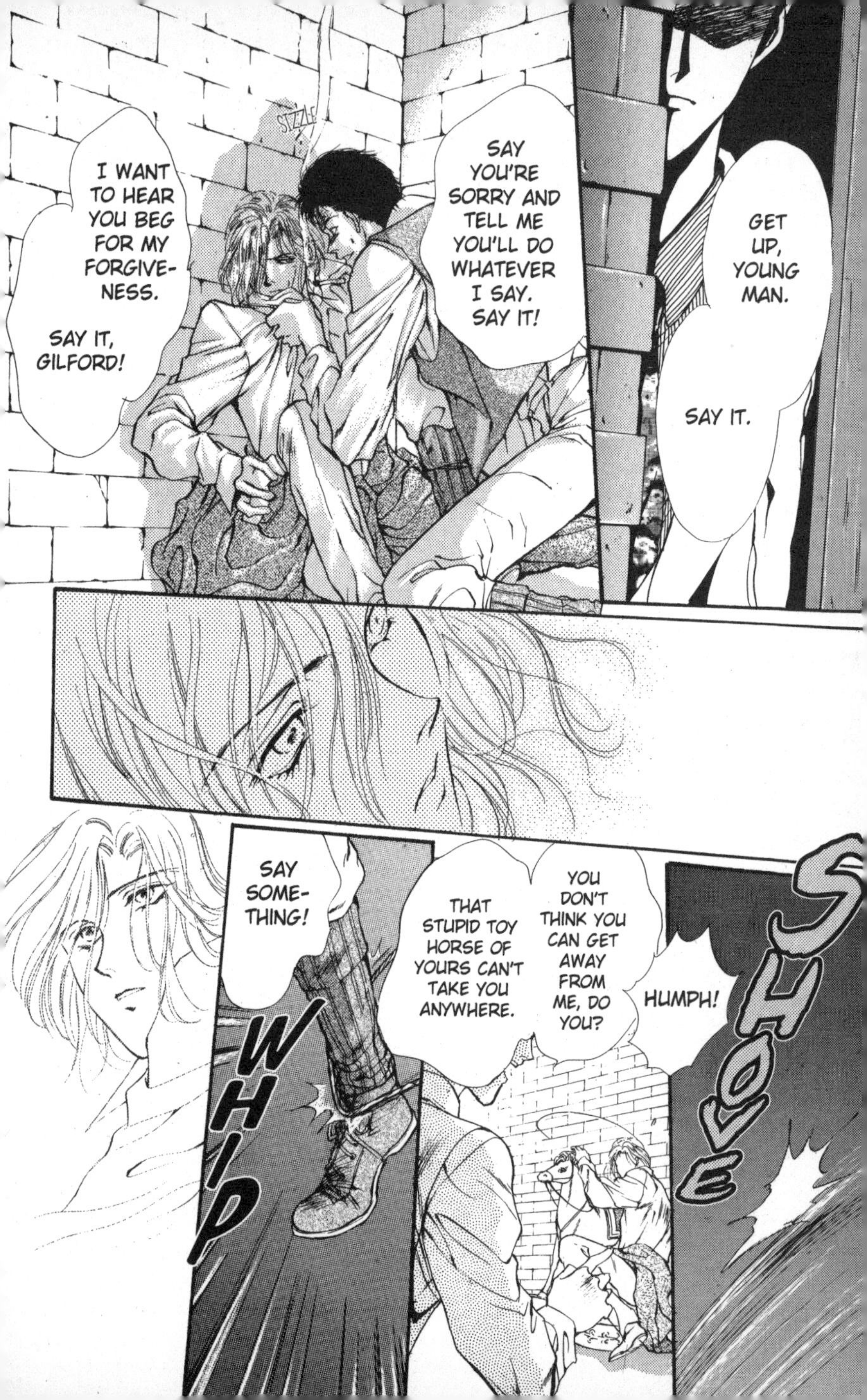
GET UP, YOUNG MAN.
SAY IT.
SIZZLE
SAY YOU'RE SORRY AND TELL ME YOU'LL DO WHATEVER I SAY. SAY IT!
I WANT TO HEAR YOU BEG FOR MY FORGIVE-NESS.
SAY IT, GILFORD!
SHOVE
HUMPH!
YOU DON'T THINK YOU CAN GET AWAY FROM ME, DO YOU?
THAT STUPID TOY HORSE OF YOURS CAN'T TAKE YOU ANYWHERE.
SAY SOME-THING!
WHIP!

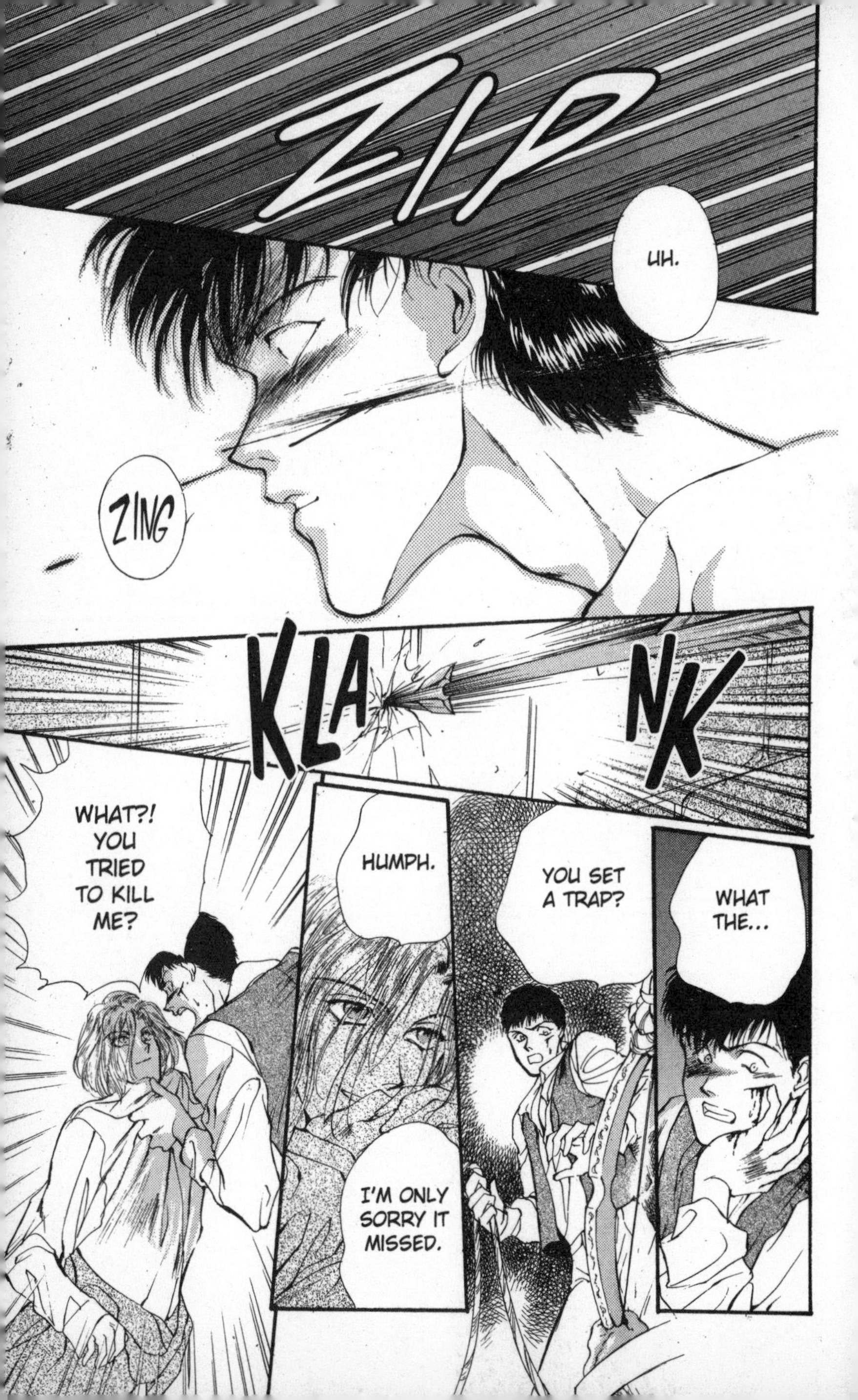
ZIP
UH.
ZING
KLANK
WHAT THE...
YOU SET A TRAP?
HUMPH.
I'M ONLY SORRY IT MISSED.
WHAT?! YOU TRIED TO KILL ME?

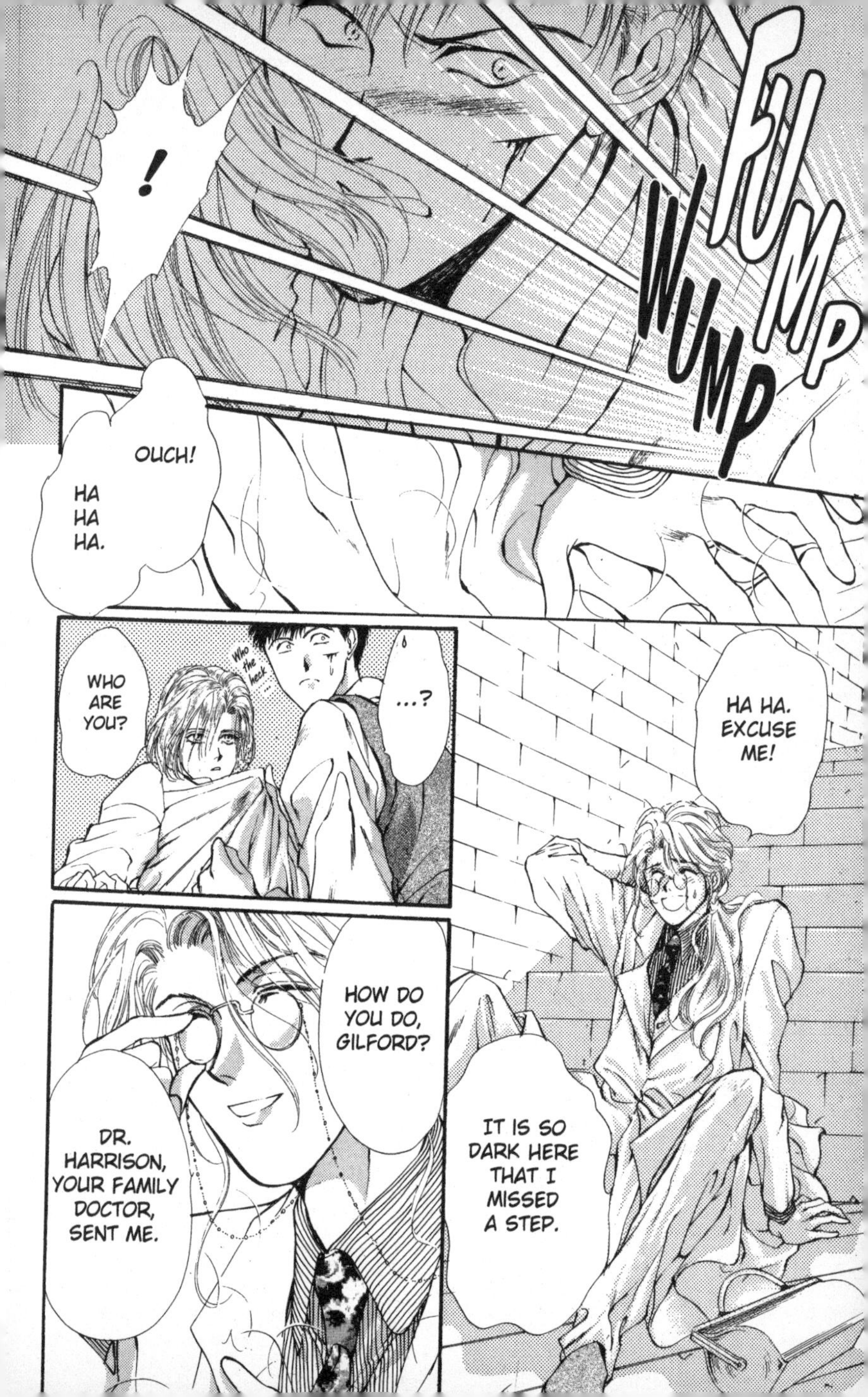
FUMP
WUMP
!
OUCH!
HA HA HA.
HA HA. EXCUSE ME!
IT IS SO DARK HERE THAT I MISSED A STEP.
...?
Who the heck...
WHO ARE YOU?
HOW DO YOU DO, GILFORD?
DR. HARRISON, YOUR FAMILY DOCTOR, SENT ME.

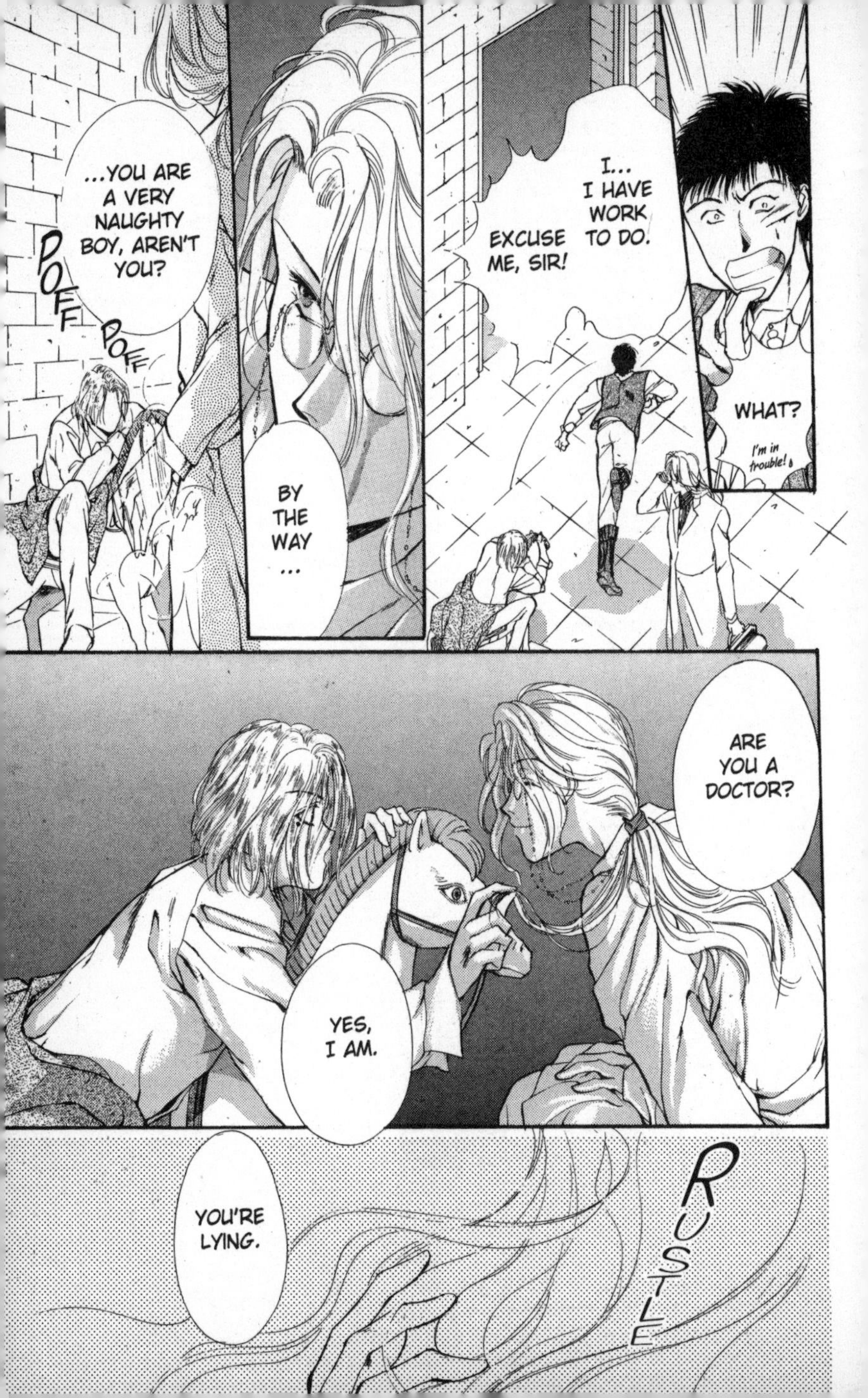
WHAT?
I'm in trouble!
I... I HAVE WORK TO DO.
EXCUSE ME, SIR!
BY THE WAY ...
...YOU ARE A VERY NAUGHTY BOY, AREN'T YOU?
POFF
POFF
ARE YOU A DOCTOR?
YES, I AM.
RUSTLE
YOU'RE LYING.

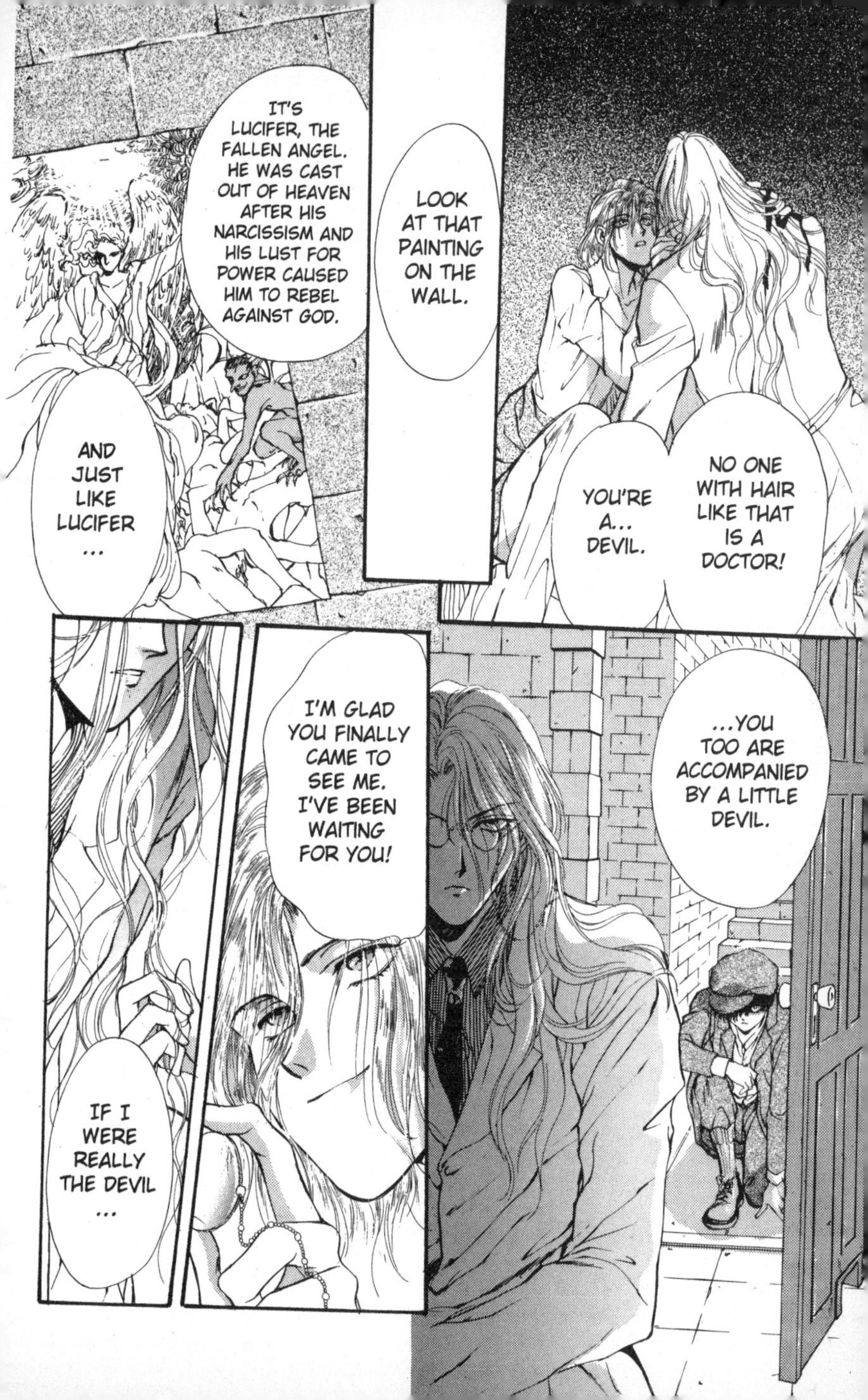

NO ONE WITH HAIR LIKE THAT IS A DOCTOR!
YOU'RE A... DEVIL.
LOOK AT THAT PAINTING ON THE WALL.
IT'S LUCIFER, THE FALLEN ANGEL. HE WAS CAST OUT OF HEAVEN AFTER HIS NARCISSISM AND HIS LUST FOR POWER CAUSED HIM TO REBEL AGAINST GOD.
AND JUST LIKE LUCIFER ...
...YOU TOO ARE ACCOMPANIED BY A LITTLE DEVIL.
I'M GLAD YOU FINALLY CAME TO SEE ME. I'VE BEEN WAITING FOR YOU!
IF I WERE REALLY THE DEVIL ...

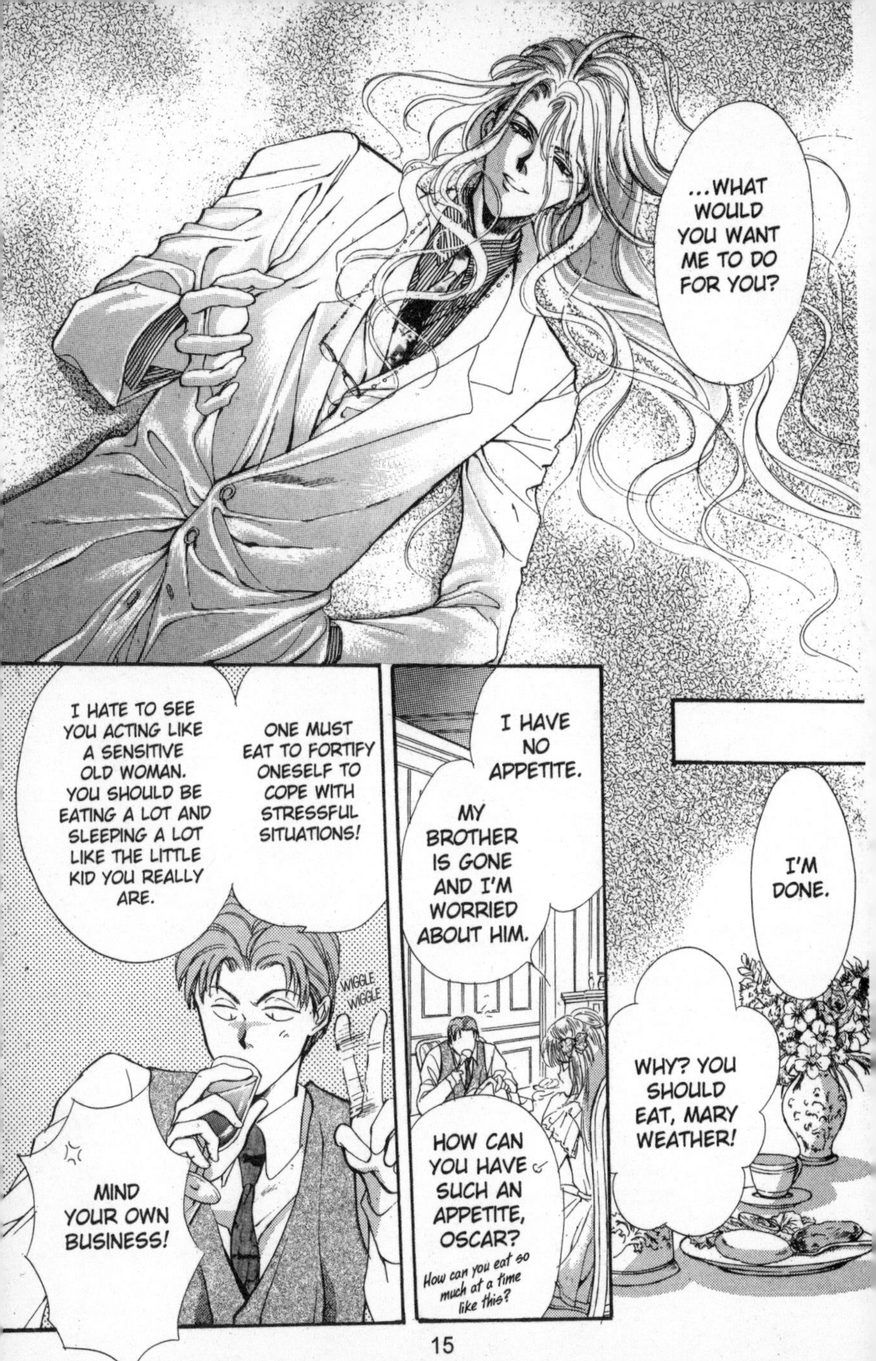
...WHAT WOULD YOU WANT ME TO DO FOR YOU?
I'M DONE.
WHY? YOU SHOULD EAT, MARY WEATHER!
I HAVE NO APPETITE.
MY BROTHER IS GONE AND I'M WORRIED ABOUT HIM.
HOW CAN YOU HAVE SUCH AN APPETITE, OSCAR?
How can you eat so much at a time like this?
ONE MUST EAT TO FORTIFY ONESELF TO COPE WITH STRESSFUL SITUATIONS!
I HATE TO SEE YOU ACTING LIKE A SENSITIVE OLD WOMAN. YOU SHOULD BE EATING A LOT AND SLEEPING A LOT LIKE THE LITTLE KID YOU REALLY ARE.
WIGGLE WIGGLE
MIND YOUR OWN BUSINESS!

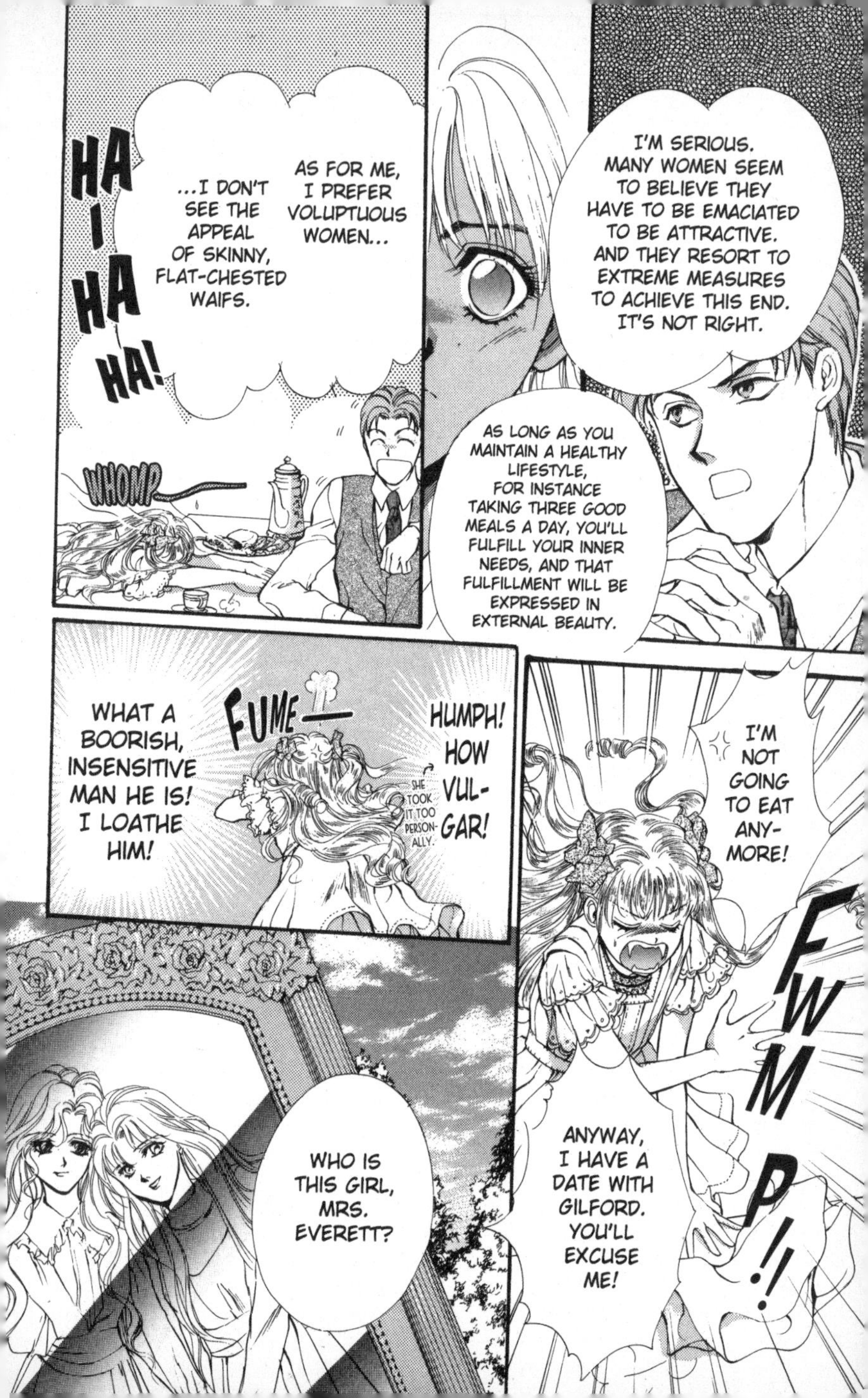
I'M SERIOUS. MANY WOMEN SEEM TO BELIEVE THEY HAVE TO BE EMACIATED TO BE ATTRACTIVE. AND THEY RESORT TO EXTREME MEASURES TO ACHIEVE THIS END. IT'S NOT RIGHT.
AS LONG AS YOU MAINTAIN A HEALTHY LIFESTYLE, FOR INSTANCE TAKING THREE GOOD MEALS A DAY, YOU'LL FULFILL YOUR INNER NEEDS, AND THAT FULFILLMENT WILL BE EXPRESSED IN EXTERNAL BEAUTY.
AS FOR ME, I PREFER VOLUPTUOUS WOMEN...
...I DON'T SEE THE APPEAL OF SKINNY, FLAT-CHESTED WAIFS.
HA I HA HA HA!
WHOMP
I'M NOT GOING TO EAT ANY-MORE!
FWMP!!
ANYWAY, I HAVE A DATE WITH GILFORD. YOU'LL EXCUSE ME!
HUMPH! HOW VUL-GAR!
SHE TOOK IT TOO PERSON-ALLY.
FUME
WHAT A BOORISH, INSENSITIVE MAN HE IS! I LOATHE HIM!
WHO IS THIS GIRL, MRS. EVERETT?

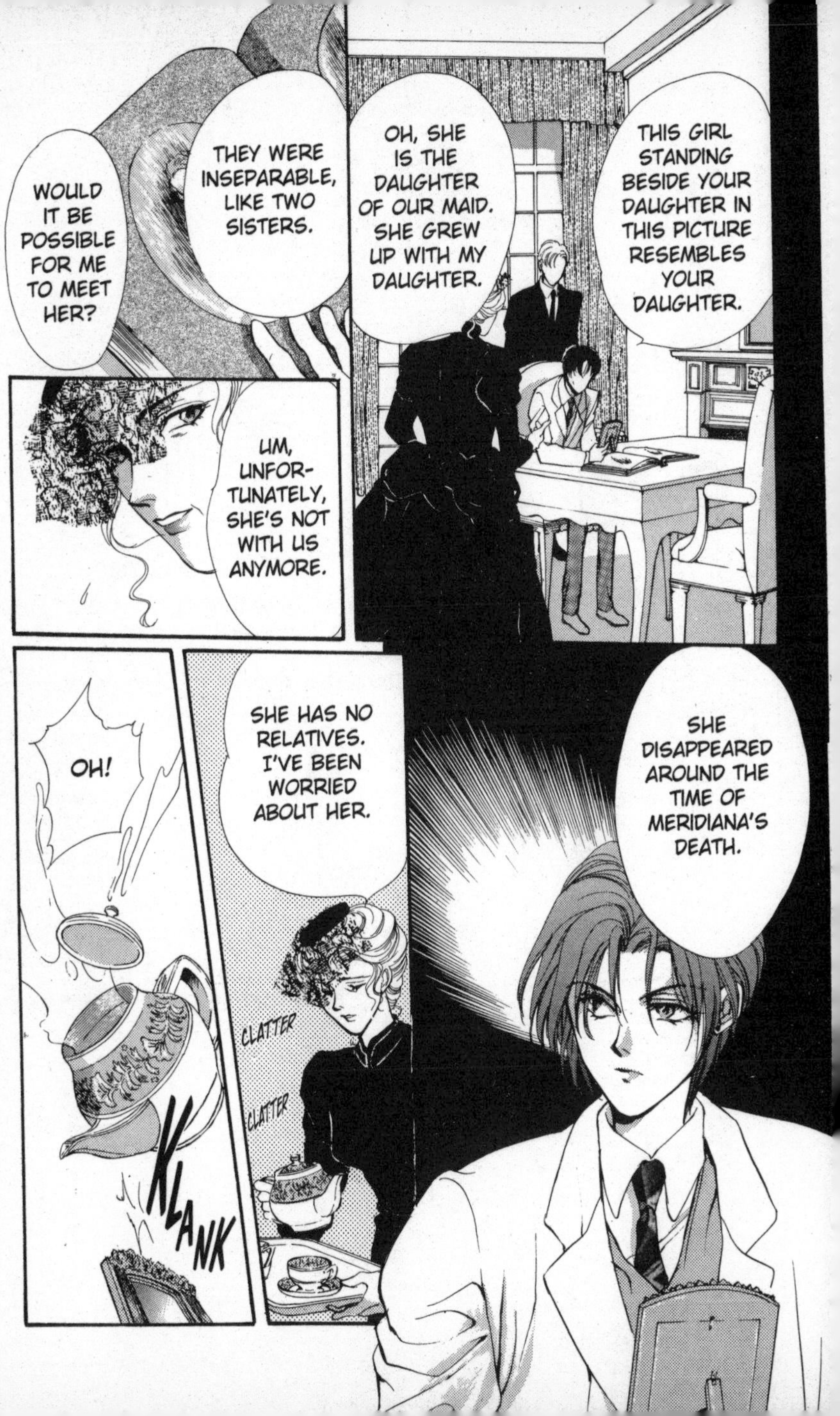
THIS GIRL STANDING BESIDE YOUR DAUGHTER IN THIS PICTURE RESEMBLES YOUR DAUGHTER.
OH, SHE IS THE DAUGHTER OF OUR MAID. SHE GREW UP WITH MY DAUGHTER.
THEY WERE INSEPARABLE, LIKE TWO SISTERS.
WOULD IT BE POSSIBLE FOR ME TO MEET HER?
UM, UNFOR-TUNATELY, SHE'S NOT WITH US ANYMORE.
SHE DISAPPEARED AROUND THE TIME OF MERIDIANA'S DEATH.
SHE HAS NO RELATIVES. I'VE BEEN WORRIED ABOUT HER.
CLATTER
CLATTER
OH!
KLANK

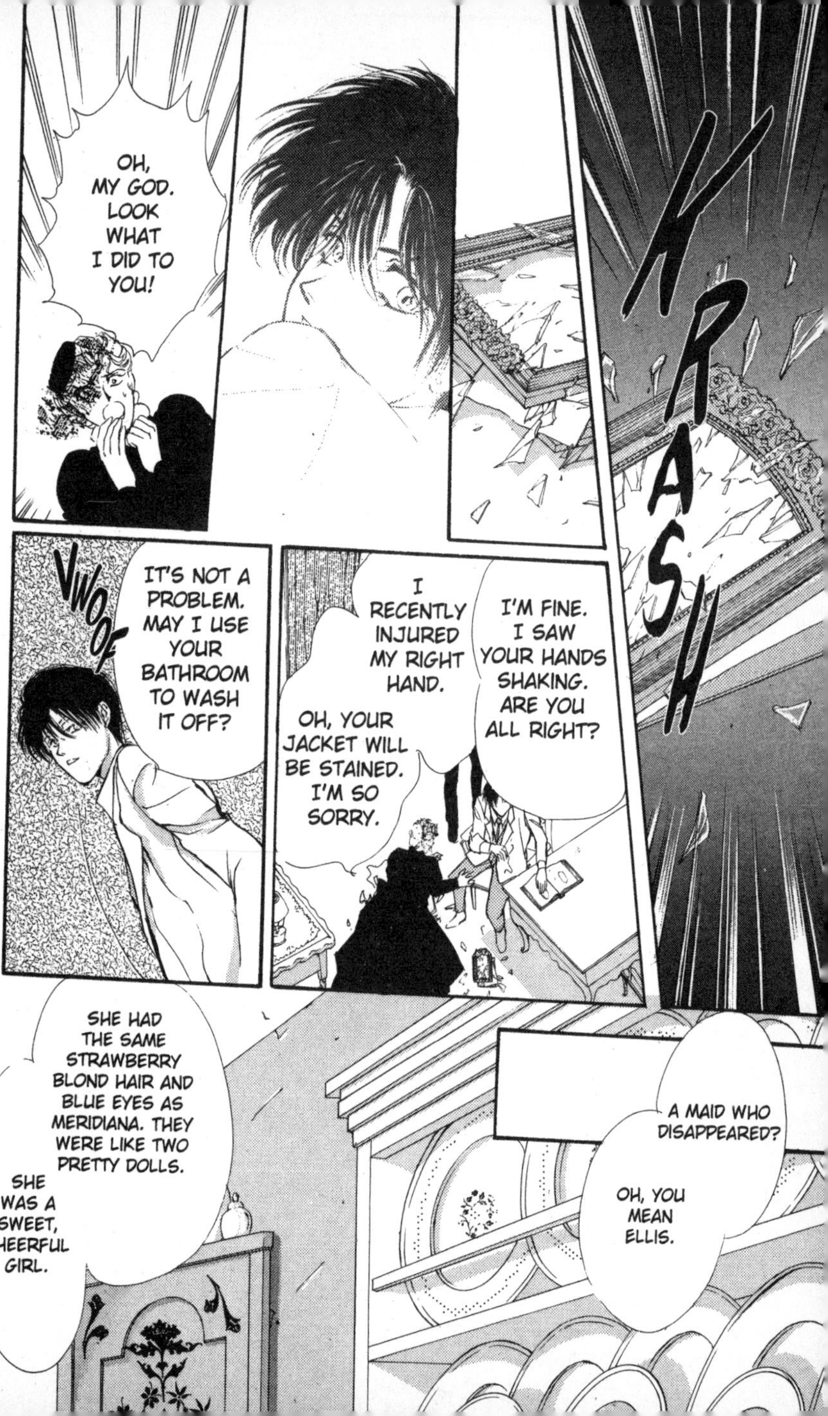
KRASH
OH, MY GOD. LOOK WHAT I DID TO YOU!
I'M FINE. I SAW YOUR HANDS SHAKING. ARE YOU ALL RIGHT?
I RECENTLY INJURED MY RIGHT HAND.
OH, YOUR JACKET WILL BE STAINED. I'M SO SORRY.
IT'S NOT A PROBLEM. MAY I USE YOUR BATHROOM TO WASH IT OFF?
VWOOF
A MAID WHO DISAPPEARED?
OH, YOU MEAN ELLIS.
SHE HAD THE SAME STRAWBERRY BLOND HAIR AND BLUE EYES AS MERIDIANA. THEY WERE LIKE TWO PRETTY DOLLS.
SHE WAS A SWEET, CHEERFUL GIRL.

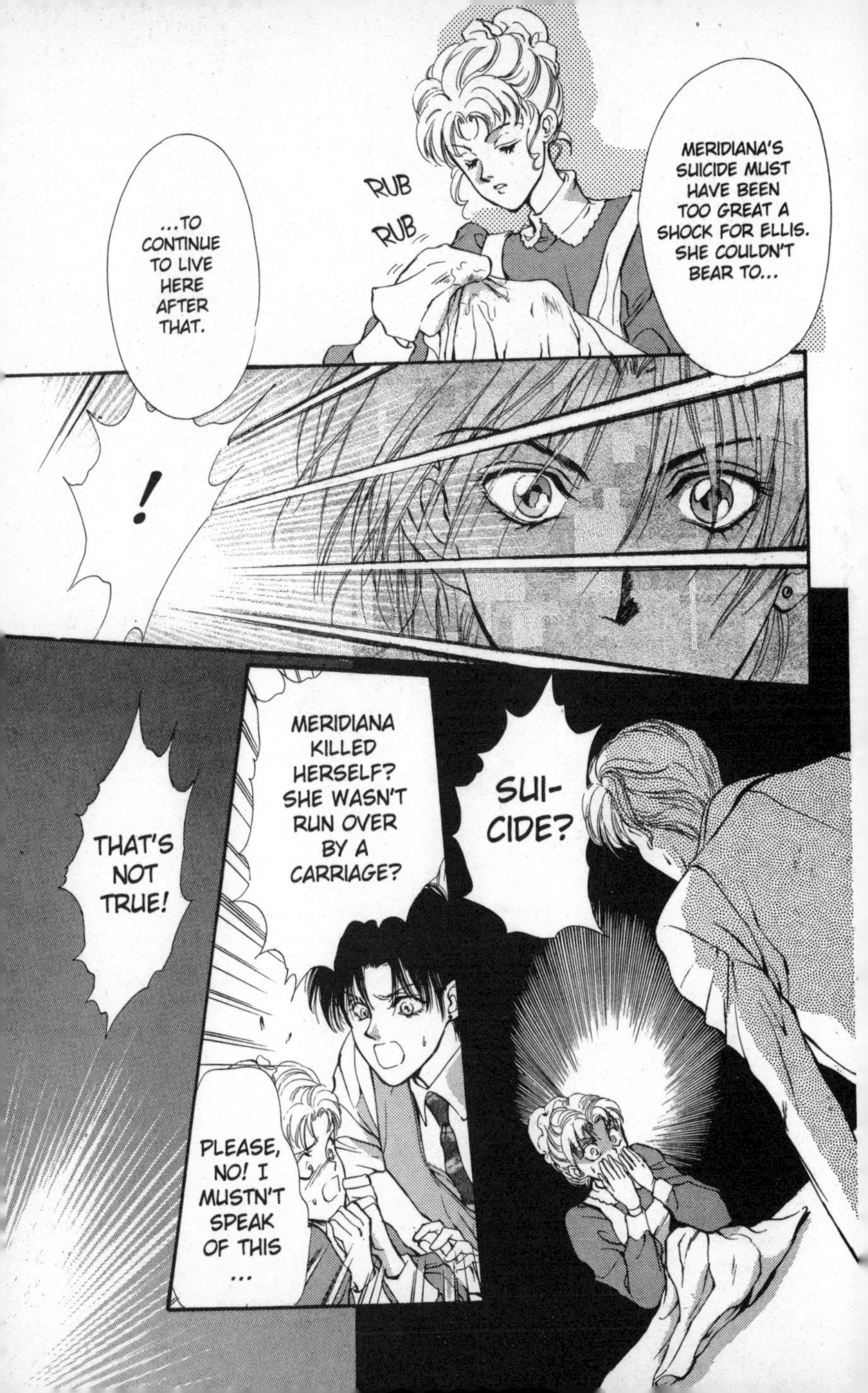
MERIDIANA'S SUICIDE MUST HAVE BEEN TOO GREAT A SHOCK FOR ELLIS. SHE COULDN'T BEAR TO...
RUB RUB
...TO CONTINUE TO LIVE HERE AFTER THAT.
!
SUI-CIDE?
MERIDIANA KILLED HERSELF? SHE WASN'T RUN OVER BY A CARRIAGE?
PLEASE, NO! I MUSTN'T SPEAK OF THIS...
THAT'S NOT TRUE!

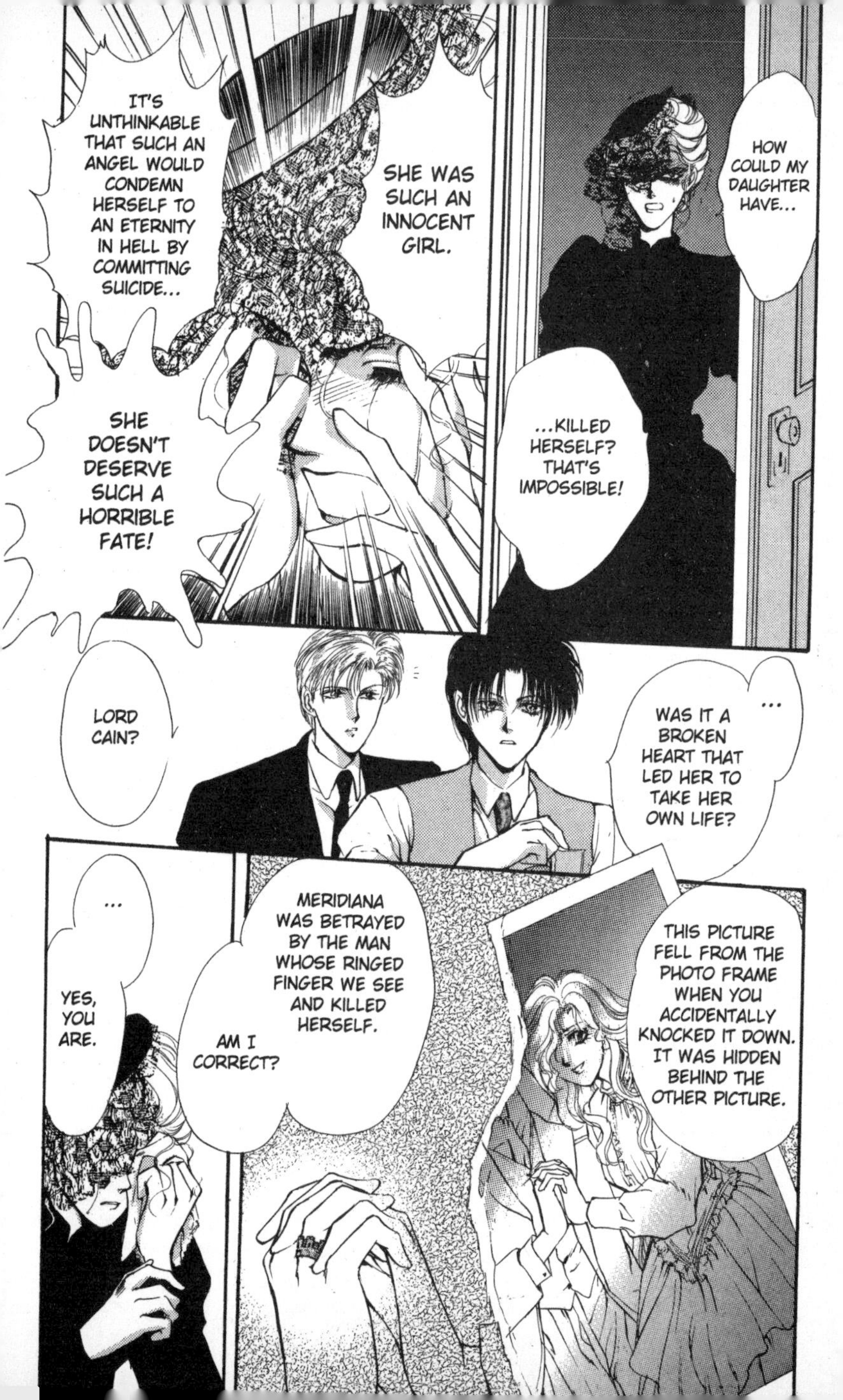
HOW COULD MY DAUGHTER HAVE...
...KILLED HERSELF? THAT'S IMPOSSIBLE!
SHE WAS SUCH AN INNOCENT GIRL.
IT'S UNTHINKABLE THAT SUCH AN ANGEL WOULD CONDEMN HERSELF TO AN ETERNITY IN HELL BY COMMITTING SUICIDE...
SHE DOESN'T DESERVE SUCH A HORRIBLE FATE!
...
WAS IT A BROKEN HEART THAT LED HER TO TAKE HER OWN LIFE?
LORD CAIN?
THIS PICTURE FELL FROM THE PHOTO FRAME WHEN YOU ACCIDENTALLY KNOCKED IT DOWN. IT WAS HIDDEN BEHIND THE OTHER PICTURE.
MERIDIANA WAS BETRAYED BY THE MAN WHOSE RINGED FINGER WE SEE AND KILLED HERSELF.
AM I CORRECT?
...
YES, YOU ARE.

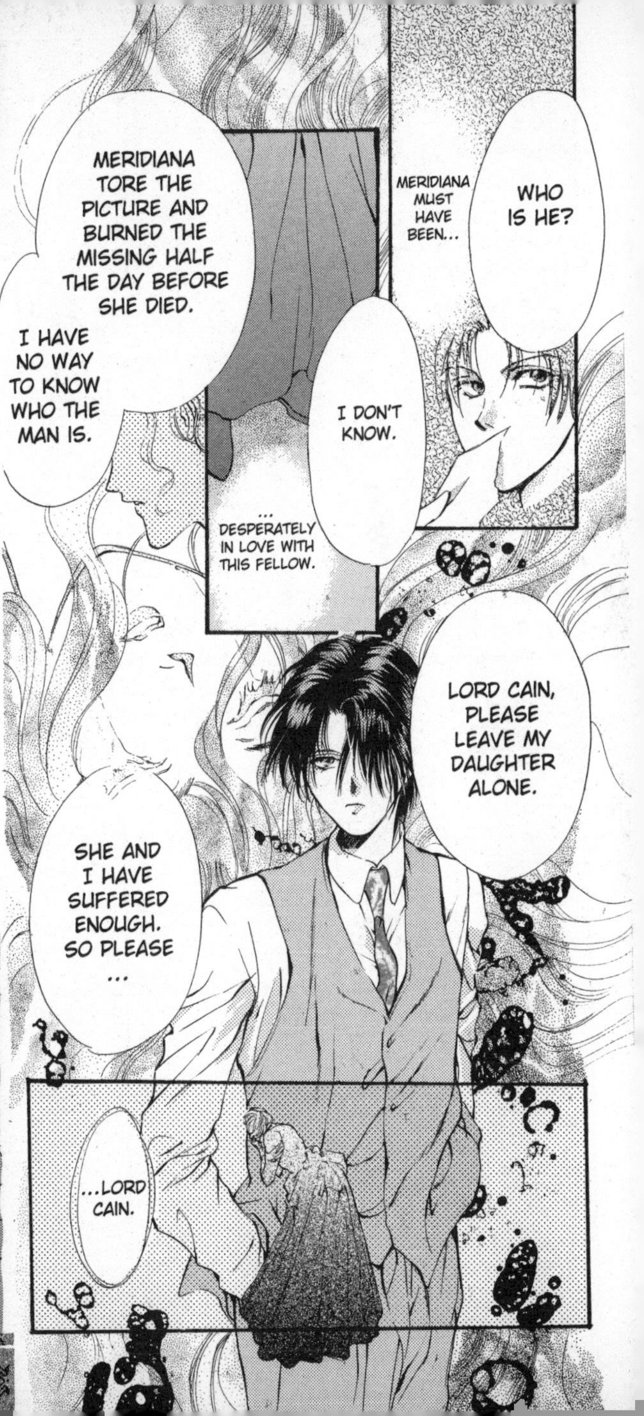
WHO IS HE?
MERIDIANA MUST HAVE BEEN...
I DON'T KNOW.
...DESPERATELY IN LOVE WITH THIS FELLOW.
MERIDIANA TORE THE PICTURE AND BURNED THE MISSING HALF THE DAY BEFORE SHE DIED.
I HAVE NO WAY TO KNOW WHO THE MAN IS.
LORD CAIN, PLEASE LEAVE MY DAUGHTER ALONE.
SHE AND I HAVE SUFFERED ENOUGH. SO PLEASE ...
...LORD CAIN.

RETURN TO
WILD TALK

This is the second volume of Earl Cain's "The Seal of theRed Ram" series and the fifth volume of the whole Earl Cain sequence. (How complicated!) I myself have no idea how many volumes this story will eventually occupy. People often ask me for personal details about the main characters, but I usually don't care much about their heights, blood types, etc. If I had to guess, I would say Cain's blood type might be B, but I have no idea about Riff's or Dr. Disraeli's. Speaking of heights, Mary Weather in the "Hana to Yume" bimonthly magazine version looks a bit too tall for her age, but, again, I didn't think too much about it. Anyway, enjoy the last half of "The Seal of the Red Ram"!

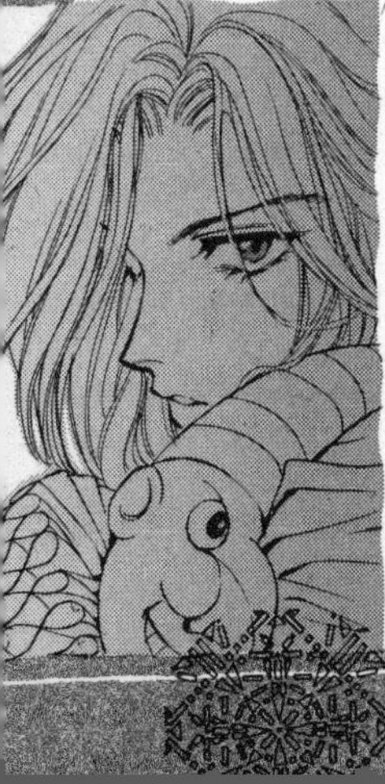

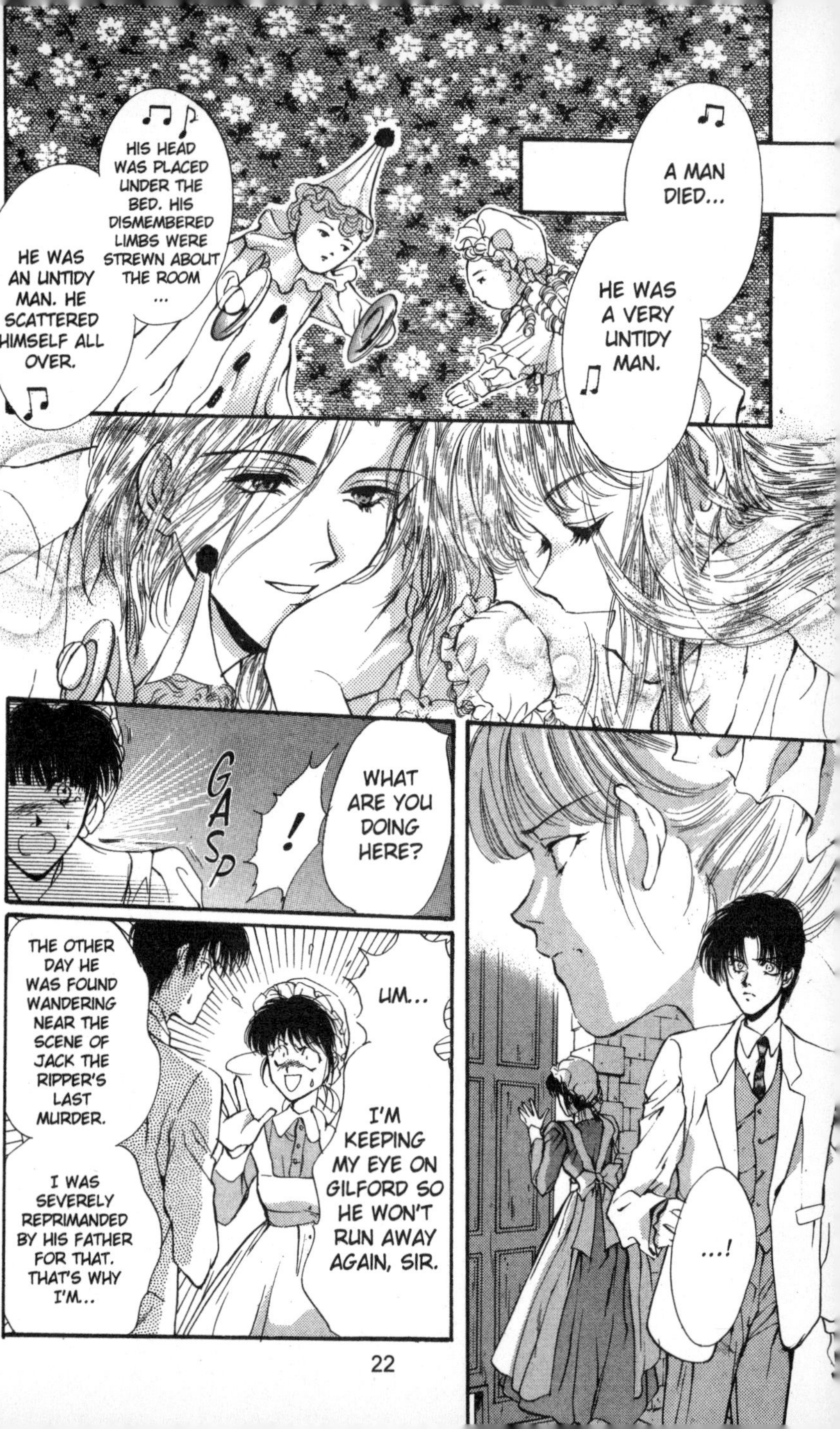
A MAN DIED...
HE WAS A VERY UNTIDY MAN.
HIS HEAD WAS PLACED UNDER THE BED. HIS DISMEMBERED LIMBS WERE STREWN ABOUT THE ROOM ...
HE WAS AN UNTIDY MAN. HE SCATTERED HIMSELF ALL OVER.
...!
GASP
!
WHAT ARE YOU DOING HERE?
UM...
I'M KEEPING MY EYE ON GILFORD SO HE WON'T RUN AWAY AGAIN, SIR.
THE OTHER DAY HE WAS FOUND WANDERING NEAR THE SCENE OF JACK THE RIPPER'S LAST MURDER.
I WAS SEVERELY REPRIMANDED BY HIS FATHER FOR THAT. THAT'S WHY I'M...

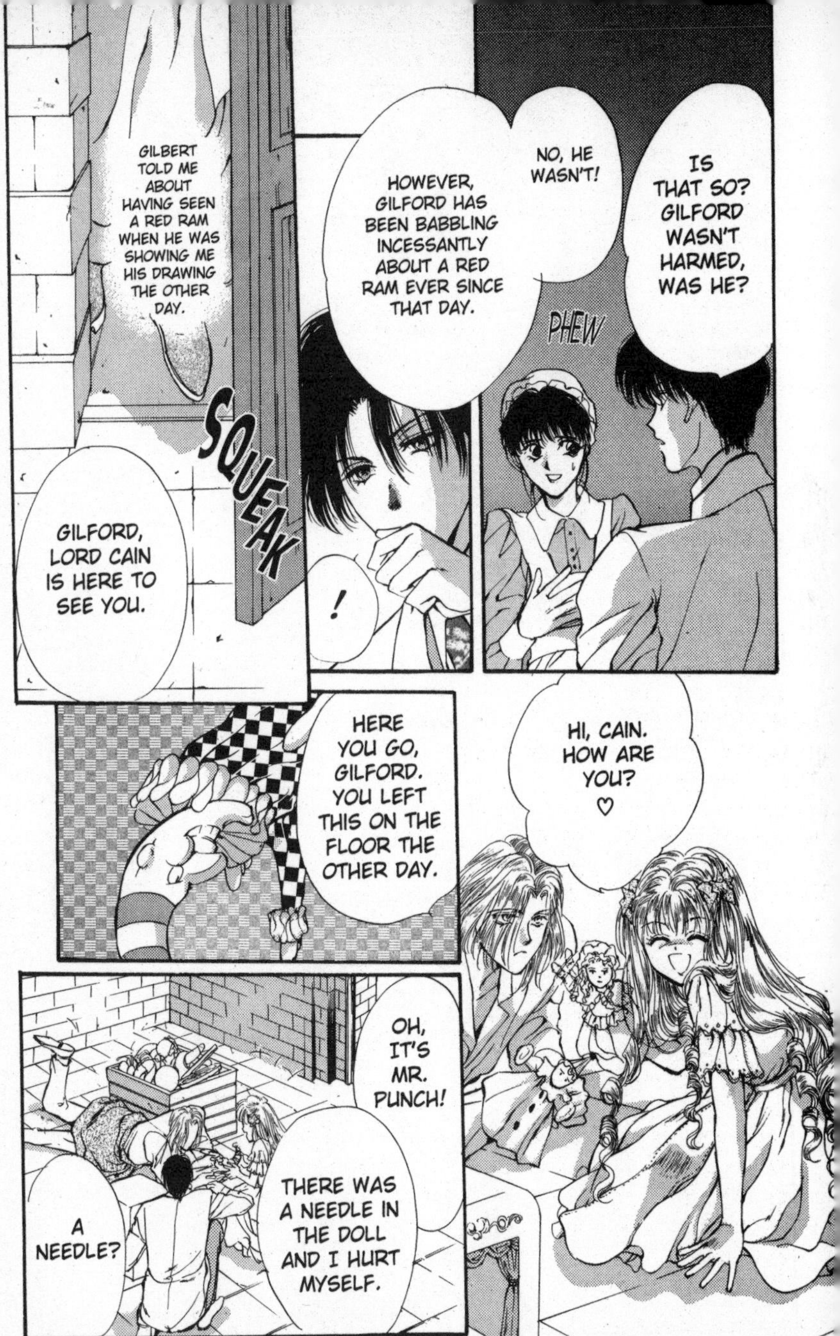
IS THAT SO? GILFORD WASN'T HARMED, WAS HE?
NO, HE WASN'T!
PHEW
HOWEVER, GILFORD HAS BEEN BABBLING INCESSANTLY ABOUT A RED RAM EVER SINCE THAT DAY.
!
GILBERT TOLD ME ABOUT HAVING SEEN A RED RAM WHEN HE WAS SHOWING ME HIS DRAWING THE OTHER DAY.
SQUEAK
GILFORD, LORD CAIN IS HERE TO SEE YOU.
HI, CAIN. HOW ARE YOU? ♡
HERE YOU GO, GILFORD. YOU LEFT THIS ON THE FLOOR THE OTHER DAY.
OH, IT'S MR. PUNCH!
THERE WAS A NEEDLE IN THE DOLL AND I HURT MYSELF.
A NEEDLE?

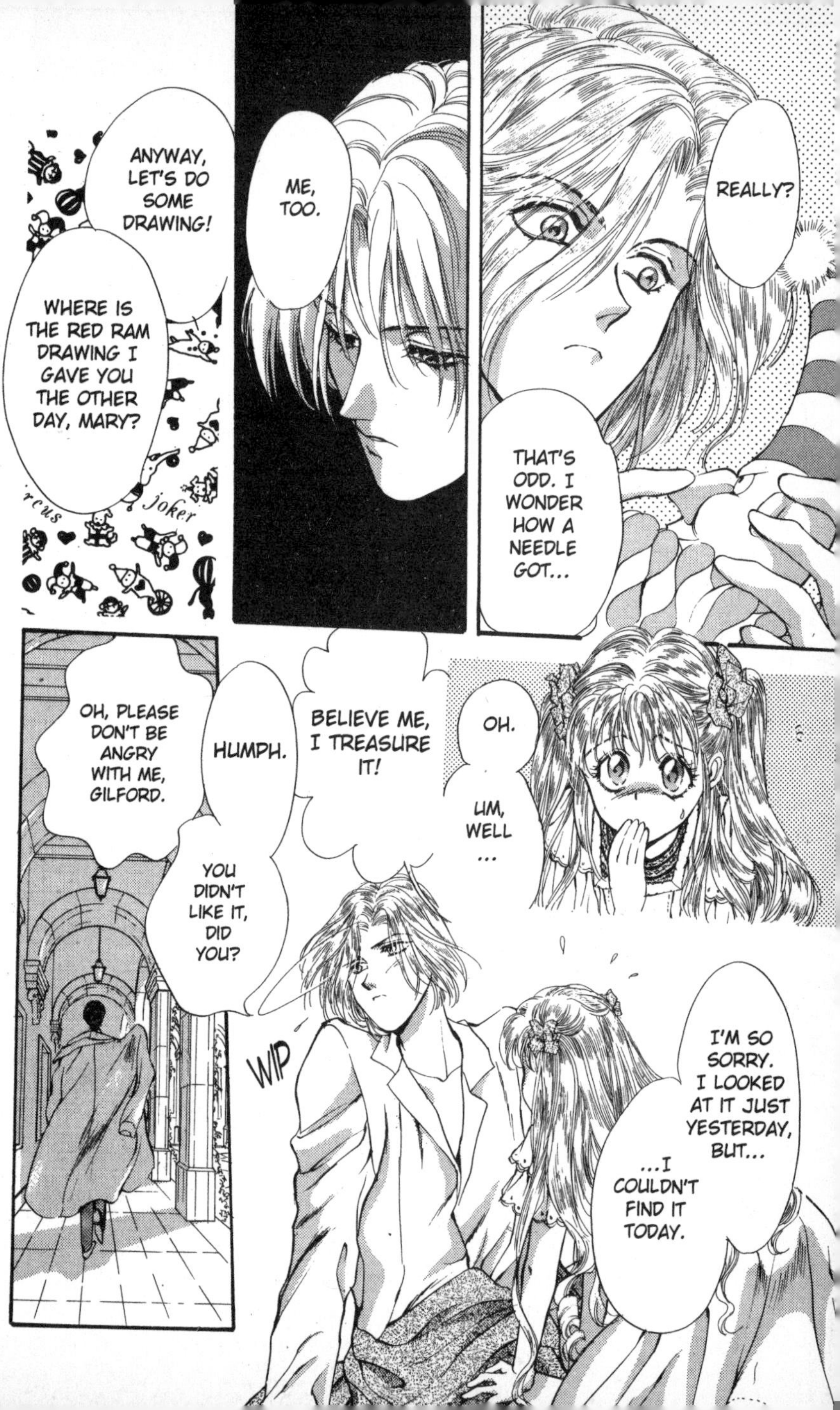
REALLY?
THAT'S ODD. I WONDER HOW A NEEDLE GOT...
ME, TOO.
ANYWAY, LET'S DO SOME DRAWING!
WHERE IS THE RED RAM DRAWING I GAVE YOU THE OTHER DAY, MARY?
OH.
UM, WELL ...
BELIEVE ME, I TREASURE IT!
HUMPH.
YOU DIDN'T LIKE IT, DID YOU?
I'M SO SORRY. I LOOKED AT IT JUST YESTERDAY, BUT...
...I COULDN'T FIND IT TODAY.
WIP
OH, PLEASE DON'T BE ANGRY WITH ME, GILFORD.

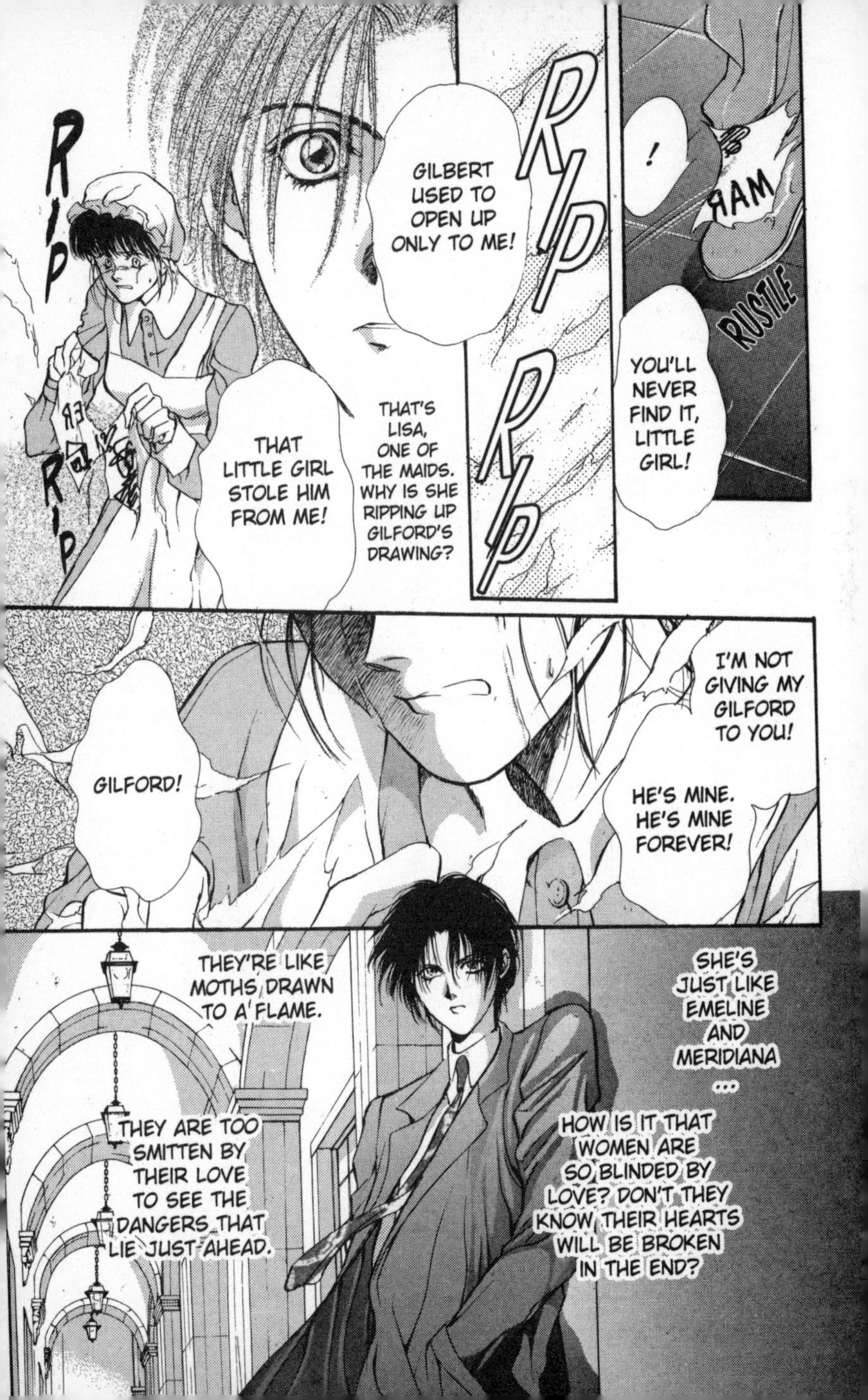
!
RUSTLE
YOU'LL NEVER FIND IT, LITTLE GIRL!
RIP
RIP
GILBERT USED TO OPEN UP ONLY TO ME!
THAT'S LISA, ONE OF THE MAIDS. WHY IS SHE RIPPING UP GILFORD'S DRAWING?
THAT LITTLE GIRL STOLE HIM FROM ME!
RIP
RIP
I'M NOT GIVING MY GILFORD TO YOU!
HE'S MINE. HE'S MINE FOREVER!
GILFORD!
SHE'S JUST LIKE EMELINE AND MERIDIANA...
HOW IS IT THAT WOMEN ARE SO BLINDED BY LOVE? DON'T THEY KNOW THEIR HEARTS WILL BE BROKEN IN THE END?
THEY'RE LIKE MOTHS DRAWN TO A FLAME.
THEY ARE TOO SMITTEN BY THEIR LOVE TO SEE THE DANGERS THAT LIE JUST AHEAD.

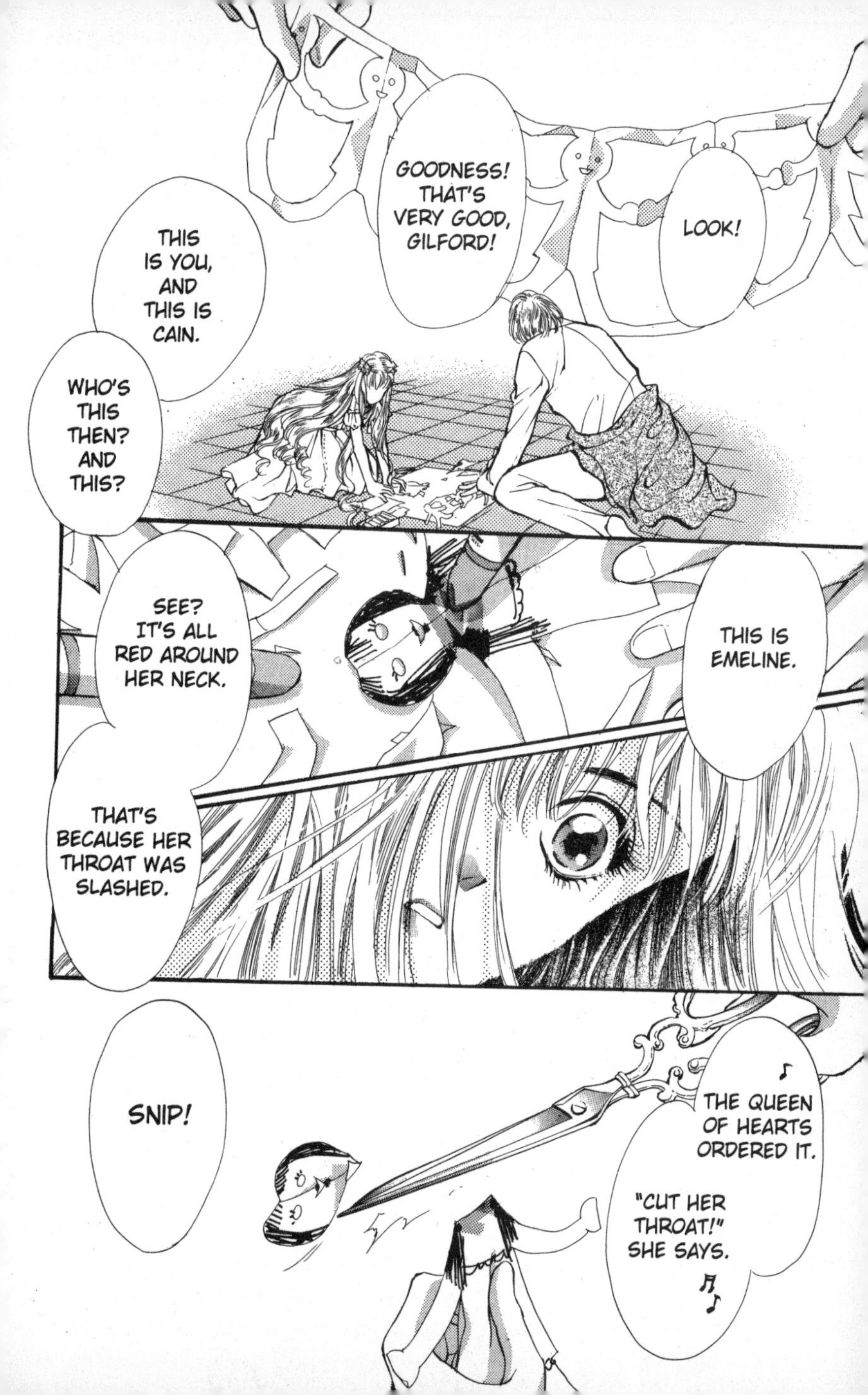
LOOK!
GOODNESS! THAT'S VERY GOOD, GILFORD!
THIS IS YOU, AND THIS IS CAIN.
WHO'S THIS THEN? AND THIS?
THIS IS EMELINE.
SEE? IT'S ALL RED AROUND HER NECK.
THAT'S BECAUSE HER THROAT WAS SLASHED.
THE QUEEN OF HEARTS ORDERED IT.
"CUT HER THROAT!" SHE SAYS.
SNIP!

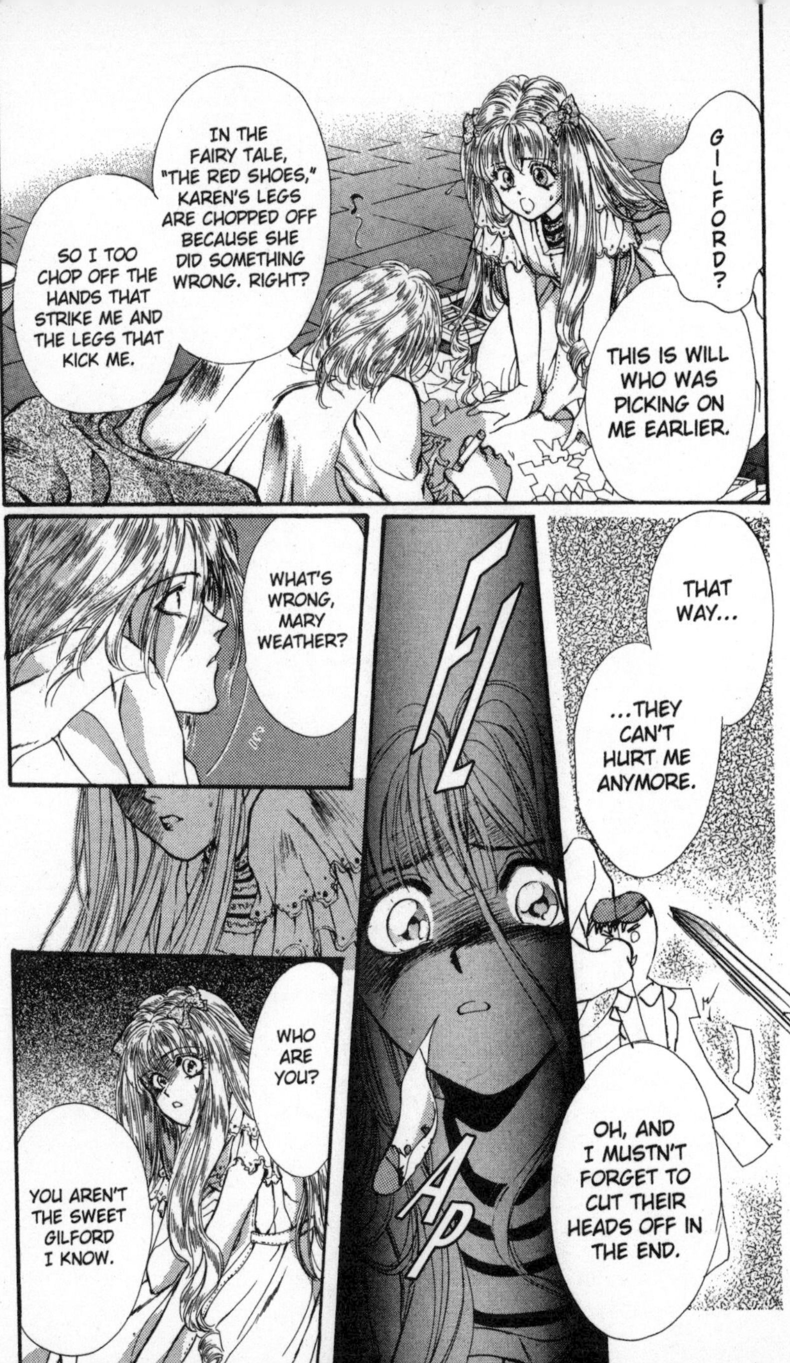
GILFORD?
THIS IS WILL WHO WAS PICKING ON ME EARLIER.
IN THE FAIRY TALE, "THE RED SHOES," KAREN'S LEGS ARE CHOPPED OFF BECAUSE SHE DID SOMETHING WRONG. RIGHT?
SO I TOO CHOP OFF THE HANDS THAT STRIKE ME AND THE LEGS THAT KICK ME.
THAT WAY...
...THEY CAN'T HURT ME ANYMORE.
OH, AND I MUSTN'T FORGET TO CUT THEIR HEADS OFF IN THE END.
FL
AP
WHAT'S WRONG, MARY WEATHER?
WHO ARE YOU?
YOU AREN'T THE SWEET GILFORD I KNOW.

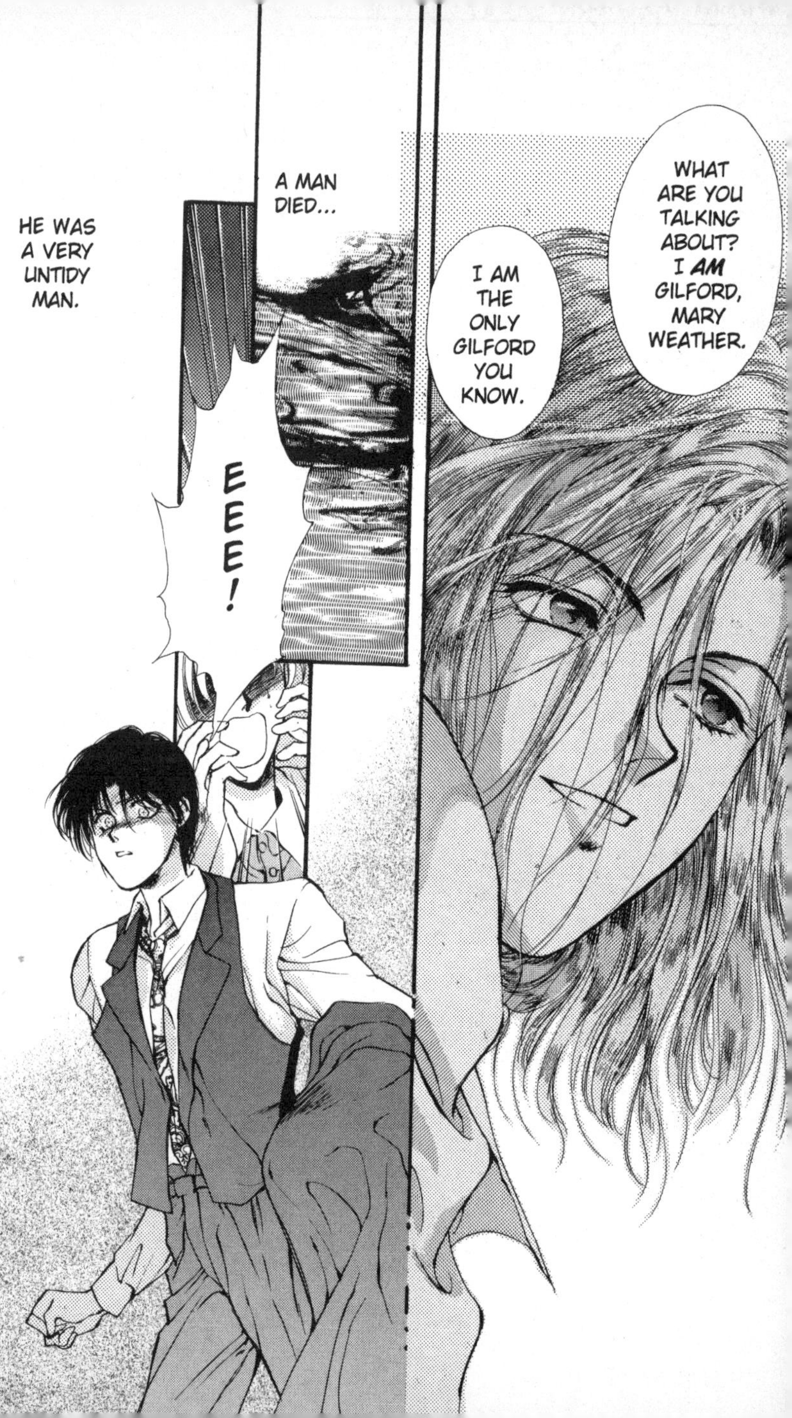
WHAT ARE YOU TALKING ABOUT? I *AM* GILFORD, MARY WEATHER.
I AM THE ONLY GILFORD YOU KNOW.
A MAN DIED...
EEE!
HE WAS A VERY UNTIDY MAN.

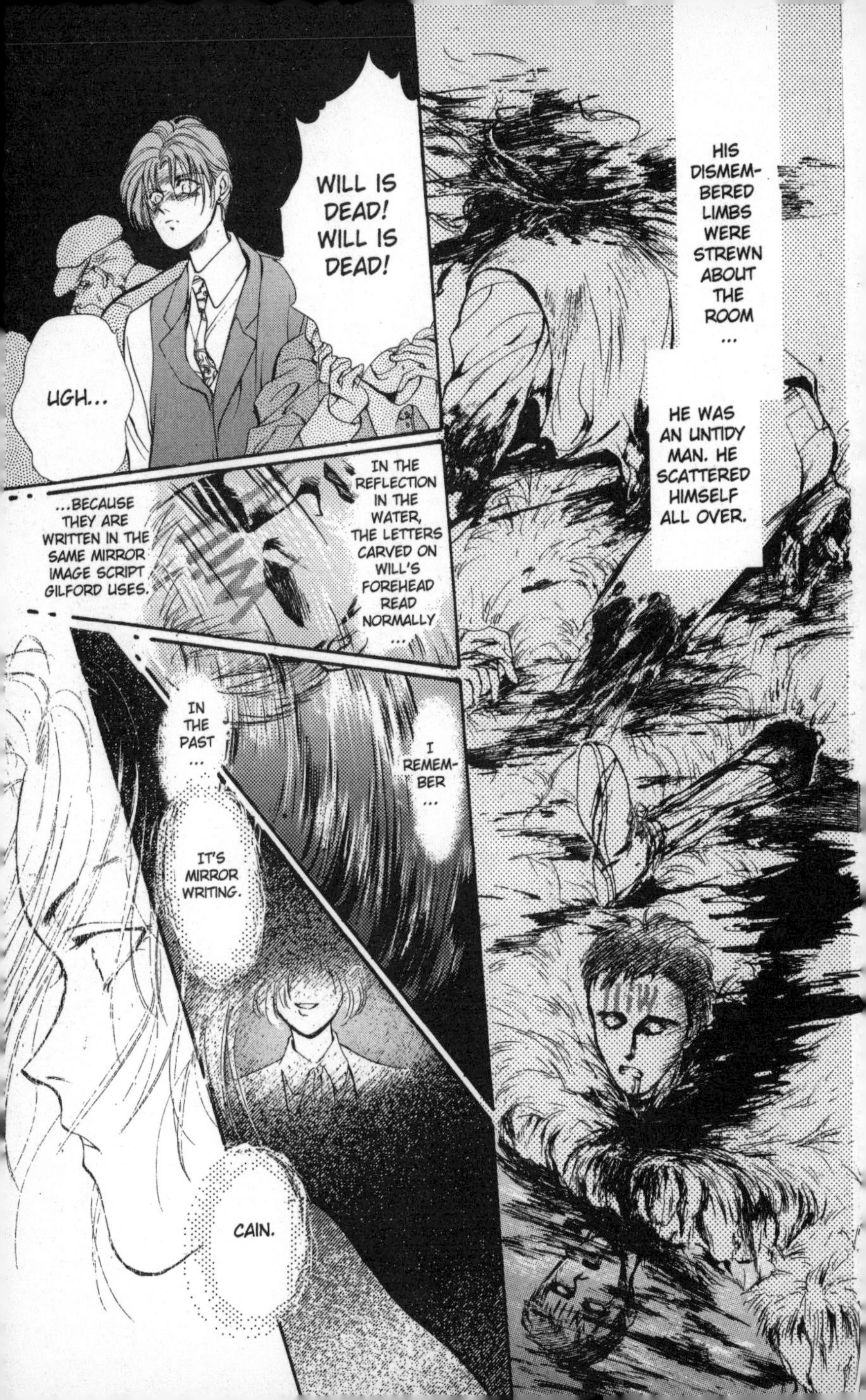
HIS DISMEMBERED LIMBS WERE STREWN ABOUT THE ROOM ...
HE WAS AN UNTIDY MAN. HE SCATTERED HIMSELF ALL OVER.
WILL IS DEAD! WILL IS DEAD!
UGH...
IN THE REFLECTION IN THE WATER, THE LETTERS CARVED ON WILL'S FOREHEAD READ NORMALLY ...
...BECAUSE THEY ARE WRITTEN IN THE SAME MIRROR IMAGE SCRIPT GILFORD USES.
I REMEMBER ...
IN THE PAST ...
IT'S MIRROR WRITING.
CAIN.

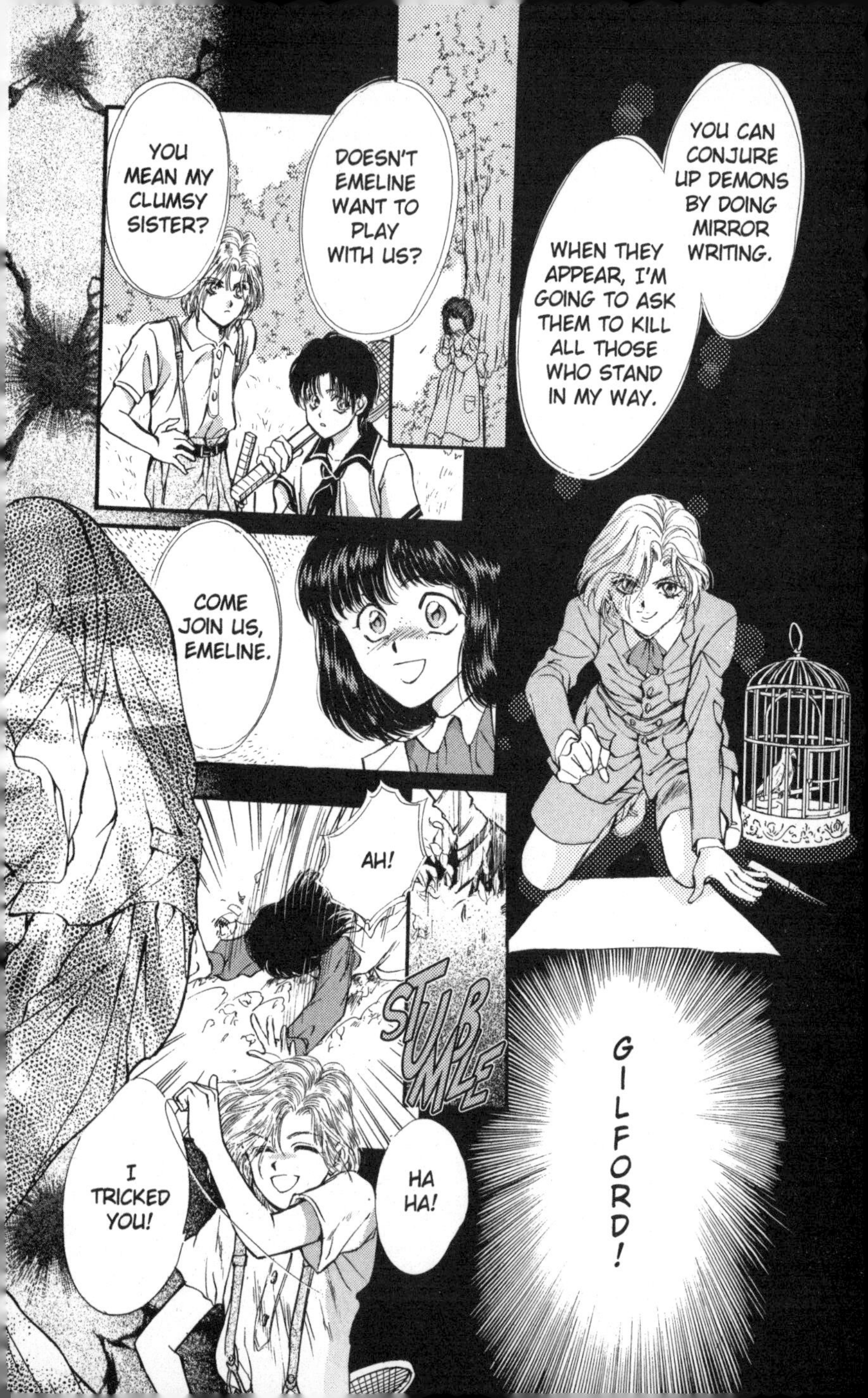
YOU CAN CONJURE UP DEMONS BY DOING MIRROR WRITING.
WHEN THEY APPEAR, I'M GOING TO ASK THEM TO KILL ALL THOSE WHO STAND IN MY WAY.
DOESN'T EMELINE WANT TO PLAY WITH US?
YOU MEAN MY CLUMSY SISTER?
COME JOIN US, EMELINE.
AH!
STUMBLE
HA HA!
I TRICKED YOU!
GILFORD!

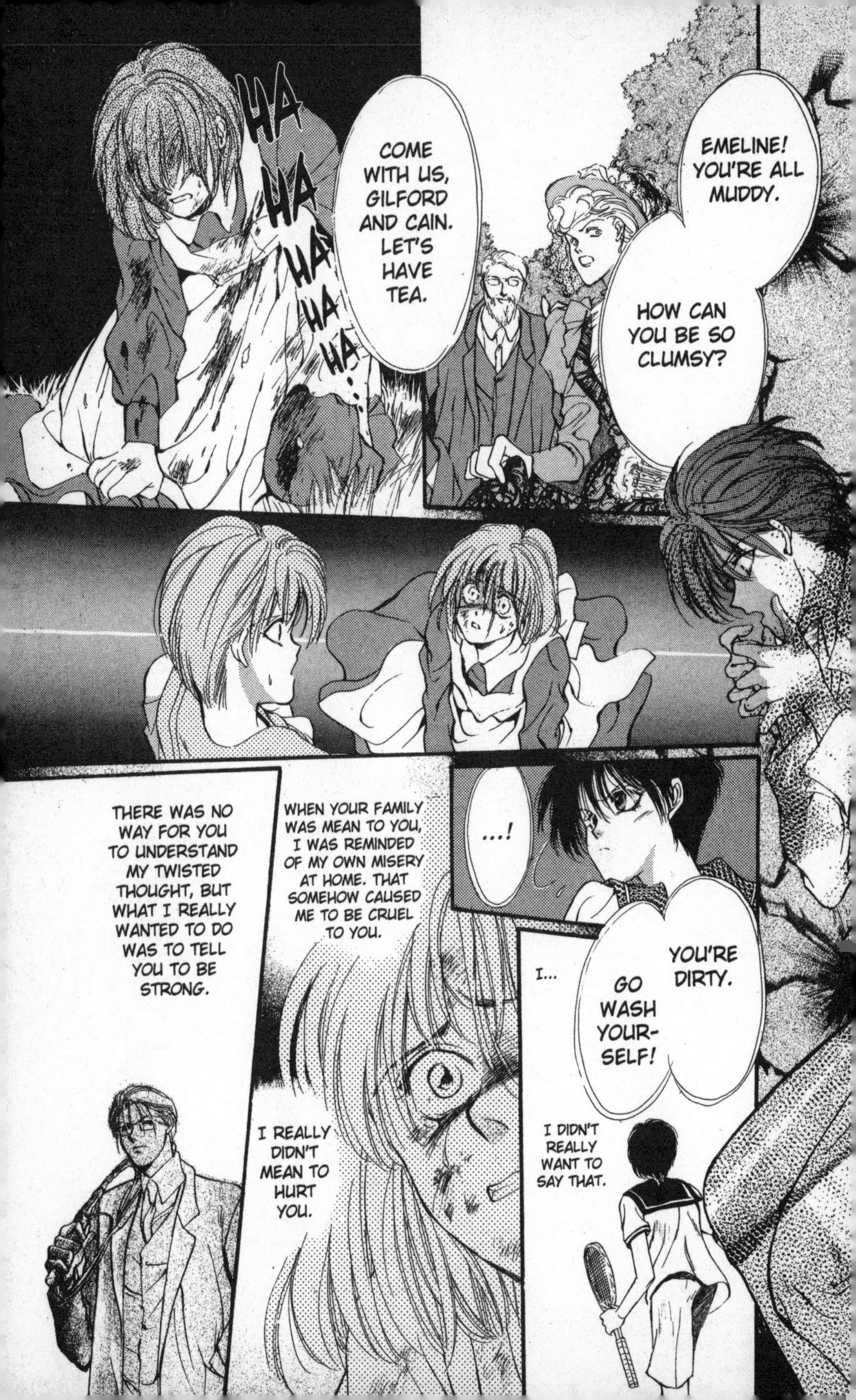
EMELINE! YOU'RE ALL MUDDY.
HOW CAN YOU BE SO CLUMSY?
COME WITH US, GILFORD AND CAIN. LET'S HAVE TEA.
HA HA HA HA HA
...!
YOU'RE DIRTY. GO WASH YOURSELF!
I...
I DIDN'T REALLY WANT TO SAY THAT.
WHEN YOUR FAMILY WAS MEAN TO YOU, I WAS REMINDED OF MY OWN MISERY AT HOME. THAT SOMEHOW CAUSED ME TO BE CRUEL TO YOU.
I REALLY DIDN'T MEAN TO HURT YOU.
THERE WAS NO WAY FOR YOU TO UNDERSTAND MY TWISTED THOUGHT, BUT WHAT I REALLY WANTED TO DO WAS TO TELL YOU TO BE STRONG.

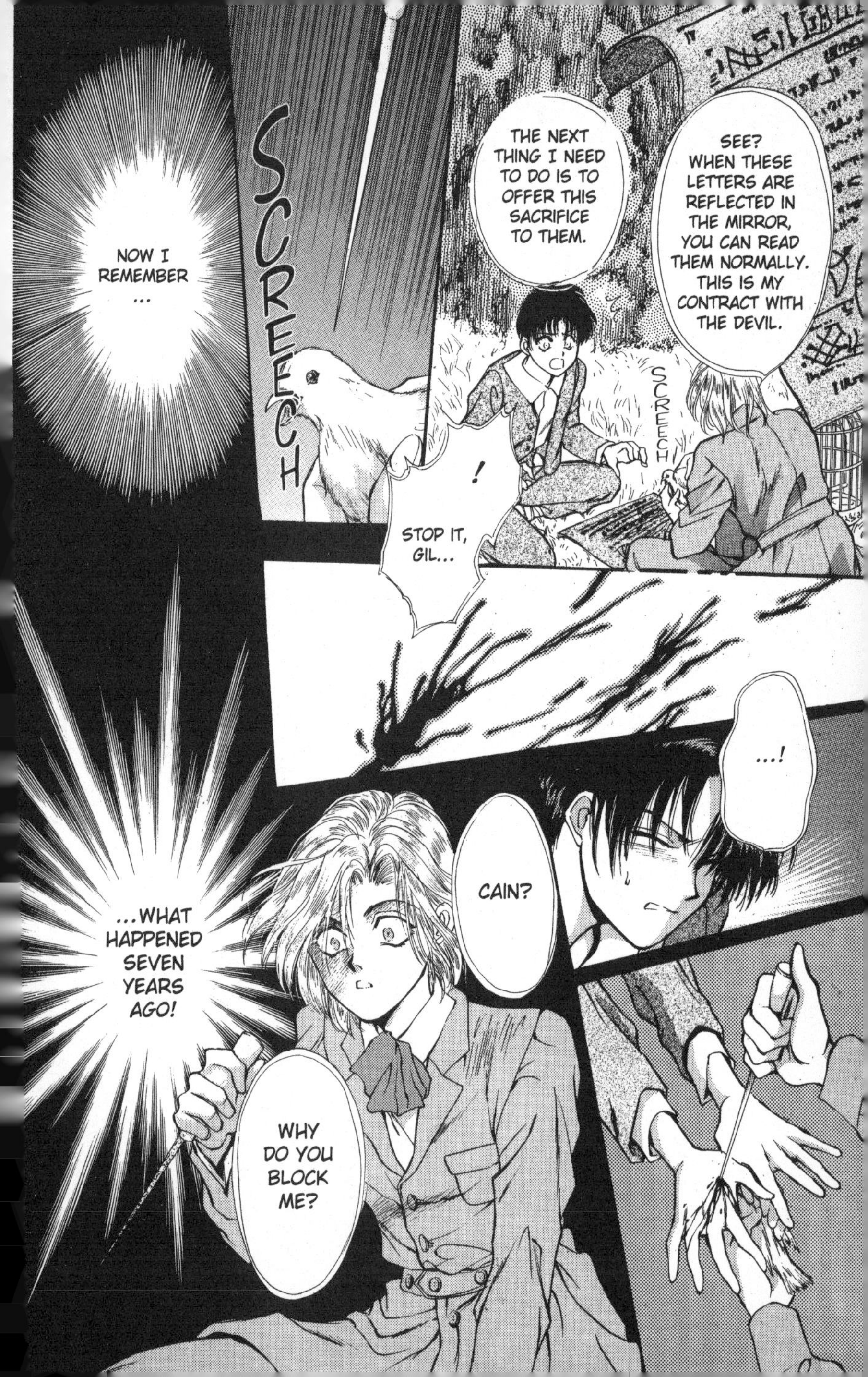
SEE? WHEN THESE LETTERS ARE REFLECTED IN THE MIRROR, YOU CAN READ THEM NORMALLY. THIS IS MY CONTRACT WITH THE DEVIL.
THE NEXT THING I NEED TO DO IS TO OFFER THIS SACRIFICE TO THEM.
SCREECH
SCREECH
!
STOP IT, GIL...
...!
CAIN?
WHY DO YOU BLOCK ME?
NOW I REMEMBER ...
...WHAT HAPPENED SEVEN YEARS AGO!

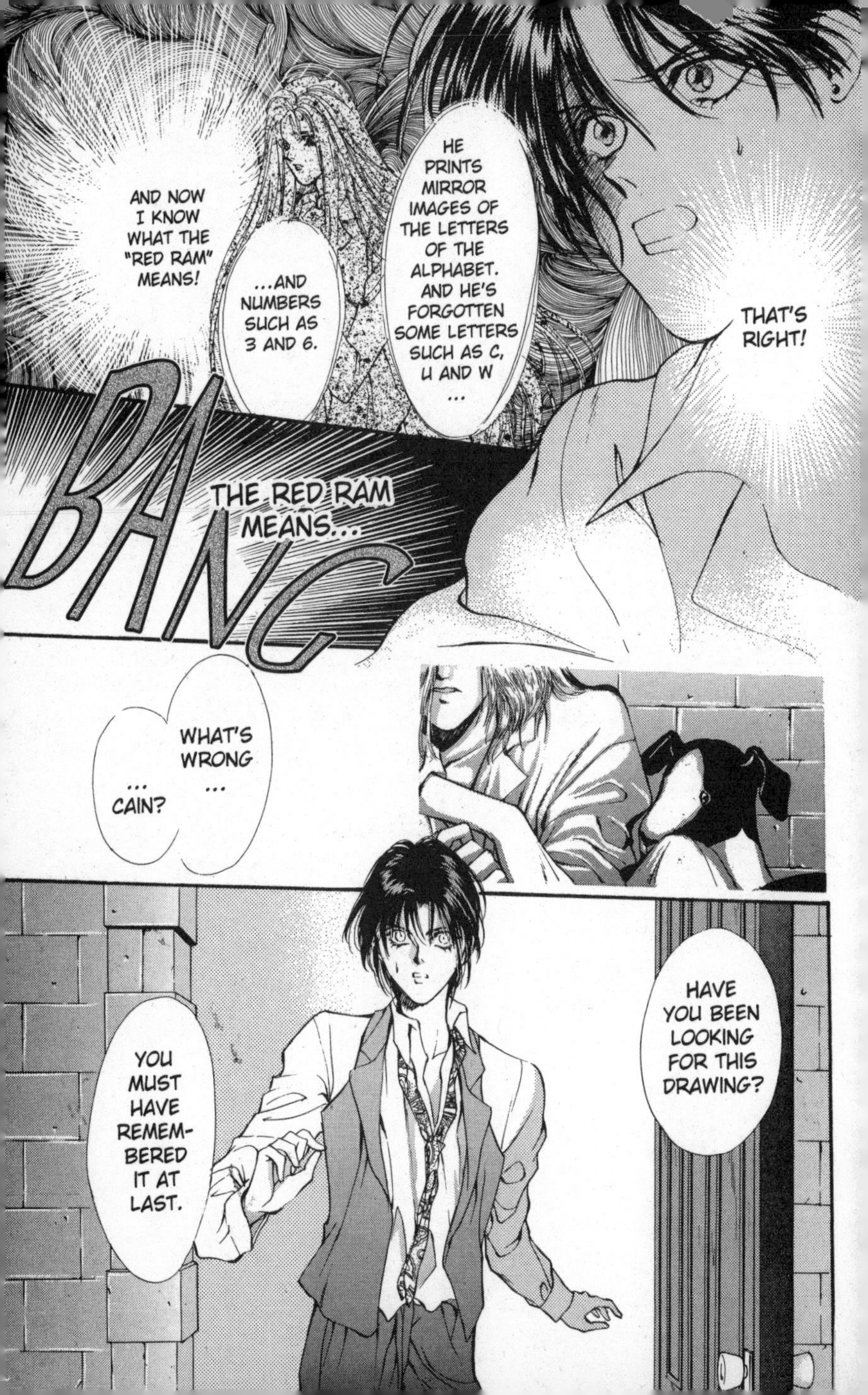
HE PRINTS MIRROR IMAGES OF THE LETTERS OF THE ALPHABET. AND HE'S FORGOTTEN SOME LETTERS SUCH AS C, U AND W ...
...AND NUMBERS SUCH AS 3 AND 6.
AND NOW I KNOW WHAT THE "RED RAM" MEANS!
THAT'S RIGHT!
THE RED RAM MEANS...
BANG
WHAT'S WRONG ...
... CAIN?
HAVE YOU BEEN LOOKING FOR THIS DRAWING?
YOU MUST HAVE REMEM-BERED IT AT LAST.

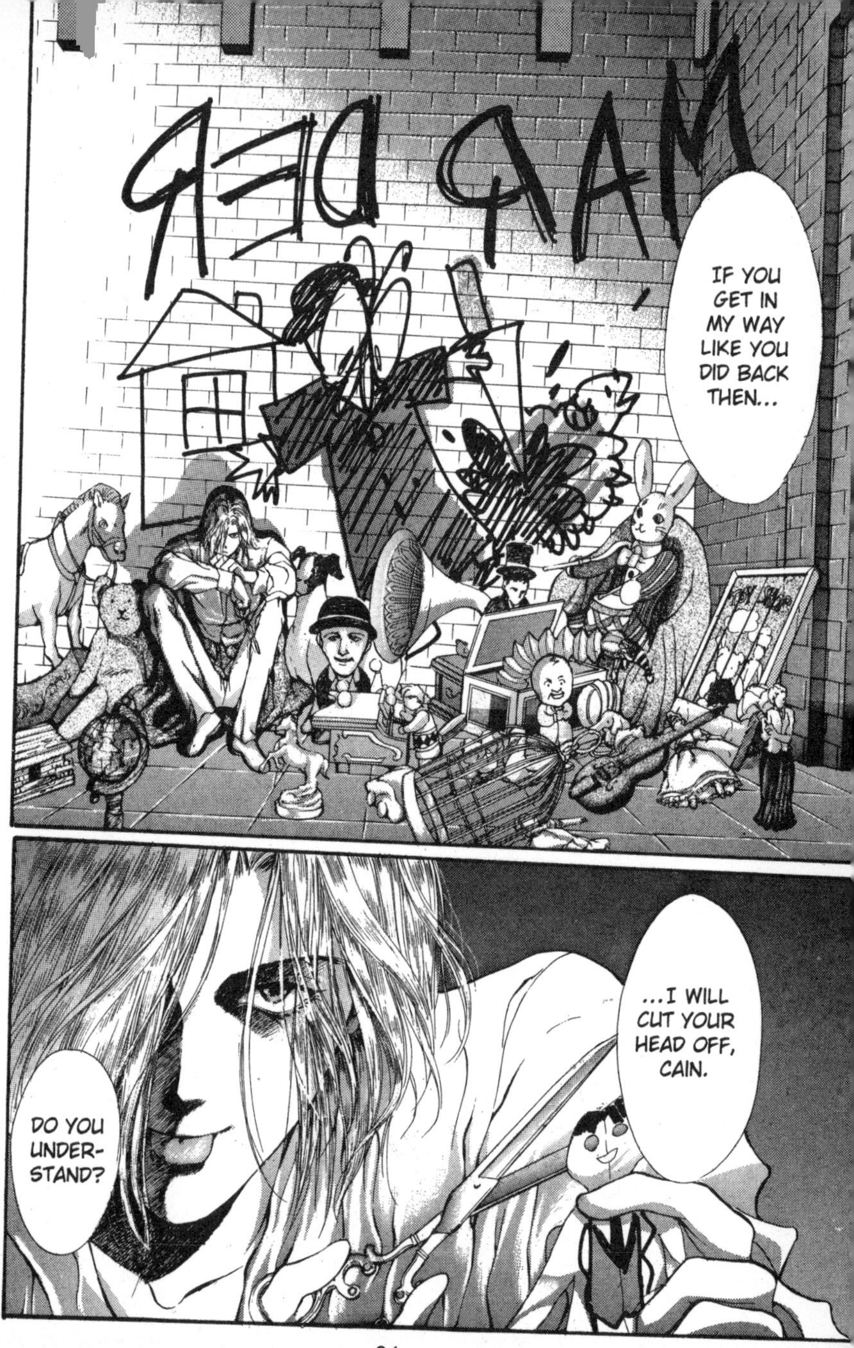
IF YOU GET IN MY WAY LIKE YOU DID BACK THEN...
...I WILL CUT YOUR HEAD OFF, CAIN.
DO YOU UNDER-STAND?

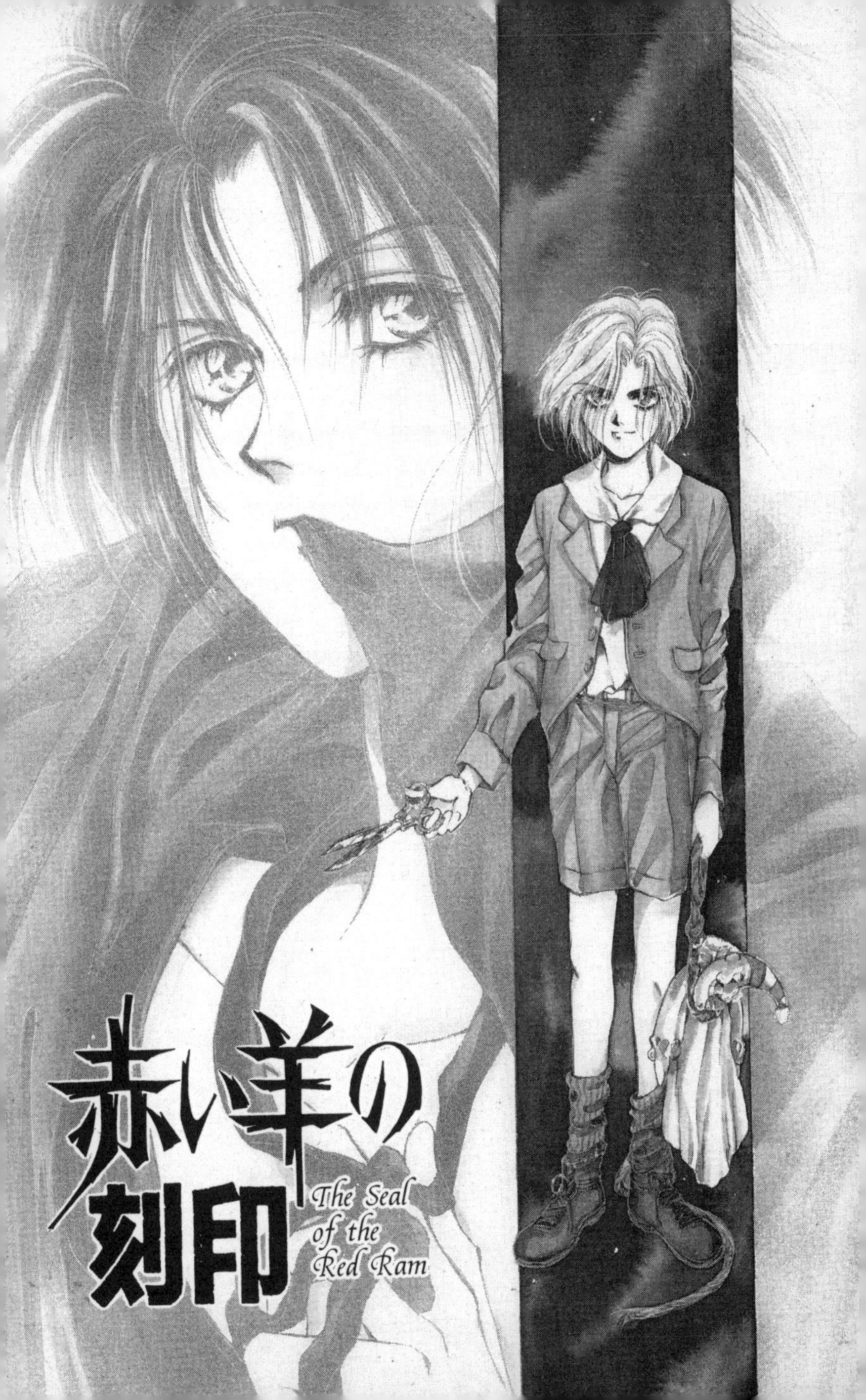
赤い羊の刻印
The Seal of the Red Ram

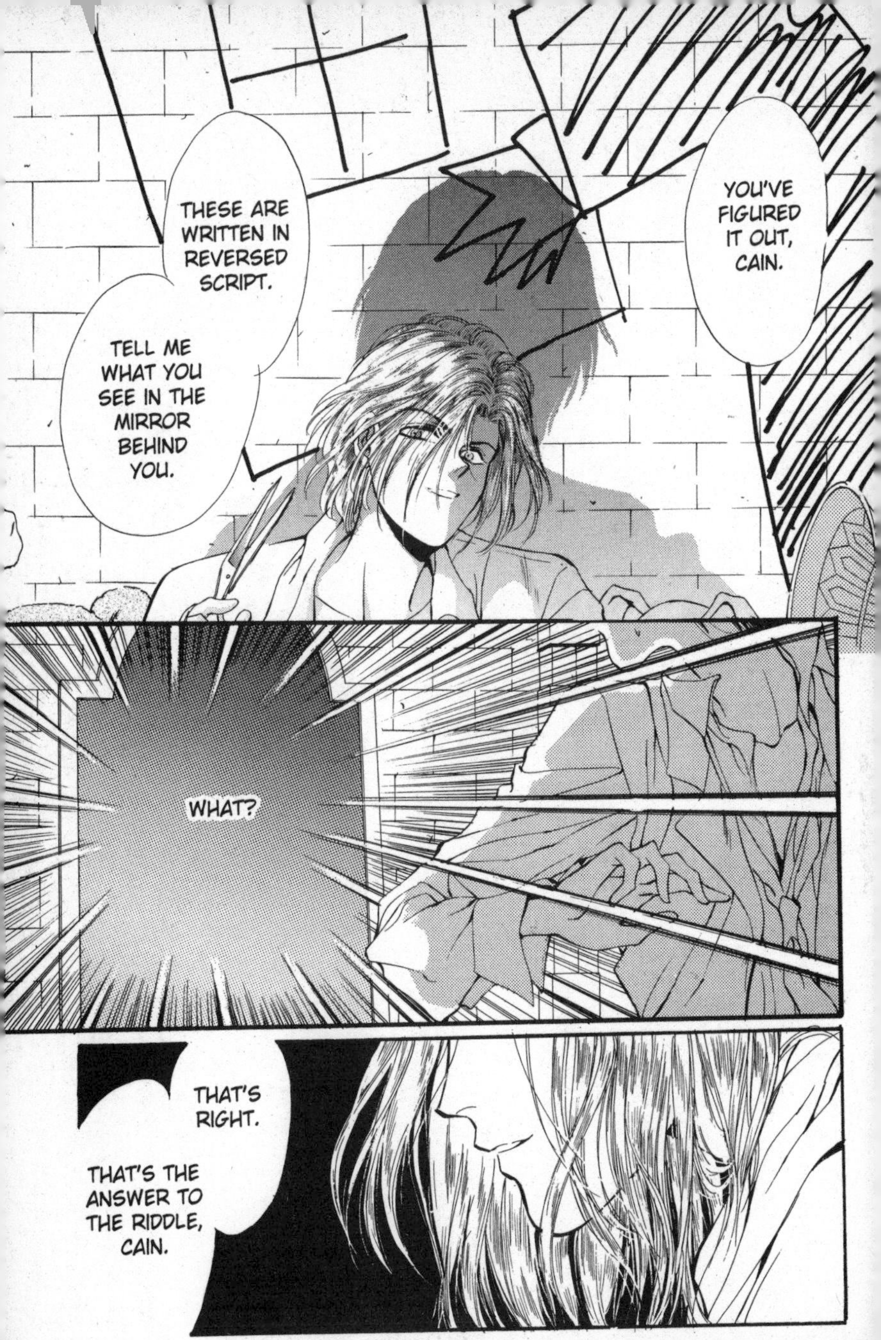
YOU'VE FIGURED IT OUT, CAIN.
THESE ARE WRITTEN IN REVERSED SCRIPT.
TELL ME WHAT YOU SEE IN THE MIRROR BEHIND YOU.
WHAT?
THAT'S RIGHT.
THAT'S THE ANSWER TO THE RIDDLE, CAIN.

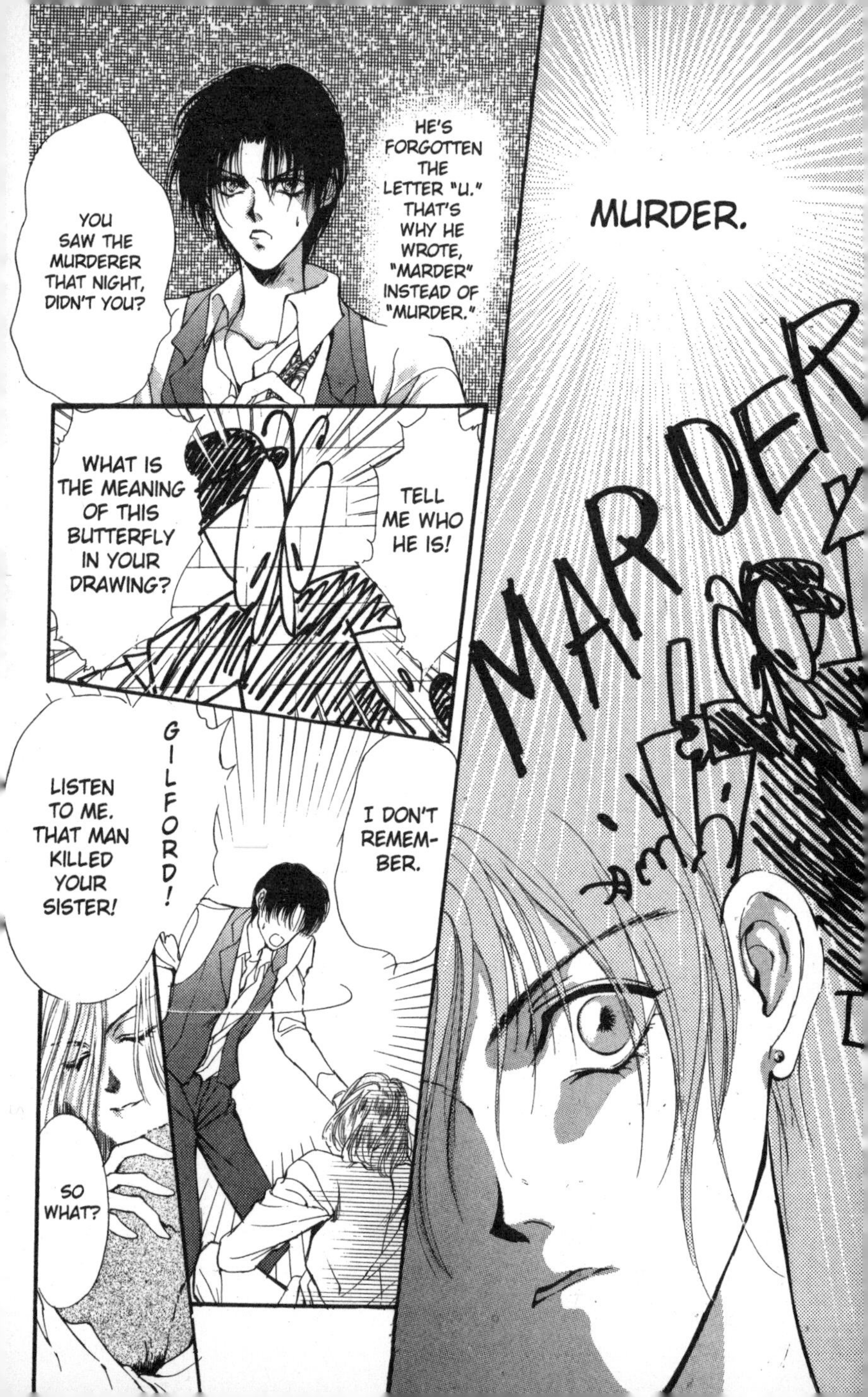
MURDER.
MAR DER
HE'S FORGOTTEN THE LETTER "U." THAT'S WHY HE WROTE, "MARDER" INSTEAD OF "MURDER."
YOU SAW THE MURDERER THAT NIGHT, DIDN'T YOU?
TELL ME WHO HE IS!
WHAT IS THE MEANING OF THIS BUTTERFLY IN YOUR DRAWING?
I DON'T REMEM-BER.
GILFORD!
LISTEN TO ME. THAT MAN KILLED YOUR SISTER!
SO WHAT?

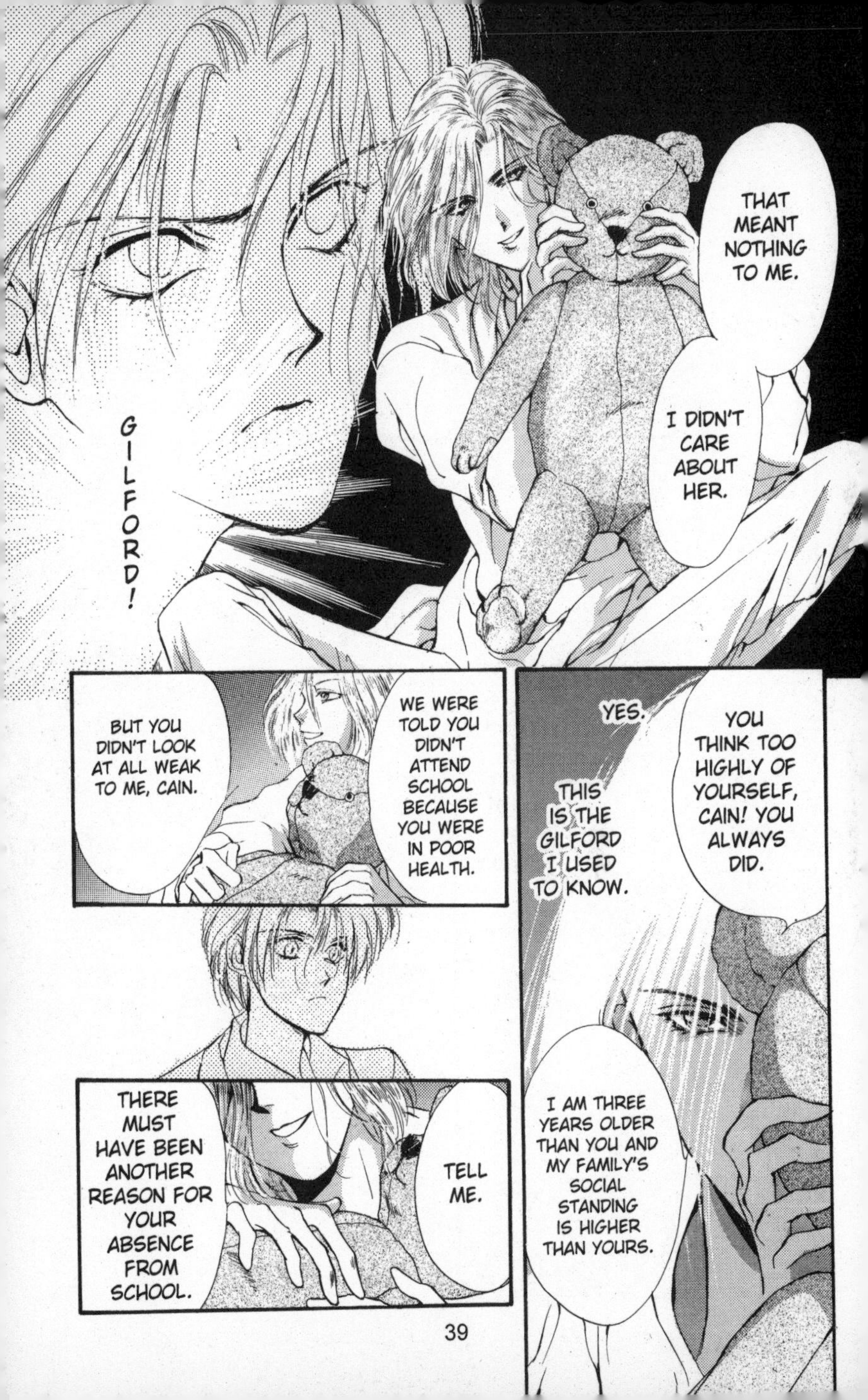
THAT MEANT NOTHING TO ME.
I DIDN'T CARE ABOUT HER.
GILFORD!
YOU THINK TOO HIGHLY OF YOURSELF, CAIN! YOU ALWAYS DID.
YES.
THIS IS THE GILFORD I USED TO KNOW.
I AM THREE YEARS OLDER THAN YOU AND MY FAMILY'S SOCIAL STANDING IS HIGHER THAN YOURS.
WE WERE TOLD YOU DIDN'T ATTEND SCHOOL BECAUSE YOU WERE IN POOR HEALTH.
BUT YOU DIDN'T LOOK AT ALL WEAK TO ME, CAIN.
TELL ME.
THERE MUST HAVE BEEN ANOTHER REASON FOR YOUR ABSENCE FROM SCHOOL.

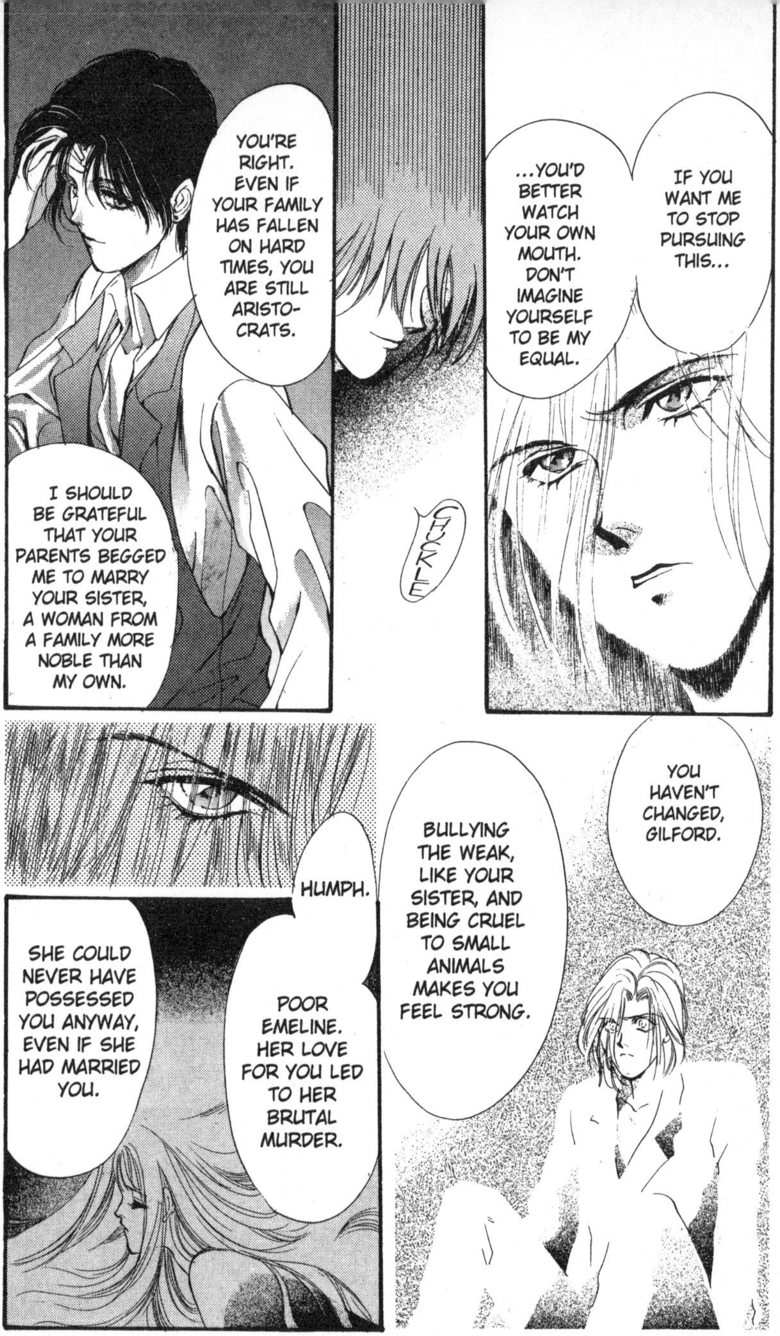
IF YOU WANT ME TO STOP PURSUING THIS...
...YOU'D BETTER WATCH YOUR OWN MOUTH. DON'T IMAGINE YOURSELF TO BE MY EQUAL.
CHUCKLE
YOU'RE RIGHT. EVEN IF YOUR FAMILY HAS FALLEN ON HARD TIMES, YOU ARE STILL ARISTO-CRATS.
I SHOULD BE GRATEFUL THAT YOUR PARENTS BEGGED ME TO MARRY YOUR SISTER, A WOMAN FROM A FAMILY MORE NOBLE THAN MY OWN.
YOU HAVEN'T CHANGED, GILFORD.
BULLYING THE WEAK, LIKE YOUR SISTER, AND BEING CRUEL TO SMALL ANIMALS MAKES YOU FEEL STRONG.
HUMPH.
POOR EMELINE. HER LOVE FOR YOU LED TO HER BRUTAL MURDER.
SHE COULD NEVER HAVE POSSESSED YOU ANYWAY, EVEN IF SHE HAD MARRIED YOU.

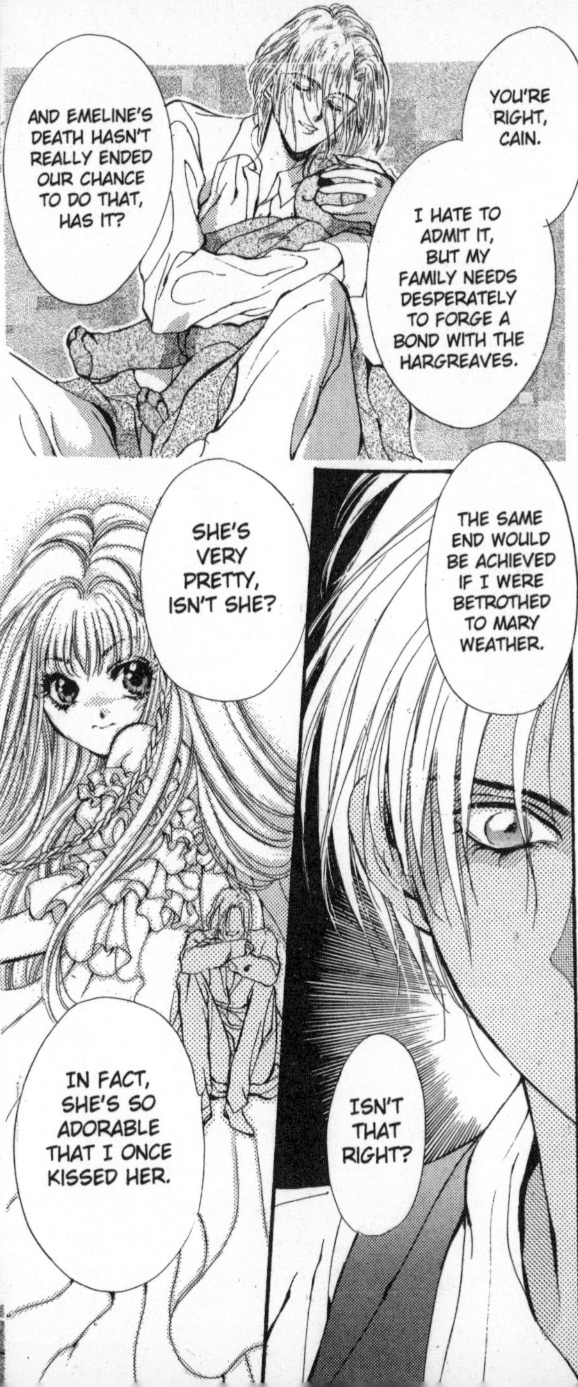
YOU'RE RIGHT, CAIN.
I HATE TO ADMIT IT, BUT MY FAMILY NEEDS DESPERATELY TO FORGE A BOND WITH THE HARGREAVES.
AND EMELINE'S DEATH HASN'T REALLY ENDED OUR CHANCE TO DO THAT, HAS IT?
THE SAME END WOULD BE ACHIEVED IF I WERE BETROTHED TO MARY WEATHER.
ISN'T THAT RIGHT?
SHE'S VERY PRETTY, ISN'T SHE?
IN FACT, SHE'S SO ADORABLE THAT I ONCE KISSED HER.

WILD TALK
PART 2

Since Gilford, a key character in the latter half of the "Red Ram", began revealing his true self, I have really enjoyed working on this story. In fact, I've been dying to begin writing this part. I love to portray evil men. I was surprised that my readers reacted so strongly to the maid, Lisa, since she isn't a major character at all. Personally, I like depicting maids because I love their uniforms. I find them very cute. Maid uniforms have a variety of designs, depending on the sort of work the maid does. Many readers responded quite strongly to Mr. Punch too. Old Mother Goose has a rhyme about Mr. Punch. Some readers said Mr. Punch reminded them of the movie, *Dolls*. I love that movie! To those who have a fear of dolls, the movie must be very horrifying. By the way, I didn't watch the movie again while preparing to write this story.

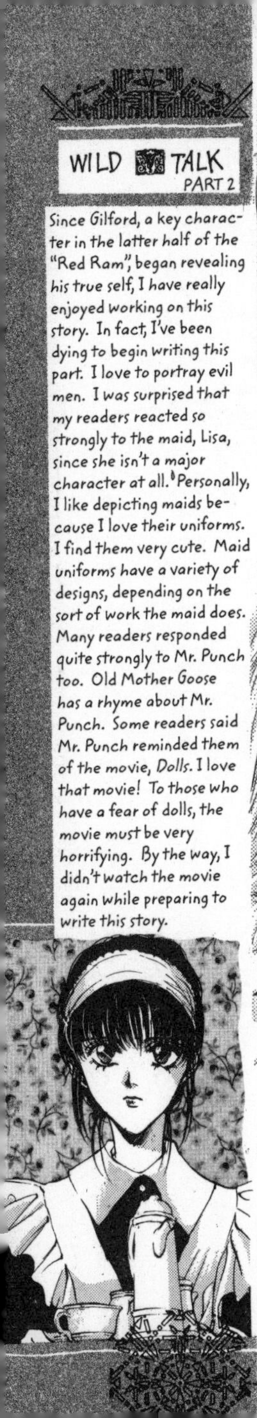

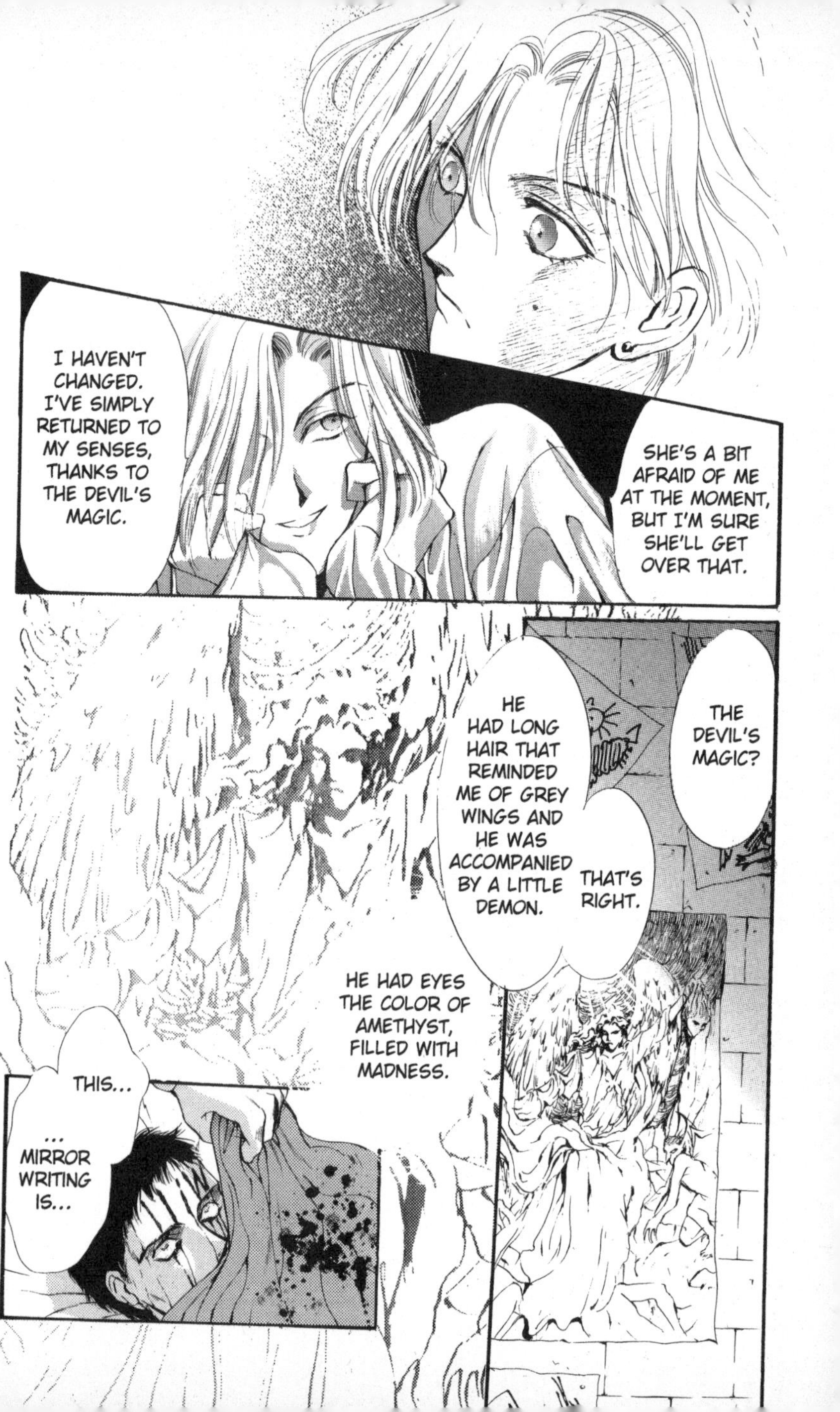

SHE'S A BIT AFRAID OF ME AT THE MOMENT, BUT I'M SURE SHE'LL GET OVER THAT.
I HAVEN'T CHANGED. I'VE SIMPLY RETURNED TO MY SENSES, THANKS TO THE DEVIL'S MAGIC.
THE DEVIL'S MAGIC?
THAT'S RIGHT.
HE HAD LONG HAIR THAT REMINDED ME OF GREY WINGS AND HE WAS ACCOMPANIED BY A LITTLE DEMON.
HE HAD EYES THE COLOR OF AMETHYST, FILLED WITH MADNESS.
THIS...
...MIRROR WRITING IS...

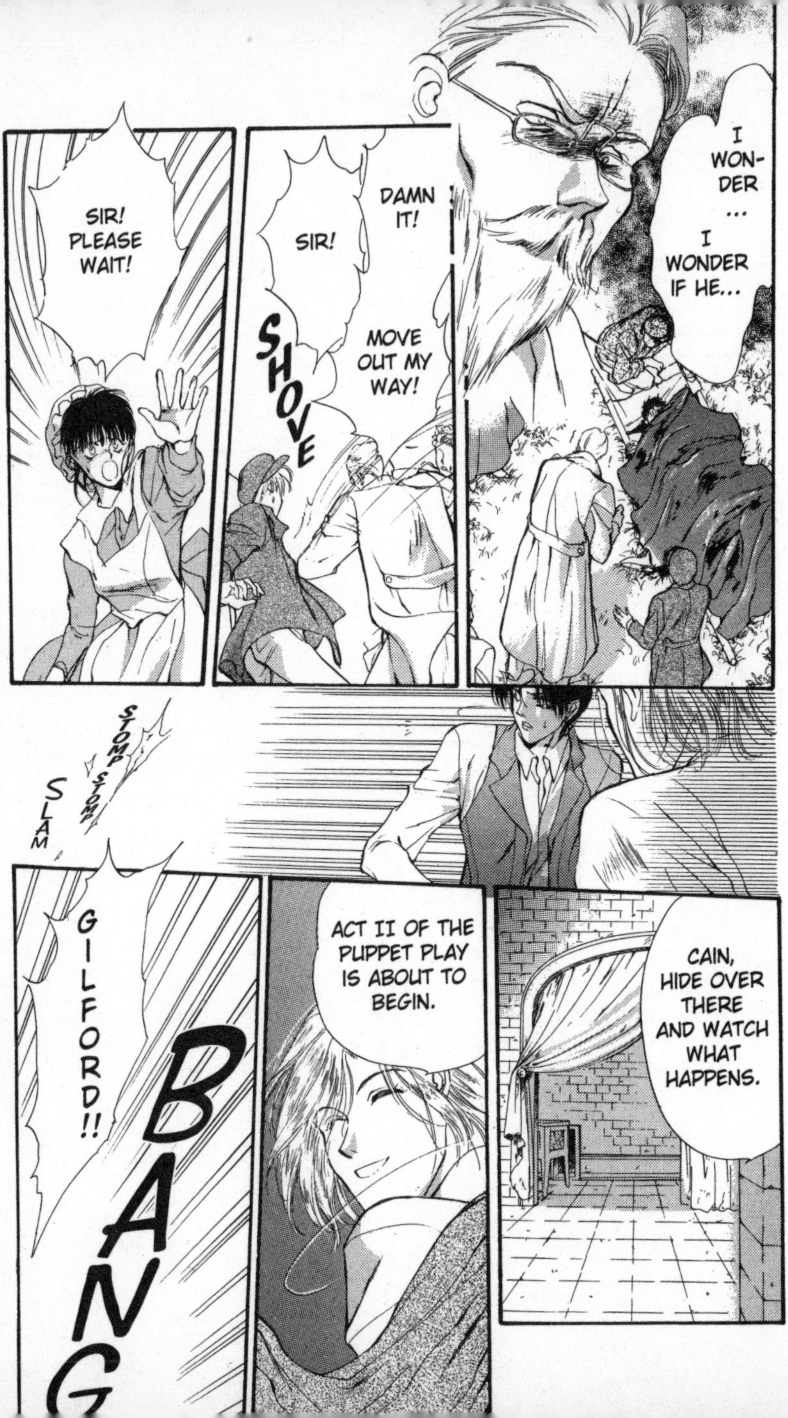
I WONDER... I WONDER IF HE...
DAMN IT!
SIR!
MOVE OUT MY WAY!
SHOVE
SIR! PLEASE WAIT!
STOMP STOMP
SLAM
CAIN, HIDE OVER THERE AND WATCH WHAT HAPPENS.
ACT II OF THE PUPPET PLAY IS ABOUT TO BEGIN.
GILFORD!!
BANG

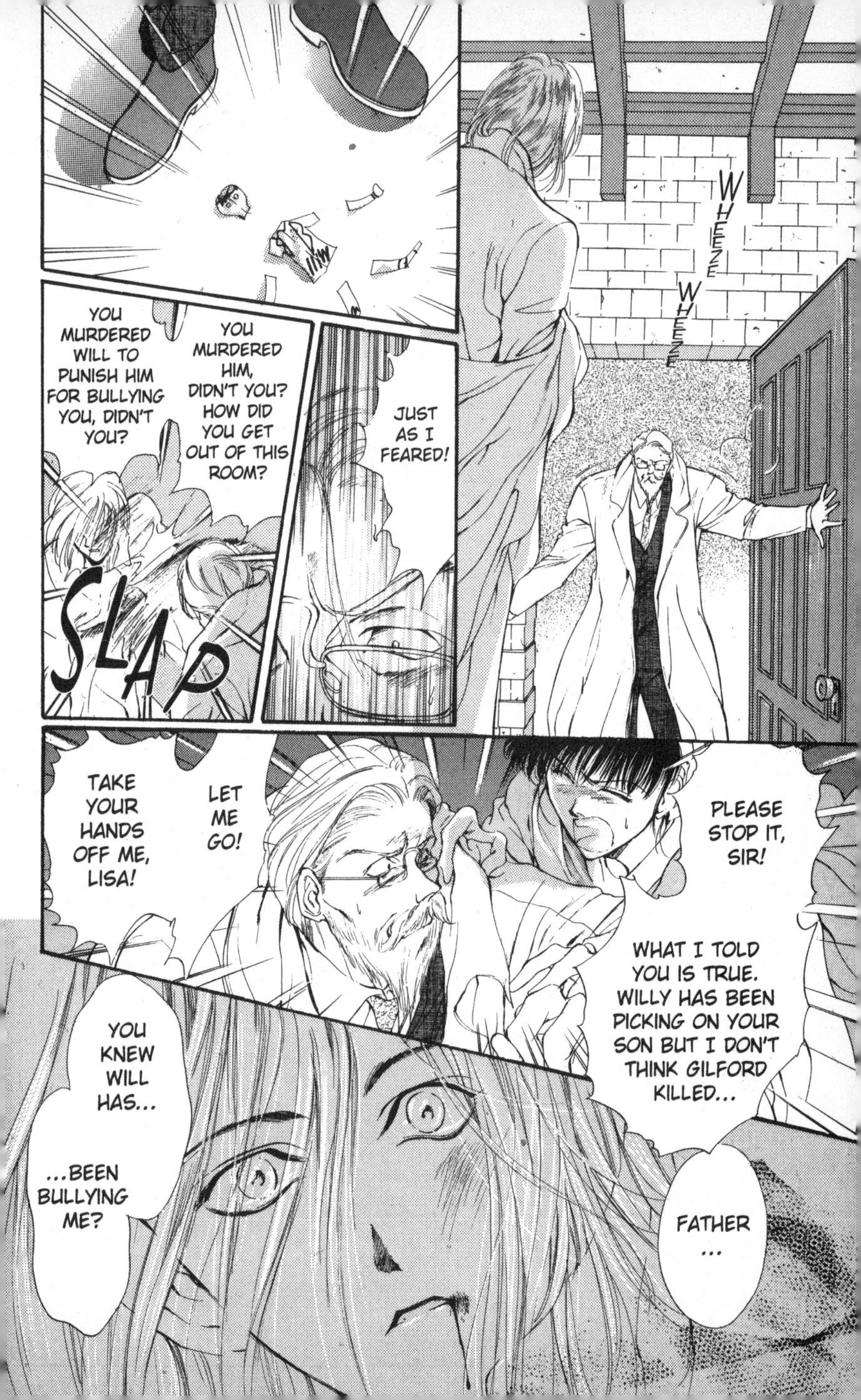
WHEEZE
WHEEZE
JUST AS I FEARED!
YOU MURDERED HIM, DIDN'T YOU? HOW DID YOU GET OUT OF THIS ROOM?
YOU MURDERED WILL TO PUNISH HIM FOR BULLYING YOU, DIDN'T YOU?
SLAP
PLEASE STOP IT, SIR!
LET ME GO!
TAKE YOUR HANDS OFF ME, LISA!
WHAT I TOLD YOU IS TRUE. WILLY HAS BEEN PICKING ON YOUR SON BUT I DON'T THINK GILFORD KILLED...
FATHER ...
YOU KNEW WILL HAS...
...BEEN BULLYING ME?

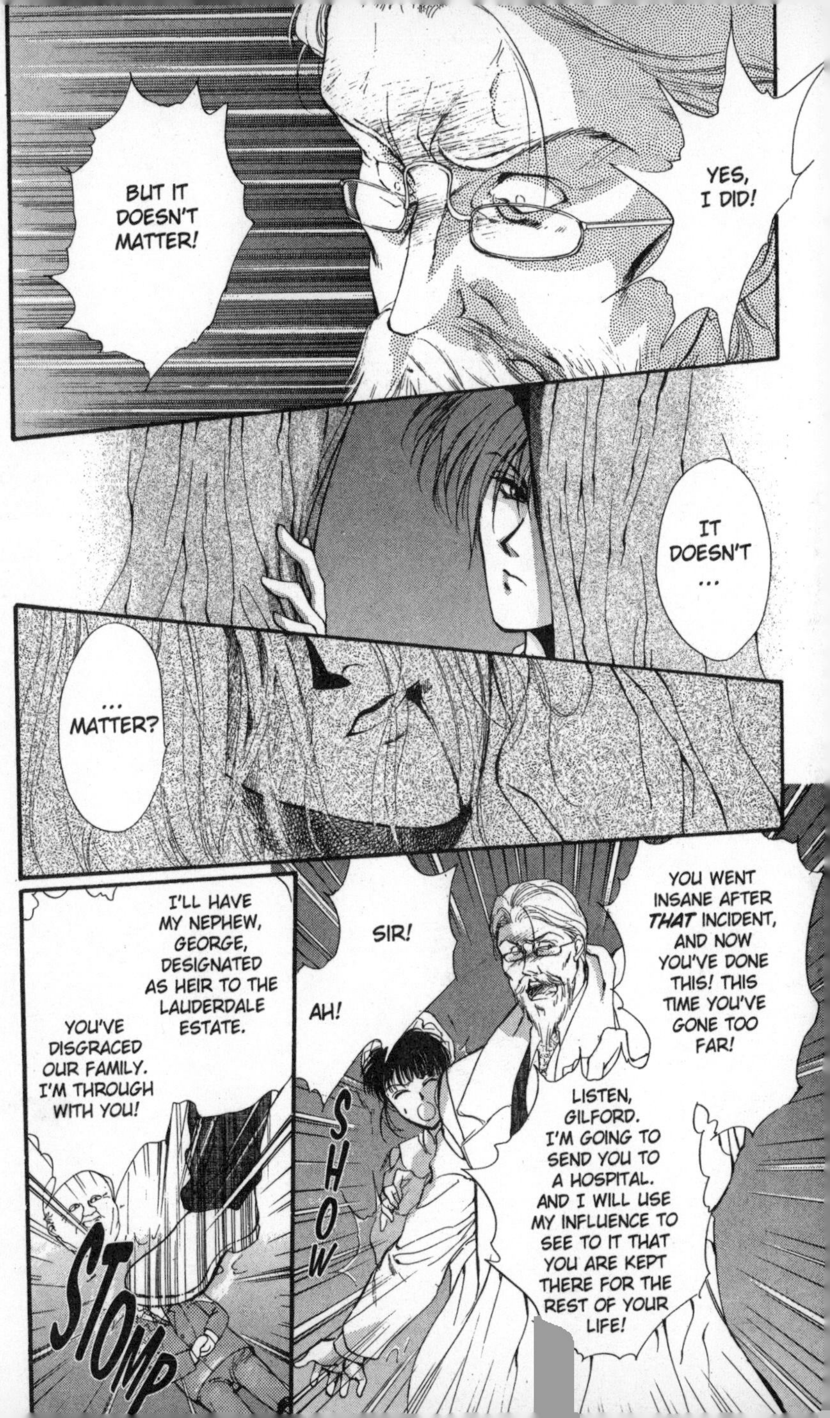
YES, I DID!
BUT IT DOESN'T MATTER!
IT DOESN'T ...
... MATTER?
YOU WENT INSANE AFTER *THAT* INCIDENT, AND NOW YOU'VE DONE THIS! THIS TIME YOU'VE GONE TOO FAR!
SIR!
AH!
LISTEN, GILFORD. I'M GOING TO SEND YOU TO A HOSPITAL. AND I WILL USE MY INFLUENCE TO SEE TO IT THAT YOU ARE KEPT THERE FOR THE REST OF YOUR LIFE!
SHOW
I'LL HAVE MY NEPHEW, GEORGE, DESIGNATED AS HEIR TO THE LAUDERDALE ESTATE.
YOU'VE DISGRACED OUR FAMILY. I'M THROUGH WITH YOU!
STOMP

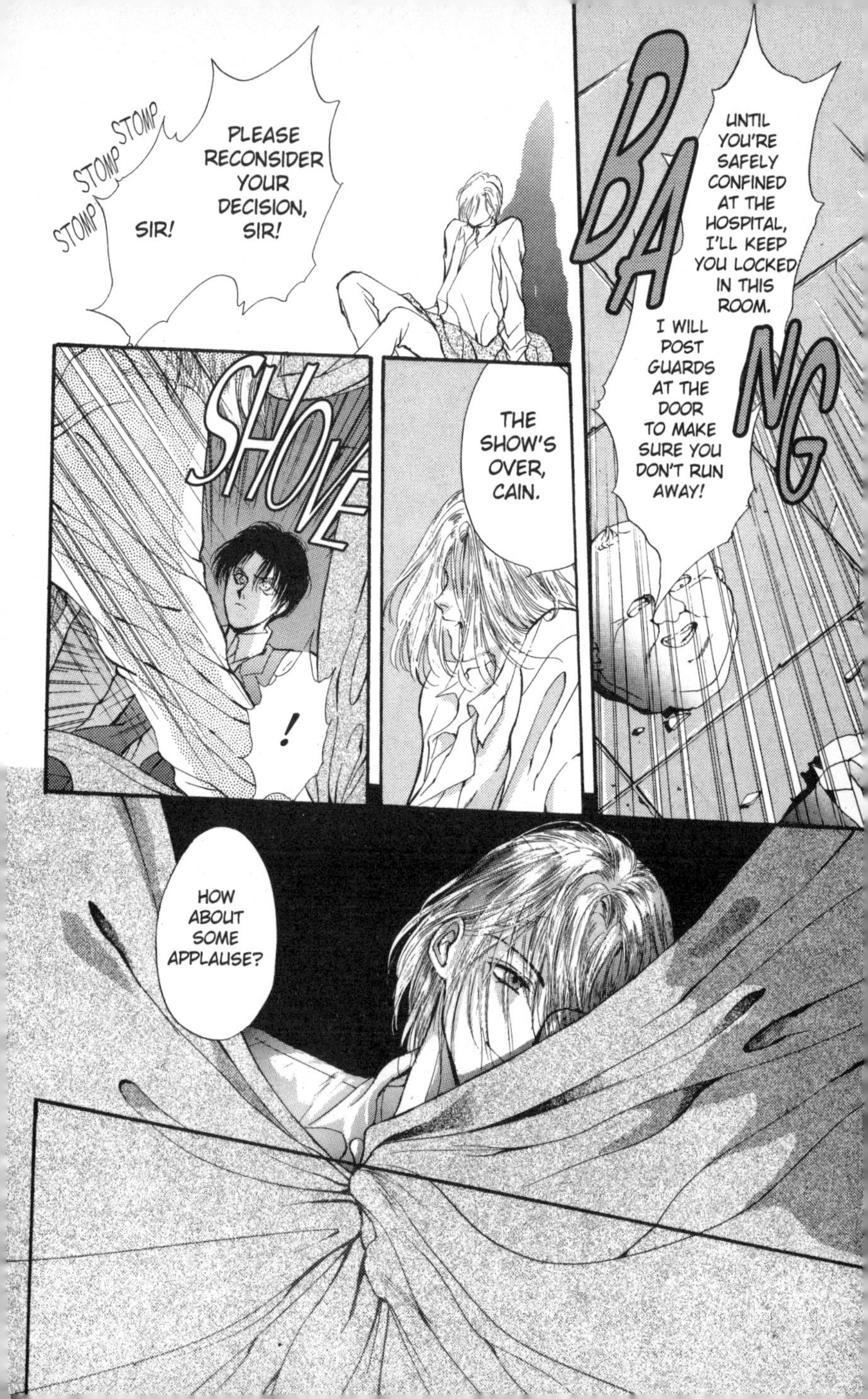
BANG
UNTIL YOU'RE SAFELY CONFINED AT THE HOSPITAL, I'LL KEEP YOU LOCKED IN THIS ROOM.
I WILL POST GUARDS AT THE DOOR TO MAKE SURE YOU DON'T RUN AWAY!
PLEASE RECONSIDER YOUR DECISION, SIR!
SIR!
STOMP STOMP STOMP
THE SHOW'S OVER, CAIN.
SHOVE
!
HOW ABOUT SOME APPLAUSE?

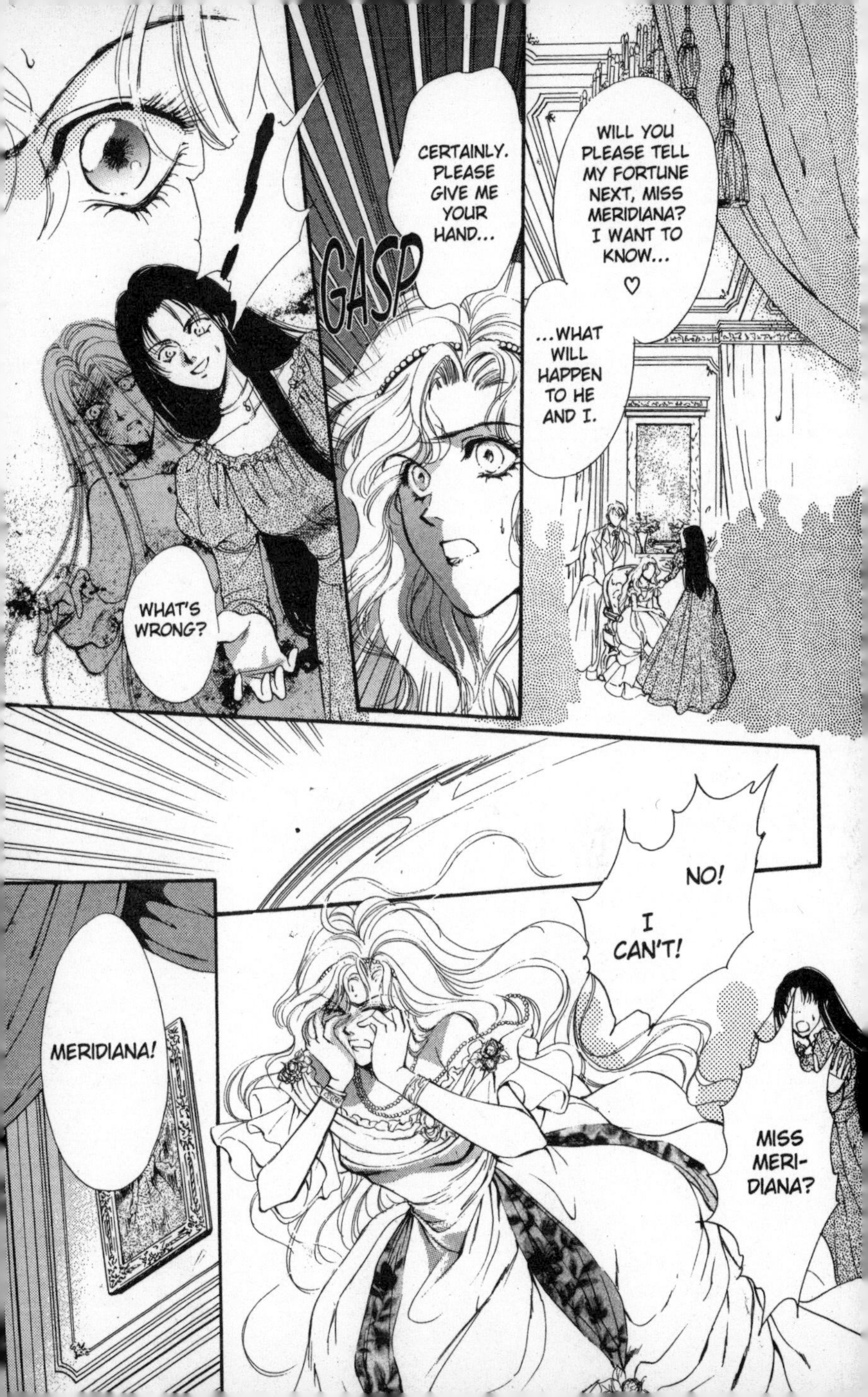
WILL YOU PLEASE TELL MY FORTUNE NEXT, MISS MERIDIANA? I WANT TO KNOW... ♡
...WHAT WILL HAPPEN TO HE AND I.
CERTAINLY. PLEASE GIVE ME YOUR HAND...
GASP
WHAT'S WRONG?
NO!
I CAN'T!
MISS MERI-DIANA?
MERIDIANA!

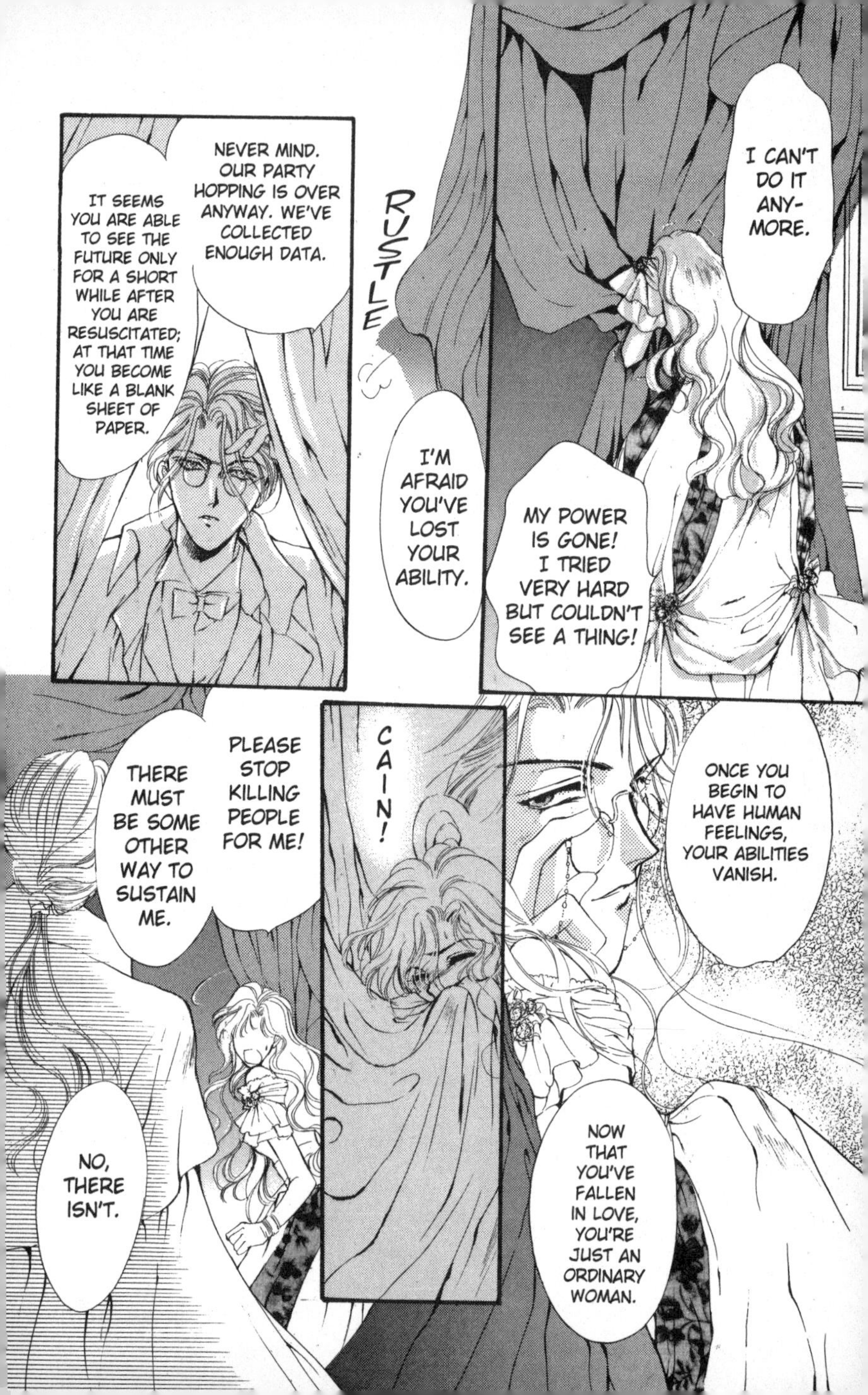
I CAN'T DO IT ANY-MORE.
MY POWER IS GONE! I TRIED VERY HARD BUT COULDN'T SEE A THING!
RUSTLE
I'M AFRAID YOU'VE LOST YOUR ABILITY.
NEVER MIND. OUR PARTY HOPPING IS OVER ANYWAY. WE'VE COLLECTED ENOUGH DATA.
IT SEEMS YOU ARE ABLE TO SEE THE FUTURE ONLY FOR A SHORT WHILE AFTER YOU ARE RESUSCITATED; AT THAT TIME YOU BECOME LIKE A BLANK SHEET OF PAPER.
ONCE YOU BEGIN TO HAVE HUMAN FEELINGS, YOUR ABILITIES VANISH.
NOW THAT YOU'VE FALLEN IN LOVE, YOU'RE JUST AN ORDINARY WOMAN.
CAIN!
PLEASE STOP KILLING PEOPLE FOR ME!
THERE MUST BE SOME OTHER WAY TO SUSTAIN ME.
NO, THERE ISN'T.

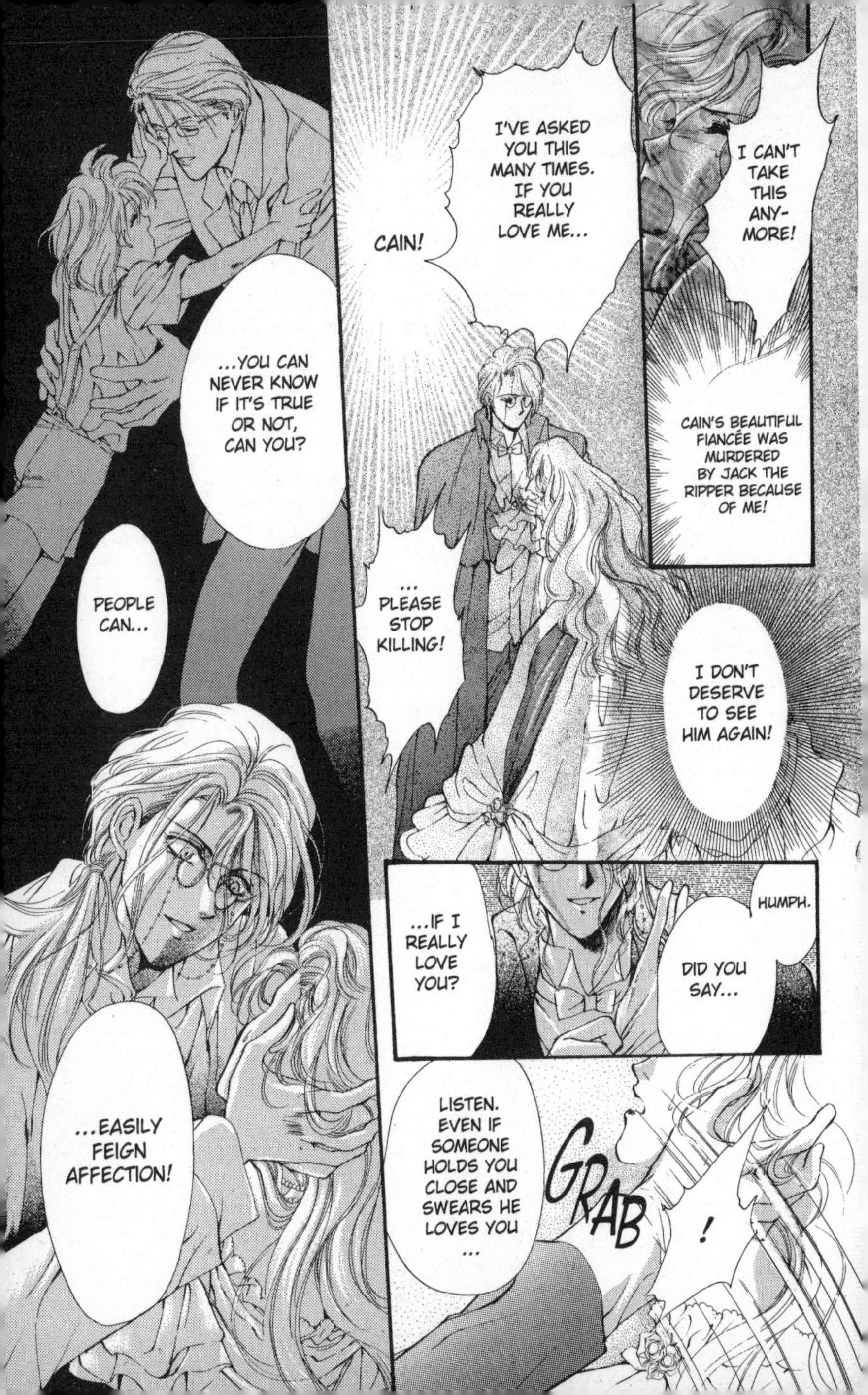
I CAN'T TAKE THIS ANY-MORE!
CAIN'S BEAUTIFUL FIANCÉE WAS MURDERED BY JACK THE RIPPER BECAUSE OF ME!
I'VE ASKED YOU THIS MANY TIMES. IF YOU REALLY LOVE ME...
CAIN!
...PLEASE STOP KILLING!
I DON'T DESERVE TO SEE HIM AGAIN!
HUMPH.
DID YOU SAY...
...IF I REALLY LOVE YOU?
LISTEN. EVEN IF SOMEONE HOLDS YOU CLOSE AND SWEARS HE LOVES YOU ...
GRAB
!
...YOU CAN NEVER KNOW IF IT'S TRUE OR NOT, CAN YOU?
PEOPLE CAN...
...EASILY FEIGN AFFECTION!

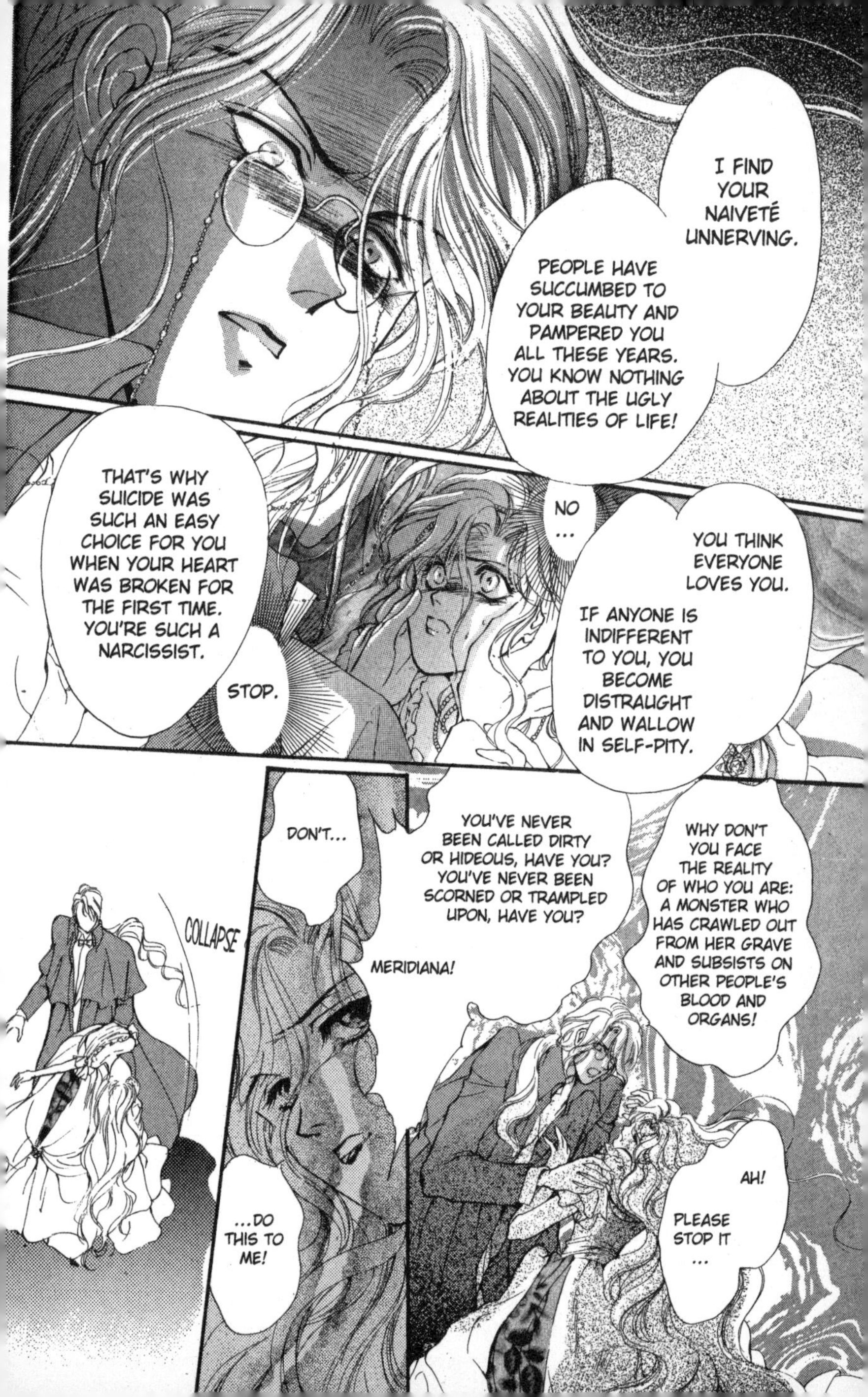
I FIND YOUR NAIVETÉ UNNERVING.
PEOPLE HAVE SUCCUMBED TO YOUR BEAUTY AND PAMPERED YOU ALL THESE YEARS. YOU KNOW NOTHING ABOUT THE UGLY REALITIES OF LIFE!
YOU THINK EVERYONE LOVES YOU.
IF ANYONE IS INDIFFERENT TO YOU, YOU BECOME DISTRAUGHT AND WALLOW IN SELF-PITY.
NO ...
THAT'S WHY SUICIDE WAS SUCH AN EASY CHOICE FOR YOU WHEN YOUR HEART WAS BROKEN FOR THE FIRST TIME. YOU'RE SUCH A NARCISSIST.
STOP.
WHY DON'T YOU FACE THE REALITY OF WHO YOU ARE: A MONSTER WHO HAS CRAWLED OUT FROM HER GRAVE AND SUBSISTS ON OTHER PEOPLE'S BLOOD AND ORGANS!
YOU'VE NEVER BEEN CALLED DIRTY OR HIDEOUS, HAVE YOU? YOU'VE NEVER BEEN SCORNED OR TRAMPLED UPON, HAVE YOU?
DON'T...
MERIDIANA!
AH!
PLEASE STOP IT ...
...DO THIS TO ME!
COLLAPSE

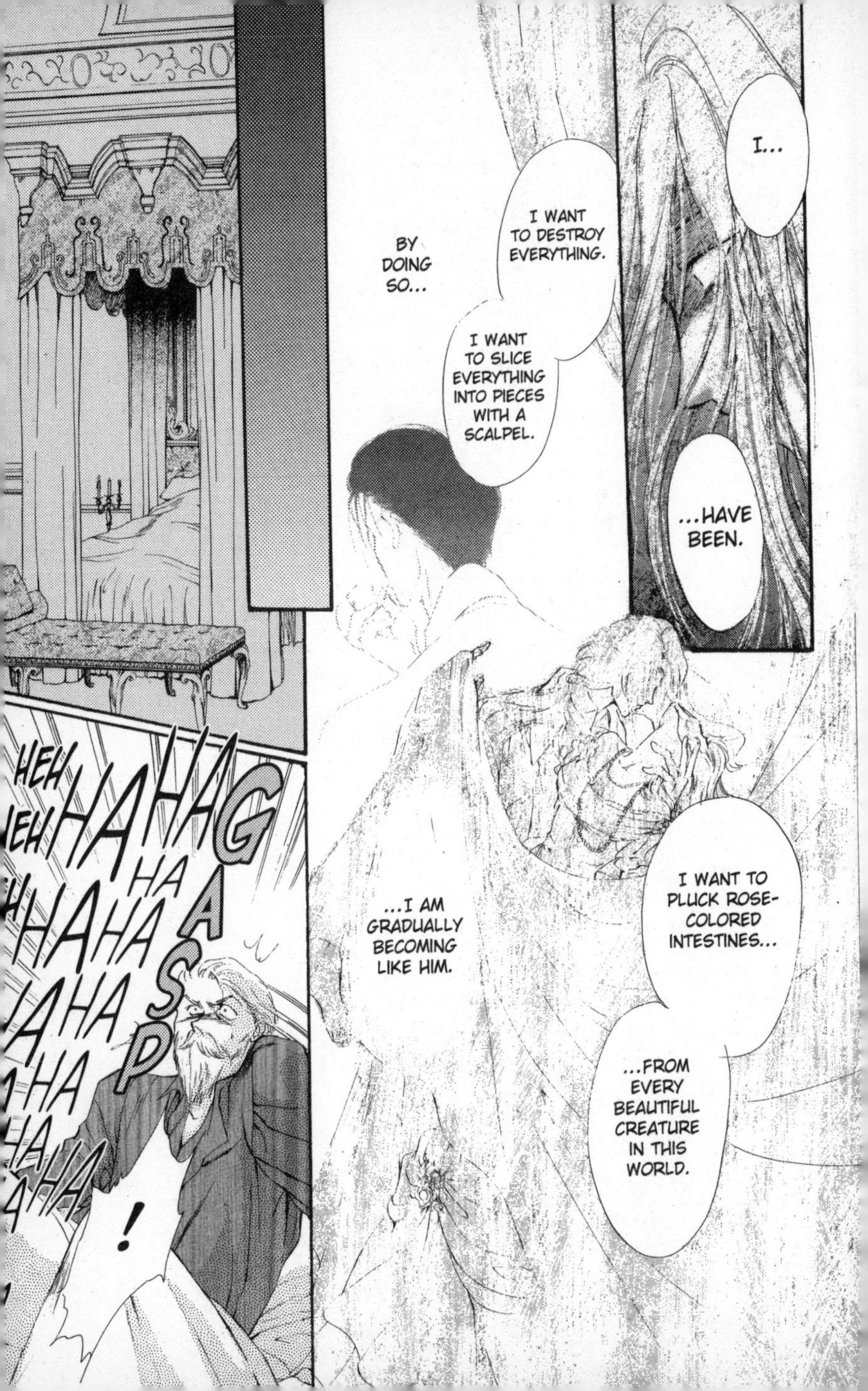
I...
...HAVE BEEN.
I WANT TO DESTROY EVERYTHING.
I WANT TO SLICE EVERYTHING INTO PIECES WITH A SCALPEL.
BY DOING SO...
I WANT TO PLUCK ROSE-COLORED INTESTINES...
...FROM EVERY BEAUTIFUL CREATURE IN THIS WORLD.
...I AM GRADUALLY BECOMING LIKE HIM.
HAG
ASP
HA HA HA HAHA HAHA HA HA HAHA HA
HEH HEH
!

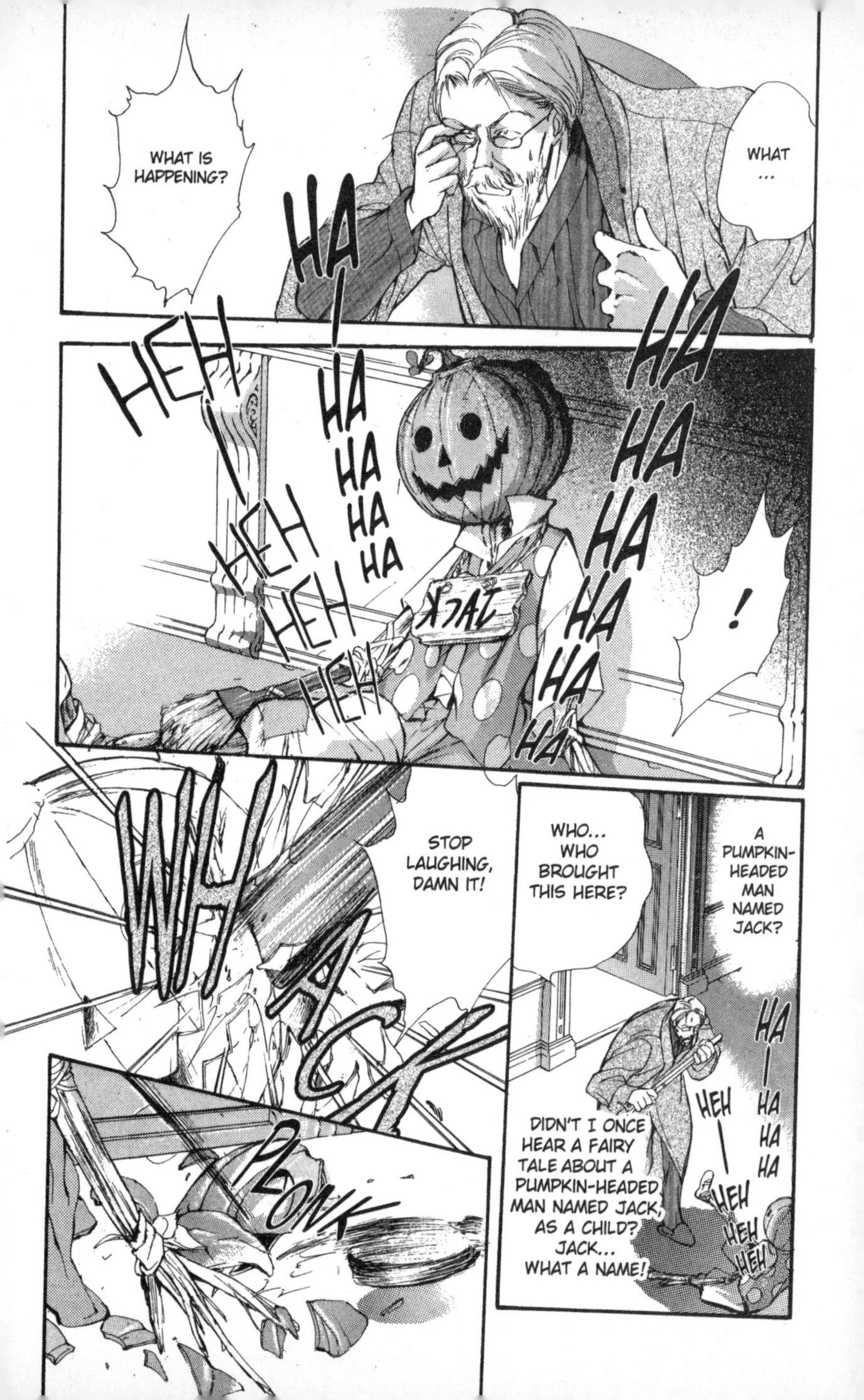
WHAT ...
WHAT IS HAPPENING?
HA-HA HA HA HA HA
HA HA HA HA HA HA HA HA HA
!
HEH-HEH HEH HEH HEH
JACK
A PUMPKIN-HEADED MAN NAMED JACK?
WHO... WHO BROUGHT THIS HERE?
DIDN'T I ONCE HEAR A FAIRY TALE ABOUT A PUMPKIN-HEADED MAN NAMED JACK, AS A CHILD? JACK... WHAT A NAME!
HA-HA HA HA HA
HEH-HEH HEH HEH
STOP LAUGHING, DAMN IT!
WHACK
PLONK

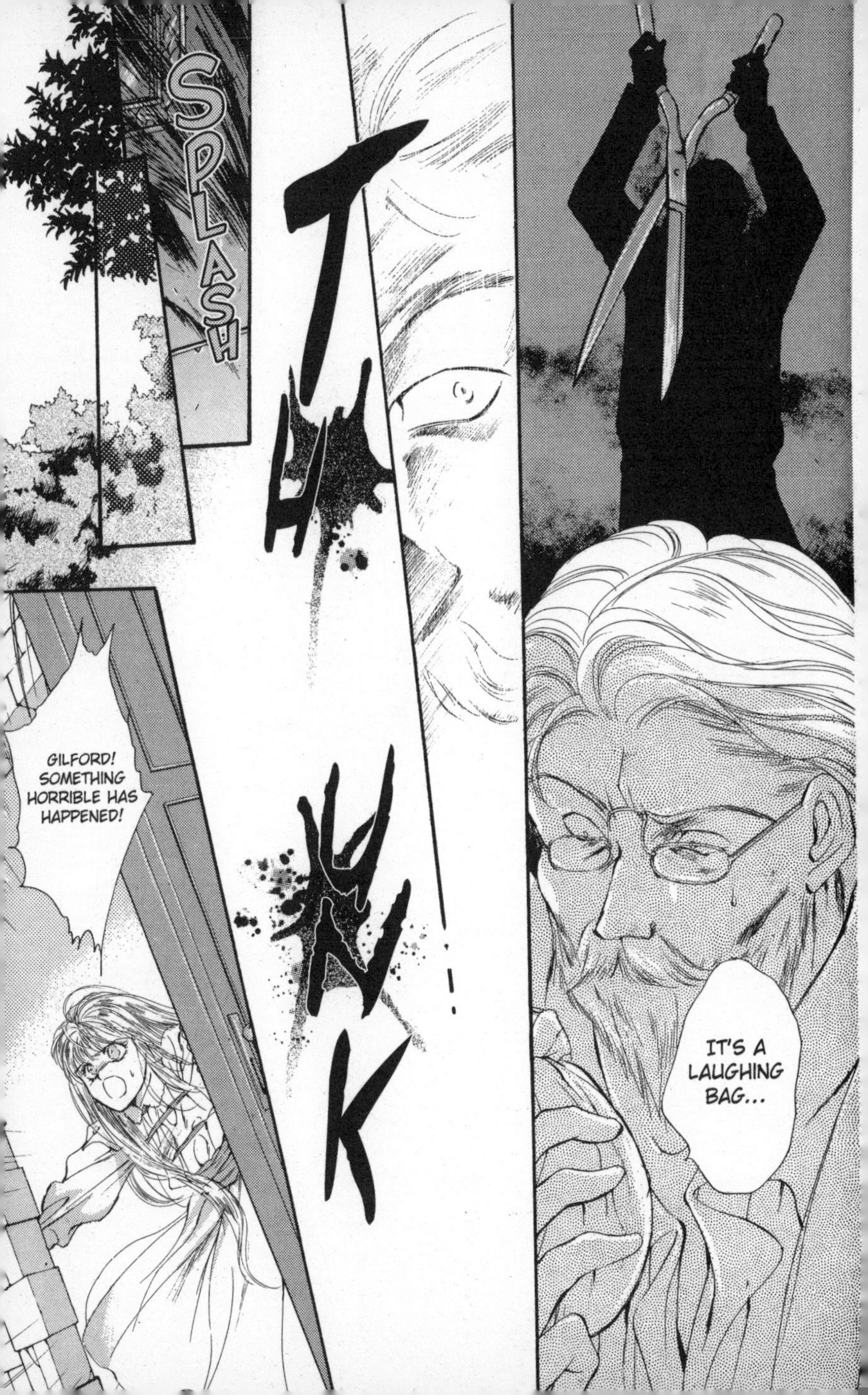

IT'S A LAUGHING BAG...
THUNK
SPLASH
GILFORD! SOMETHING HORRIBLE HAS HAPPENED!

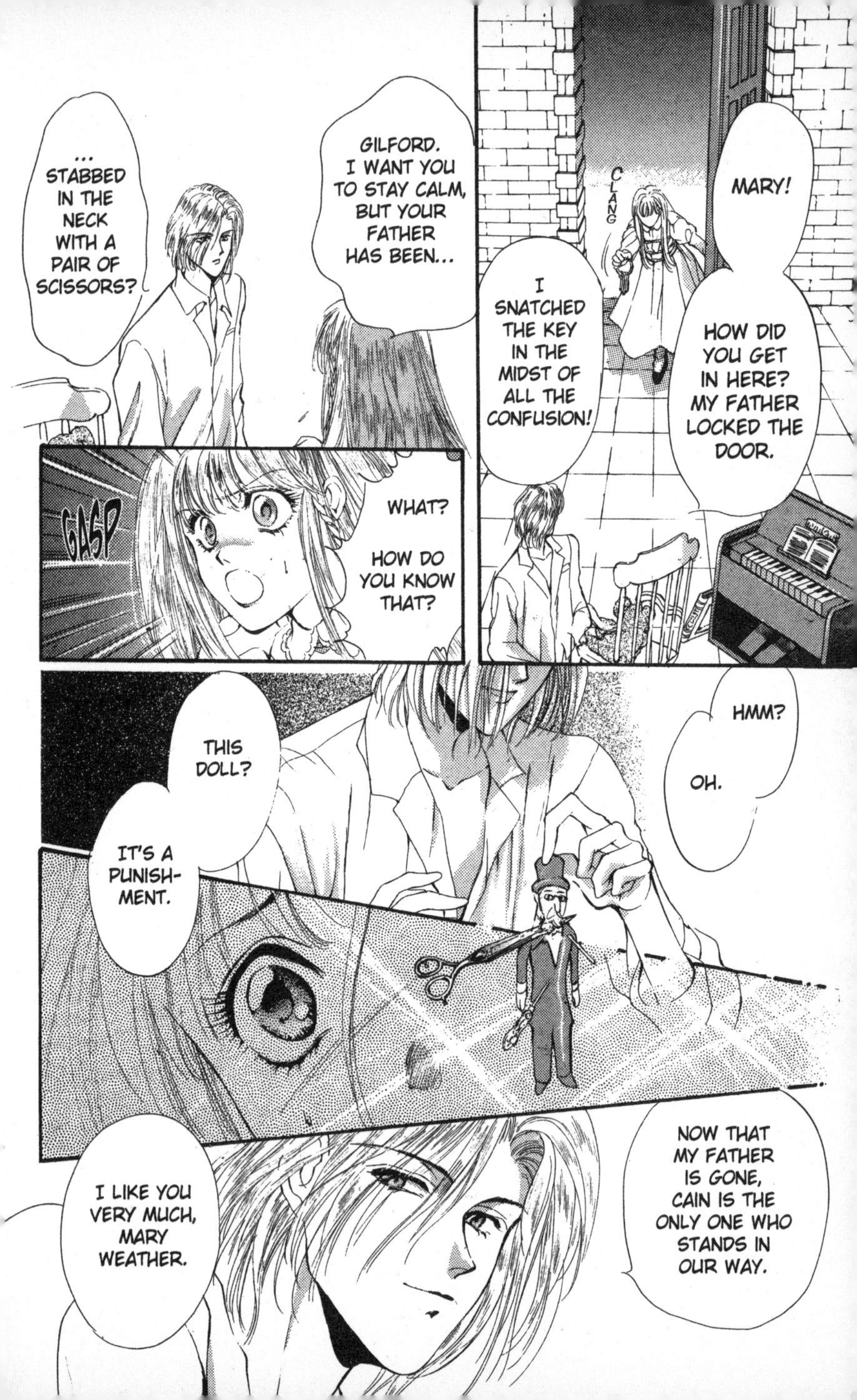
MARY!
CLANG
HOW DID YOU GET IN HERE? MY FATHER LOCKED THE DOOR.
I SNATCHED THE KEY IN THE MIDST OF ALL THE CONFUSION!
GILFORD. I WANT YOU TO STAY CALM, BUT YOUR FATHER HAS BEEN...
...STABBED IN THE NECK WITH A PAIR OF SCISSORS?
GASP
WHAT?
HOW DO YOU KNOW THAT?
HMM?
OH.
THIS DOLL?
IT'S A PUNISH-MENT.
NOW THAT MY FATHER IS GONE, CAIN IS THE ONLY ONE WHO STANDS IN OUR WAY.
I LIKE YOU VERY MUCH, MARY WEATHER.

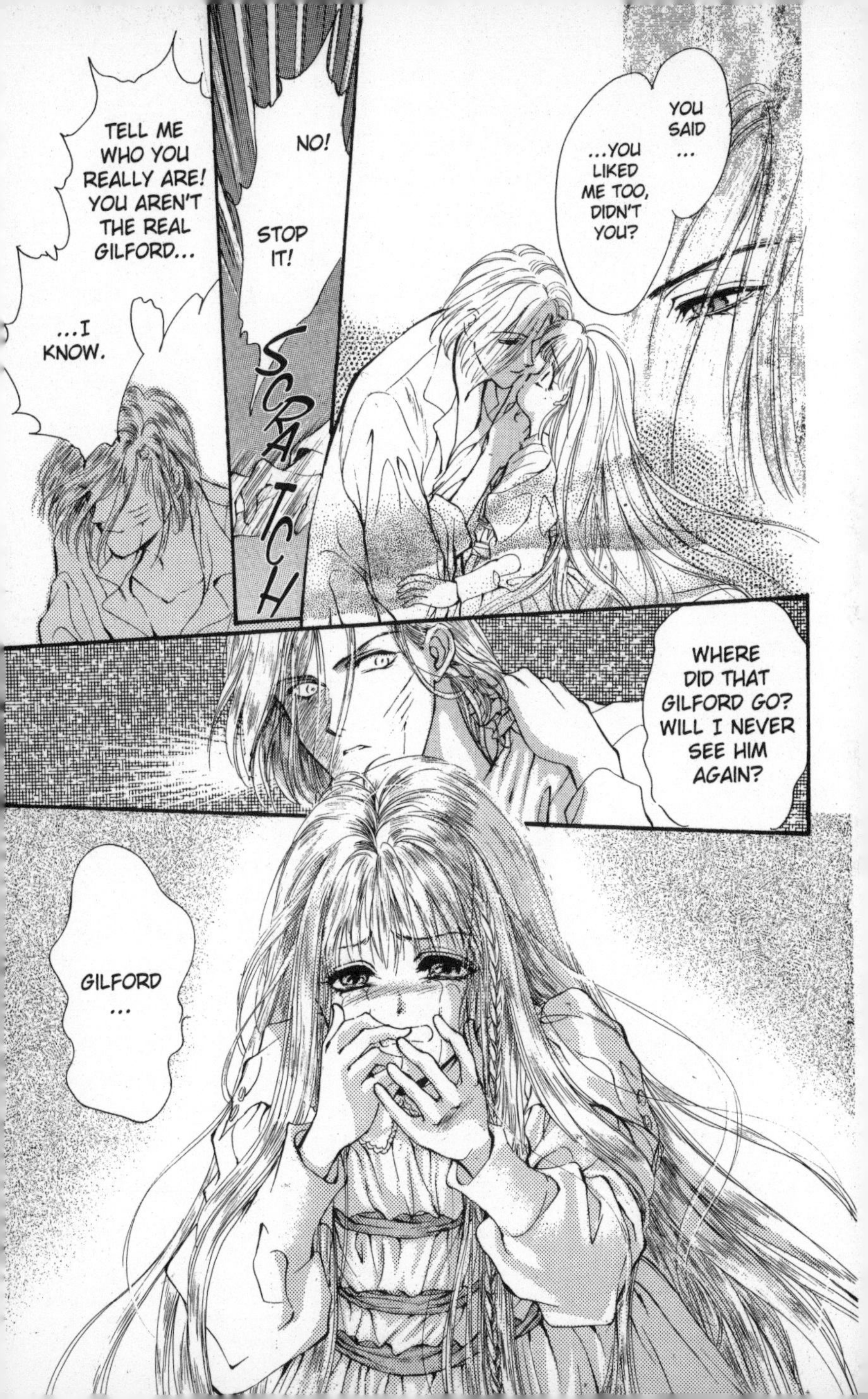
YOU SAID ... ...YOU LIKED ME TOO, DIDN'T YOU?
NO!
STOP IT!
SCRATCH
TELL ME WHO YOU REALLY ARE! YOU AREN'T THE REAL GILFORD...
...I KNOW.
WHERE DID THAT GILFORD GO? WILL I NEVER SEE HIM AGAIN?
GILFORD ...

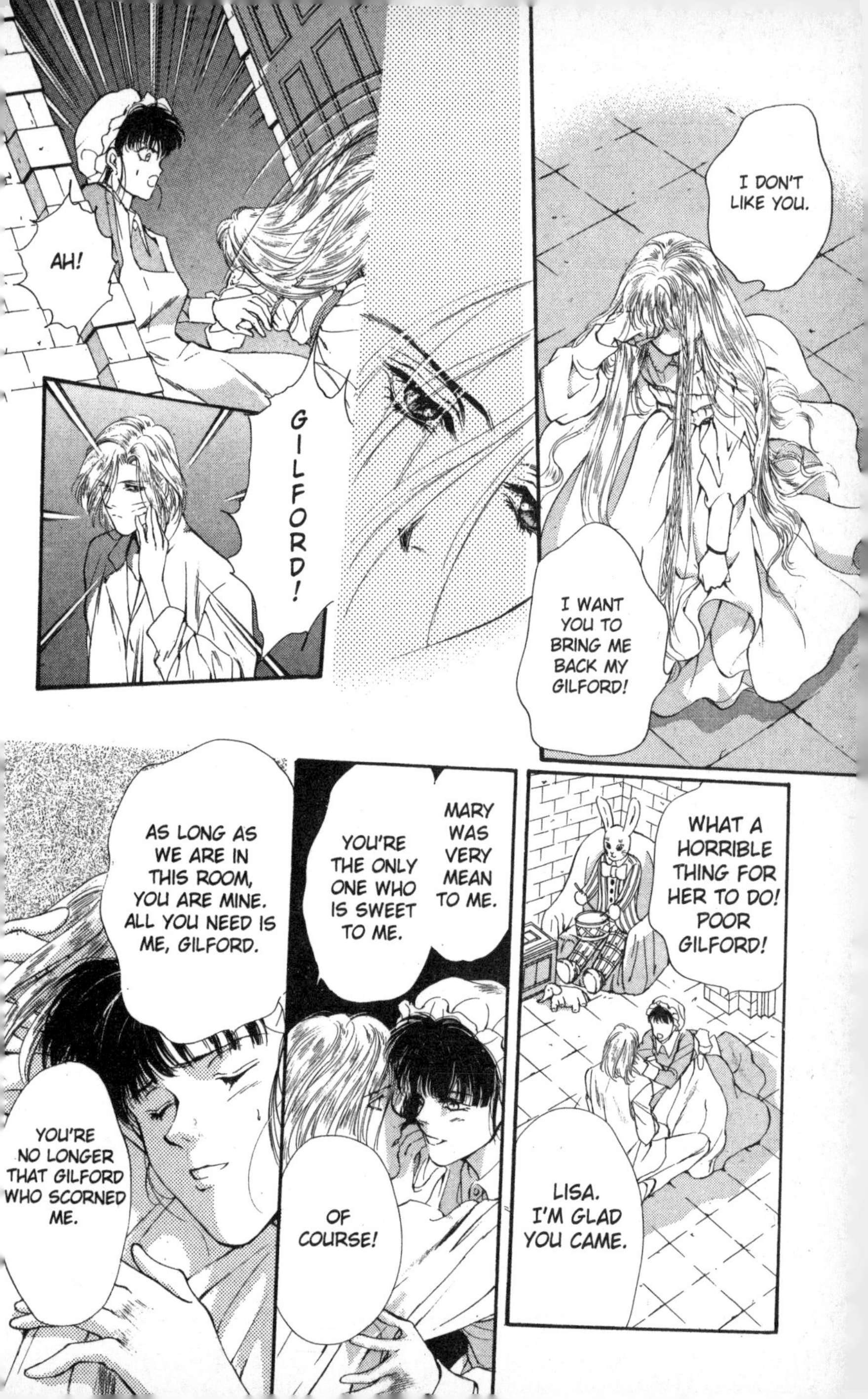

I DON'T LIKE YOU.
I WANT YOU TO BRING ME BACK MY GILFORD!
AH!
GILFORD!
WHAT A HORRIBLE THING FOR HER TO DO! POOR GILFORD!
LISA. I'M GLAD YOU CAME.
MARY WAS VERY MEAN TO ME.
YOU'RE THE ONLY ONE WHO IS SWEET TO ME.
OF COURSE!
AS LONG AS WE ARE IN THIS ROOM, YOU ARE MINE. ALL YOU NEED IS ME, GILFORD.
YOU'RE NO LONGER THAT GILFORD WHO SCORNED ME.

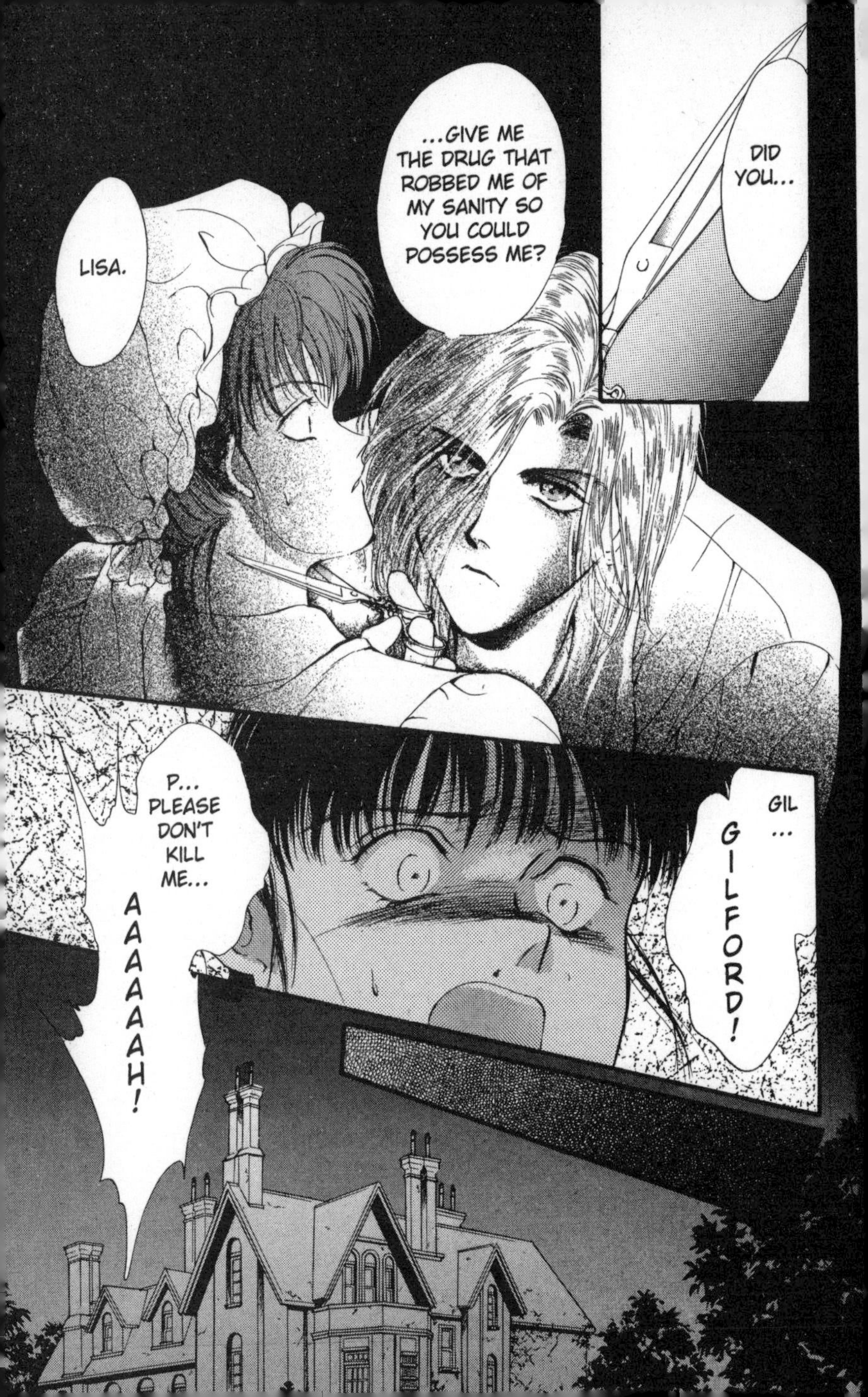
DID YOU...
...GIVE ME THE DRUG THAT ROBBED ME OF MY SANITY SO YOU COULD POSSESS ME?
LISA.
GIL...
GILFORD!
P... PLEASE DON'T KILL ME...
AAAAAAAH!

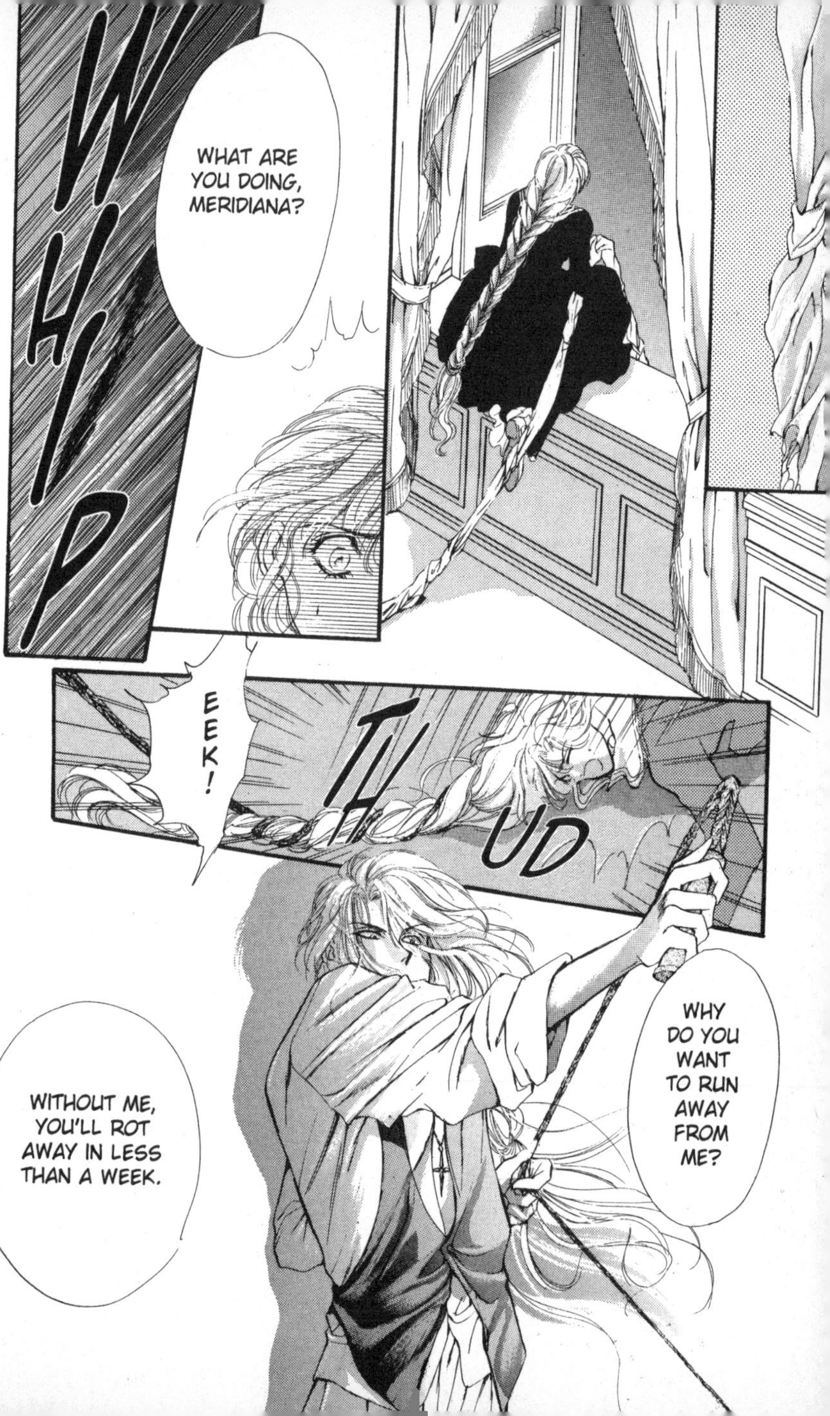
WHAT ARE YOU DOING, MERIDIANA?
WHIP
THUD
EEK!
WHY DO YOU WANT TO RUN AWAY FROM ME?
WITHOUT ME, YOU'LL ROT AWAY IN LESS THAN A WEEK.

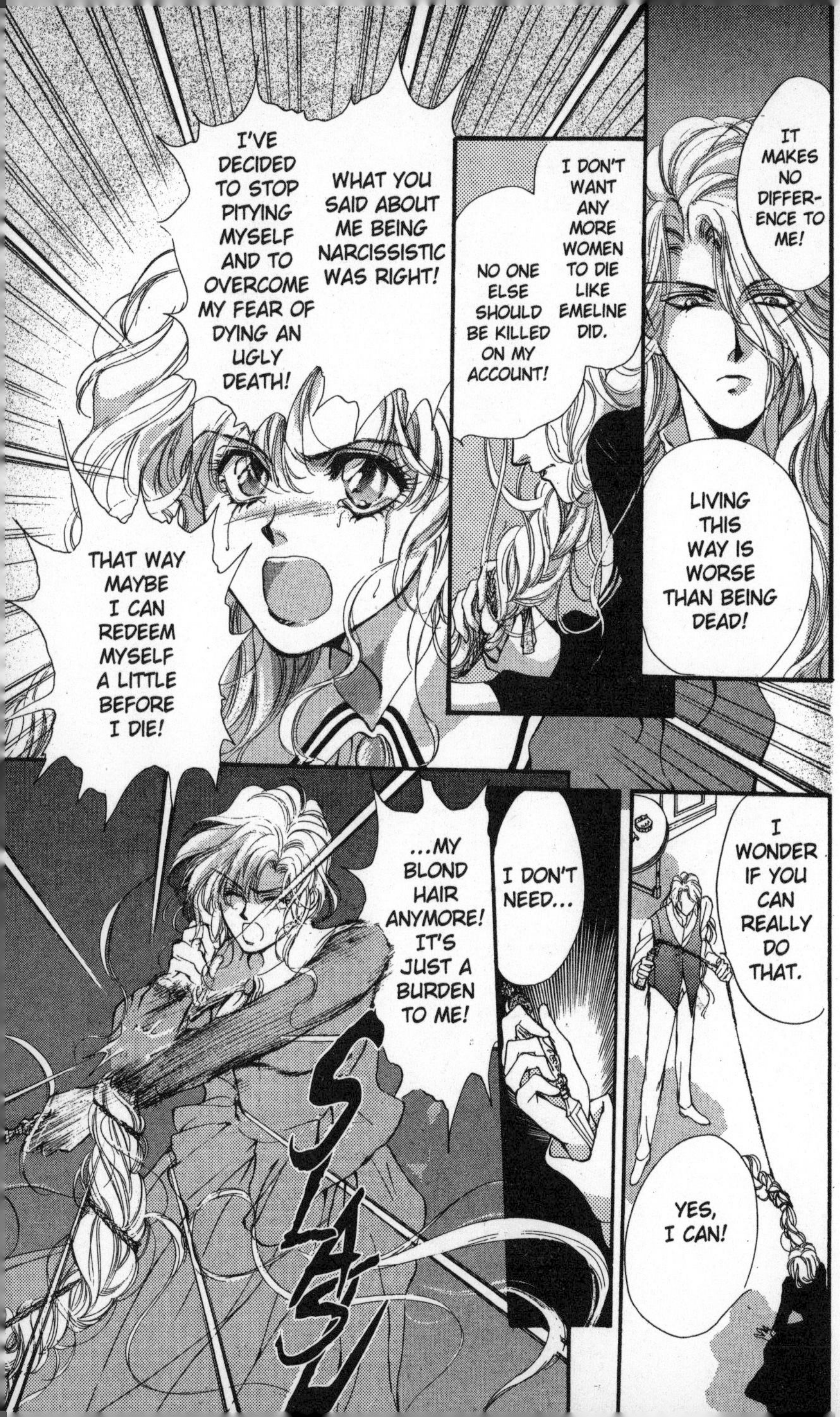
IT MAKES NO DIFFER-ENCE TO ME!
LIVING THIS WAY IS WORSE THAN BEING DEAD!
I DON'T WANT ANY MORE WOMEN TO DIE LIKE EMELINE DID.
NO ONE ELSE SHOULD BE KILLED ON MY ACCOUNT!
WHAT YOU SAID ABOUT ME BEING NARCISSISTIC WAS RIGHT!
I'VE DECIDED TO STOP PITYING MYSELF AND TO OVERCOME MY FEAR OF DYING AN UGLY DEATH!
THAT WAY MAYBE I CAN REDEEM MYSELF A LITTLE BEFORE I DIE!
I WONDER IF YOU CAN REALLY DO THAT.
YES, I CAN!
I DON'T NEED...
...MY BLOND HAIR ANYMORE! IT'S JUST A BURDEN TO ME!
SLASH

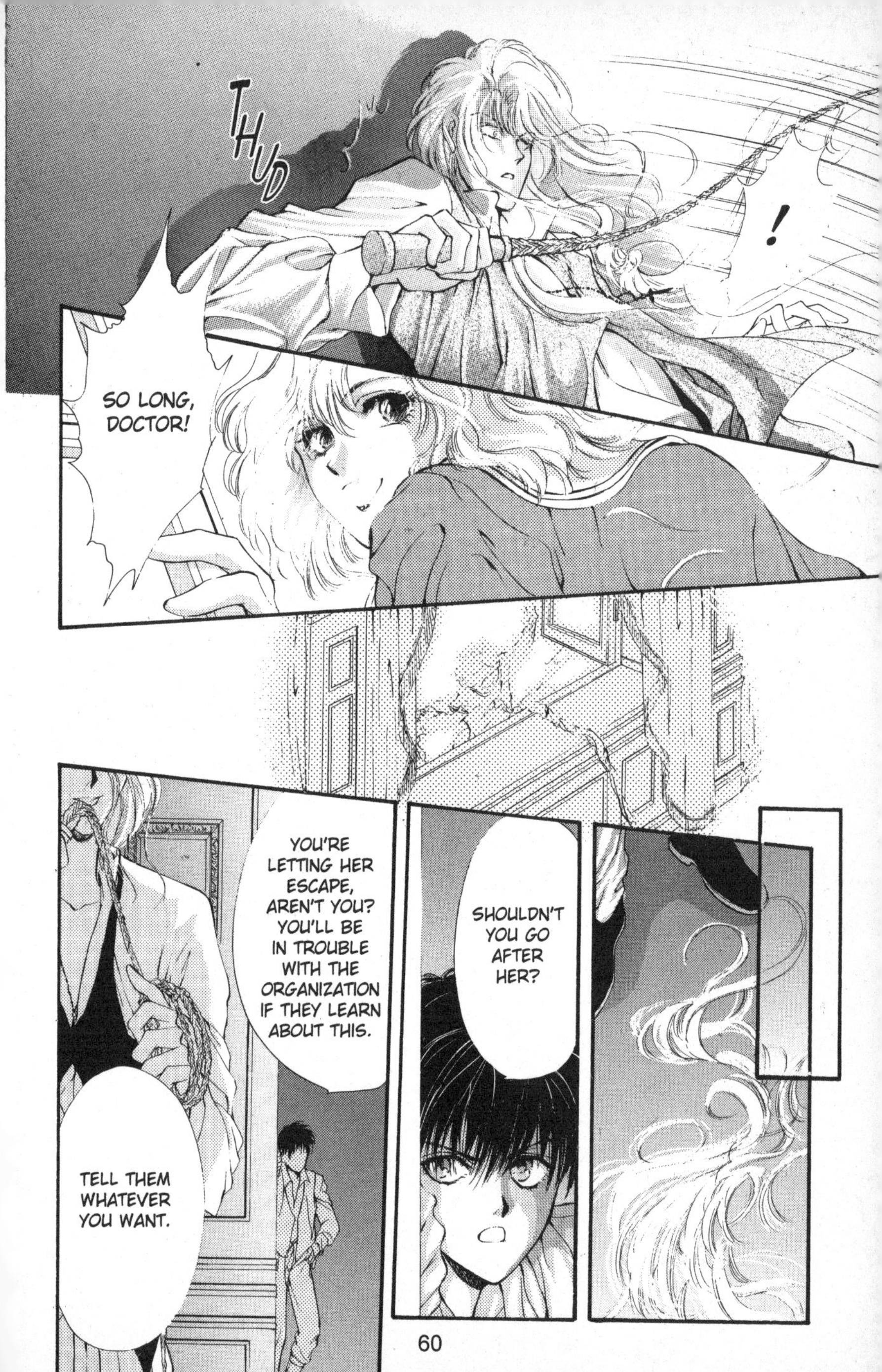
THUD
!
SO LONG, DOCTOR!
SHOULDN'T YOU GO AFTER HER?
YOU'RE LETTING HER ESCAPE, AREN'T YOU? YOU'LL BE IN TROUBLE WITH THE ORGANIZATION IF THEY LEARN ABOUT THIS.
TELL THEM WHATEVER YOU WANT.

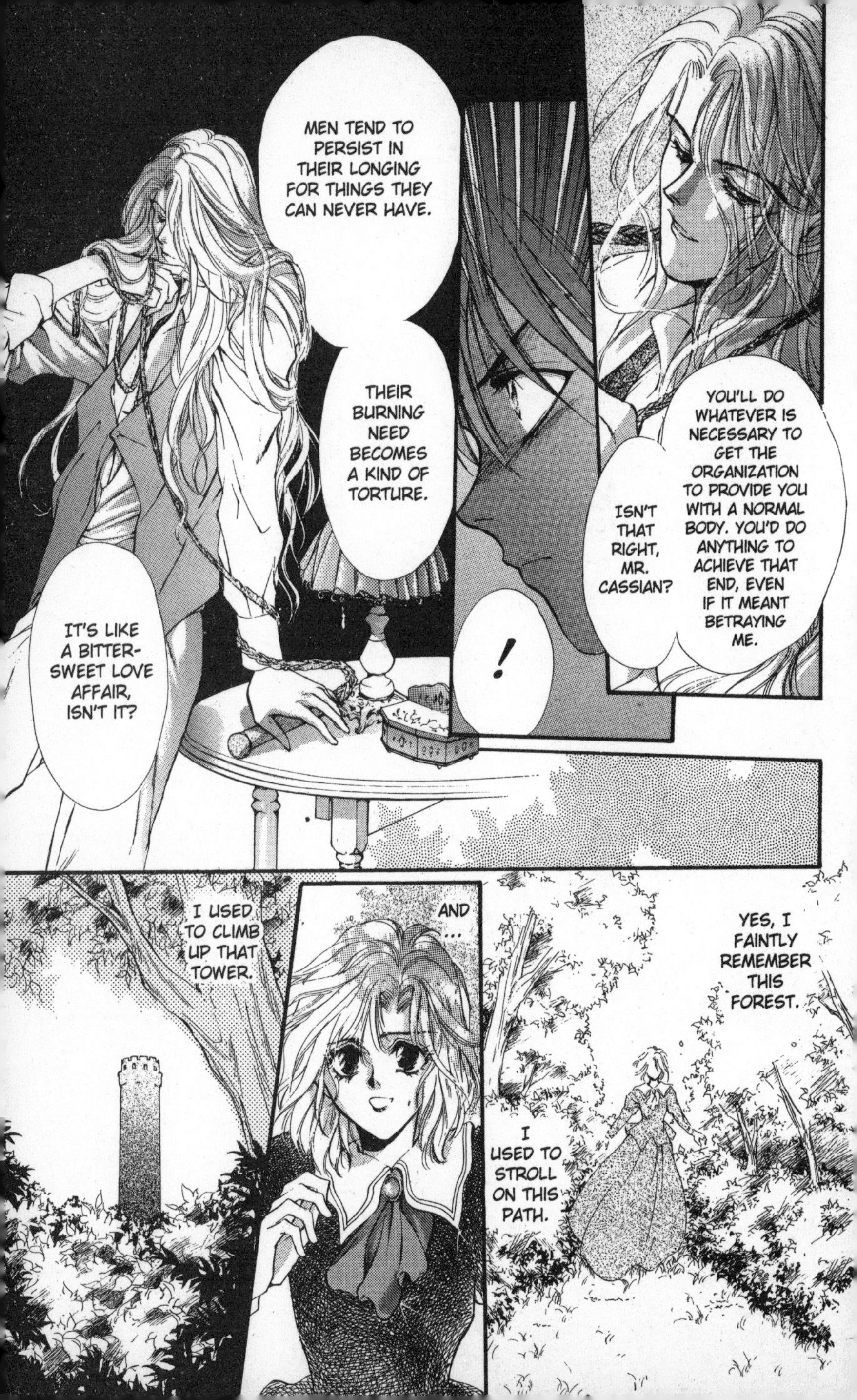
YOU'LL DO WHATEVER IS NECESSARY TO GET THE ORGANIZATION TO PROVIDE YOU WITH A NORMAL BODY. YOU'D DO ANYTHING TO ACHIEVE THAT END, EVEN IF IT MEANT BETRAYING ME.
ISN'T THAT RIGHT, MR. CASSIAN?
!
MEN TEND TO PERSIST IN THEIR LONGING FOR THINGS THEY CAN NEVER HAVE.
THEIR BURNING NEED BECOMES A KIND OF TORTURE.
IT'S LIKE A BITTER-SWEET LOVE AFFAIR, ISN'T IT?
YES, I FAINTLY REMEMBER THIS FOREST.
I USED TO STROLL ON THIS PATH.
AND ...
I USED TO CLIMB UP THAT TOWER.

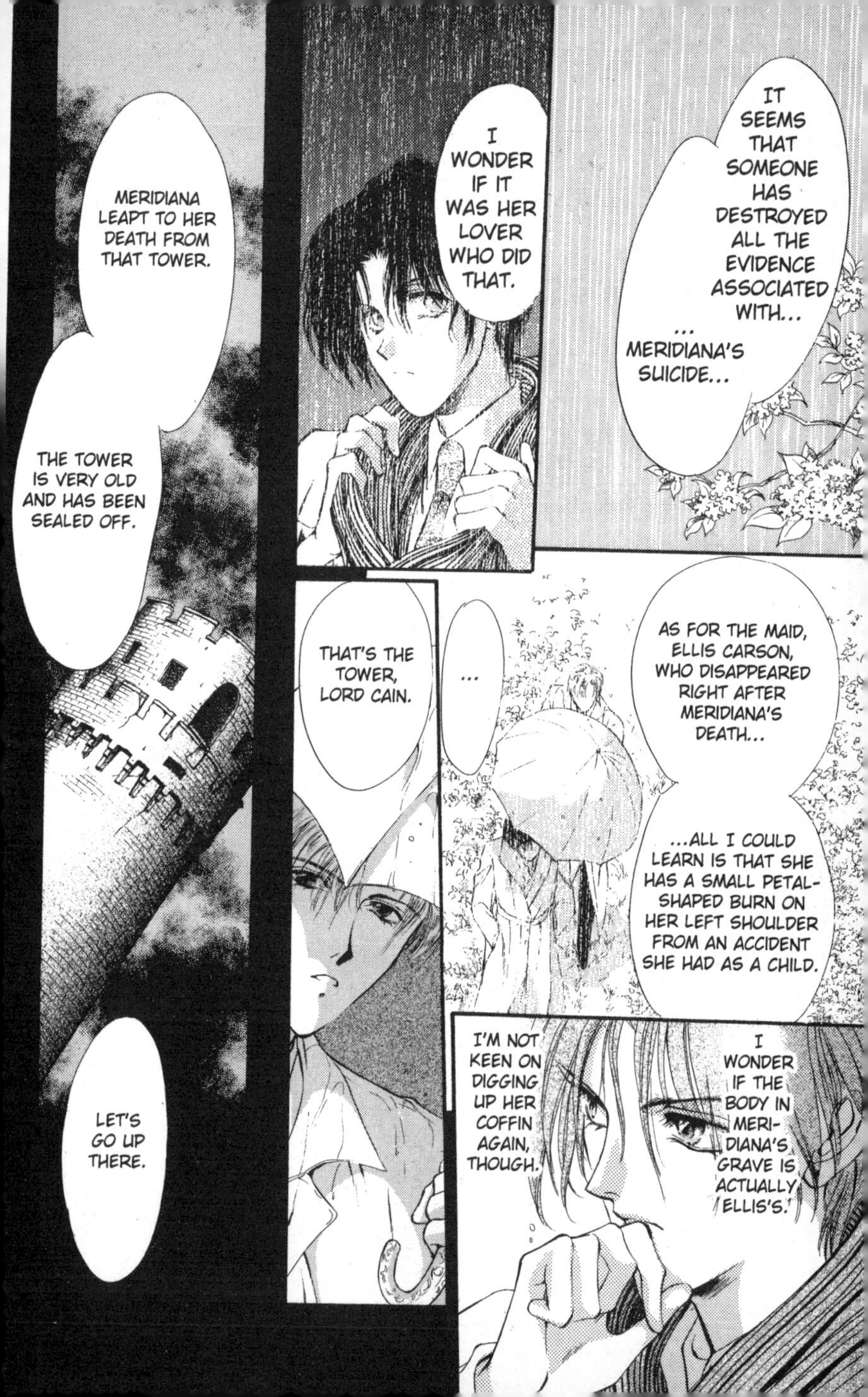
IT SEEMS THAT SOMEONE HAS DESTROYED ALL THE EVIDENCE ASSOCIATED WITH... ...MERIDIANA'S SUICIDE...
I WONDER IF IT WAS HER LOVER WHO DID THAT.
AS FOR THE MAID, ELLIS CARSON, WHO DISAPPEARED RIGHT AFTER MERIDIANA'S DEATH...
...ALL I COULD LEARN IS THAT SHE HAS A SMALL PETAL-SHAPED BURN ON HER LEFT SHOULDER FROM AN ACCIDENT SHE HAD AS A CHILD.
I WONDER IF THE BODY IN MERIDIANA'S GRAVE IS ACTUALLY ELLIS'S.
I'M NOT KEEN ON DIGGING UP HER COFFIN AGAIN, THOUGH.
...
THAT'S THE TOWER, LORD CAIN.
MERIDIANA LEAPT TO HER DEATH FROM THAT TOWER.
THE TOWER IS VERY OLD AND HAS BEEN SEALED OFF.
LET'S GO UP THERE.

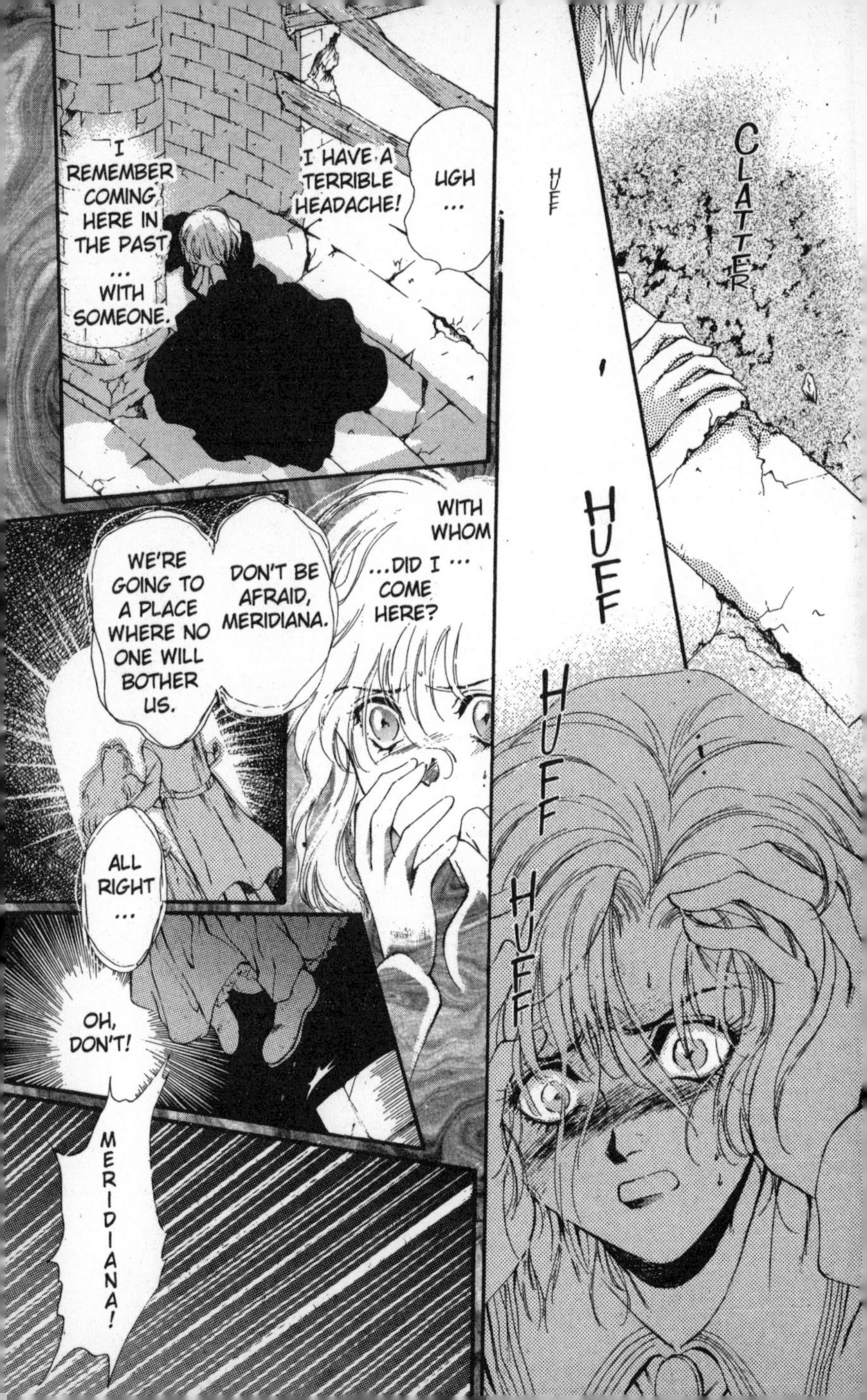
CLATTER
HUFF
HUFF
HUFF
HUFF
HUFF
UGH ...
I HAVE A TERRIBLE HEADACHE!
I REMEMBER COMING HERE IN THE PAST ... WITH SOMEONE.
WITH WHOM
...DID I ... COME HERE?
DON'T BE AFRAID, MERIDIANA.
WE'RE GOING TO A PLACE WHERE NO ONE WILL BOTHER US.
ALL RIGHT ...
OH, DON'T!
MERIDIANA!

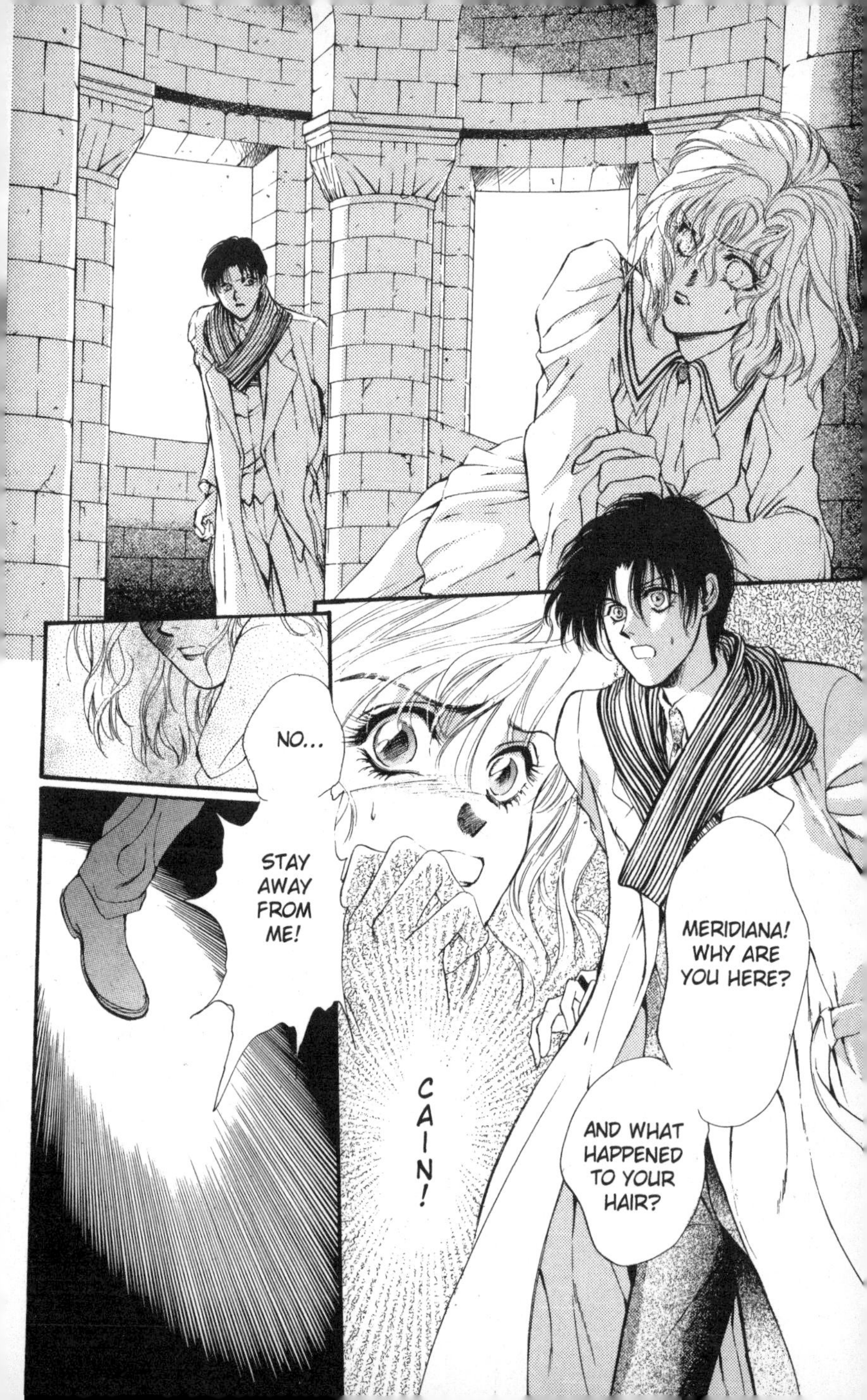
MERIDIANA! WHY ARE YOU HERE?
AND WHAT HAPPENED TO YOUR HAIR?
CAIN!
NO...
STAY AWAY FROM ME!

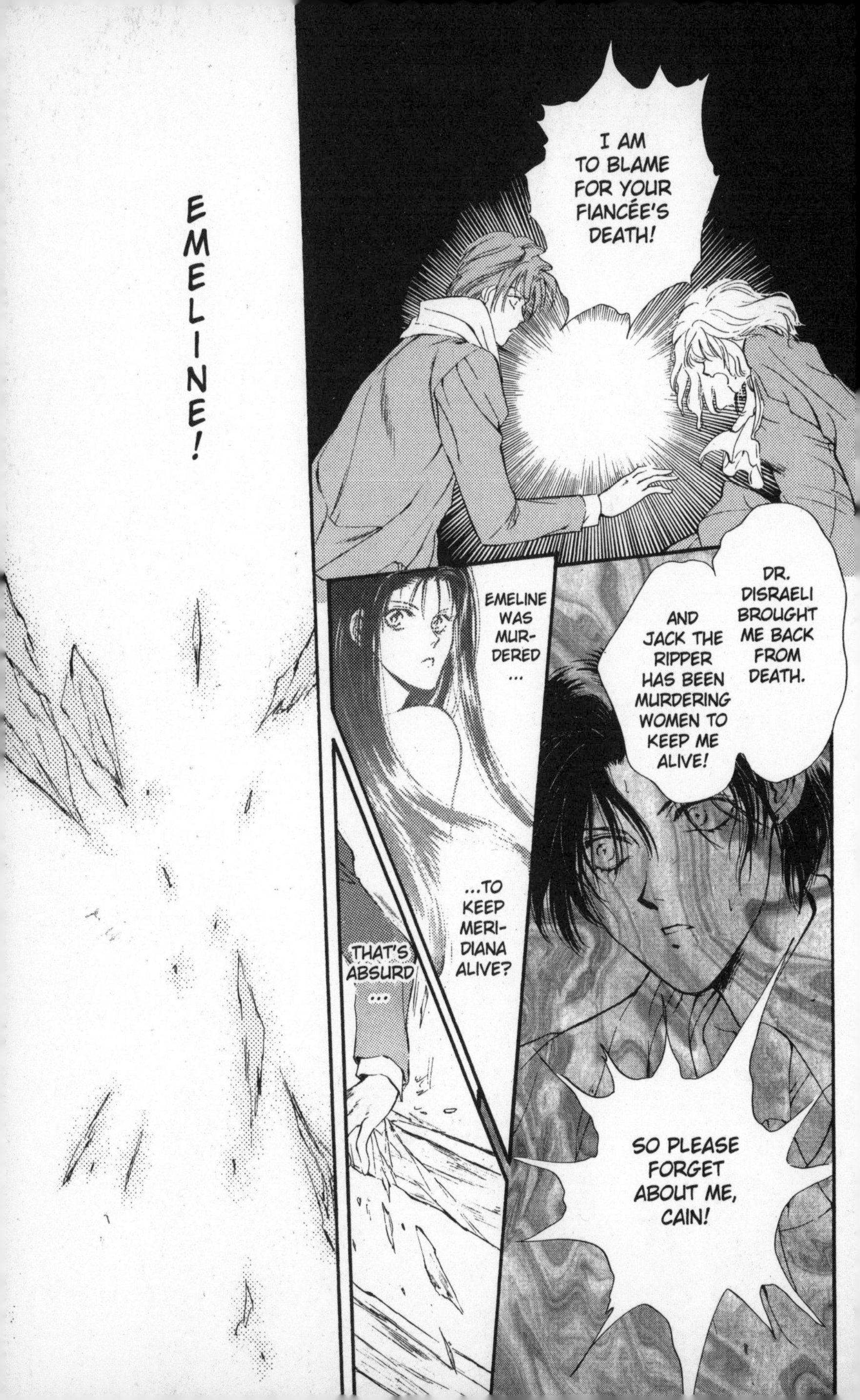
I AM TO BLAME FOR YOUR FIANCÉE'S DEATH!
DR. DISRAELI BROUGHT ME BACK FROM DEATH.
AND JACK THE RIPPER HAS BEEN MURDERING WOMEN TO KEEP ME ALIVE!
EMELINE WAS MUR-DERED...
...TO KEEP MERI-DIANA ALIVE?
THAT'S ABSURD...
SO PLEASE FORGET ABOUT ME, CAIN!
EMELINE!

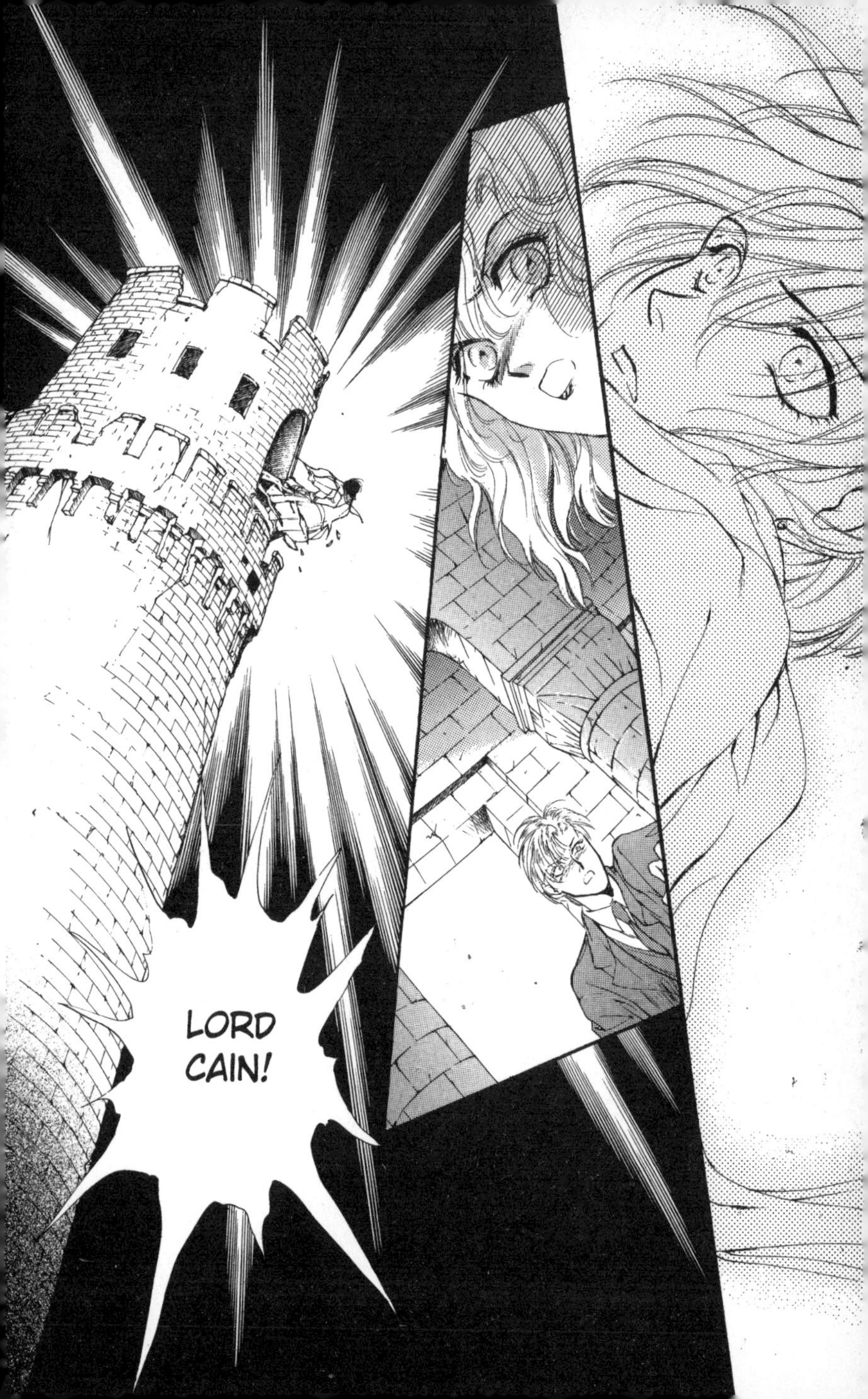
LORD
CAIN!

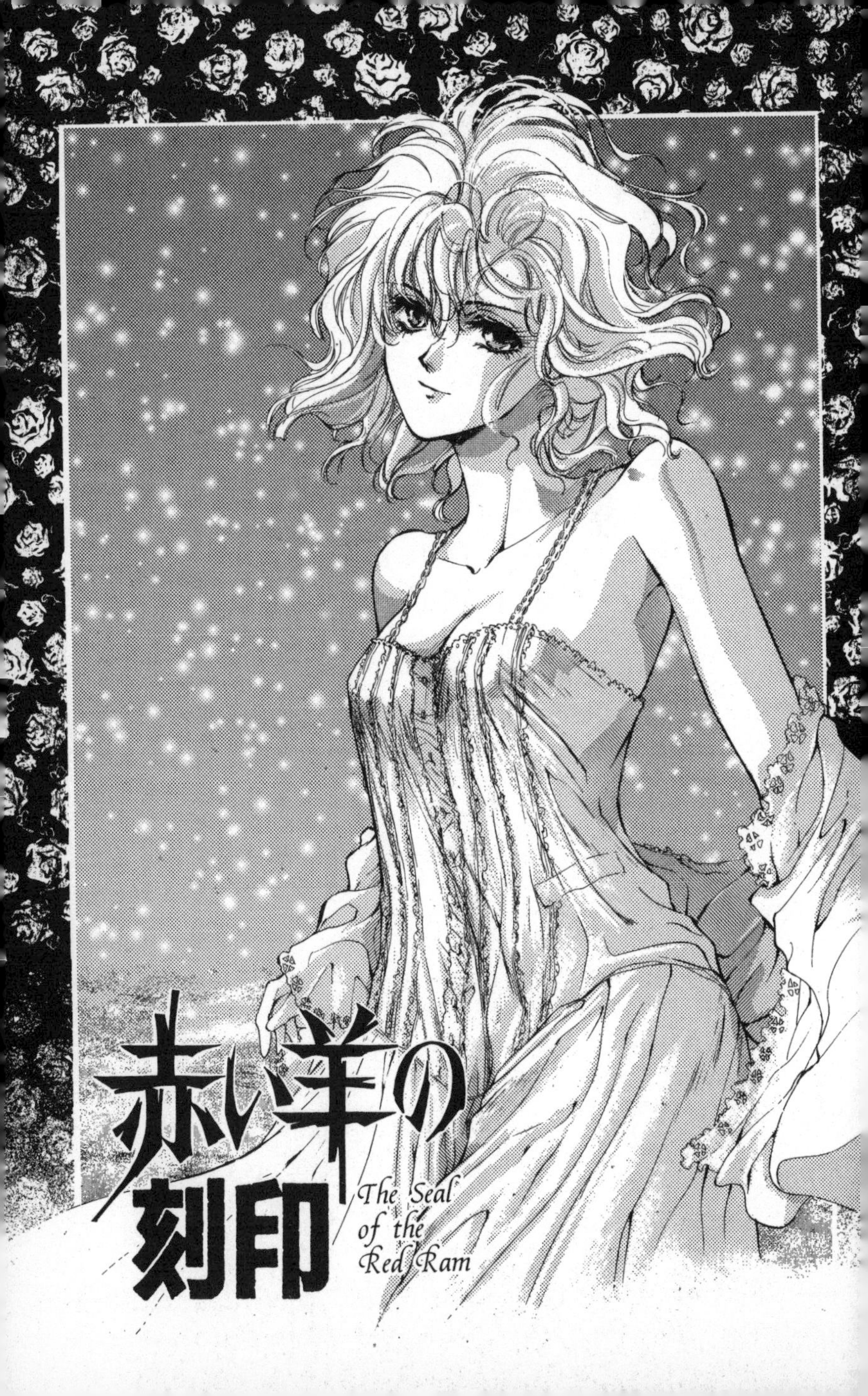

赤い羊の刻印
The Seal of the Red Ram

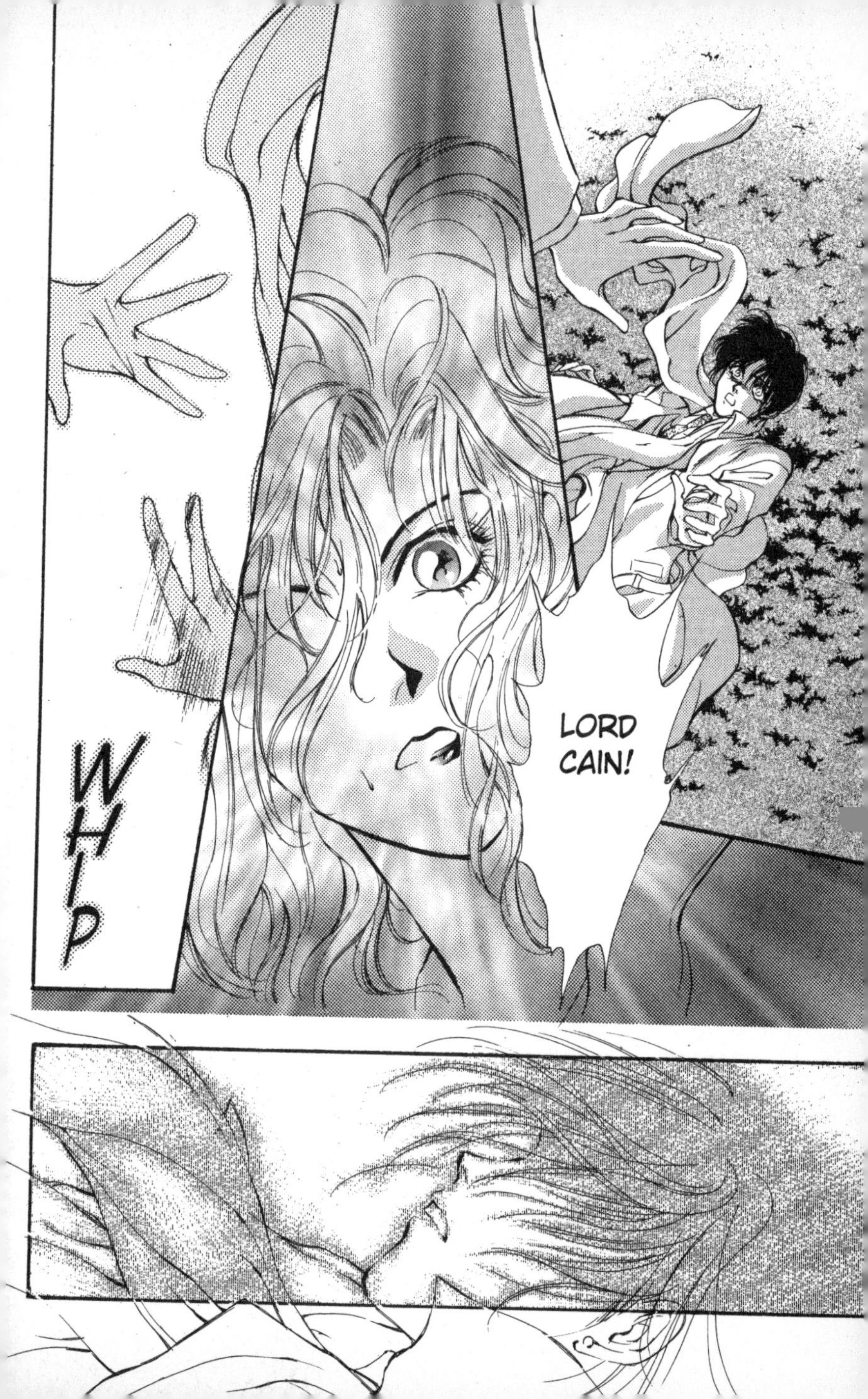
LORD CAIN!
WHIP

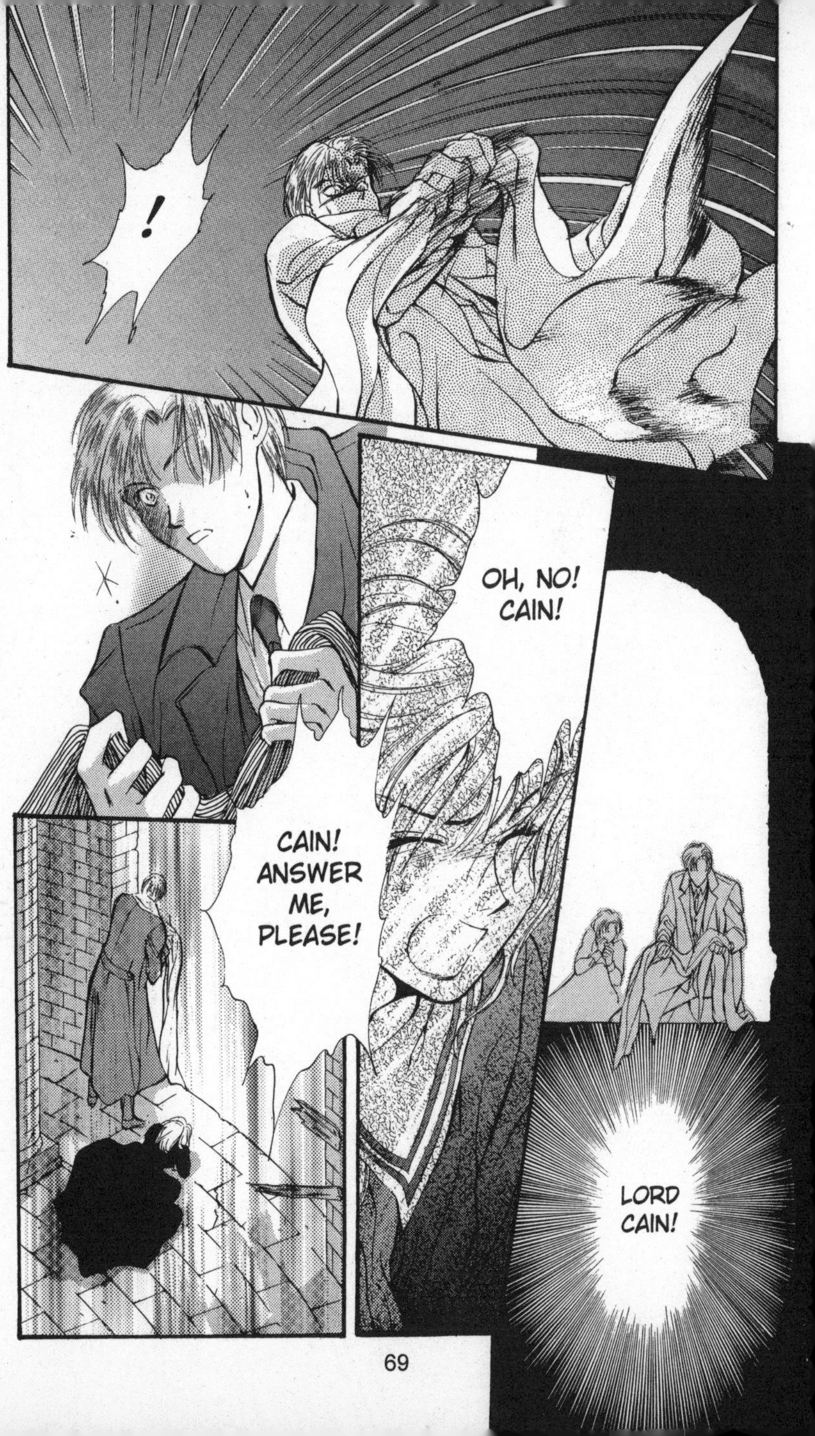
!
OH, NO! CAIN!
CAIN! ANSWER ME, PLEASE!
LORD CAIN!

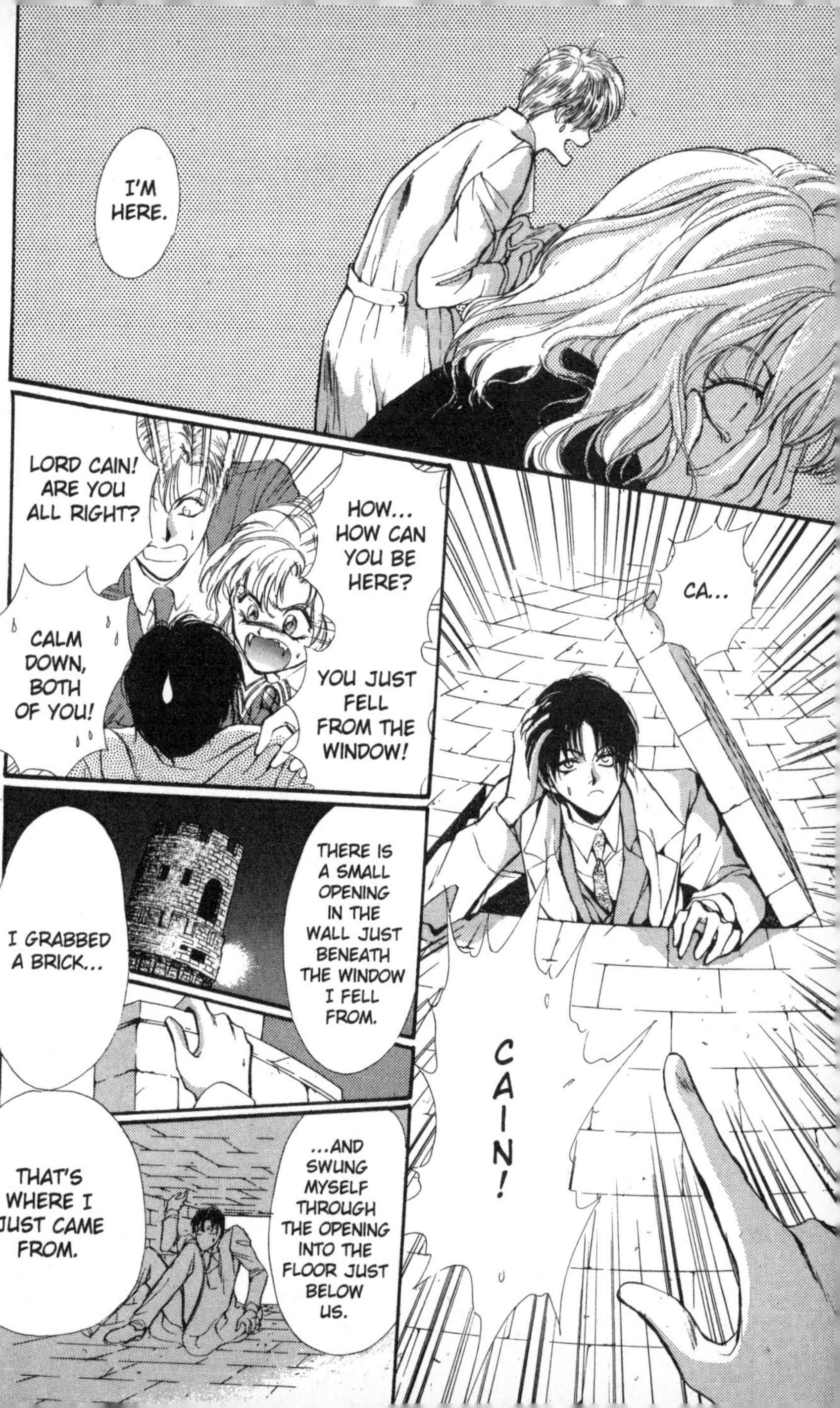
I'M HERE.
CA...
CAIN!
HOW... HOW CAN YOU BE HERE?
LORD CAIN! ARE YOU ALL RIGHT?
YOU JUST FELL FROM THE WINDOW!
CALM DOWN, BOTH OF YOU!
THERE IS A SMALL OPENING IN THE WALL JUST BENEATH THE WINDOW I FELL FROM.
I GRABBED A BRICK...
...AND SWUNG MYSELF THROUGH THE OPENING INTO THE FLOOR JUST BELOW US.
THAT'S WHERE I JUST CAME FROM.

WILD TALK
PART 3

Meridiana hacked her hair short as if to rid herself of the narcissism that Dr. Disraeli angrily accused her of. I had planned this segment, in which the doctor berates Meridiana, from the very beginning, but, when I actually began depicting the scene, I thought I'd better change Meridiana's looks slightly because so many readers disliked her. I personally feel sorry for Meridiana because of all she's been through. Don't you? I'm not sure if cutting her hair short made her more likable, but she gained some popularity toward the end of the story. By the way, whose eyes do you think Meridiana's resemble? You'll find out about that much later.

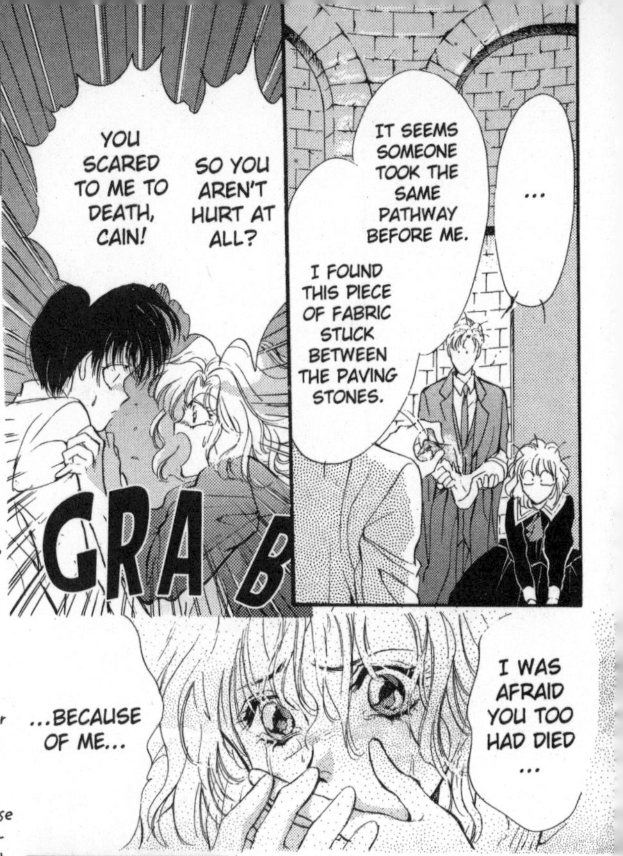
...
IT SEEMS SOMEONE TOOK THE SAME PATHWAY BEFORE ME.
I FOUND THIS PIECE OF FABRIC STUCK BETWEEN THE PAVING STONES.
SO YOU AREN'T HURT AT ALL?
YOU SCARED TO ME TO DEATH, CAIN!
GRAB
I WAS AFRAID YOU TOO HAD DIED ...
...BECAUSE OF ME...

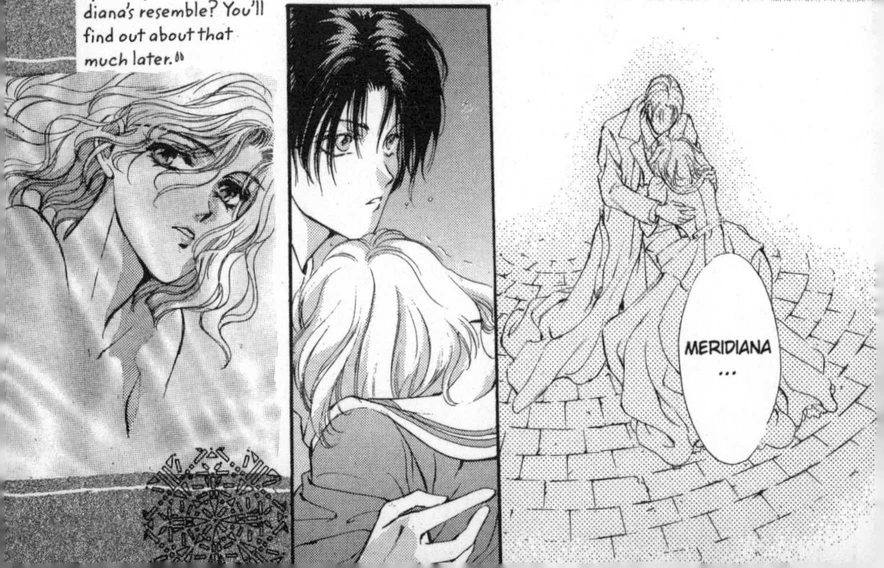
MERIDIANA ...

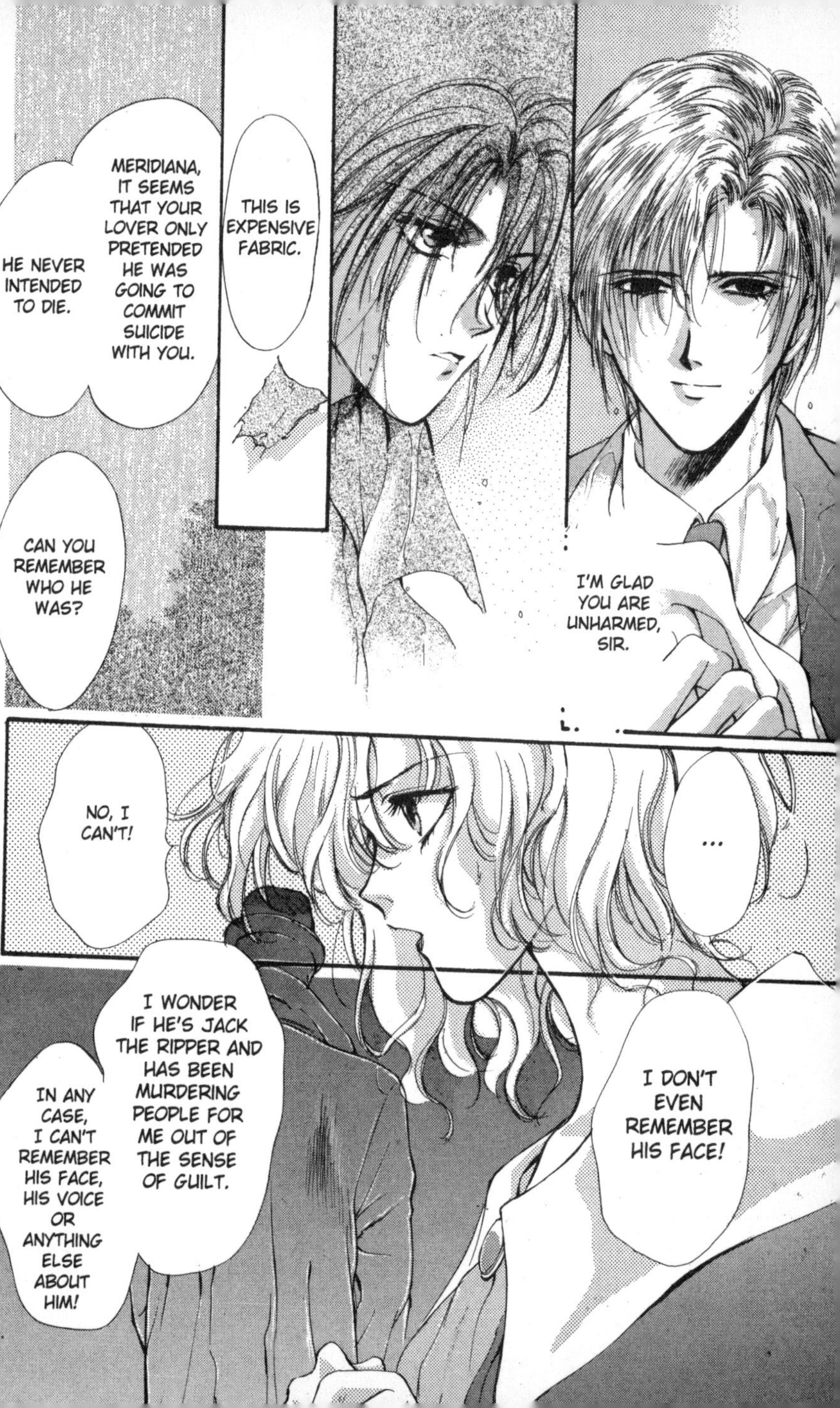
I'M GLAD YOU ARE UNHARMED, SIR.
THIS IS EXPENSIVE FABRIC.
MERIDIANA, IT SEEMS THAT YOUR LOVER ONLY PRETENDED HE WAS GOING TO COMMIT SUICIDE WITH YOU.
HE NEVER INTENDED TO DIE.
CAN YOU REMEMBER WHO HE WAS?
...
NO, I CAN'T!
I DON'T EVEN REMEMBER HIS FACE!
I WONDER IF HE'S JACK THE RIPPER AND HAS BEEN MURDERING PEOPLE FOR ME OUT OF THE SENSE OF GUILT.
IN ANY CASE, I CAN'T REMEMBER HIS FACE, HIS VOICE OR ANYTHING ELSE ABOUT HIM!

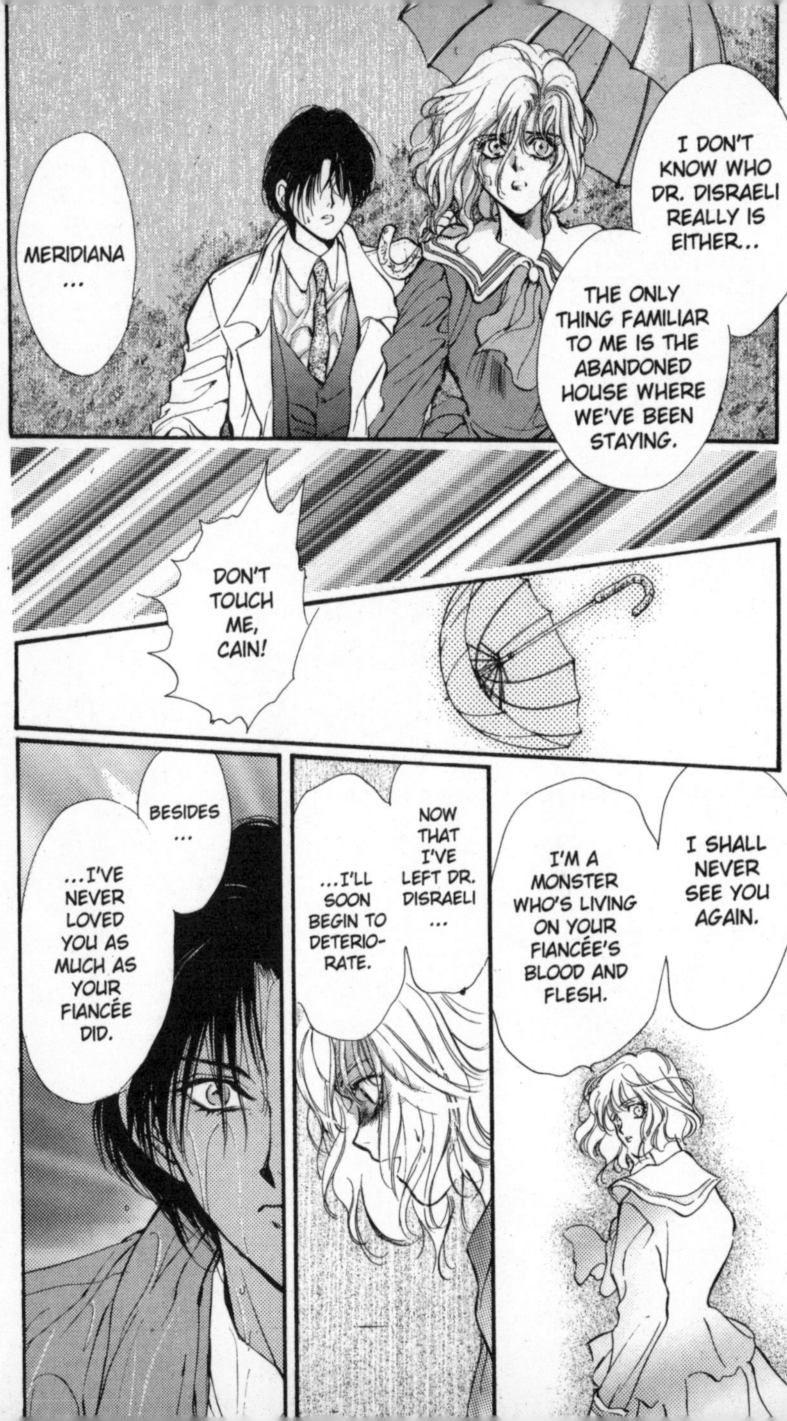
I DON'T KNOW WHO DR. DISRAELI REALLY IS EITHER...
THE ONLY THING FAMILIAR TO ME IS THE ABANDONED HOUSE WHERE WE'VE BEEN STAYING.
MERIDIANA ...
DON'T TOUCH ME, CAIN!
I SHALL NEVER SEE YOU AGAIN.
I'M A MONSTER WHO'S LIVING ON YOUR FIANCÉE'S BLOOD AND FLESH.
NOW THAT I'VE LEFT DR. DISRAELI ...
...I'LL SOON BEGIN TO DETERIO-RATE.
BESIDES ...
...I'VE NEVER LOVED YOU AS MUCH AS YOUR FIANCÉE DID.

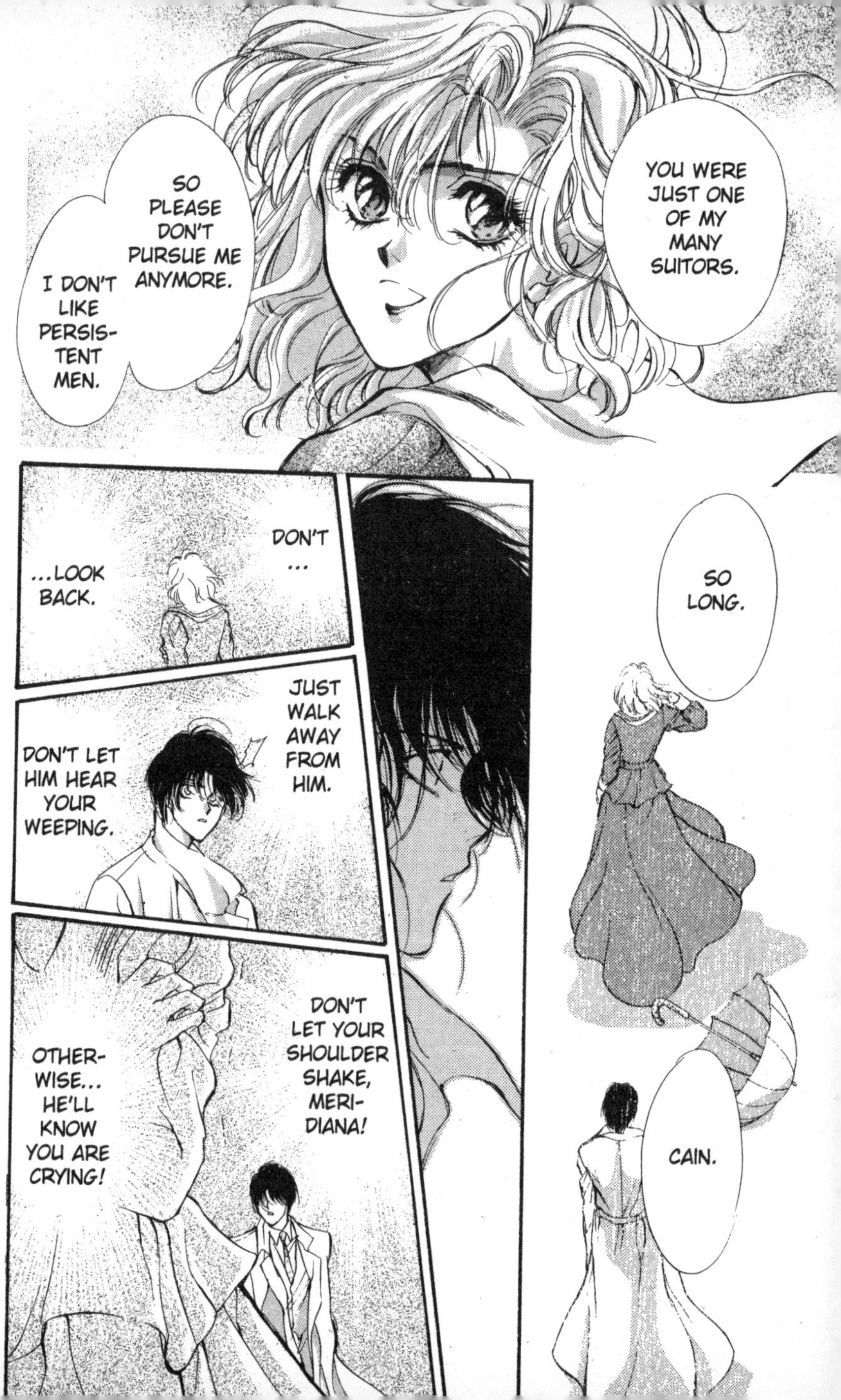

YOU WERE JUST ONE OF MY MANY SUITORS.
SO PLEASE DON'T PURSUE ME ANYMORE.
I DON'T LIKE PERSIS-TENT MEN.
SO LONG.
CAIN.
DON'T ...
...LOOK BACK.
JUST WALK AWAY FROM HIM.
DON'T LET HIM HEAR YOUR WEEPING.
DON'T LET YOUR SHOULDER SHAKE, MERI-DIANA!
OTHER-WISE... HE'LL KNOW YOU ARE CRYING!

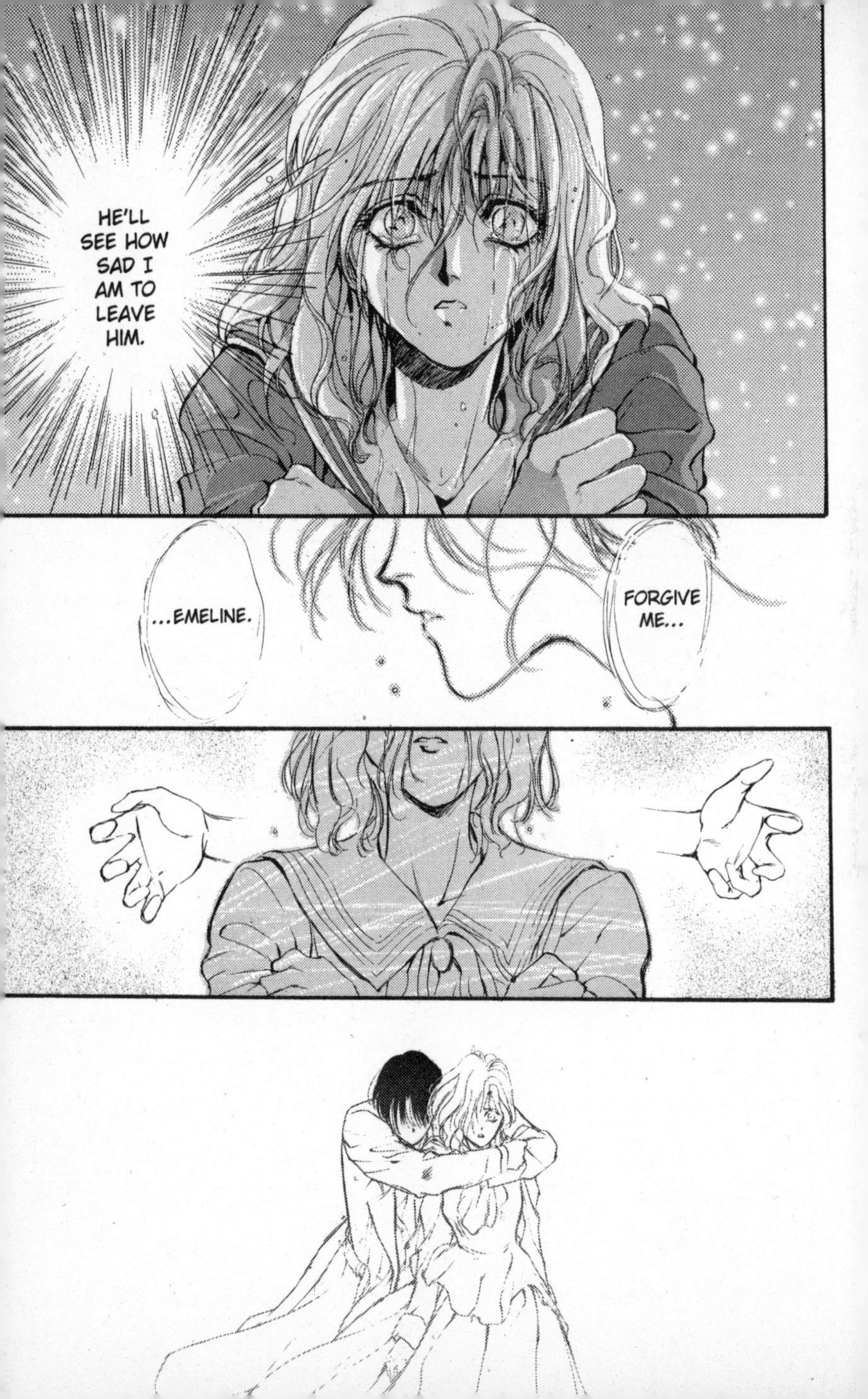
HE'LL SEE HOW SAD I AM TO LEAVE HIM.
FORGIVE ME...
...EMELINE.

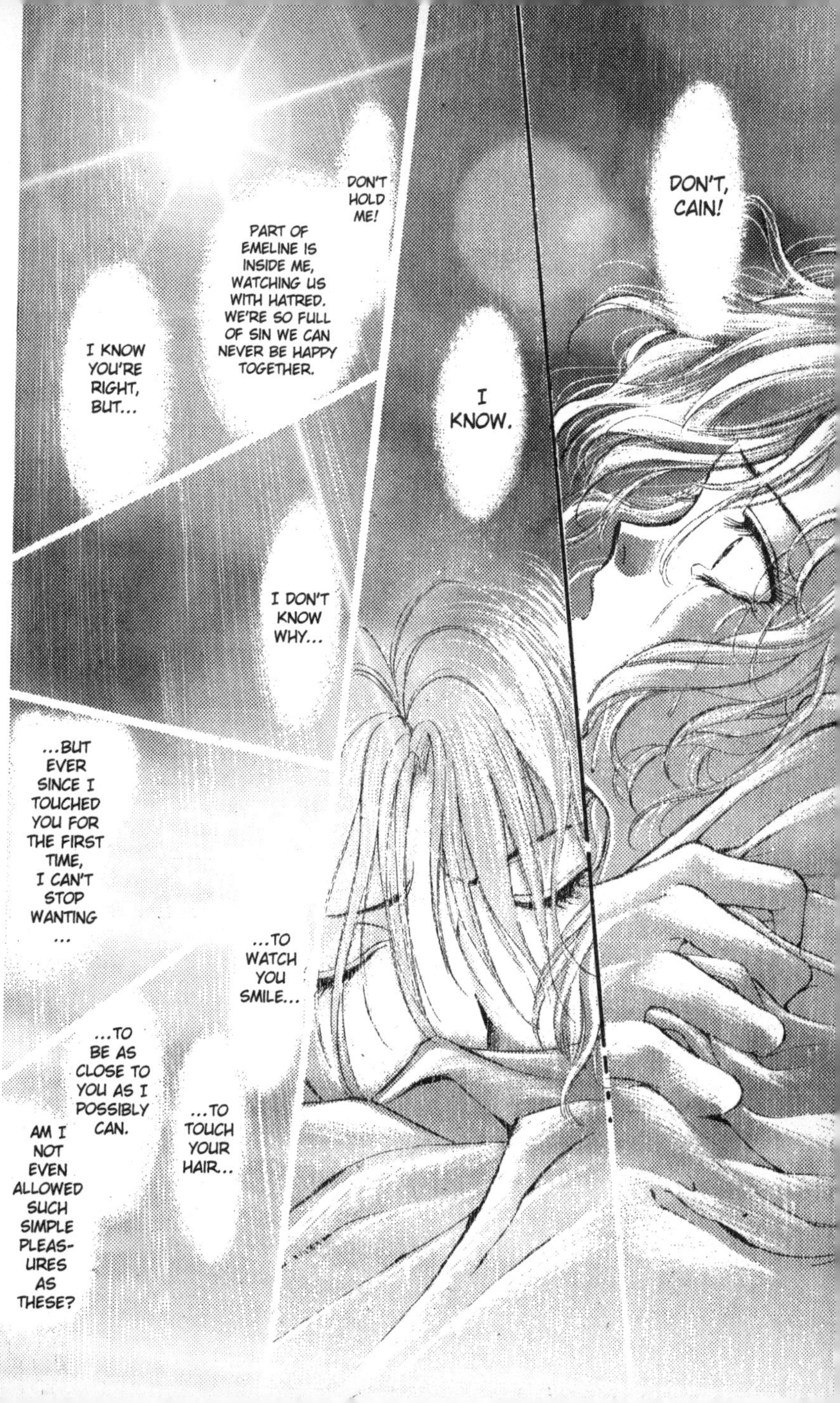
DON'T, CAIN!
I KNOW.
DON'T HOLD ME!
PART OF EMELINE IS INSIDE ME, WATCHING US WITH HATRED. WE'RE SO FULL OF SIN WE CAN NEVER BE HAPPY TOGETHER.
I KNOW YOU'RE RIGHT, BUT...
I DON'T KNOW WHY...
...BUT EVER SINCE I TOUCHED YOU FOR THE FIRST TIME, I CAN'T STOP WANTING...
...TO WATCH YOU SMILE...
...TO BE AS CLOSE TO YOU AS I POSSIBLY CAN.
...TO TOUCH YOUR HAIR...
AM I NOT EVEN ALLOWED SUCH SIMPLE PLEASURES AS THESE?

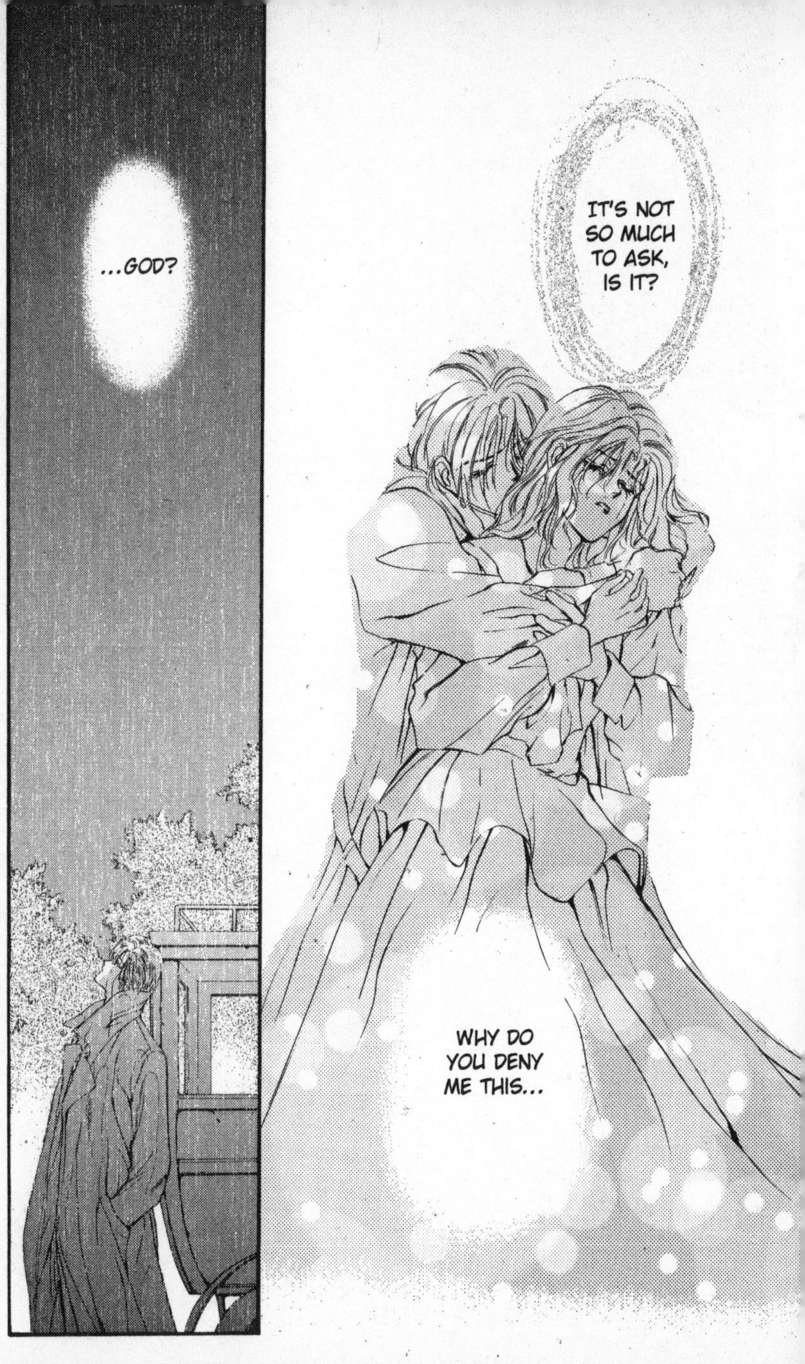
IT'S NOT SO MUCH TO ASK, IS IT?
WHY DO YOU DENY ME THIS...
...GOD?

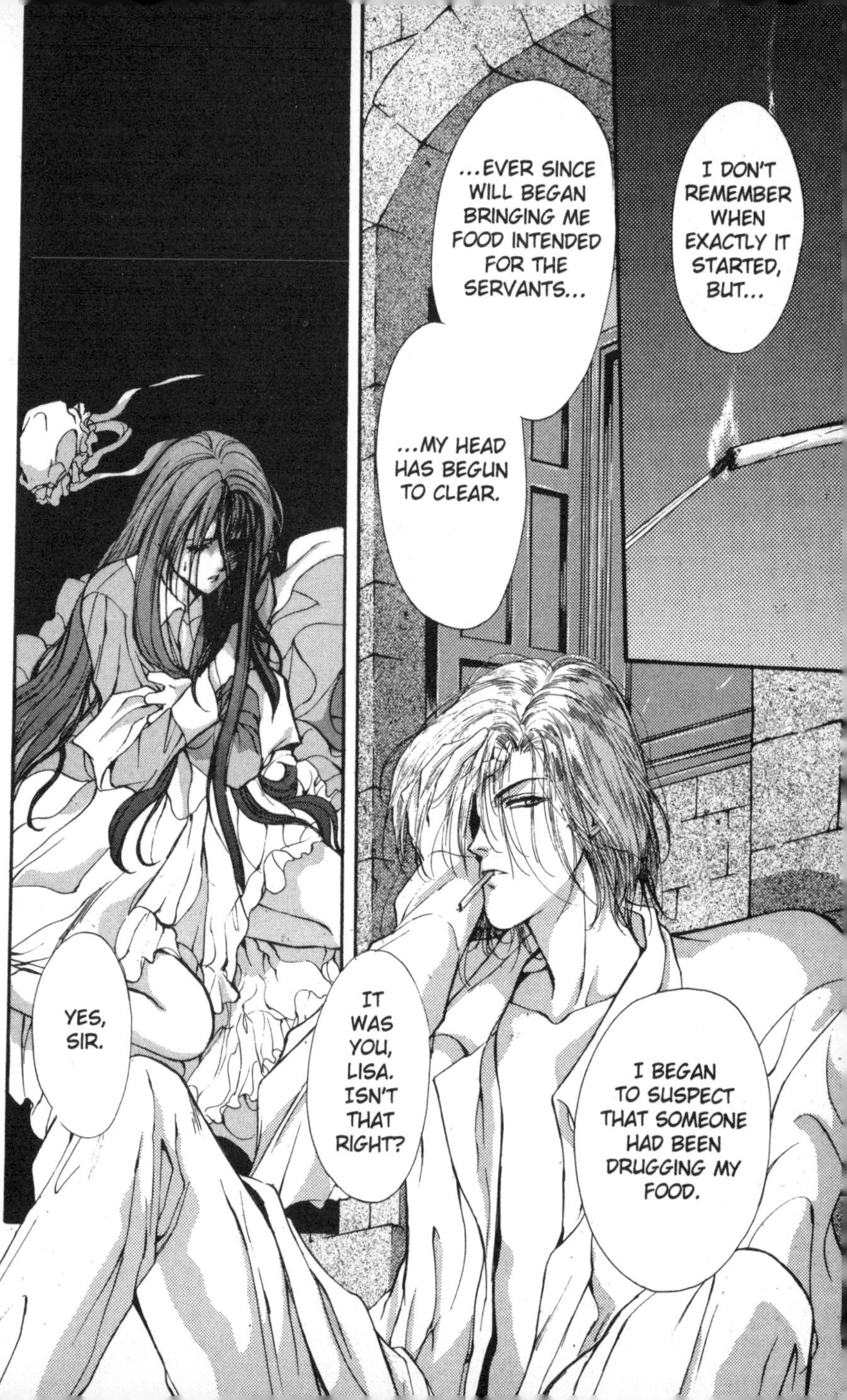
I DON'T REMEMBER WHEN EXACTLY IT STARTED, BUT...
...EVER SINCE WILL BEGAN BRINGING ME FOOD INTENDED FOR THE SERVANTS...
...MY HEAD HAS BEGUN TO CLEAR.
I BEGAN TO SUSPECT THAT SOMEONE HAD BEEN DRUGGING MY FOOD.
IT WAS YOU, LISA. ISN'T THAT RIGHT?
YES, SIR.

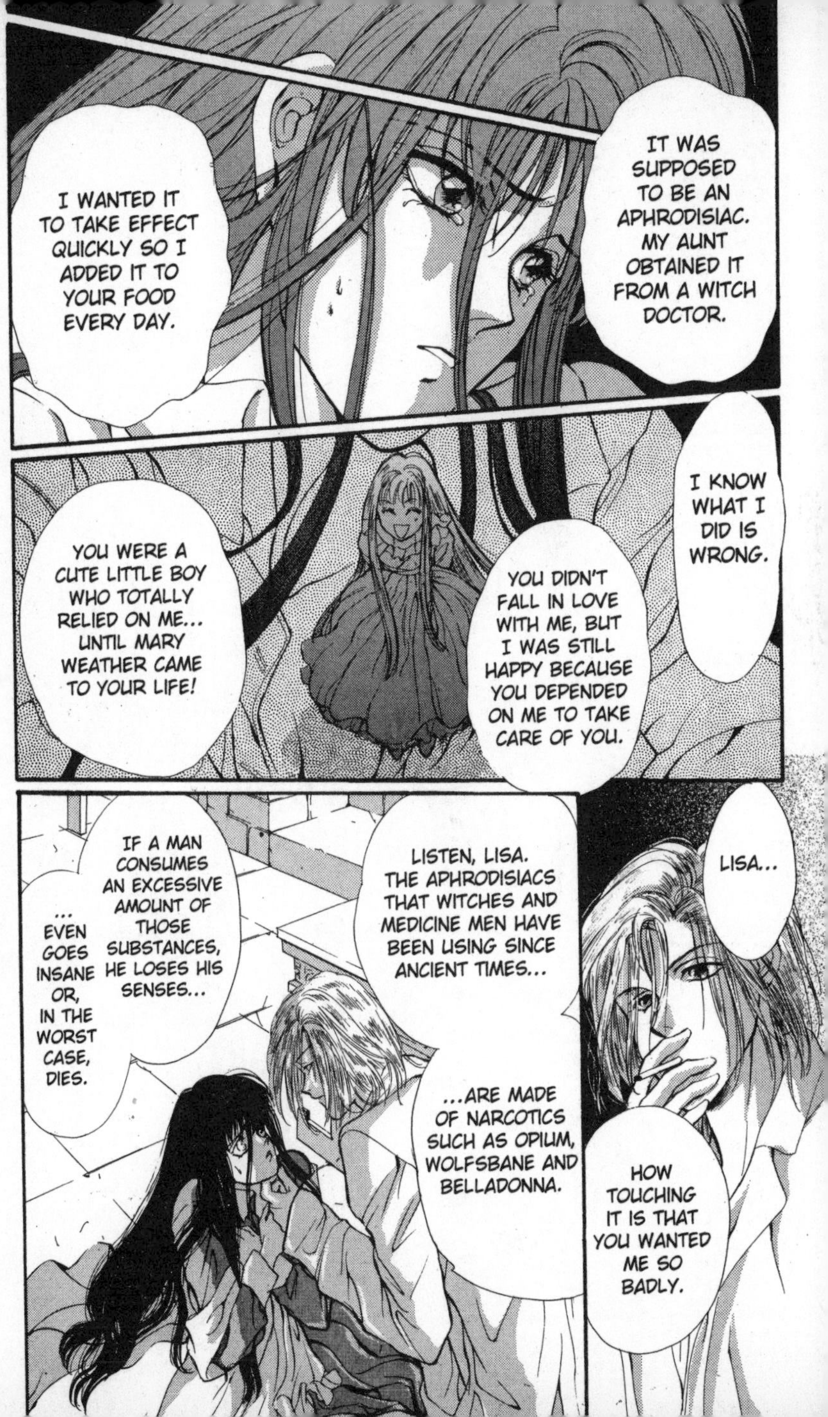
IT WAS SUPPOSED TO BE AN APHRODISIAC. MY AUNT OBTAINED IT FROM A WITCH DOCTOR.
I WANTED IT TO TAKE EFFECT QUICKLY SO I ADDED IT TO YOUR FOOD EVERY DAY.
I KNOW WHAT I DID IS WRONG.
YOU DIDN'T FALL IN LOVE WITH ME, BUT I WAS STILL HAPPY BECAUSE YOU DEPENDED ON ME TO TAKE CARE OF YOU.
YOU WERE A CUTE LITTLE BOY WHO TOTALLY RELIED ON ME... UNTIL MARY WEATHER CAME TO YOUR LIFE!
LISA...
HOW TOUCHING IT IS THAT YOU WANTED ME SO BADLY.
LISTEN, LISA. THE APHRODISIACS THAT WITCHES AND MEDICINE MEN HAVE BEEN USING SINCE ANCIENT TIMES...
...ARE MADE OF NARCOTICS SUCH AS OPIUM, WOLFSBANE AND BELLADONNA.
IF A MAN CONSUMES AN EXCESSIVE AMOUNT OF THOSE SUBSTANCES, HE LOSES HIS SENSES...
...EVEN GOES INSANE OR, IN THE WORST CASE, DIES.

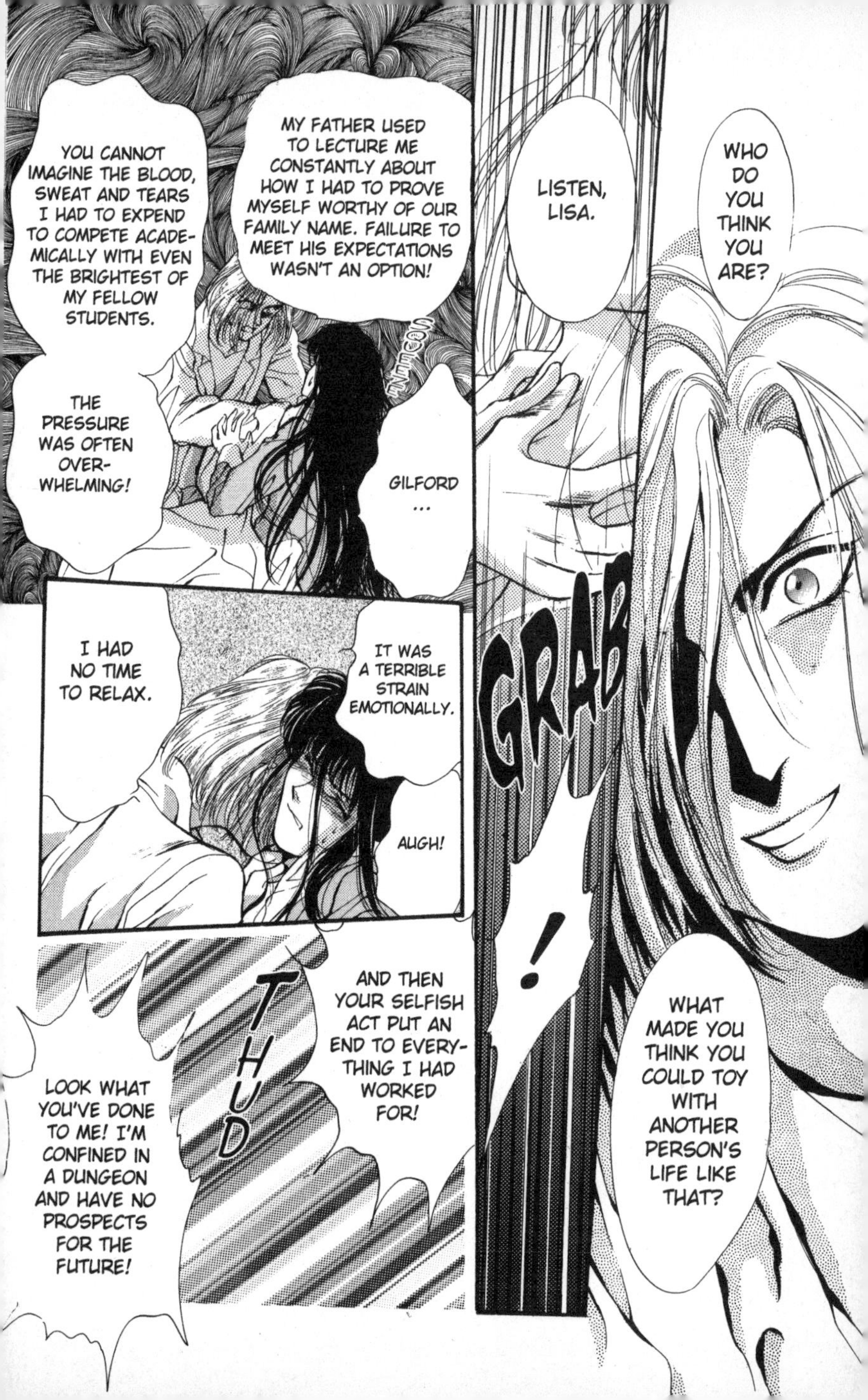

LISTEN, LISA.
WHO DO YOU THINK YOU ARE?
GRAB
!
WHAT MADE YOU THINK YOU COULD TOY WITH ANOTHER PERSON'S LIFE LIKE THAT?
MY FATHER USED TO LECTURE ME CONSTANTLY ABOUT HOW I HAD TO PROVE MYSELF WORTHY OF OUR FAMILY NAME. FAILURE TO MEET HIS EXPECTATIONS WASN'T AN OPTION!
YOU CANNOT IMAGINE THE BLOOD, SWEAT AND TEARS I HAD TO EXPEND TO COMPETE ACADEMICALLY WITH EVEN THE BRIGHTEST OF MY FELLOW STUDENTS.
GILFORD ...
THE PRESSURE WAS OFTEN OVERWHELMING!
IT WAS A TERRIBLE STRAIN EMOTIONALLY.
I HAD NO TIME TO RELAX.
AUGH!
AND THEN YOUR SELFISH ACT PUT AN END TO EVERYTHING I HAD WORKED FOR!
THUD
LOOK WHAT YOU'VE DONE TO ME! I'M CONFINED IN A DUNGEON AND HAVE NO PROSPECTS FOR THE FUTURE!

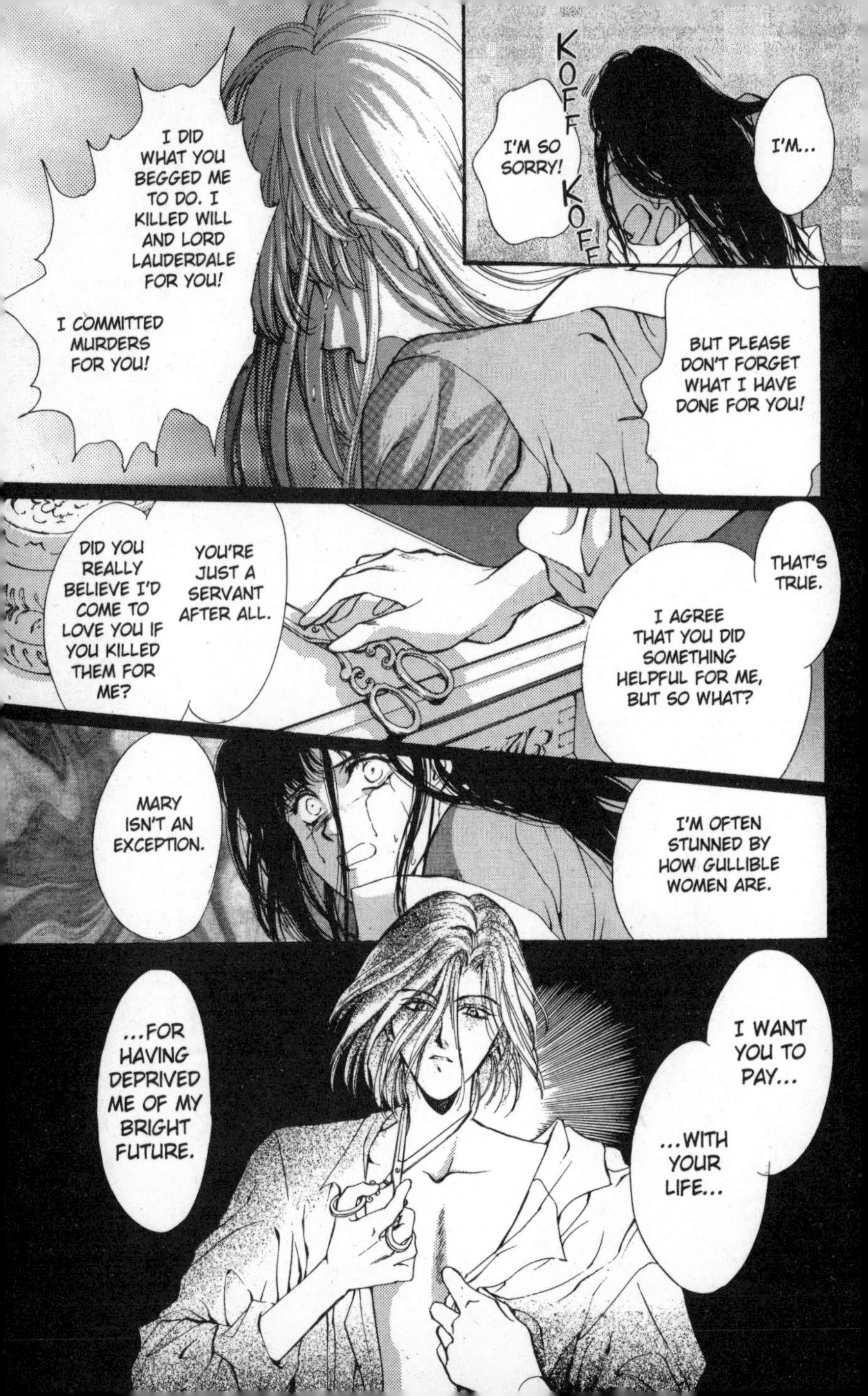
I'M...
KOFF
I'M SO SORRY!
KOFF
I DID WHAT YOU BEGGED ME TO DO. I KILLED WILL AND LORD LAUDERDALE FOR YOU!
I COMMITTED MURDERS FOR YOU!
BUT PLEASE DON'T FORGET WHAT I HAVE DONE FOR YOU!
THAT'S TRUE.
I AGREE THAT YOU DID SOMETHING HELPFUL FOR ME, BUT SO WHAT?
YOU'RE JUST A SERVANT AFTER ALL.
DID YOU REALLY BELIEVE I'D COME TO LOVE YOU IF YOU KILLED THEM FOR ME?
I'M OFTEN STUNNED BY HOW GULLIBLE WOMEN ARE.
MARY ISN'T AN EXCEPTION.
I WANT YOU TO PAY...
...WITH YOUR LIFE...
...FOR HAVING DEPRIVED ME OF MY BRIGHT FUTURE.

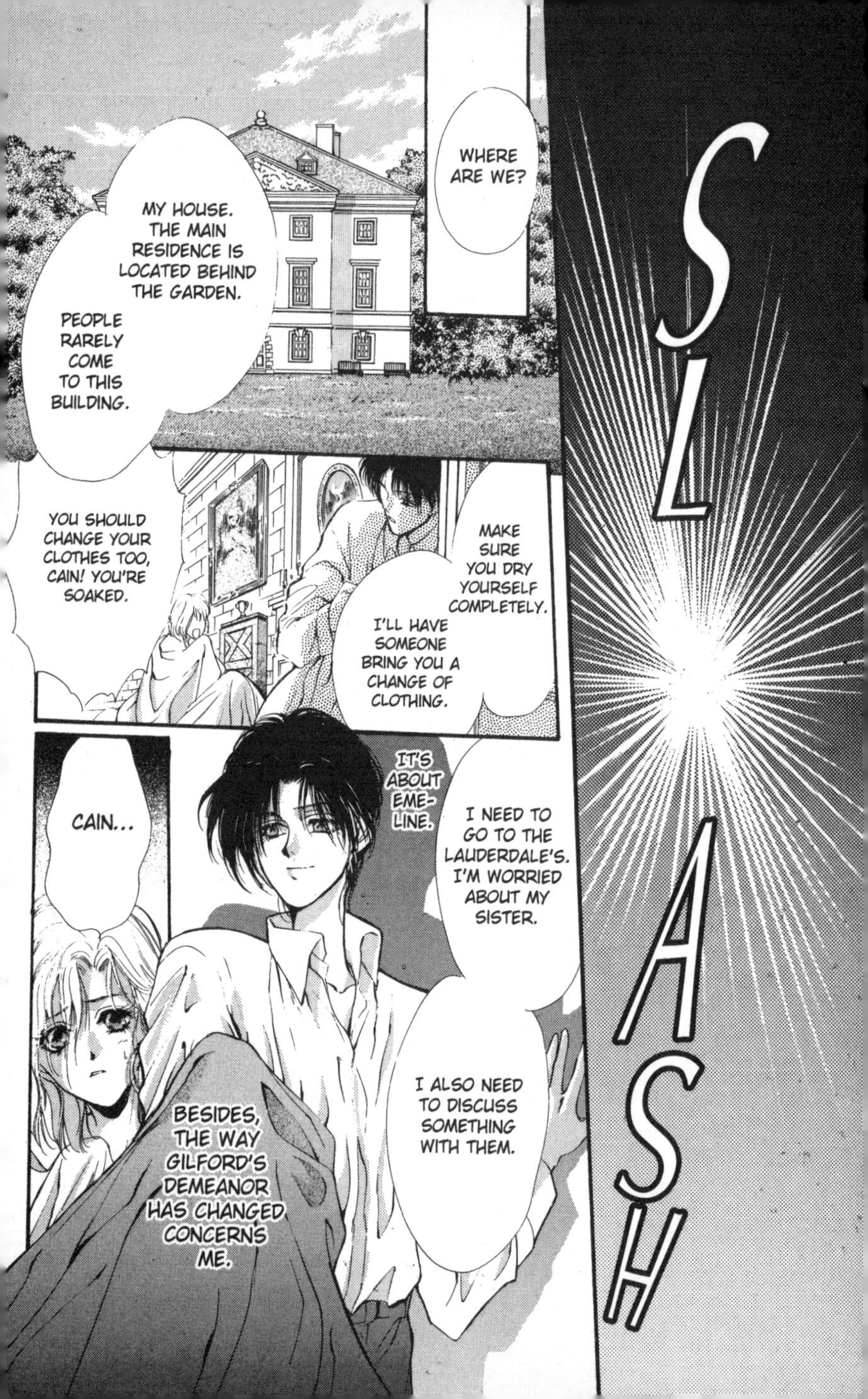
SLASH
WHERE ARE WE?
MY HOUSE. THE MAIN RESIDENCE IS LOCATED BEHIND THE GARDEN.
PEOPLE RARELY COME TO THIS BUILDING.
MAKE SURE YOU DRY YOURSELF COMPLETELY.
I'LL HAVE SOMEONE BRING YOU A CHANGE OF CLOTHING.
YOU SHOULD CHANGE YOUR CLOTHES TOO, CAIN! YOU'RE SOAKED.
I NEED TO GO TO THE LAUDERDALE'S. I'M WORRIED ABOUT MY SISTER.
IT'S ABOUT EME-LINE.
CAIN...
I ALSO NEED TO DISCUSS SOMETHING WITH THEM.
BESIDES, THE WAY GILFORD'S DEMEANOR HAS CHANGED CONCERNS ME.

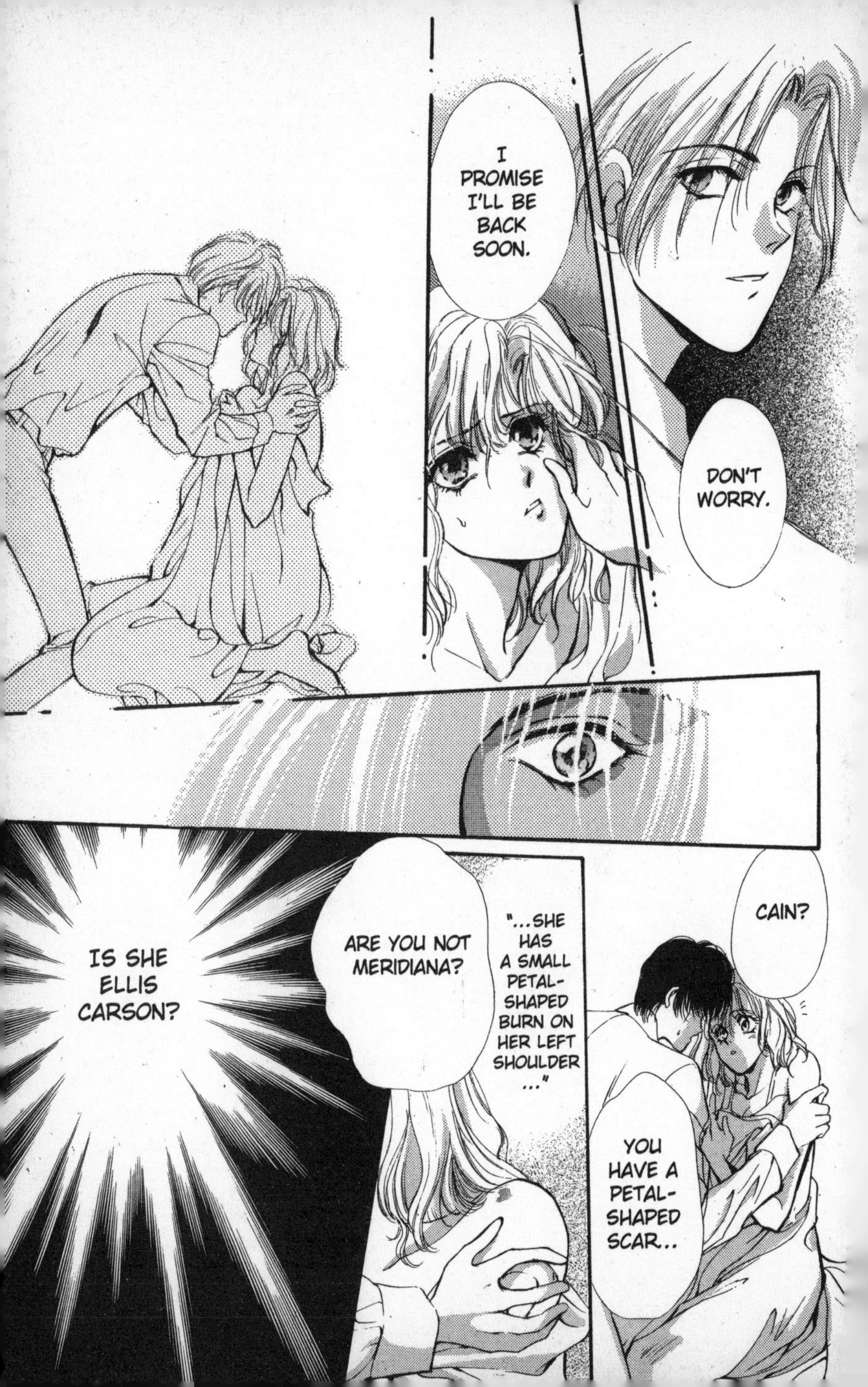
I PROMISE I'LL BE BACK SOON.
DON'T WORRY.
CAIN?
YOU HAVE A PETAL-SHAPED SCAR...
"...SHE HAS A SMALL PETAL-SHAPED BURN ON HER LEFT SHOULDER..."
ARE YOU NOT MERIDIANA?
IS SHE ELLIS CARSON?

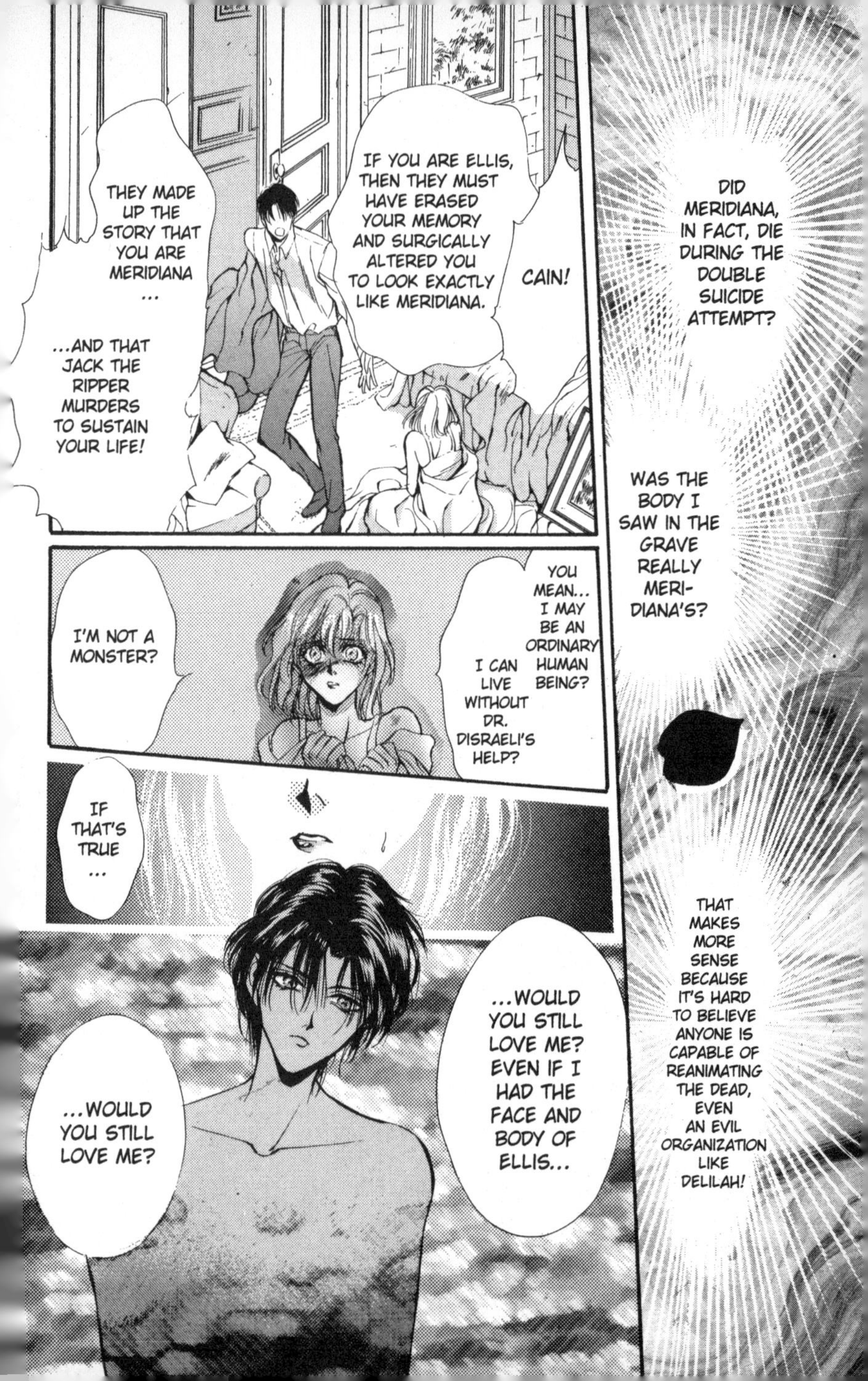
DID MERIDIANA, IN FACT, DIE DURING THE DOUBLE SUICIDE ATTEMPT?
WAS THE BODY I SAW IN THE GRAVE REALLY MERI-DIANA'S?
THAT MAKES MORE SENSE BECAUSE IT'S HARD TO BELIEVE ANYONE IS CAPABLE OF REANIMATING THE DEAD, EVEN AN EVIL ORGANIZATION LIKE DELILAH!
CAIN!
IF YOU ARE ELLIS, THEN THEY MUST HAVE ERASED YOUR MEMORY AND SURGICALLY ALTERED YOU TO LOOK EXACTLY LIKE MERIDIANA.
THEY MADE UP THE STORY THAT YOU ARE MERIDIANA ...
...AND THAT JACK THE RIPPER MURDERS TO SUSTAIN YOUR LIFE!
YOU MEAN... I MAY BE AN ORDINARY HUMAN BEING?
I CAN LIVE WITHOUT DR. DISRAELI'S HELP?
I'M NOT A MONSTER?
IF THAT'S TRUE ...
...WOULD YOU STILL LOVE ME? EVEN IF I HAD THE FACE AND BODY OF ELLIS...
...WOULD YOU STILL LOVE ME?

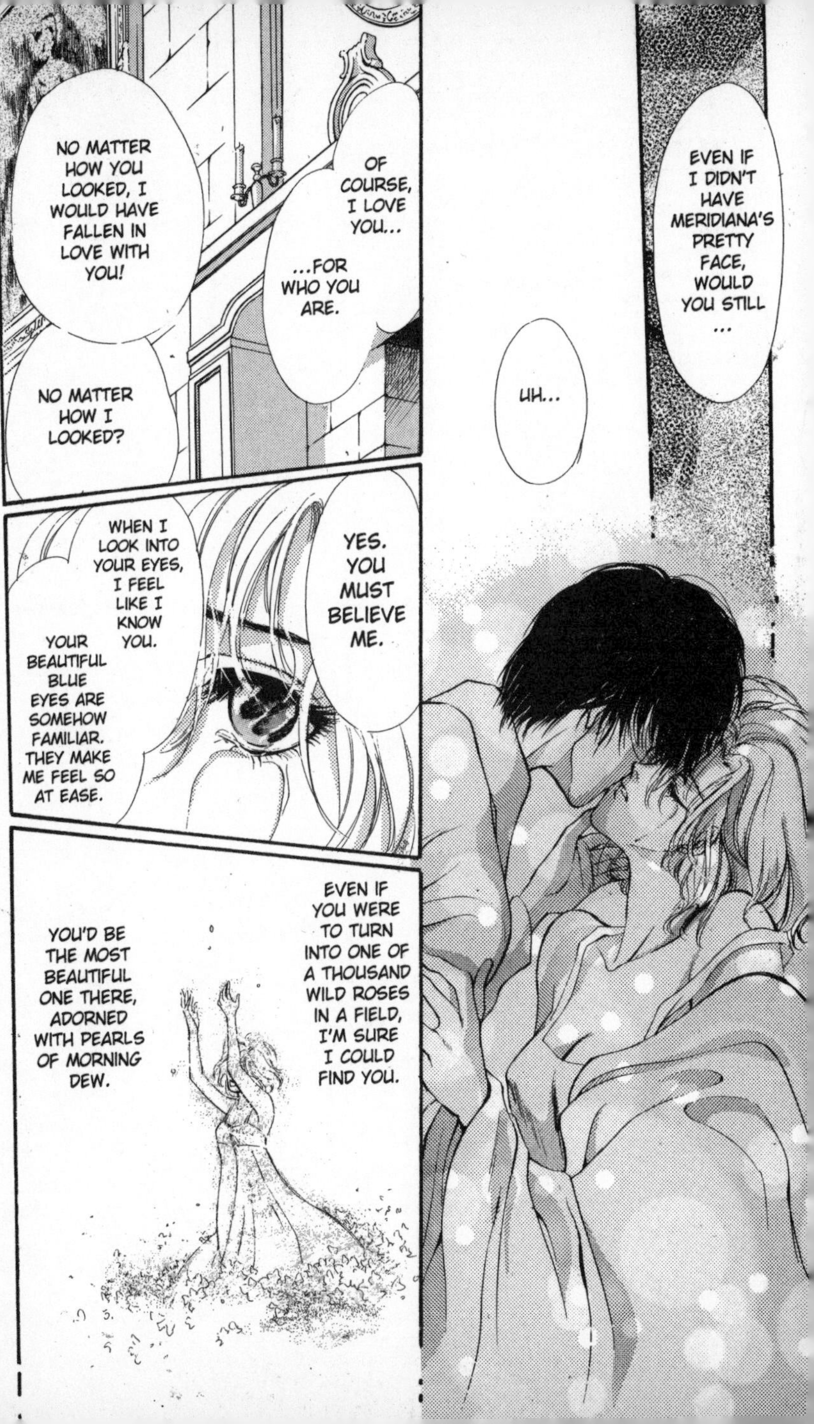
EVEN IF I DIDN'T HAVE MERIDIANA'S PRETTY FACE, WOULD YOU STILL ...
UH...
OF COURSE, I LOVE YOU...
...FOR WHO YOU ARE.
NO MATTER HOW YOU LOOKED, I WOULD HAVE FALLEN IN LOVE WITH YOU!
NO MATTER HOW I LOOKED?
YES. YOU MUST BELIEVE ME.
WHEN I LOOK INTO YOUR EYES, I FEEL LIKE I KNOW YOU.
YOUR BEAUTIFUL BLUE EYES ARE SOMEHOW FAMILIAR. THEY MAKE ME FEEL SO AT EASE.
EVEN IF YOU WERE TO TURN INTO ONE OF A THOUSAND WILD ROSES IN A FIELD, I'M SURE I COULD FIND YOU.
YOU'D BE THE MOST BEAUTIFUL ONE THERE, ADORNED WITH PEARLS OF MORNING DEW.

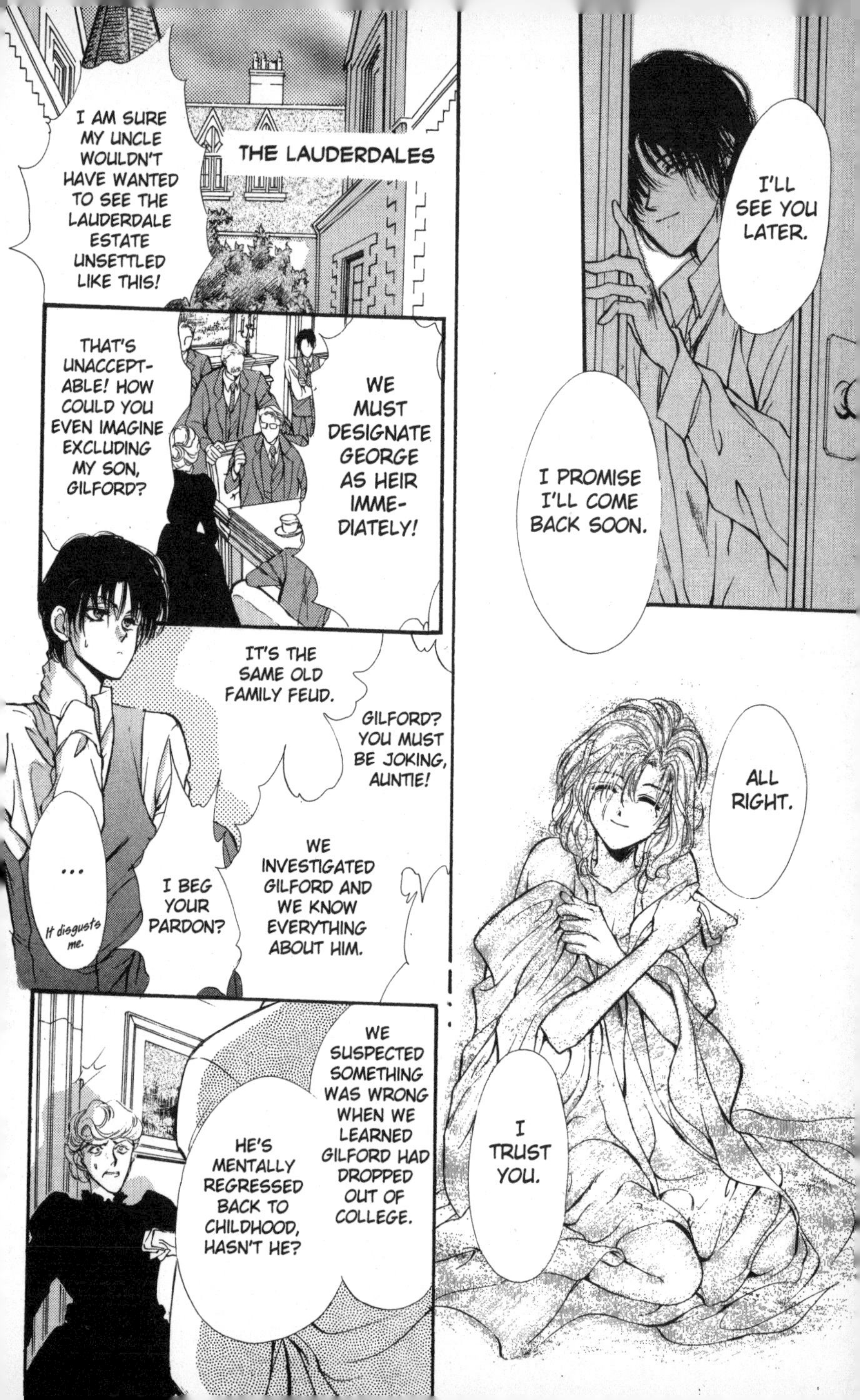
I'LL SEE YOU LATER.
I PROMISE I'LL COME BACK SOON.
ALL RIGHT.
I TRUST YOU.
THE LAUDERDALES
I AM SURE MY UNCLE WOULDN'T HAVE WANTED TO SEE THE LAUDERDALE ESTATE UNSETTLED LIKE THIS!
WE MUST DESIGNATE GEORGE AS HEIR IMME-DIATELY!
THAT'S UNACCEPT-ABLE! HOW COULD YOU EVEN IMAGINE EXCLUDING MY SON, GILFORD?
IT'S THE SAME OLD FAMILY FEUD.
GILFORD? YOU MUST BE JOKING, AUNTIE!
WE INVESTIGATED GILFORD AND WE KNOW EVERYTHING ABOUT HIM.
I BEG YOUR PARDON?
...
It disgusts me.
WE SUSPECTED SOMETHING WAS WRONG WHEN WE LEARNED GILFORD HAD DROPPED OUT OF COLLEGE.
HE'S MENTALLY REGRESSED BACK TO CHILDHOOD, HASN'T HE?

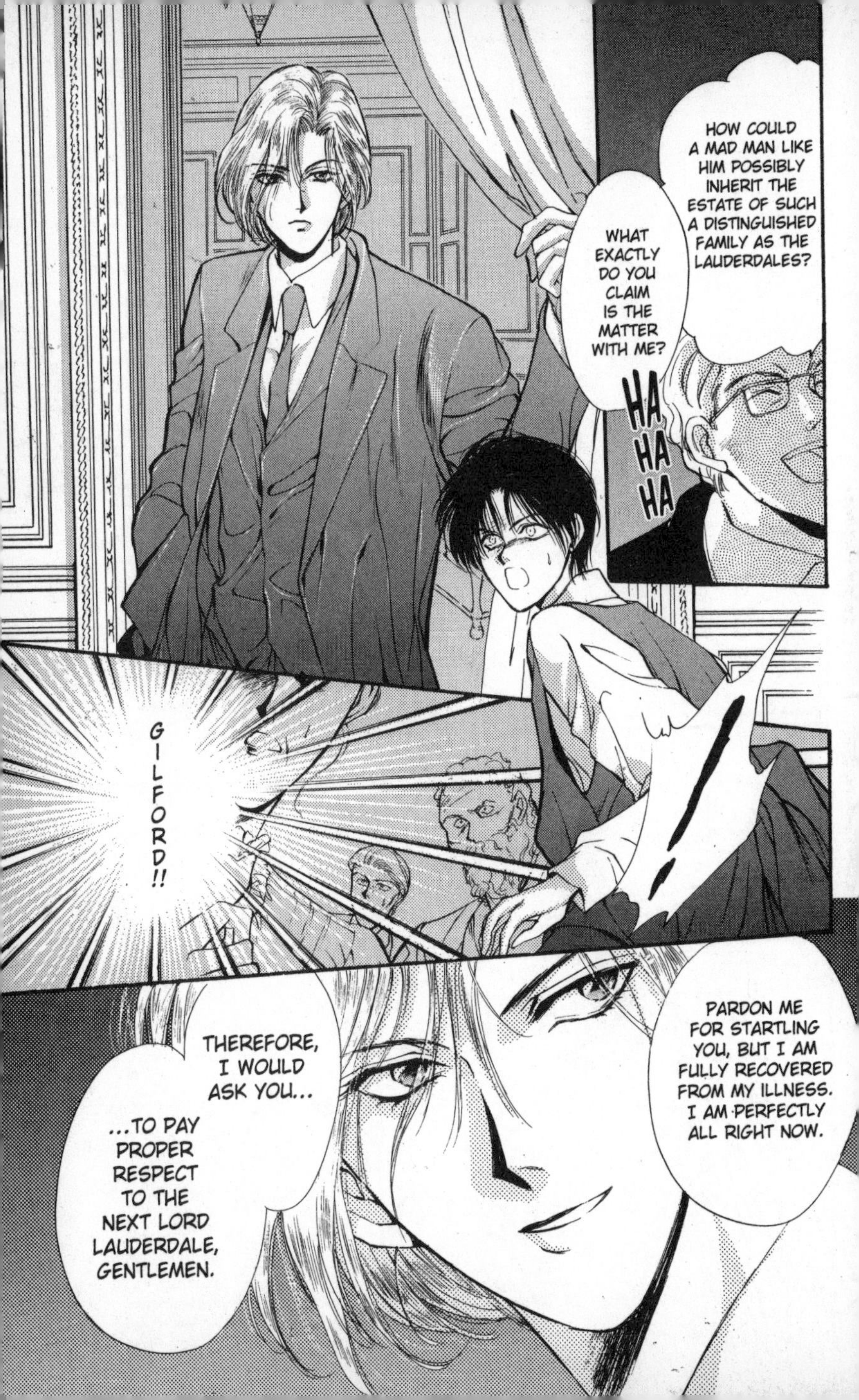
HOW COULD A MAD MAN LIKE HIM POSSIBLY INHERIT THE ESTATE OF SUCH A DISTINGUISHED FAMILY AS THE LAUDERDALES?
HA HA HA
WHAT EXACTLY DO YOU CLAIM IS THE MATTER WITH ME?
GILFORD!!
PARDON ME FOR STARTLING YOU, BUT I AM FULLY RECOVERED FROM MY ILLNESS. I AM PERFECTLY ALL RIGHT NOW.
THEREFORE, I WOULD ASK YOU...
...TO PAY PROPER RESPECT TO THE NEXT LORD LAUDERDALE, GENTLEMEN.

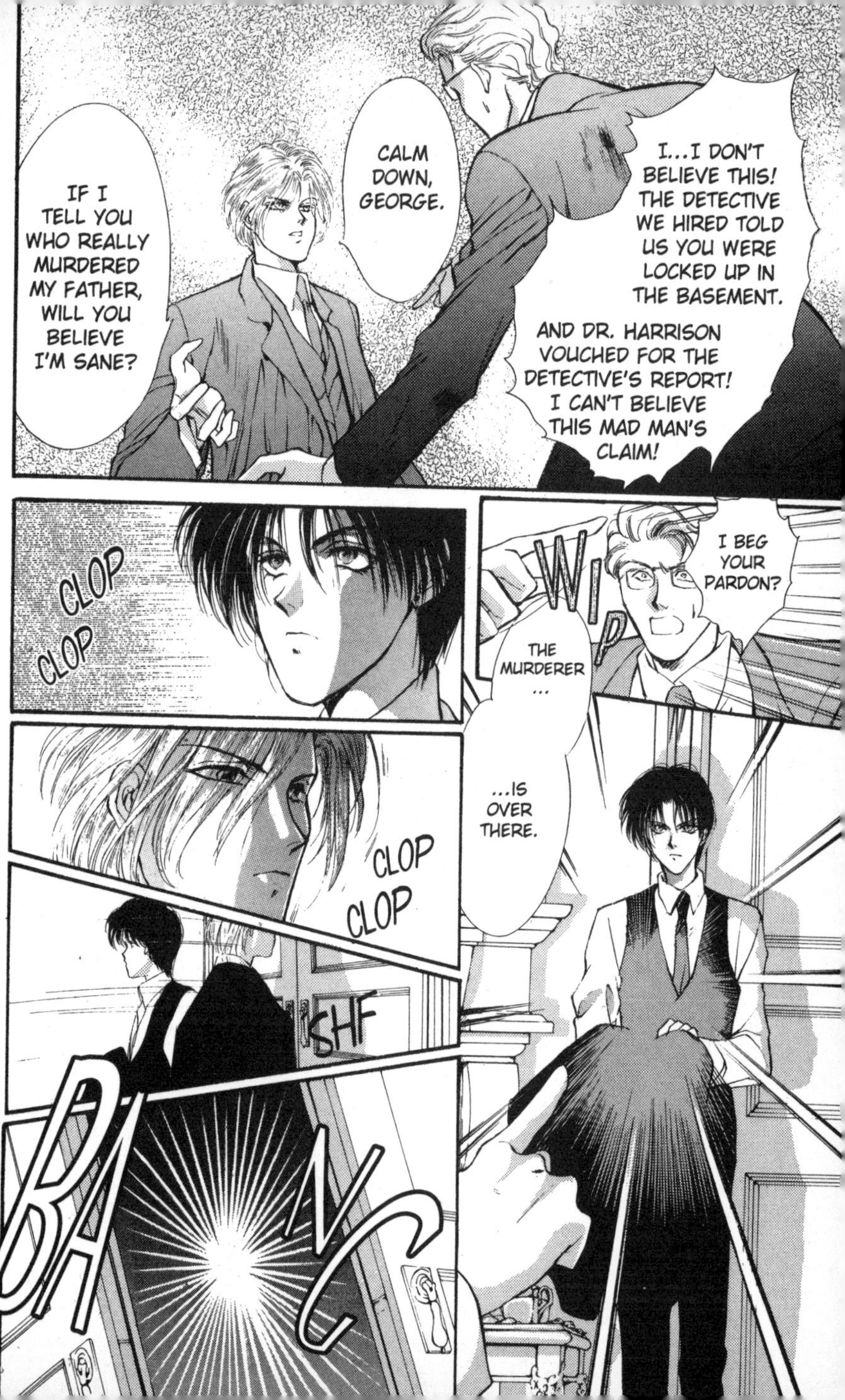
I...I DON'T BELIEVE THIS! THE DETECTIVE WE HIRED TOLD US YOU WERE LOCKED UP IN THE BASEMENT.
AND DR. HARRISON VOUCHED FOR THE DETECTIVE'S REPORT! I CAN'T BELIEVE THIS MAD MAN'S CLAIM!
CALM DOWN, GEORGE.
IF I TELL YOU WHO REALLY MURDERED MY FATHER, WILL YOU BELIEVE I'M SANE?
WIP
I BEG YOUR PARDON?
THE MURDERER...
...IS OVER THERE.
CLOP CLOP
CLOP CLOP
SHF
BANG

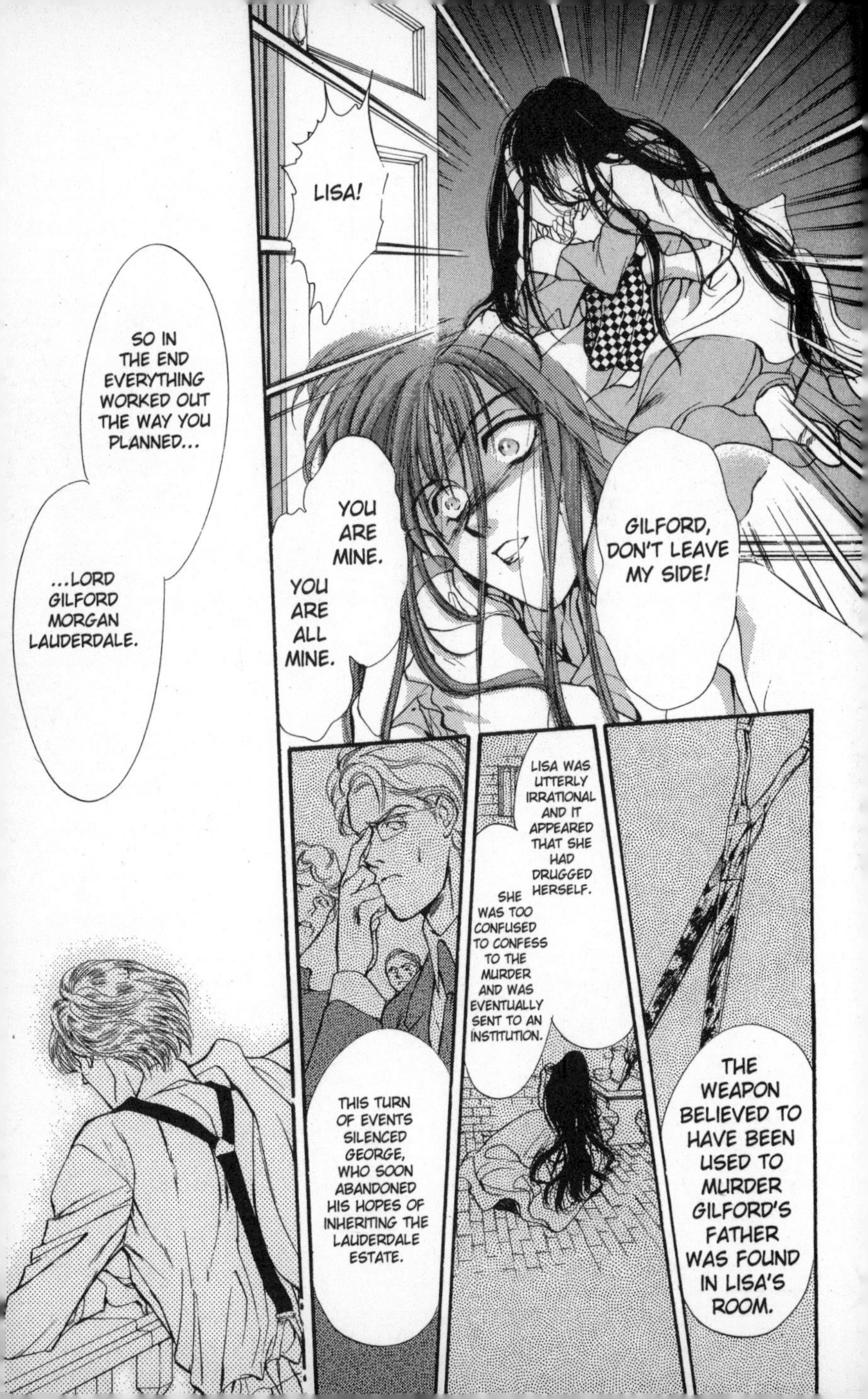
LISA!
GILFORD, DON'T LEAVE MY SIDE!
YOU ARE MINE.
YOU ARE ALL MINE.
THE WEAPON BELIEVED TO HAVE BEEN USED TO MURDER GILFORD'S FATHER WAS FOUND IN LISA'S ROOM.
LISA WAS UTTERLY IRRATIONAL AND IT APPEARED THAT SHE HAD DRUGGED HERSELF.
SHE WAS TOO CONFUSED TO CONFESS TO THE MURDER AND WAS EVENTUALLY SENT TO AN INSTITUTION.
THIS TURN OF EVENTS SILENCED GEORGE, WHO SOON ABANDONED HIS HOPES OF INHERITING THE LAUDERDALE ESTATE.
SO IN THE END EVERYTHING WORKED OUT THE WAY YOU PLANNED...
...LORD GILFORD MORGAN LAUDERDALE.

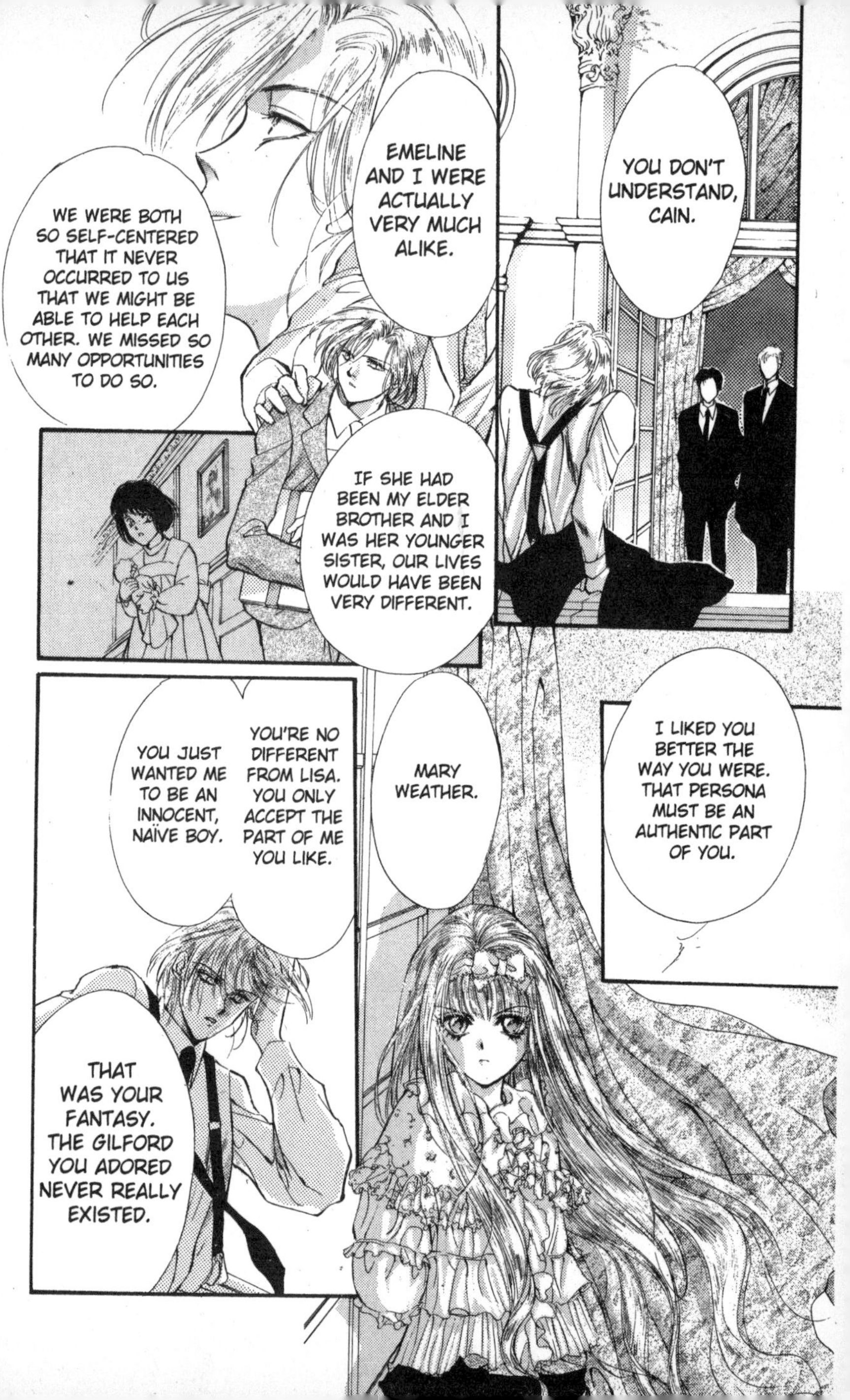
YOU DON'T UNDERSTAND, CAIN.
EMELINE AND I WERE ACTUALLY VERY MUCH ALIKE.
WE WERE BOTH SO SELF-CENTERED THAT IT NEVER OCCURRED TO US THAT WE MIGHT BE ABLE TO HELP EACH OTHER. WE MISSED SO MANY OPPORTUNITIES TO DO SO.
IF SHE HAD BEEN MY ELDER BROTHER AND I WAS HER YOUNGER SISTER, OUR LIVES WOULD HAVE BEEN VERY DIFFERENT.
I LIKED YOU BETTER THE WAY YOU WERE. THAT PERSONA MUST BE AN AUTHENTIC PART OF YOU.
MARY WEATHER.
YOU'RE NO DIFFERENT FROM LISA. YOU ONLY ACCEPT THE PART OF ME YOU LIKE.
YOU JUST WANTED ME TO BE AN INNOCENT, NAÏVE BOY.
THAT WAS YOUR FANTASY. THE GILFORD YOU ADORED NEVER REALLY EXISTED.

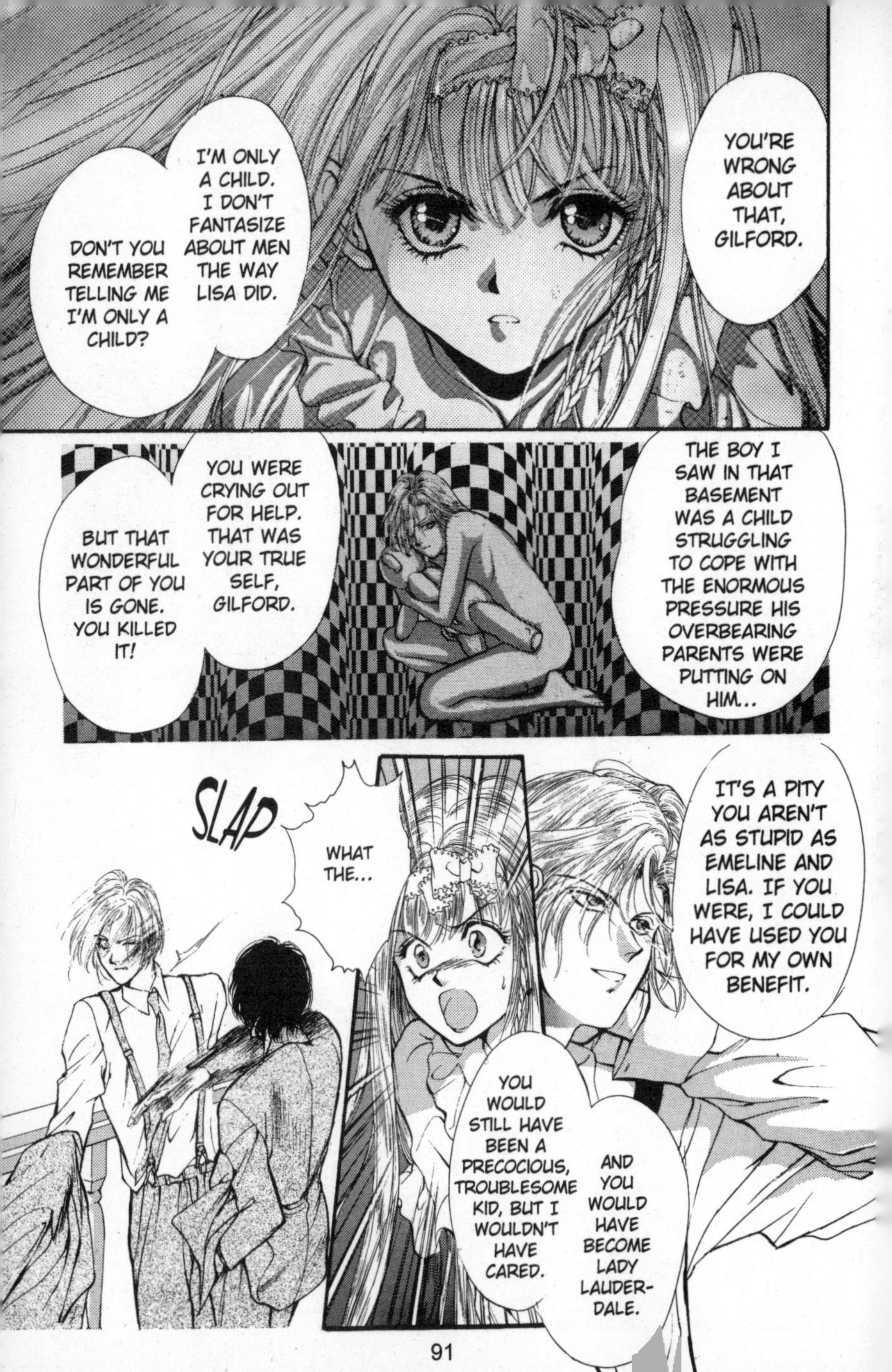
YOU'RE WRONG ABOUT THAT, GILFORD.
I'M ONLY A CHILD. I DON'T FANTASIZE ABOUT MEN THE WAY LISA DID.
DON'T YOU REMEMBER TELLING ME I'M ONLY A CHILD?
THE BOY I SAW IN THAT BASEMENT WAS A CHILD STRUGGLING TO COPE WITH THE ENORMOUS PRESSURE HIS OVERBEARING PARENTS WERE PUTTING ON HIM...
YOU WERE CRYING OUT FOR HELP. THAT WAS YOUR TRUE SELF, GILFORD.
BUT THAT WONDERFUL PART OF YOU IS GONE. YOU KILLED IT!
IT'S A PITY YOU AREN'T AS STUPID AS EMELINE AND LISA. IF YOU WERE, I COULD HAVE USED YOU FOR MY OWN BENEFIT.
YOU WOULD STILL HAVE BEEN A PRECOCIOUS, TROUBLESOME KID, BUT I WOULDN'T HAVE CARED.
AND YOU WOULD HAVE BECOME LADY LAUDER-DALE.
SLAP
WHAT THE...

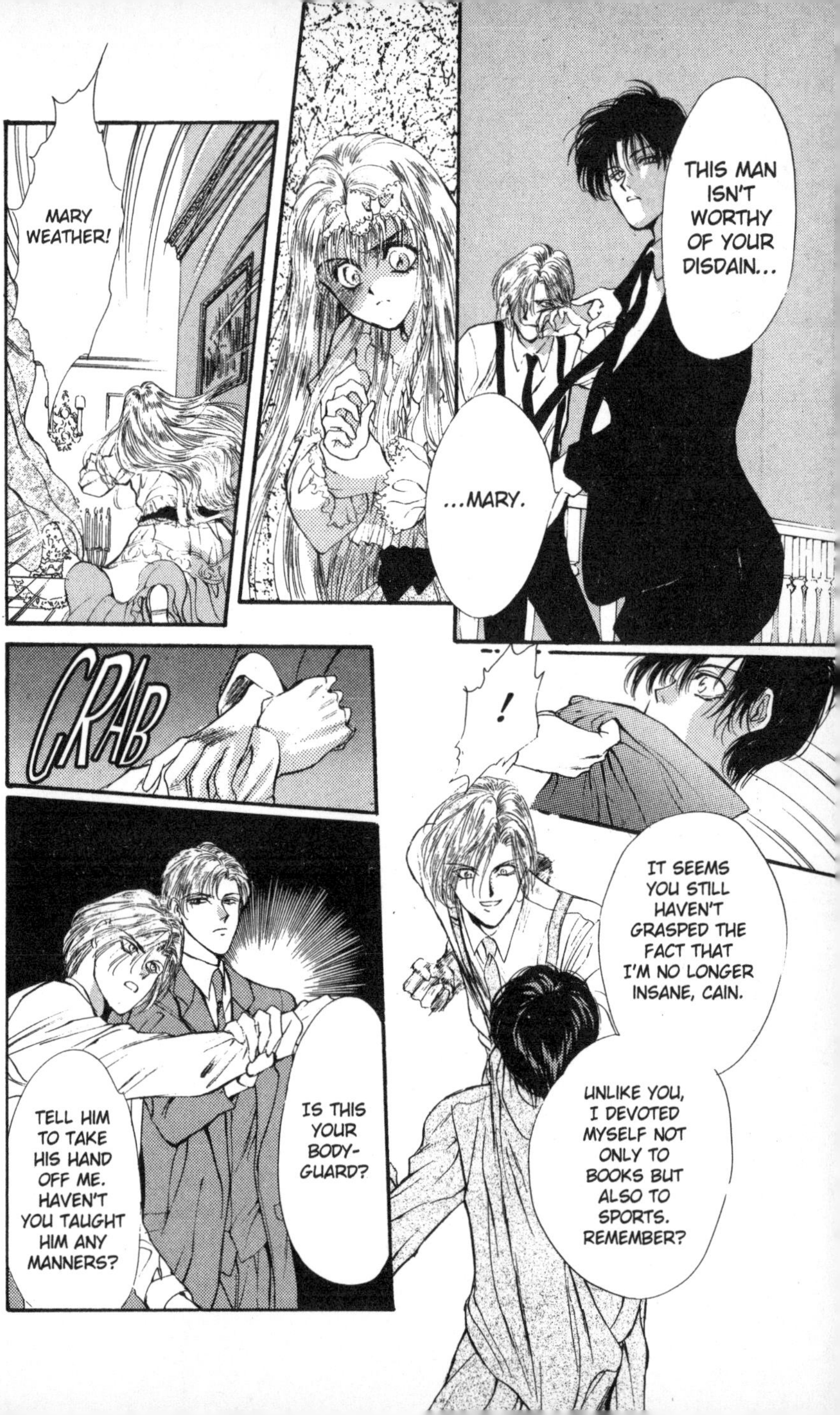
THIS MAN ISN'T WORTHY OF YOUR DISDAIN...
...MARY.
MARY WEATHER!
!
IT SEEMS YOU STILL HAVEN'T GRASPED THE FACT THAT I'M NO LONGER INSANE, CAIN.
UNLIKE YOU, I DEVOTED MYSELF NOT ONLY TO BOOKS BUT ALSO TO SPORTS. REMEMBER?
GRAB
IS THIS YOUR BODY-GUARD?
TELL HIM TO TAKE HIS HAND OFF ME. HAVEN'T YOU TAUGHT HIM ANY MANNERS?

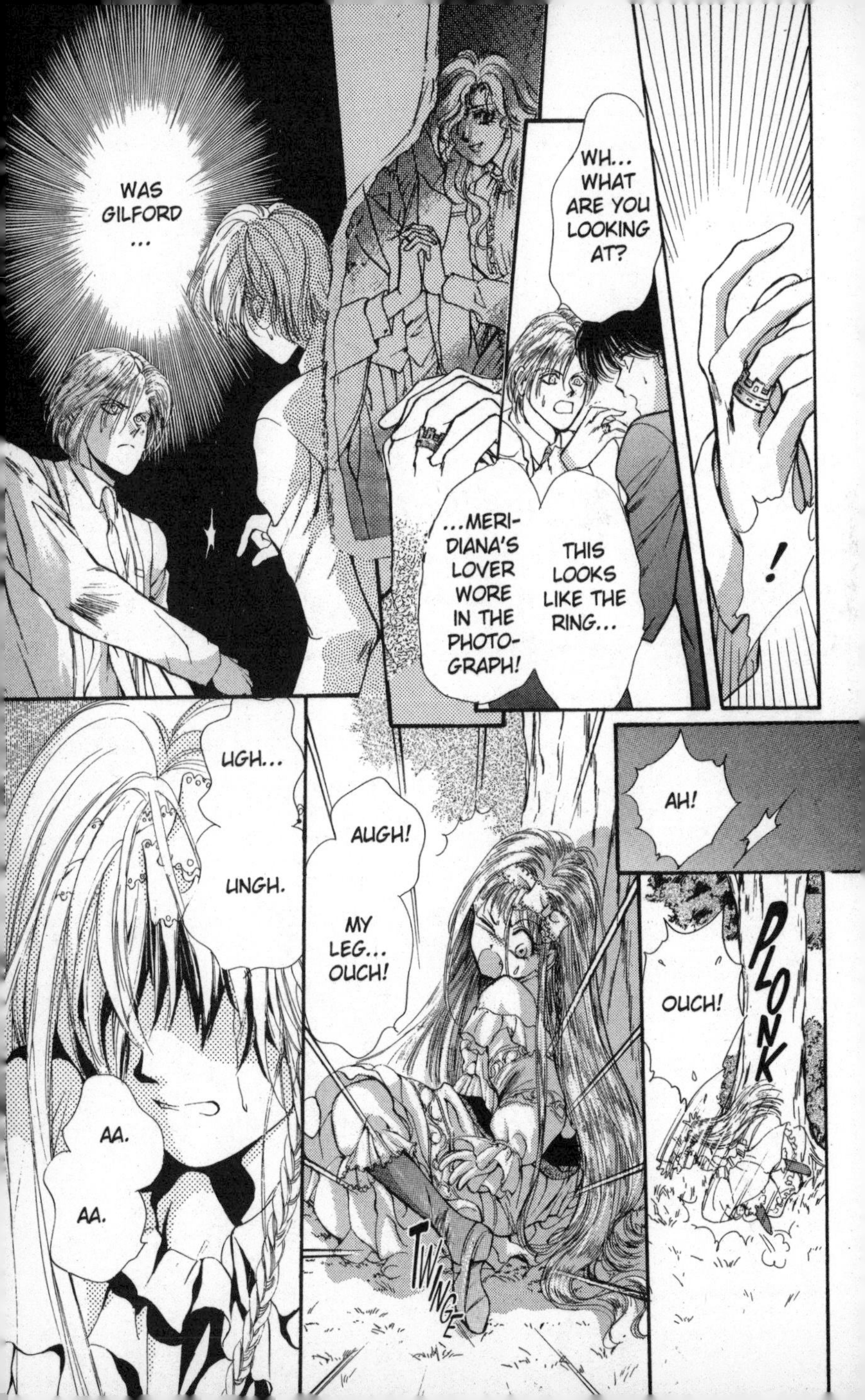
!
WH... WHAT ARE YOU LOOKING AT?
THIS LOOKS LIKE THE RING...
...MERI-DIANA'S LOVER WORE IN THE PHOTOGRAPH!
WAS GILFORD ...
AH!
PLONK
OUCH!
AUGH!
MY LEG... OUCH!
TWINGE
UGH...
UNGH.
AA.
AA.

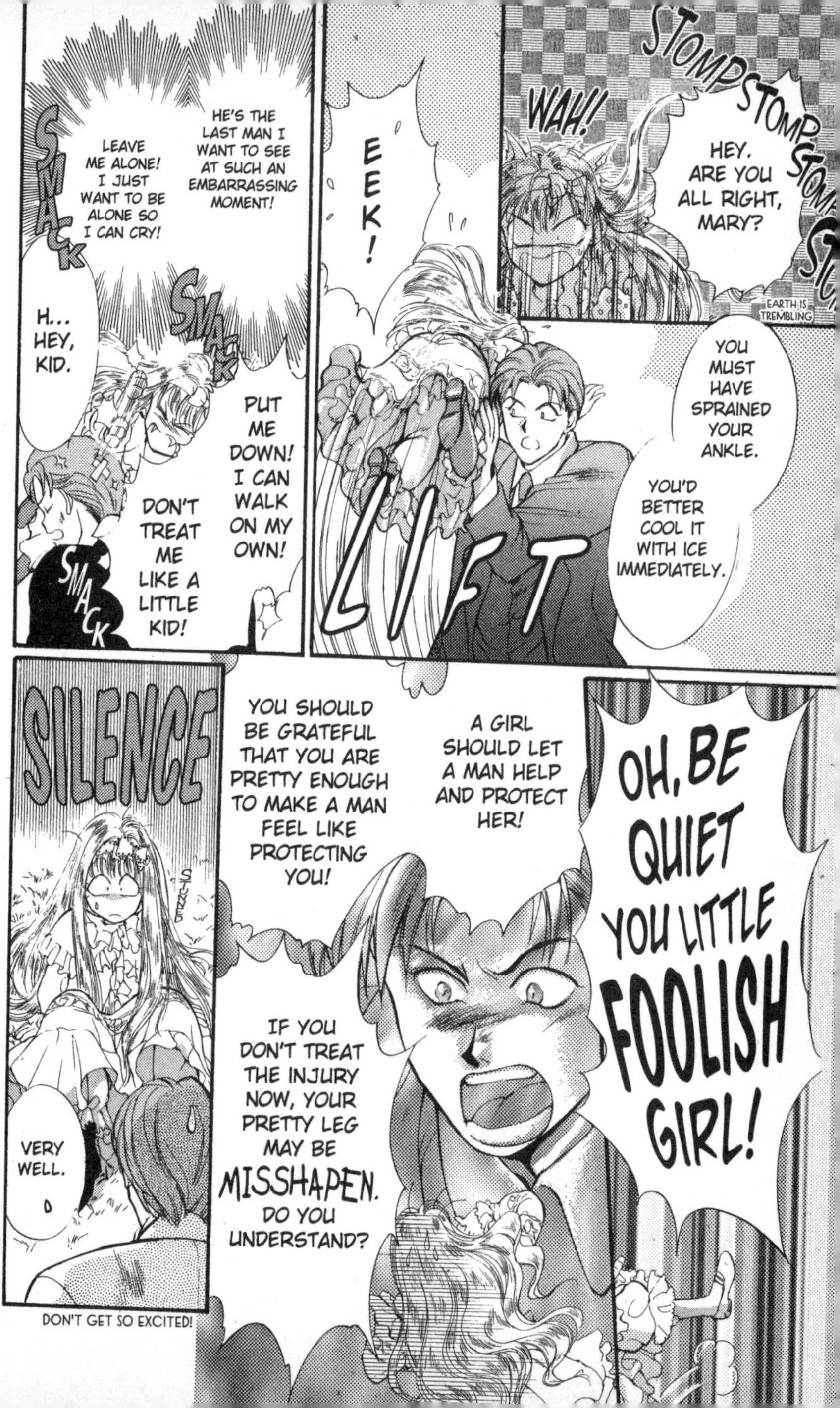
STOMP STOMP STOMP STOMP
WAH!
HEY. ARE YOU ALL RIGHT, MARY?
EARTH IS TREMBLING
YOU MUST HAVE SPRAINED YOUR ANKLE.
YOU'D BETTER COOL IT WITH ICE IMMEDIATELY.
LIFT
EEK!
HE'S THE LAST MAN I WANT TO SEE AT SUCH AN EMBARRASSING MOMENT!
LEAVE ME ALONE! I JUST WANT TO BE ALONE SO I CAN CRY!
SMACK
SMACK
H... HEY, KID.
PUT ME DOWN! I CAN WALK ON MY OWN!
DON'T TREAT ME LIKE A LITTLE KID!
SMACK
OH, BE QUIET YOU LITTLE FOOLISH GIRL!
A GIRL SHOULD LET A MAN HELP AND PROTECT HER!
YOU SHOULD BE GRATEFUL THAT YOU ARE PRETTY ENOUGH TO MAKE A MAN FEEL LIKE PROTECTING YOU!
IF YOU DON'T TREAT THE INJURY NOW, YOUR PRETTY LEG MAY BE MISSHAPEN. DO YOU UNDERSTAND?
SILENCE
STUNNED
VERY WELL.
DON'T GET SO EXCITED!

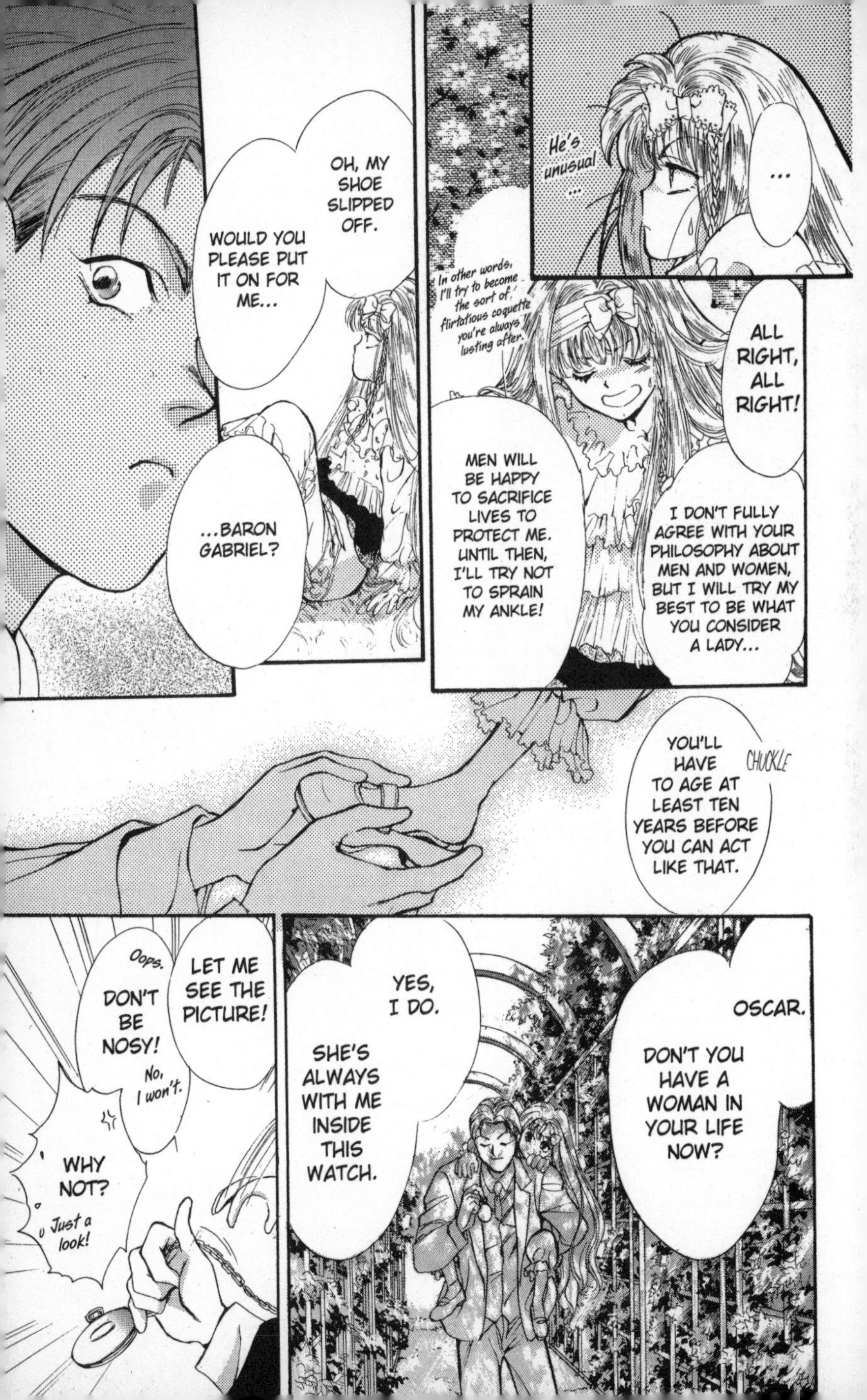
...
He's unusual...
In other words, I'll try to become the sort of flirtatious coquette you're always lusting after.
ALL RIGHT, ALL RIGHT!
I DON'T FULLY AGREE WITH YOUR PHILOSOPHY ABOUT MEN AND WOMEN, BUT I WILL TRY MY BEST TO BE WHAT YOU CONSIDER A LADY...
MEN WILL BE HAPPY TO SACRIFICE LIVES TO PROTECT ME. UNTIL THEN, I'LL TRY NOT TO SPRAIN MY ANKLE!
OH, MY SHOE SLIPPED OFF.
WOULD YOU PLEASE PUT IT ON FOR ME...
...BARON GABRIEL?
CHUCKLE
YOU'LL HAVE TO AGE AT LEAST TEN YEARS BEFORE YOU CAN ACT LIKE THAT.
OSCAR.
DON'T YOU HAVE A WOMAN IN YOUR LIFE NOW?
YES, I DO.
SHE'S ALWAYS WITH ME INSIDE THIS WATCH.
LET ME SEE THE PICTURE!
Oops.
DON'T BE NOSY!
No, I won't.
WHY NOT?
Just a look!

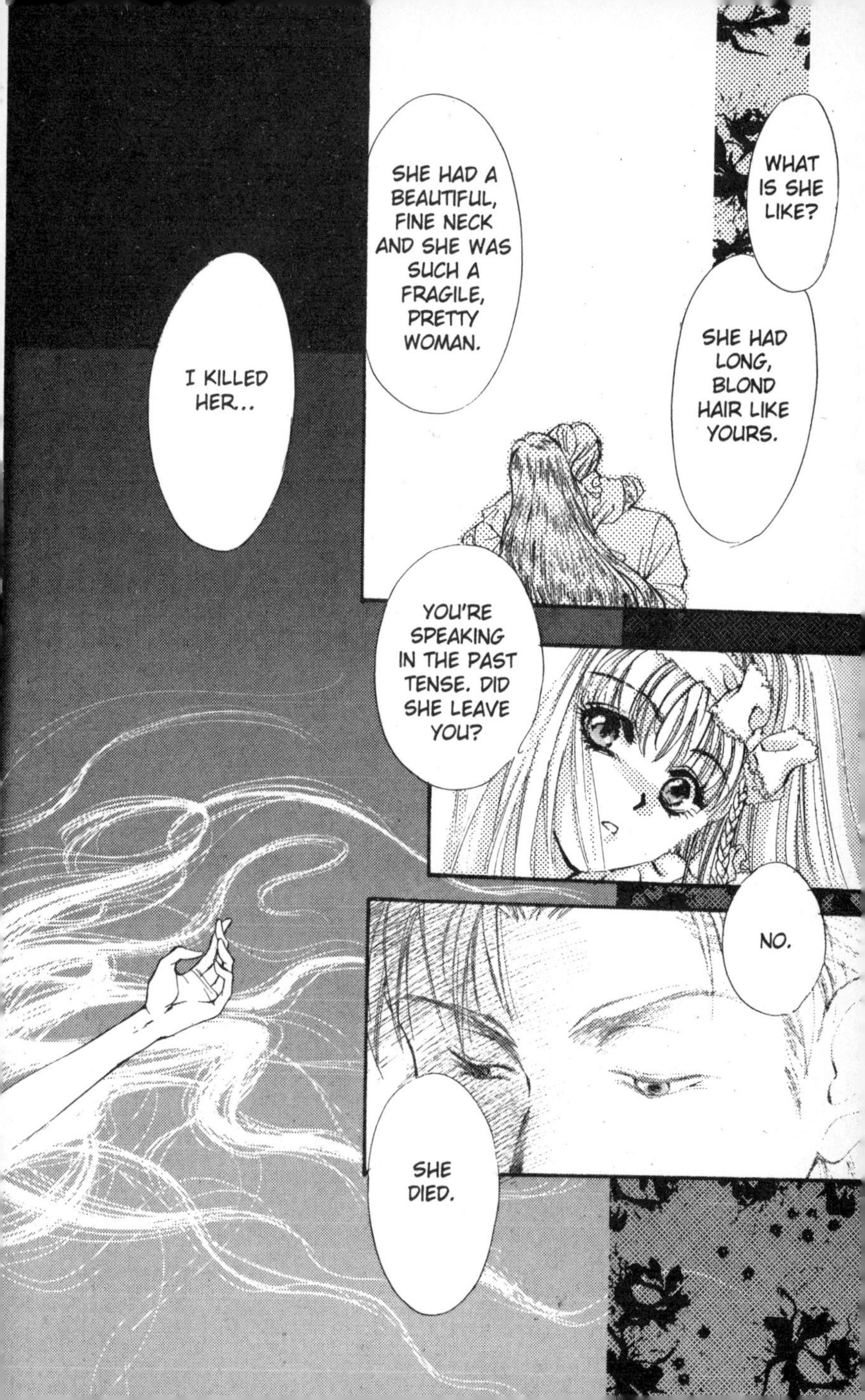
WHAT IS SHE LIKE?
SHE HAD LONG, BLOND HAIR LIKE YOURS.
SHE HAD A BEAUTIFUL, FINE NECK AND SHE WAS SUCH A FRAGILE, PRETTY WOMAN.
YOU'RE SPEAKING IN THE PAST TENSE. DID SHE LEAVE YOU?
NO.
SHE DIED.
I KILLED HER...

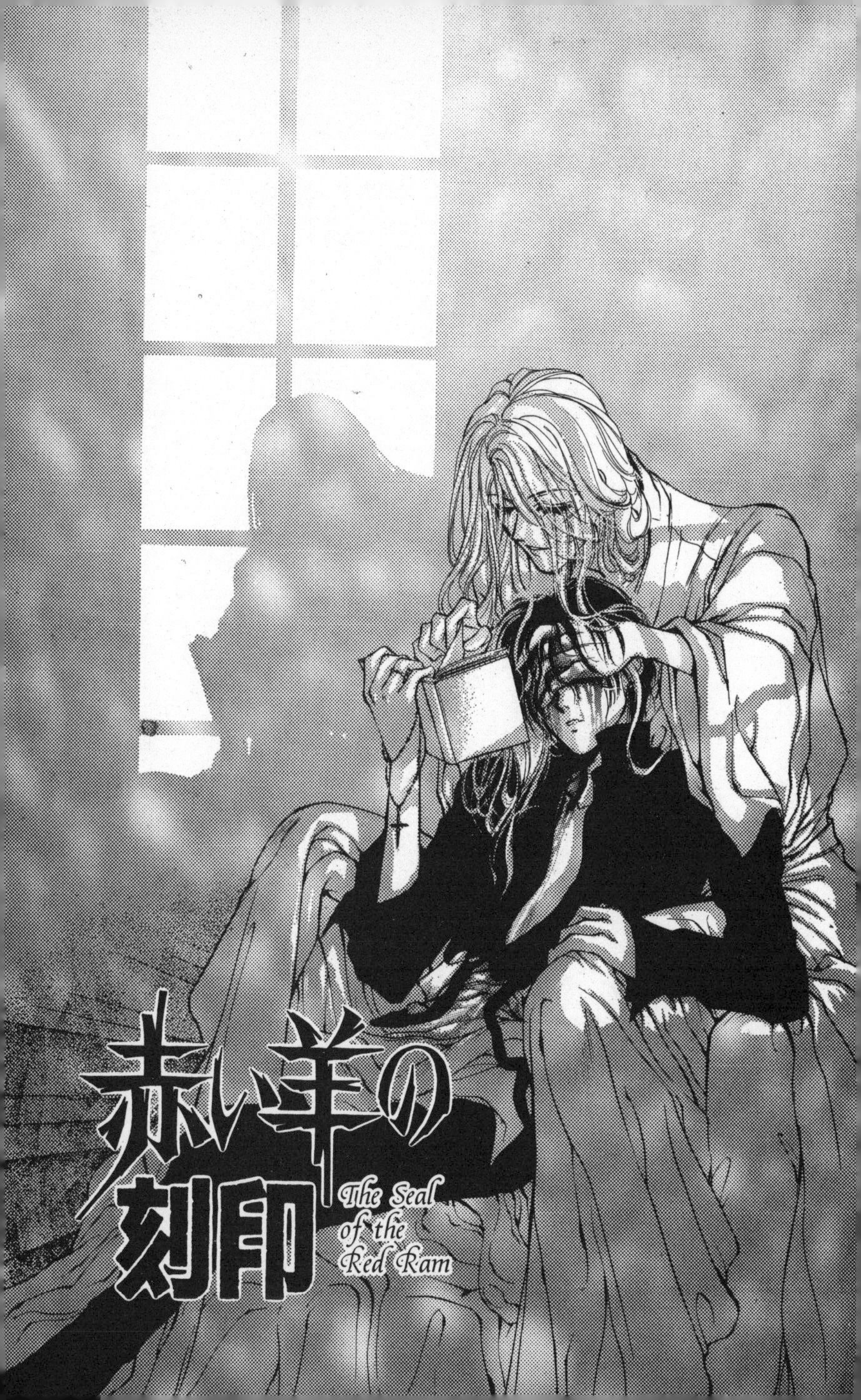
赤い羊の刻印
The Seal of the Red Ram

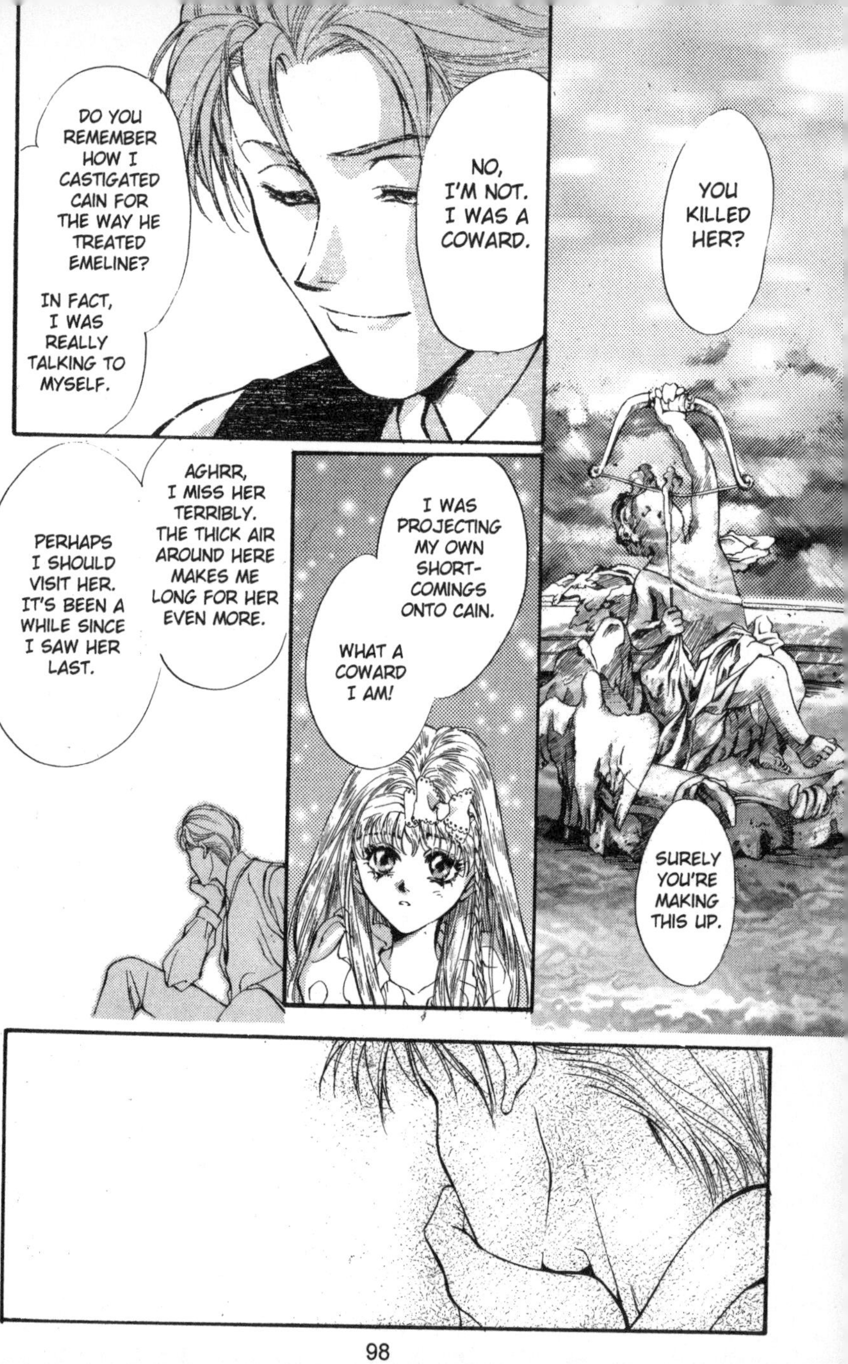
YOU KILLED HER?
SURELY YOU'RE MAKING THIS UP.
NO, I'M NOT. I WAS A COWARD.
DO YOU REMEMBER HOW I CASTIGATED CAIN FOR THE WAY HE TREATED EMELINE?
IN FACT, I WAS REALLY TALKING TO MYSELF.
I WAS PROJECTING MY OWN SHORT-COMINGS ONTO CAIN.
WHAT A COWARD I AM!
AGHRR, I MISS HER TERRIBLY. THE THICK AIR AROUND HERE MAKES ME LONG FOR HER EVEN MORE.
PERHAPS I SHOULD VISIT HER. IT'S BEEN A WHILE SINCE I SAW HER LAST.

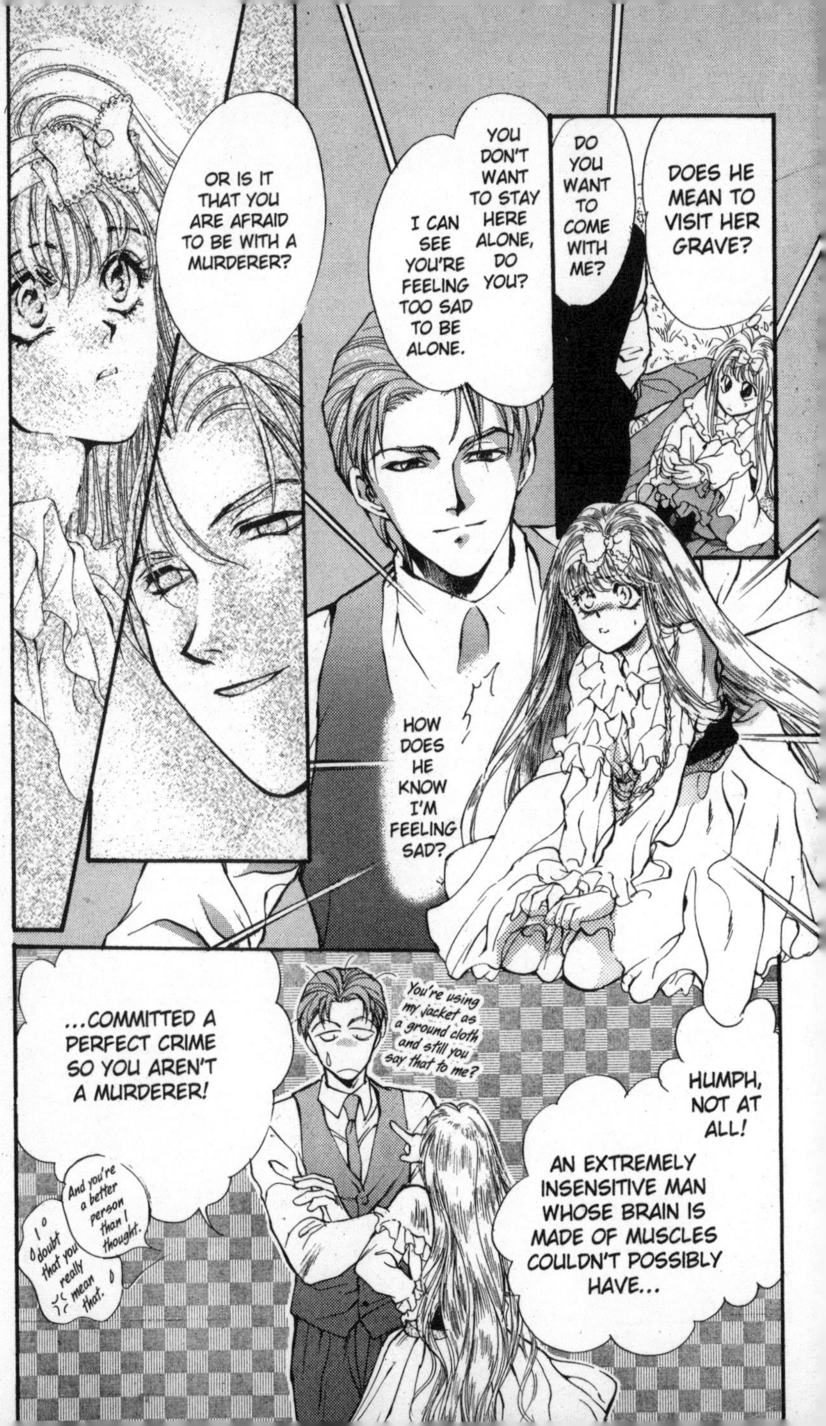
DOES HE MEAN TO VISIT HER GRAVE?
DO YOU WANT TO COME WITH ME?
YOU DON'T WANT TO STAY HERE ALONE, DO YOU?
I CAN SEE YOU'RE FEELING TOO SAD TO BE ALONE.
HOW DOES HE KNOW I'M FEELING SAD?
OR IS IT THAT YOU ARE AFRAID TO BE WITH A MURDERER?
HUMPH, NOT AT ALL!
AN EXTREMELY INSENSITIVE MAN WHOSE BRAIN IS MADE OF MUSCLES COULDN'T POSSIBLY HAVE...
You're using my jacket as a ground cloth and still you say that to me?
...COMMITTED A PERFECT CRIME SO YOU AREN'T A MURDERER!
And you're a better person than I thought.
I doubt that you really mean that.

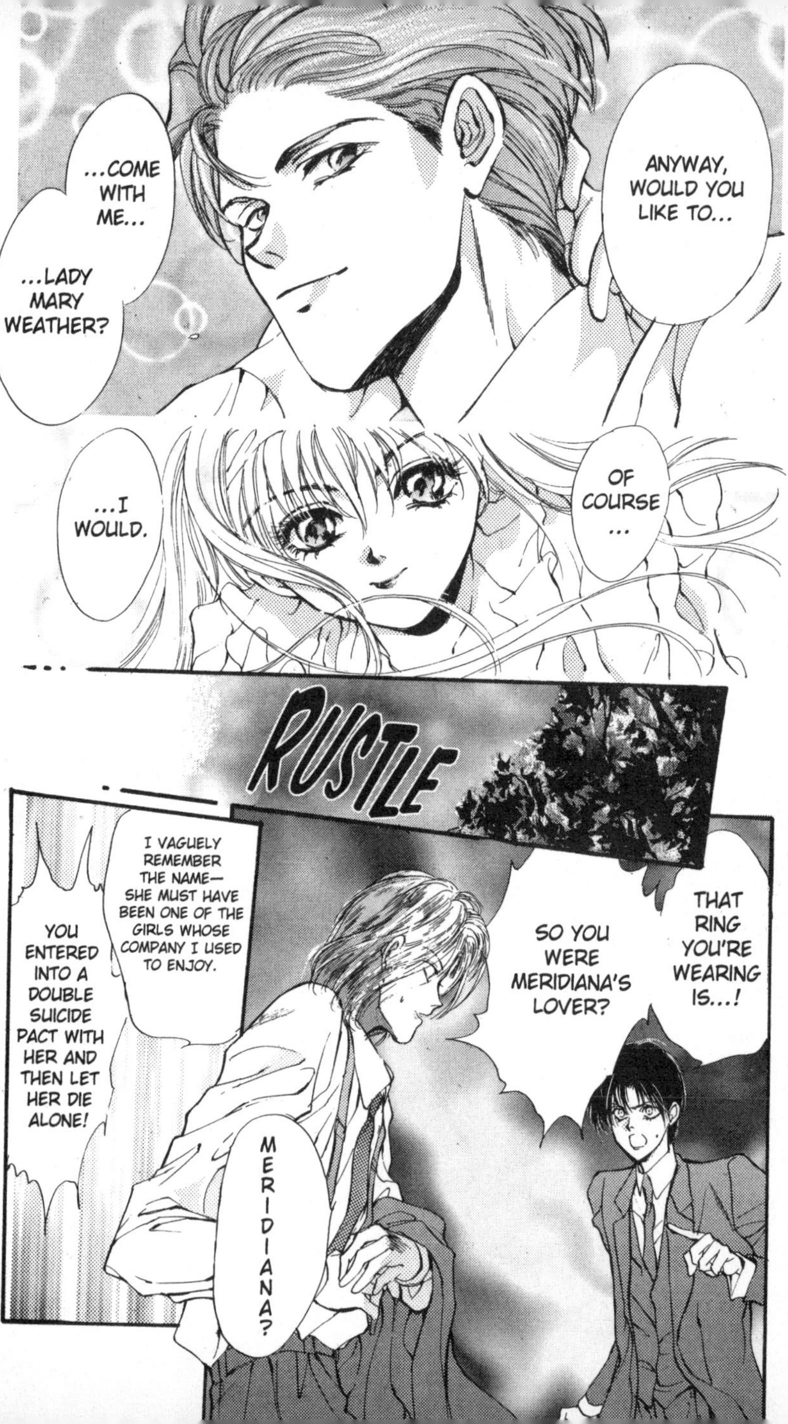
ANYWAY, WOULD YOU LIKE TO...
...COME WITH ME...
...LADY MARY WEATHER?
OF COURSE...
...I WOULD.
RUSTLE
THAT RING YOU'RE WEARING IS...!
SO YOU WERE MERIDIANA'S LOVER?
MERIDIANA?
I VAGUELY REMEMBER THE NAME— SHE MUST HAVE BEEN ONE OF THE GIRLS WHOSE COMPANY I USED TO ENJOY.
YOU ENTERED INTO A DOUBLE SUICIDE PACT WITH HER AND THEN LET HER DIE ALONE!

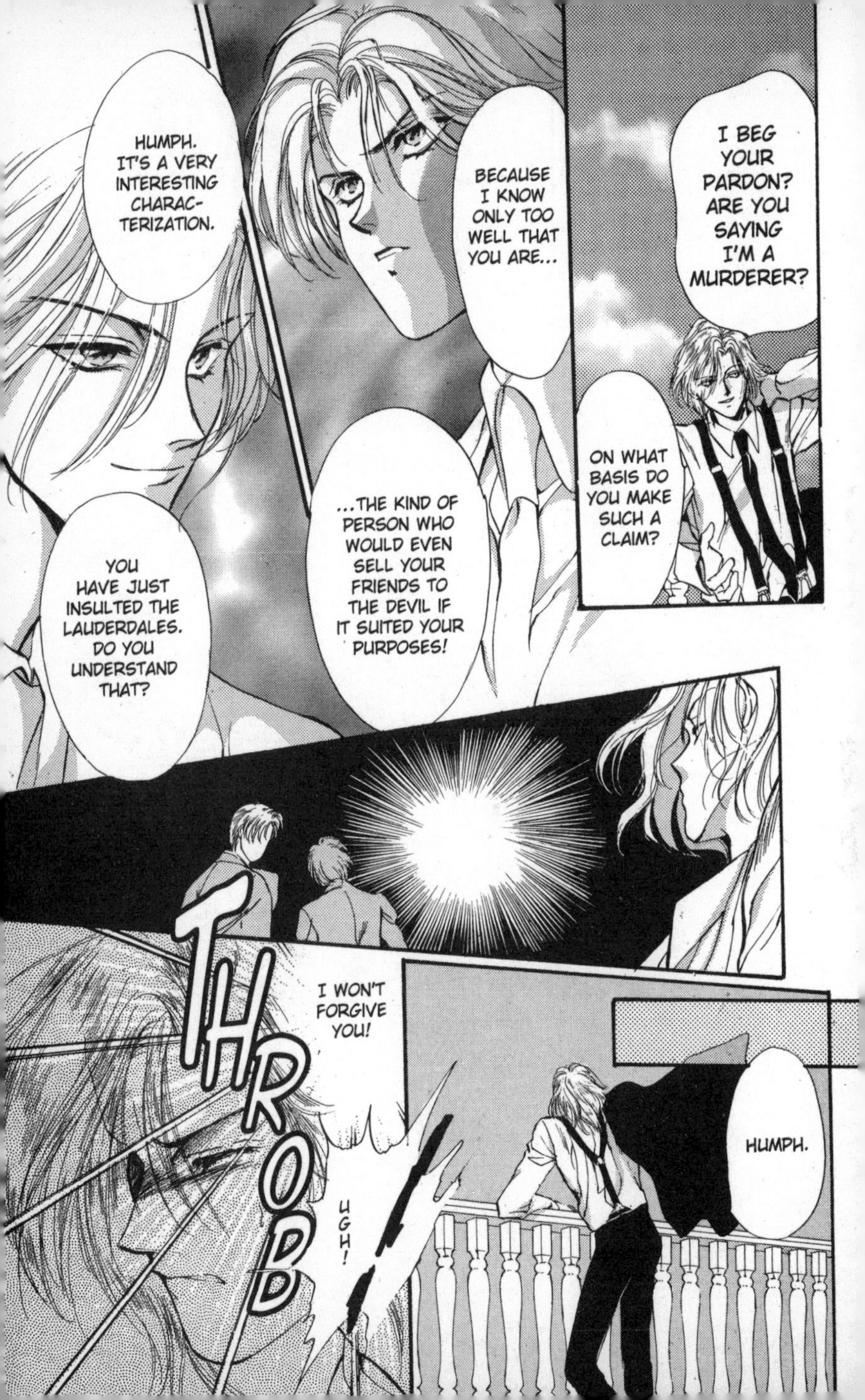
I BEG YOUR PARDON? ARE YOU SAYING I'M A MURDERER?
ON WHAT BASIS DO YOU MAKE SUCH A CLAIM?
BECAUSE I KNOW ONLY TOO WELL THAT YOU ARE...
...THE KIND OF PERSON WHO WOULD EVEN SELL YOUR FRIENDS TO THE DEVIL IF IT SUITED YOUR PURPOSES!
HUMPH. IT'S A VERY INTERESTING CHARAC-TERIZATION.
YOU HAVE JUST INSULTED THE LAUDERDALES. DO YOU UNDERSTAND THAT?
HUMPH.
I WON'T FORGIVE YOU!
THROB
UGH!

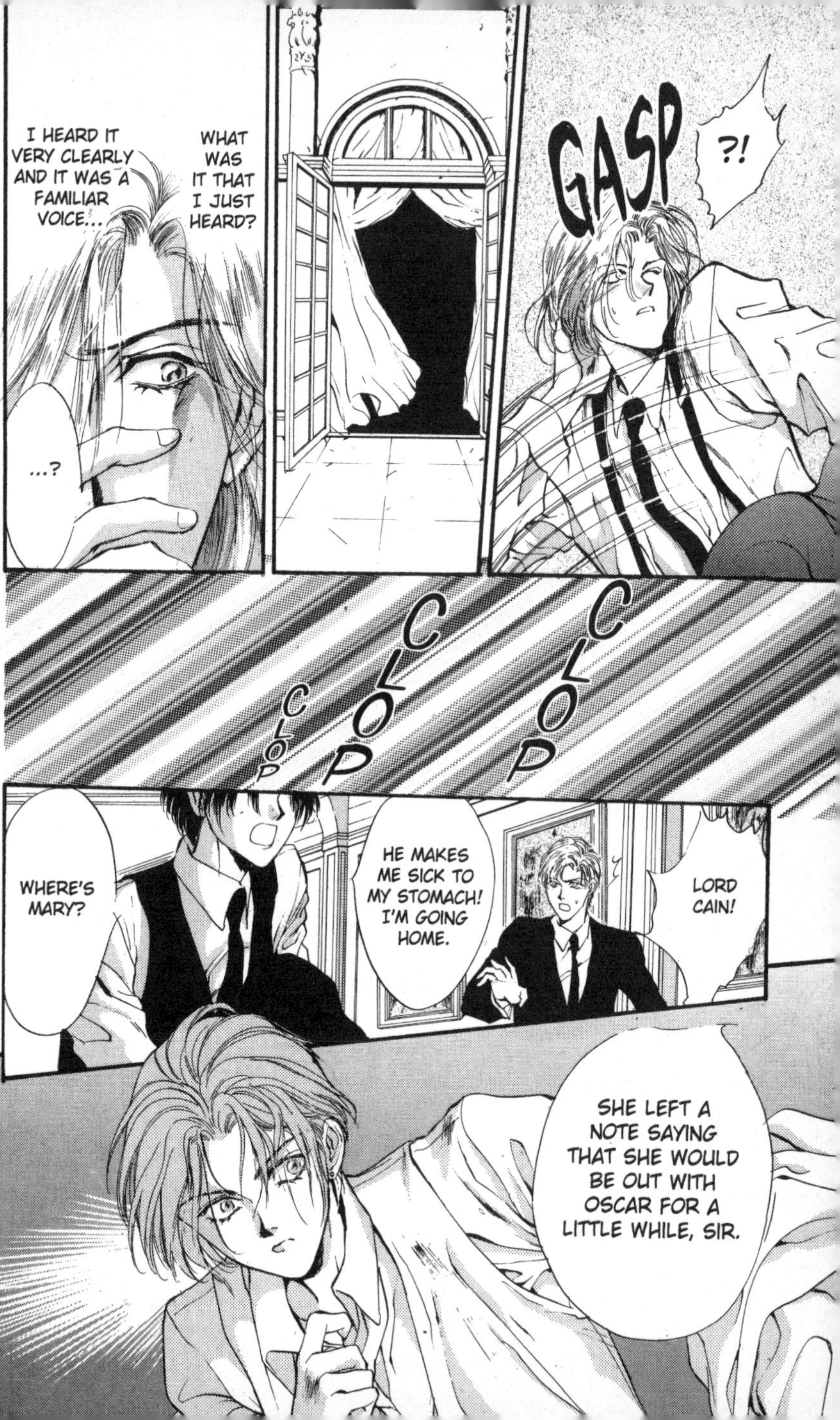
GASP
?!
WHAT WAS IT THAT I JUST HEARD?
I HEARD IT VERY CLEARLY AND IT WAS A FAMILIAR VOICE...
...?
CLOP
CLOP
CLOP
LORD CAIN!
HE MAKES ME SICK TO MY STOMACH! I'M GOING HOME.
WHERE'S MARY?
SHE LEFT A NOTE SAYING THAT SHE WOULD BE OUT WITH OSCAR FOR A LITTLE WHILE, SIR.

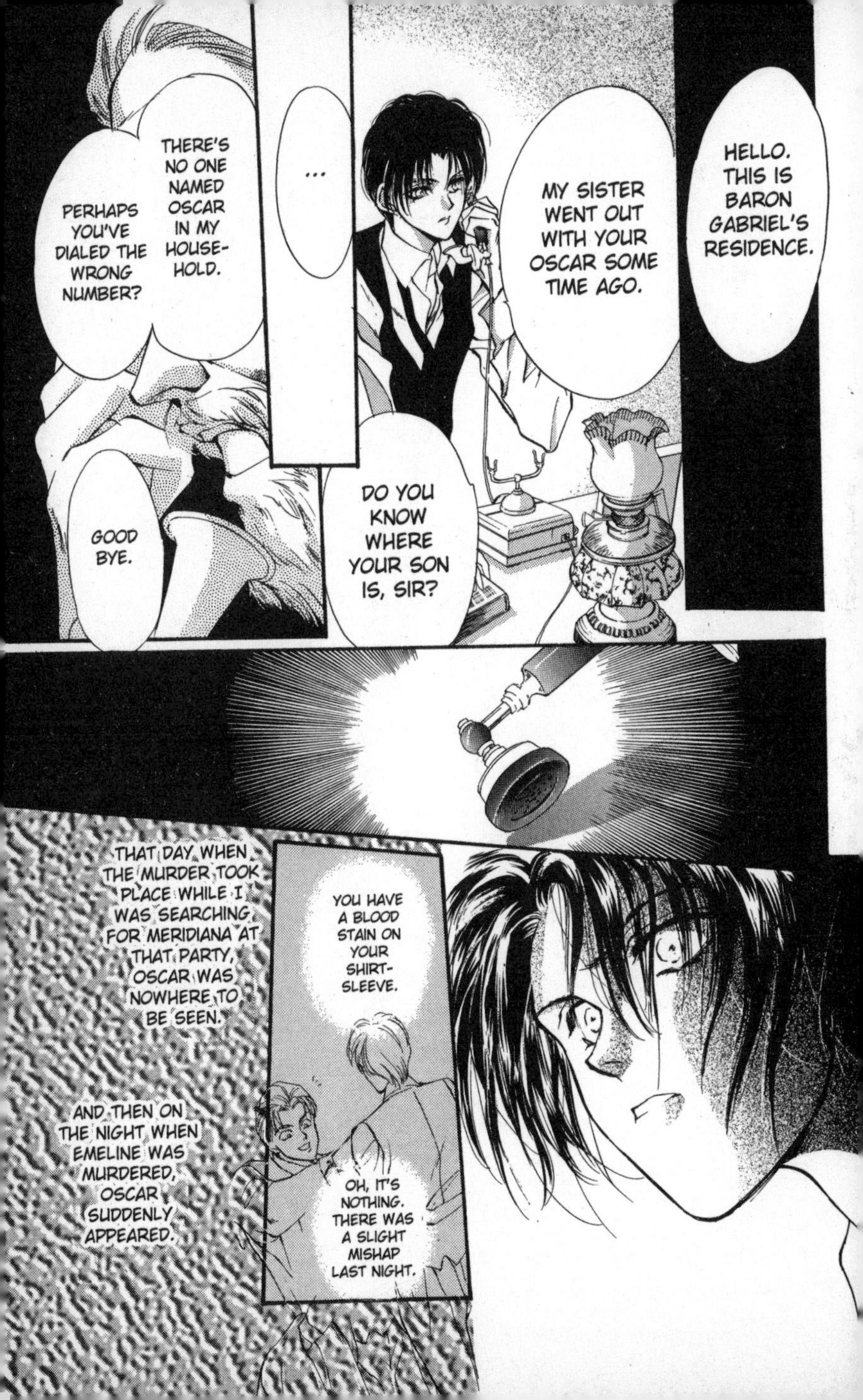
HELLO. THIS IS BARON GABRIEL'S RESIDENCE.
MY SISTER WENT OUT WITH YOUR OSCAR SOME TIME AGO.
DO YOU KNOW WHERE YOUR SON IS, SIR?
...
THERE'S NO ONE NAMED OSCAR IN MY HOUSE-HOLD.
PERHAPS YOU'VE DIALED THE WRONG NUMBER?
GOOD BYE.
THAT DAY WHEN THE MURDER TOOK PLACE WHILE I WAS SEARCHING FOR MERIDIANA AT THAT PARTY, OSCAR WAS NOWHERE TO BE SEEN.
YOU HAVE A BLOOD STAIN ON YOUR SHIRT-SLEEVE.
AND THEN ON THE NIGHT WHEN EMELINE WAS MURDERED, OSCAR SUDDENLY APPEARED.
OH, IT'S NOTHING. THERE WAS A SLIGHT MISHAP LAST NIGHT.

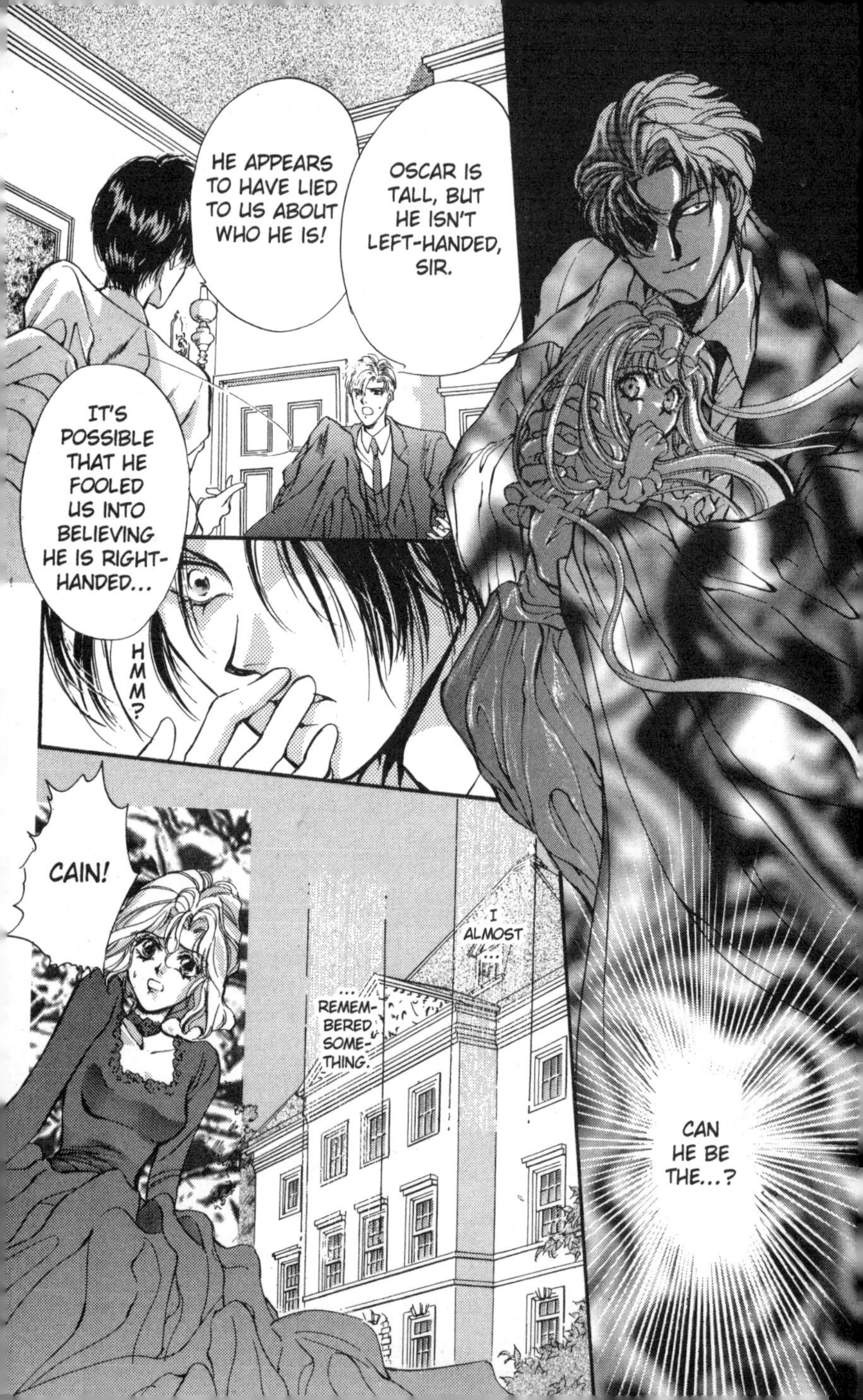
CAN HE BE THE...?
OSCAR IS TALL, BUT HE ISN'T LEFT-HANDED, SIR.
HE APPEARS TO HAVE LIED TO US ABOUT WHO HE IS!
IT'S POSSIBLE THAT HE FOOLED US INTO BELIEVING HE IS RIGHT-HANDED...
HMMM?
I ALMOST
...REMEMBERED SOMETHING.
CAIN!

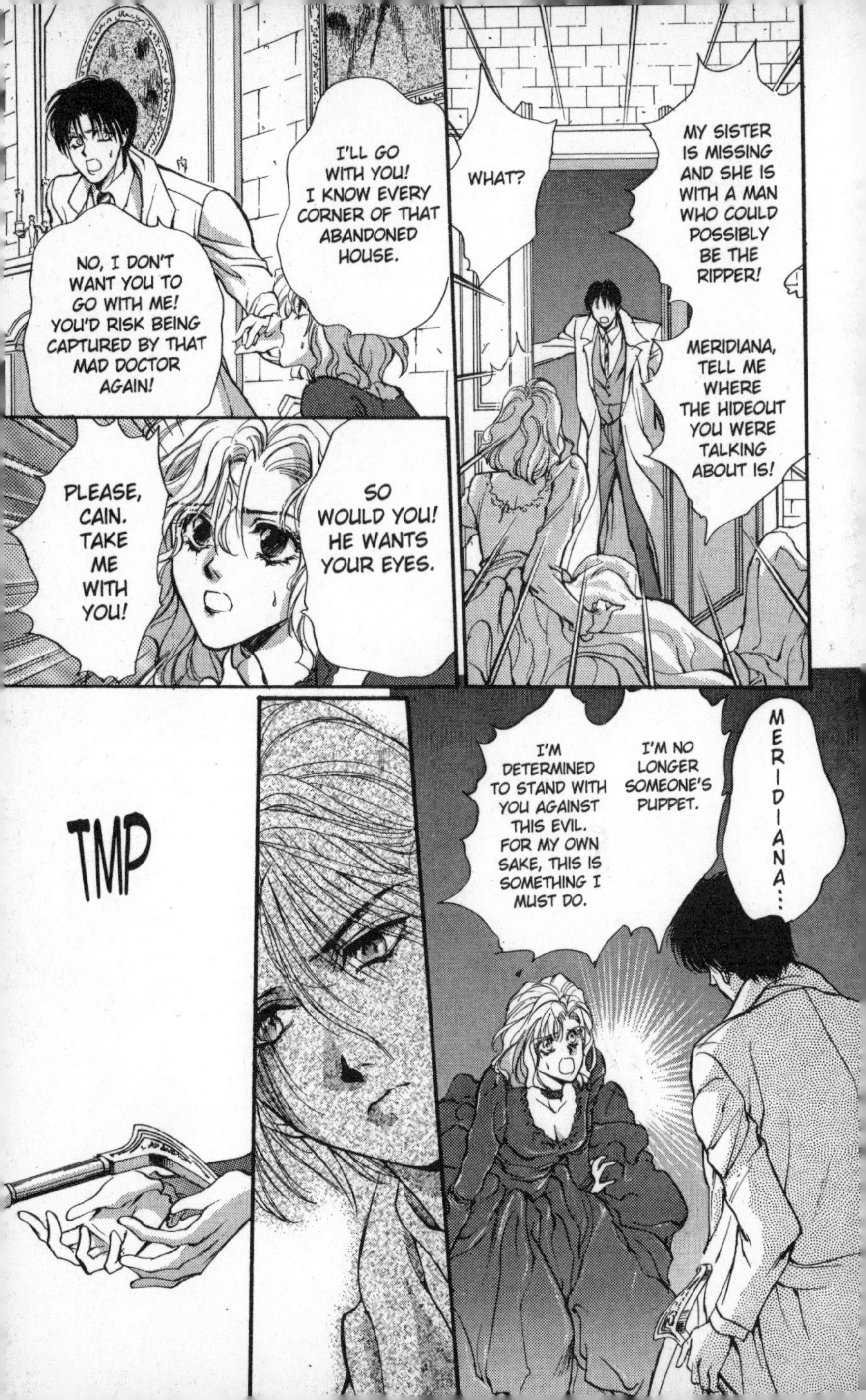

MY SISTER IS MISSING AND SHE IS WITH A MAN WHO COULD POSSIBLY BE THE RIPPER!
WHAT?
MERIDIANA, TELL ME WHERE THE HIDEOUT YOU WERE TALKING ABOUT IS!
I'LL GO WITH YOU! I KNOW EVERY CORNER OF THAT ABANDONED HOUSE.
NO, I DON'T WANT YOU TO GO WITH ME! YOU'D RISK BEING CAPTURED BY THAT MAD DOCTOR AGAIN!
SO WOULD YOU! HE WANTS YOUR EYES.
PLEASE, CAIN. TAKE ME WITH YOU!
MERIDIANA...
I'M NO LONGER SOMEONE'S PUPPET.
I'M DETERMINED TO STAND WITH YOU AGAINST THIS EVIL. FOR MY OWN SAKE, THIS IS SOMETHING I MUST DO.
TMP

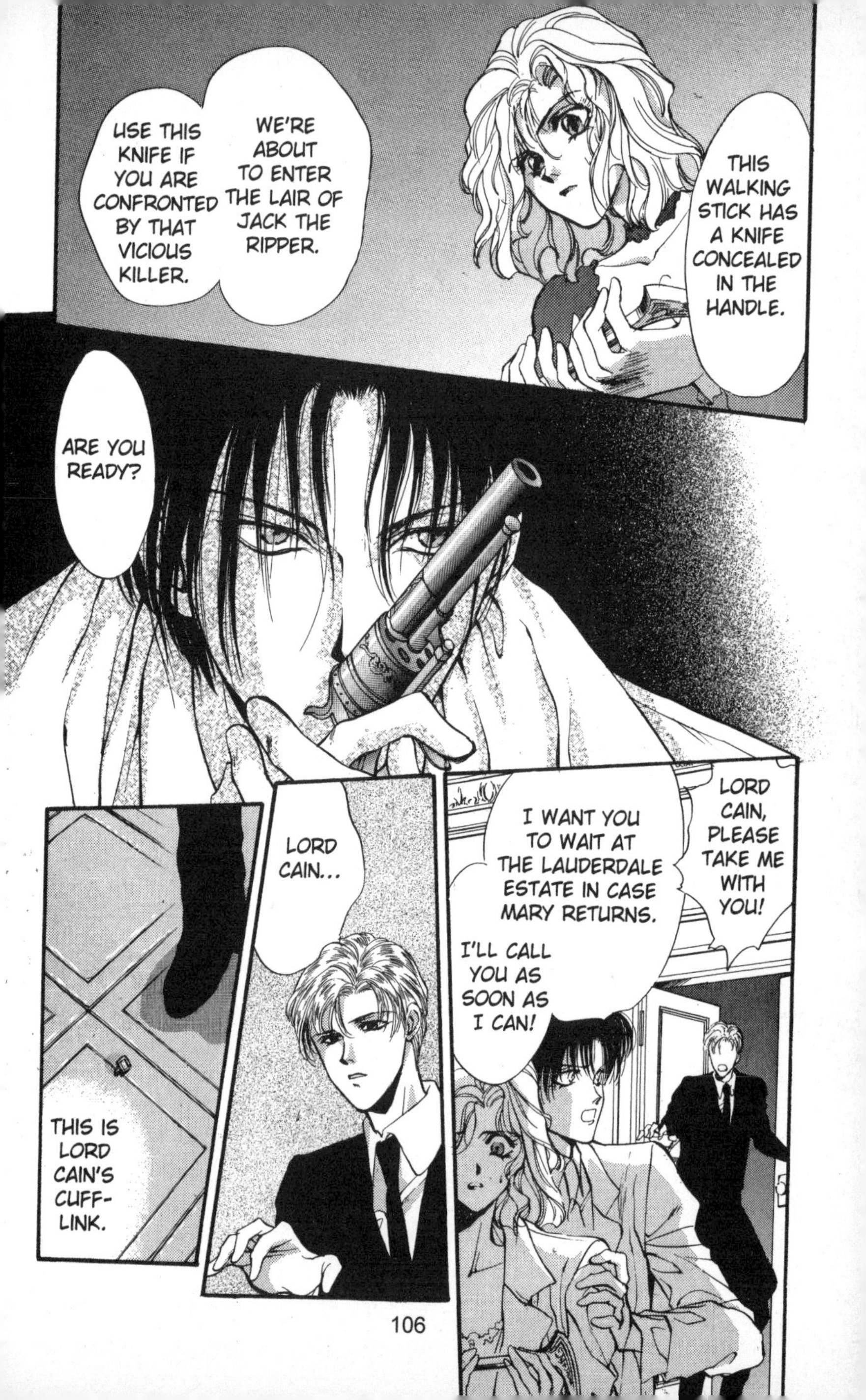
THIS WALKING STICK HAS A KNIFE CONCEALED IN THE HANDLE.
WE'RE ABOUT TO ENTER THE LAIR OF JACK THE RIPPER.
USE THIS KNIFE IF YOU ARE CONFRONTED BY THAT VICIOUS KILLER.
ARE YOU READY?
LORD CAIN, PLEASE TAKE ME WITH YOU!
I WANT YOU TO WAIT AT THE LAUDERDALE ESTATE IN CASE MARY RETURNS.
I'LL CALL YOU AS SOON AS I CAN!
LORD CAIN...
THIS IS LORD CAIN'S CUFF-LINK.

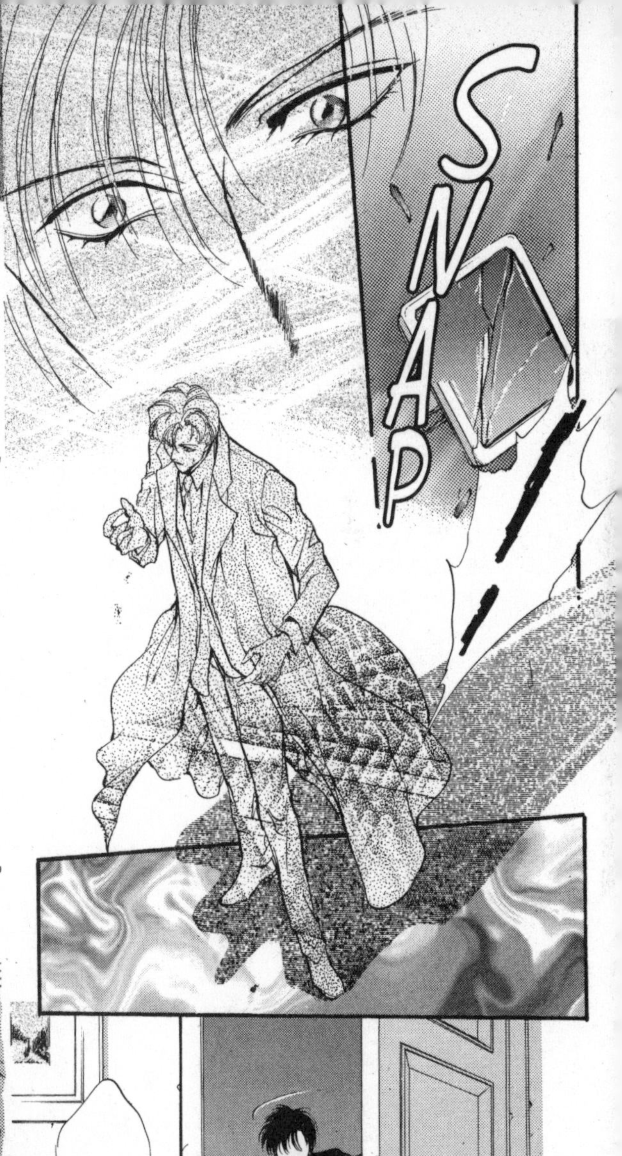
SNAP
DOCTOR ...

WILD TALK
PART 4

Some people asked why Dr. Disraeli is often seen in kimono. Answer: He likes to wear it as a gown. Did they have kimono in this period of time in Britain? It looks like they did. However, **it's hard to believe men wore them!** Anyway, Disraeli strikes me as the kind of guy who'd collect Japanese furniture and other knick-knacks — he's a collector after all. I was surprised to learn that some readers adore Disraeli. In fact, someone even sent me a fan publication devoted entirely to him. In this magazine, Disraeli is called by many different names such as 'the doctor,' 'Jiza' and 'Nishikanda.' I asked the author, Ms. Tachibana, if she has ever received any fan letters telling her that Disraeli resembles Nishikanda. She said she never had. Anyway, even if it's true that these two characters look alike, Disraeli isn't as narcissistic as Nishikanda, as far as I'm concerned.

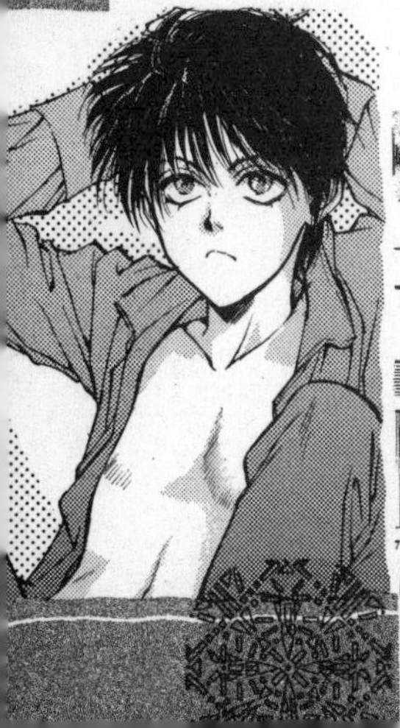

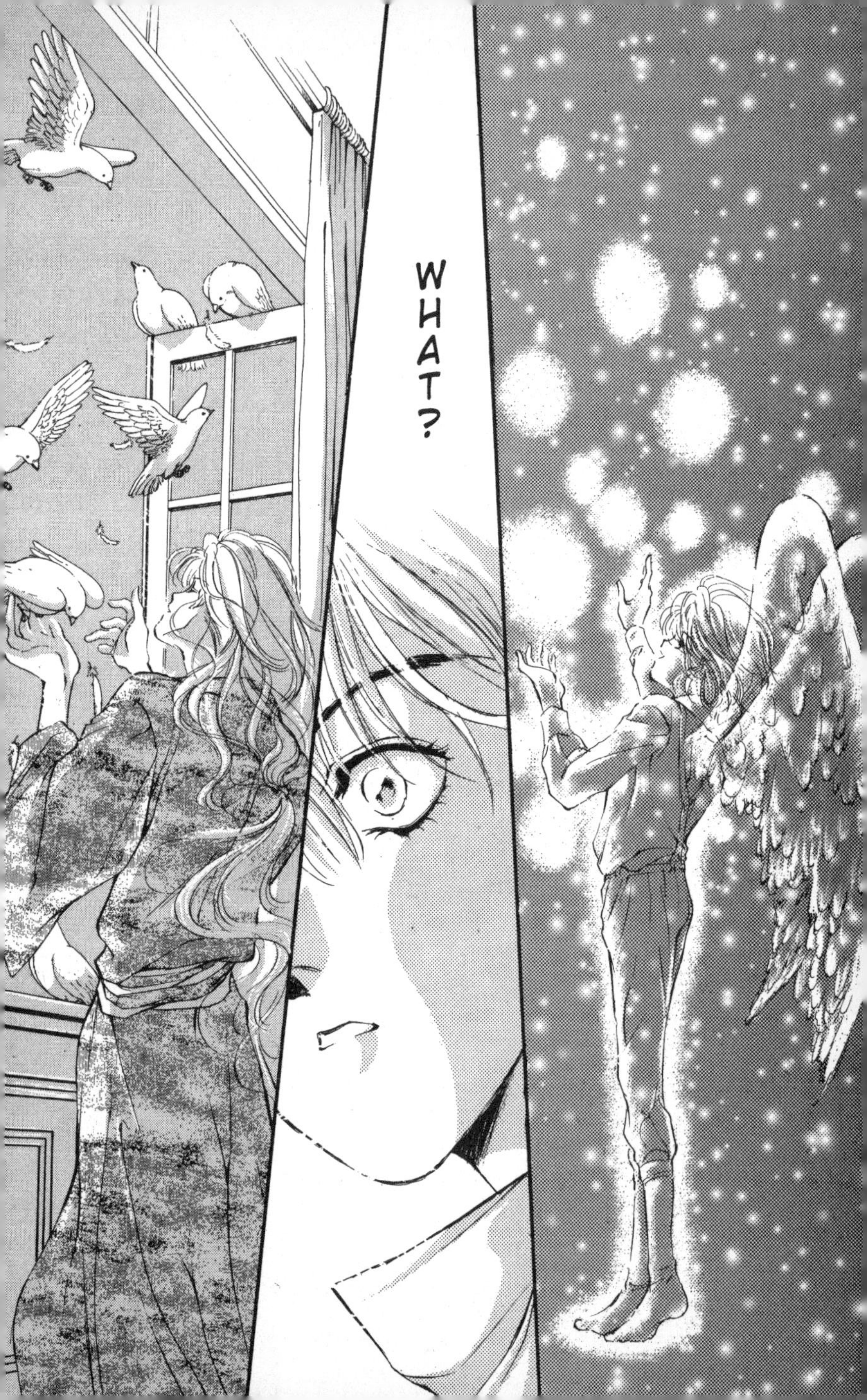
WHAT?

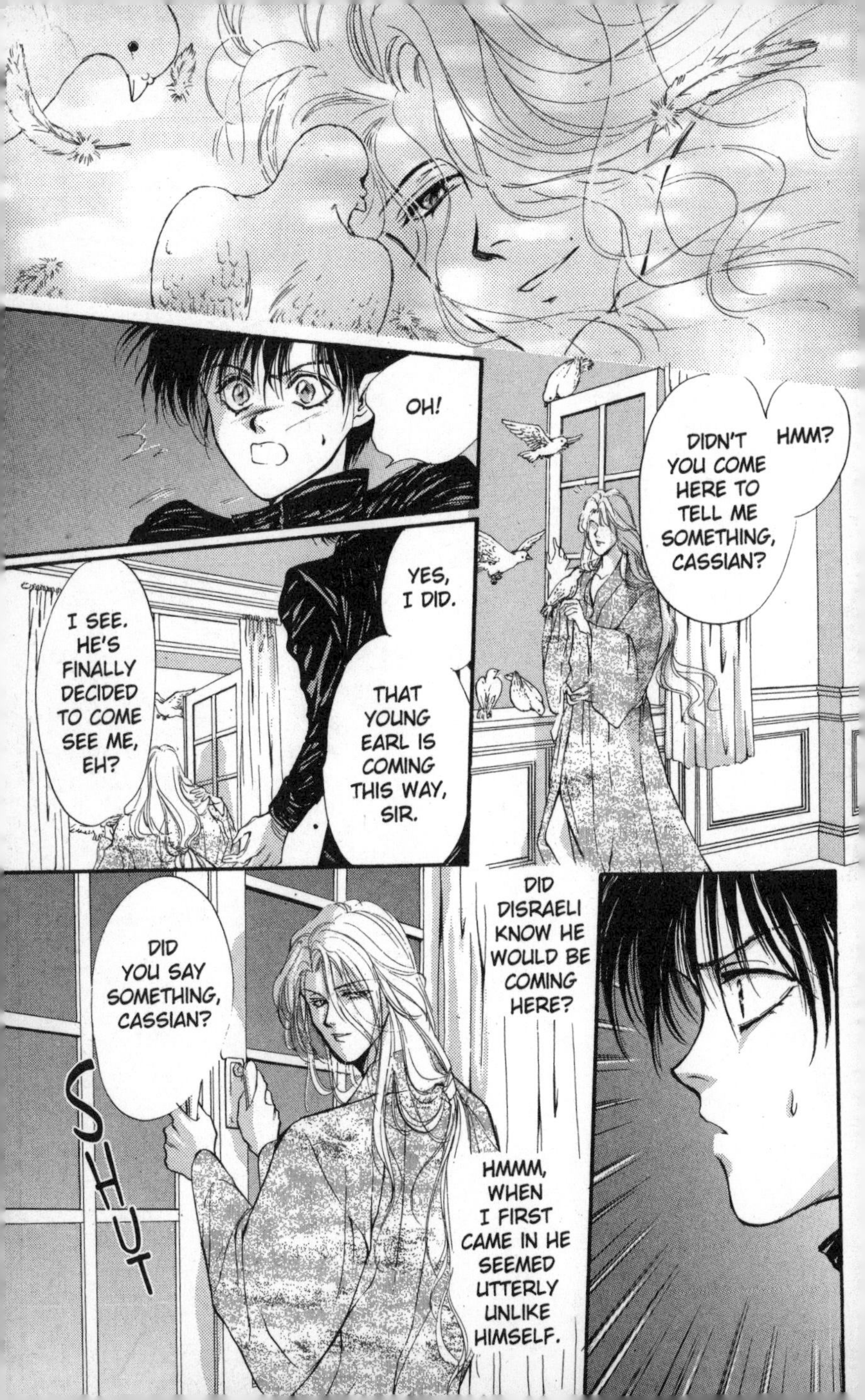
HMM?
DIDN'T YOU COME HERE TO TELL ME SOMETHING, CASSIAN?
OH!
YES, I DID.
THAT YOUNG EARL IS COMING THIS WAY, SIR.
I SEE. HE'S FINALLY DECIDED TO COME SEE ME, EH?
DID DISRAELI KNOW HE WOULD BE COMING HERE?
HMMM, WHEN I FIRST CAME IN HE SEEMED UTTERLY UNLIKE HIMSELF.
DID YOU SAY SOMETHING, CASSIAN?
SHUT

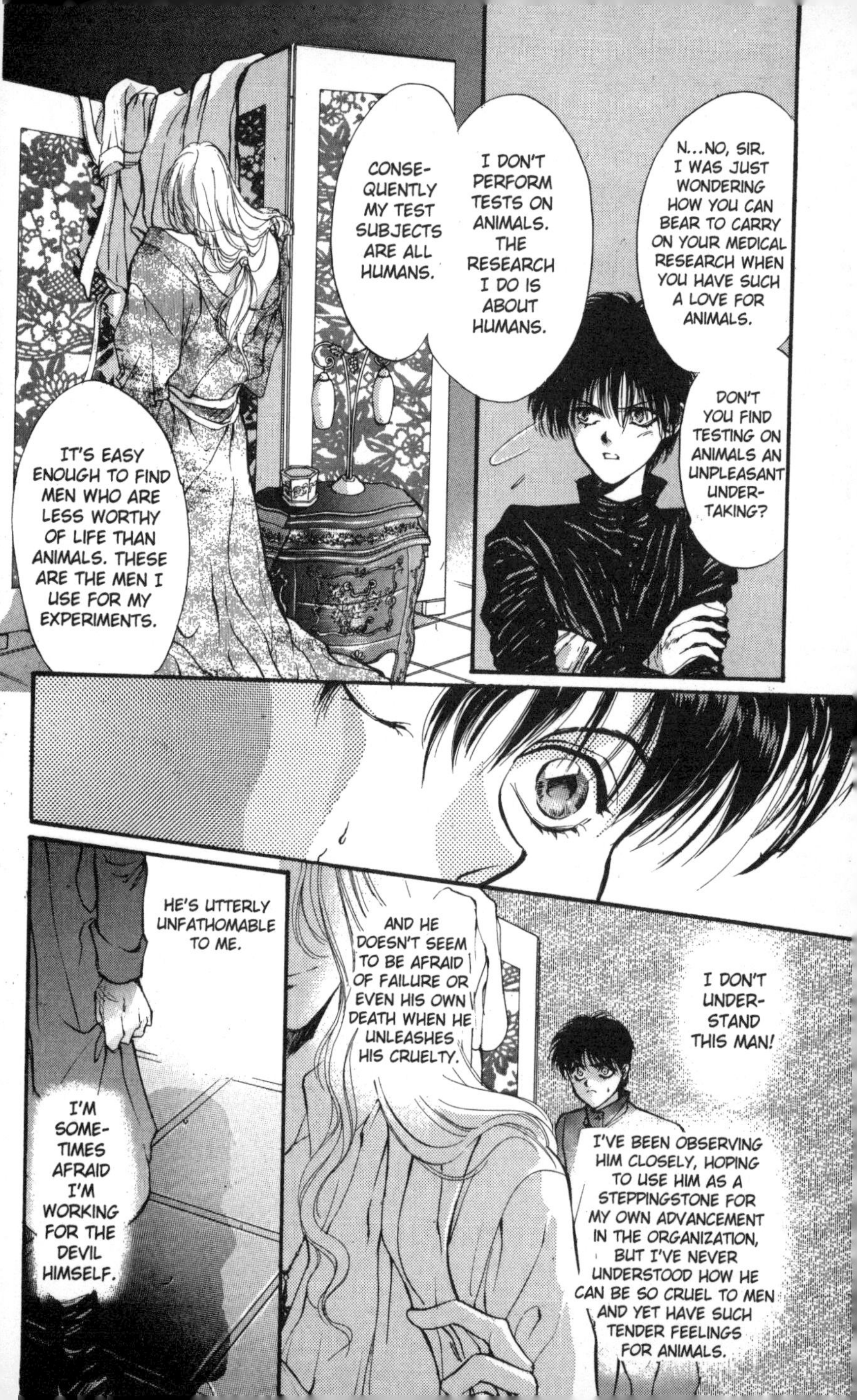
N...NO, SIR. I WAS JUST WONDERING HOW YOU CAN BEAR TO CARRY ON YOUR MEDICAL RESEARCH WHEN YOU HAVE SUCH A LOVE FOR ANIMALS.
DON'T YOU FIND TESTING ON ANIMALS AN UNPLEASANT UNDER-TAKING?
I DON'T PERFORM TESTS ON ANIMALS. THE RESEARCH I DO IS ABOUT HUMANS.
CONSE-QUENTLY MY TEST SUBJECTS ARE ALL HUMANS.
IT'S EASY ENOUGH TO FIND MEN WHO ARE LESS WORTHY OF LIFE THAN ANIMALS. THESE ARE THE MEN I USE FOR MY EXPERIMENTS.
I DON'T UNDER-STAND THIS MAN!
I'VE BEEN OBSERVING HIM CLOSELY, HOPING TO USE HIM AS A STEPPINGSTONE FOR MY OWN ADVANCEMENT IN THE ORGANIZATION, BUT I'VE NEVER UNDERSTOOD HOW HE CAN BE SO CRUEL TO MEN AND YET HAVE SUCH TENDER FEELINGS FOR ANIMALS.
AND HE DOESN'T SEEM TO BE AFRAID OF FAILURE OR EVEN HIS OWN DEATH WHEN HE UNLEASHES HIS CRUELTY.
HE'S UTTERLY UNFATHOMABLE TO ME.
I'M SOME-TIMES AFRAID I'M WORKING FOR THE DEVIL HIMSELF.

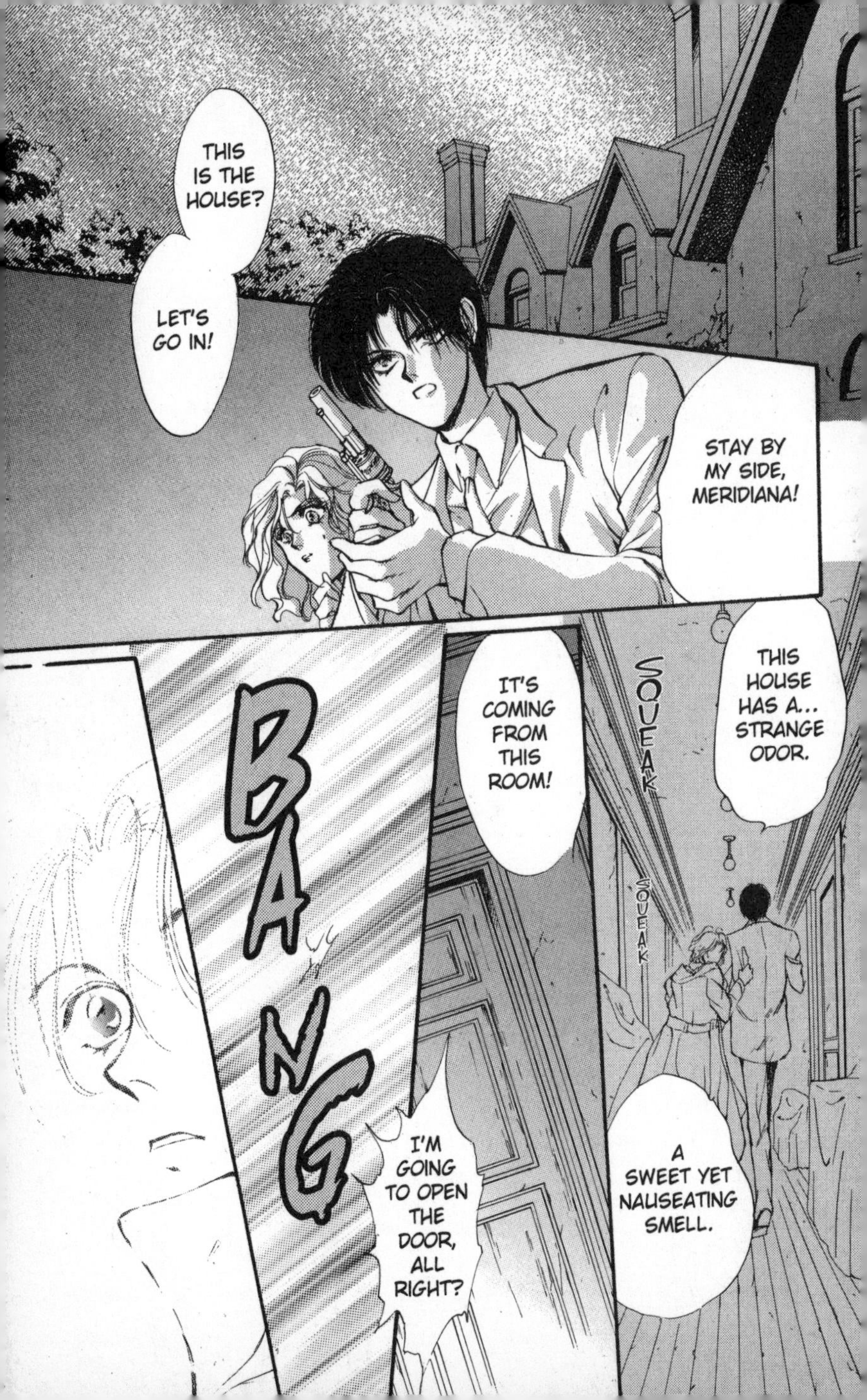
THIS IS THE HOUSE?
LET'S GO IN!
STAY BY MY SIDE, MERIDIANA!
THIS HOUSE HAS A... STRANGE ODOR.
SQUEAK
SQUEAK
A SWEET YET NAUSEATING SMELL.
IT'S COMING FROM THIS ROOM!
I'M GOING TO OPEN THE DOOR, ALL RIGHT?
BANG

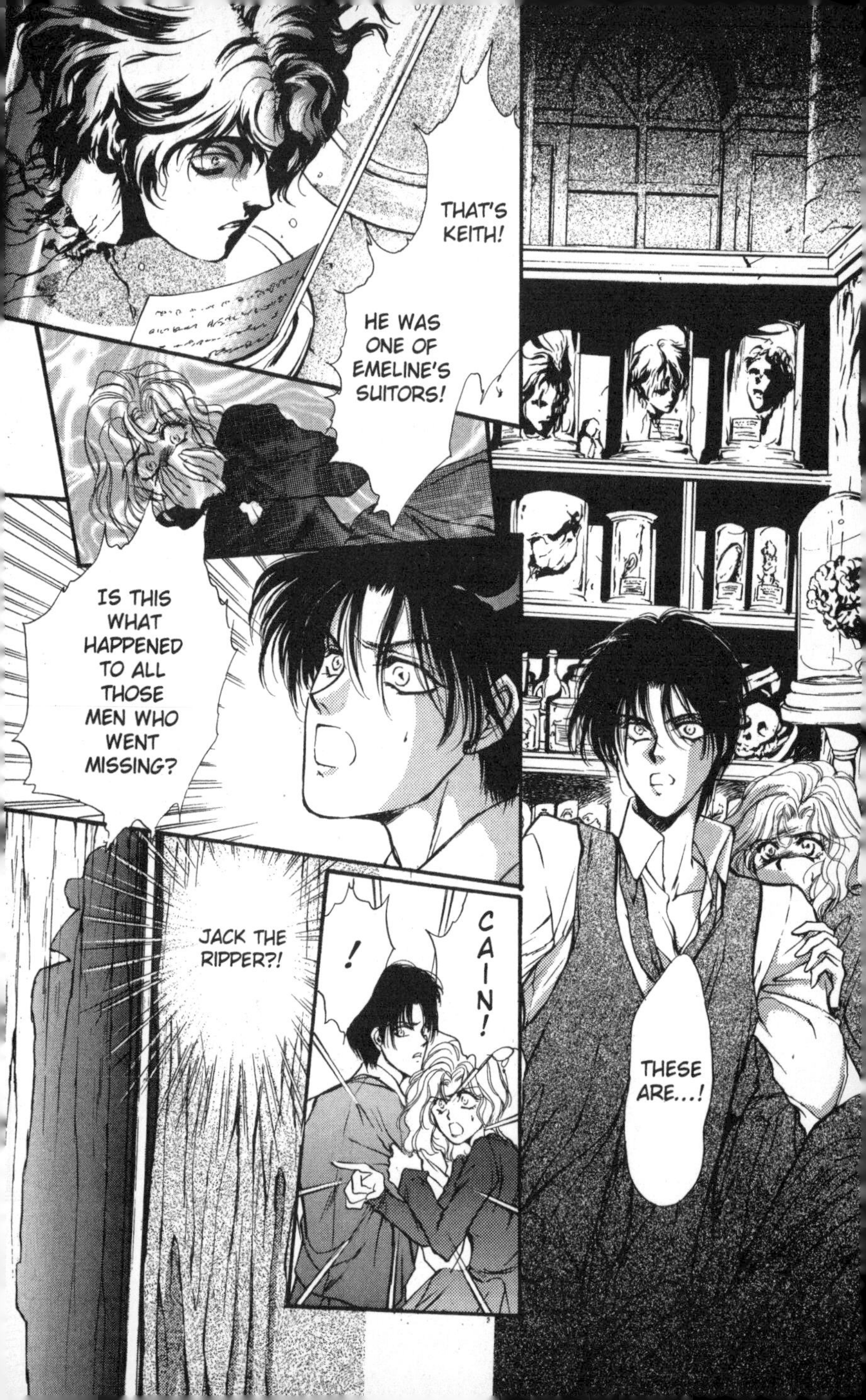
THESE ARE...!
THAT'S KEITH!
HE WAS ONE OF EMELINE'S SUITORS!
IS THIS WHAT HAPPENED TO ALL THOSE MEN WHO WENT MISSING?
CAIN!
!
JACK THE RIPPER?!

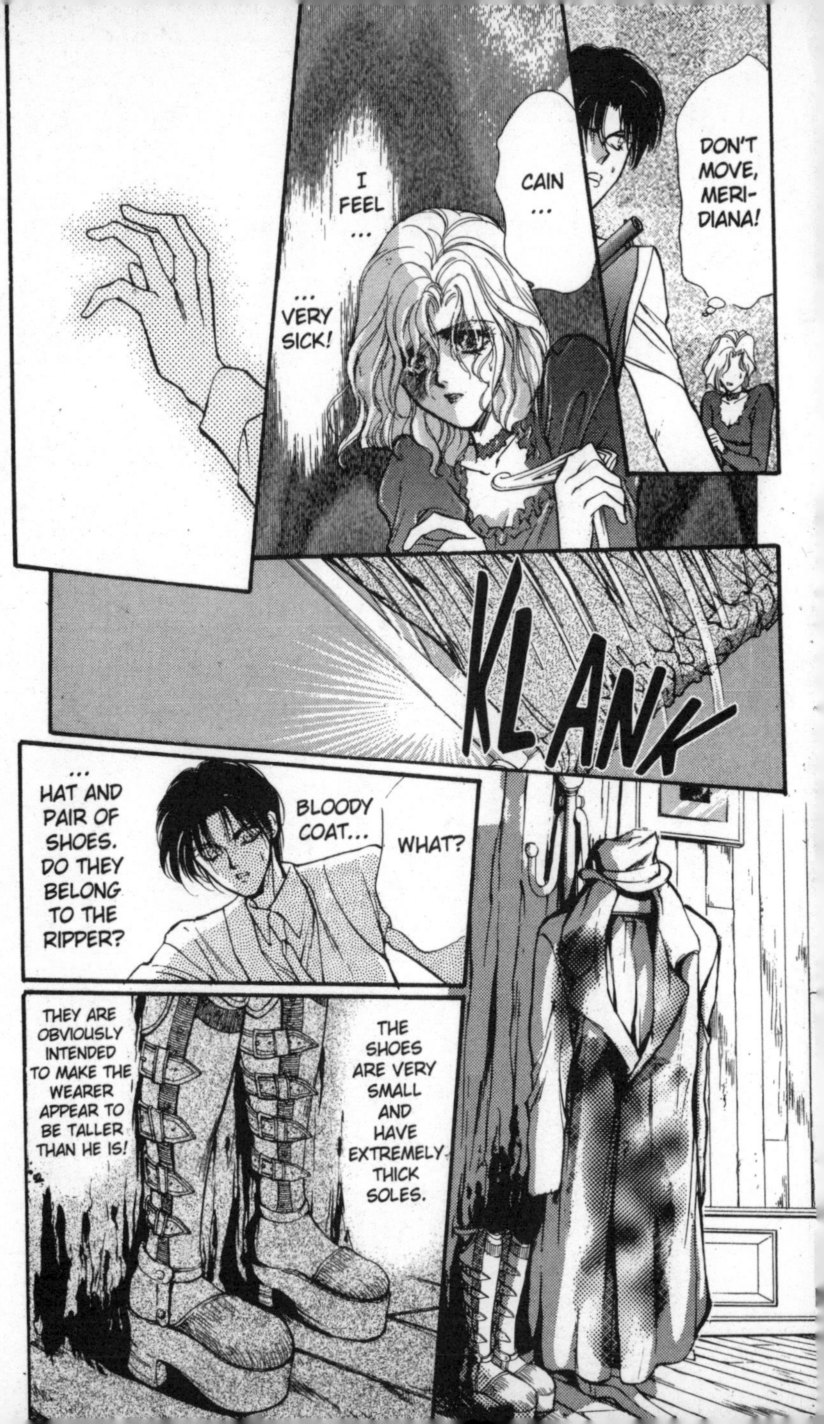
DON'T MOVE, MERIDIANA!
CAIN ...
I FEEL ...
... VERY SICK!
KLANK
WHAT?
BLOODY COAT...
... HAT AND PAIR OF SHOES. DO THEY BELONG TO THE RIPPER?
THE SHOES ARE VERY SMALL AND HAVE EXTREMELY THICK SOLES.
THEY ARE OBVIOUSLY INTENDED TO MAKE THE WEARER APPEAR TO BE TALLER THAN HE IS!

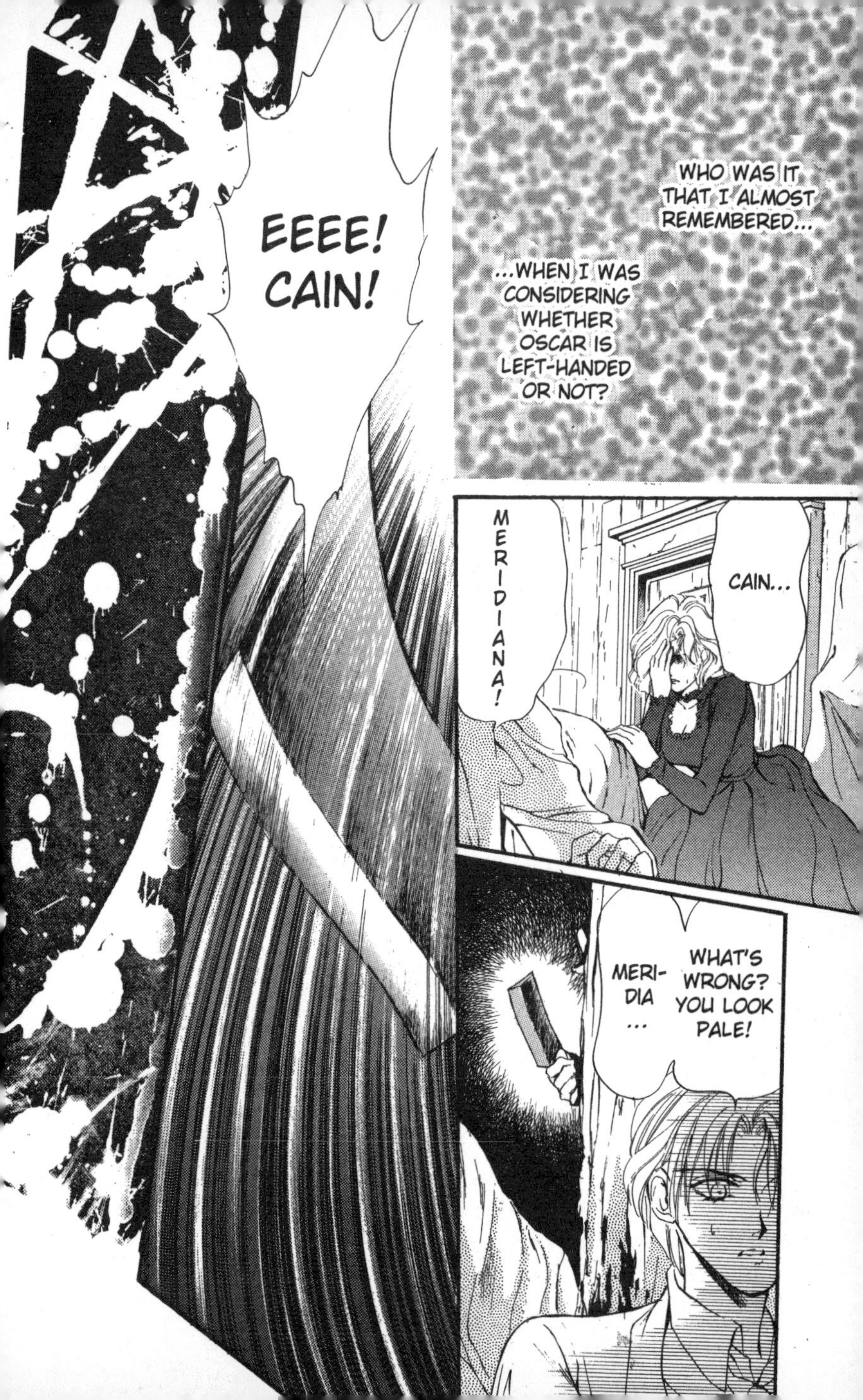
WHO WAS IT THAT I ALMOST REMEMBERED...
...WHEN I WAS CONSIDERING WHETHER OSCAR IS LEFT-HANDED OR NOT?
CAIN...
MERIDIANA!
WHAT'S WRONG? YOU LOOK PALE!
MERI-DIA...
EEEE! CAIN!

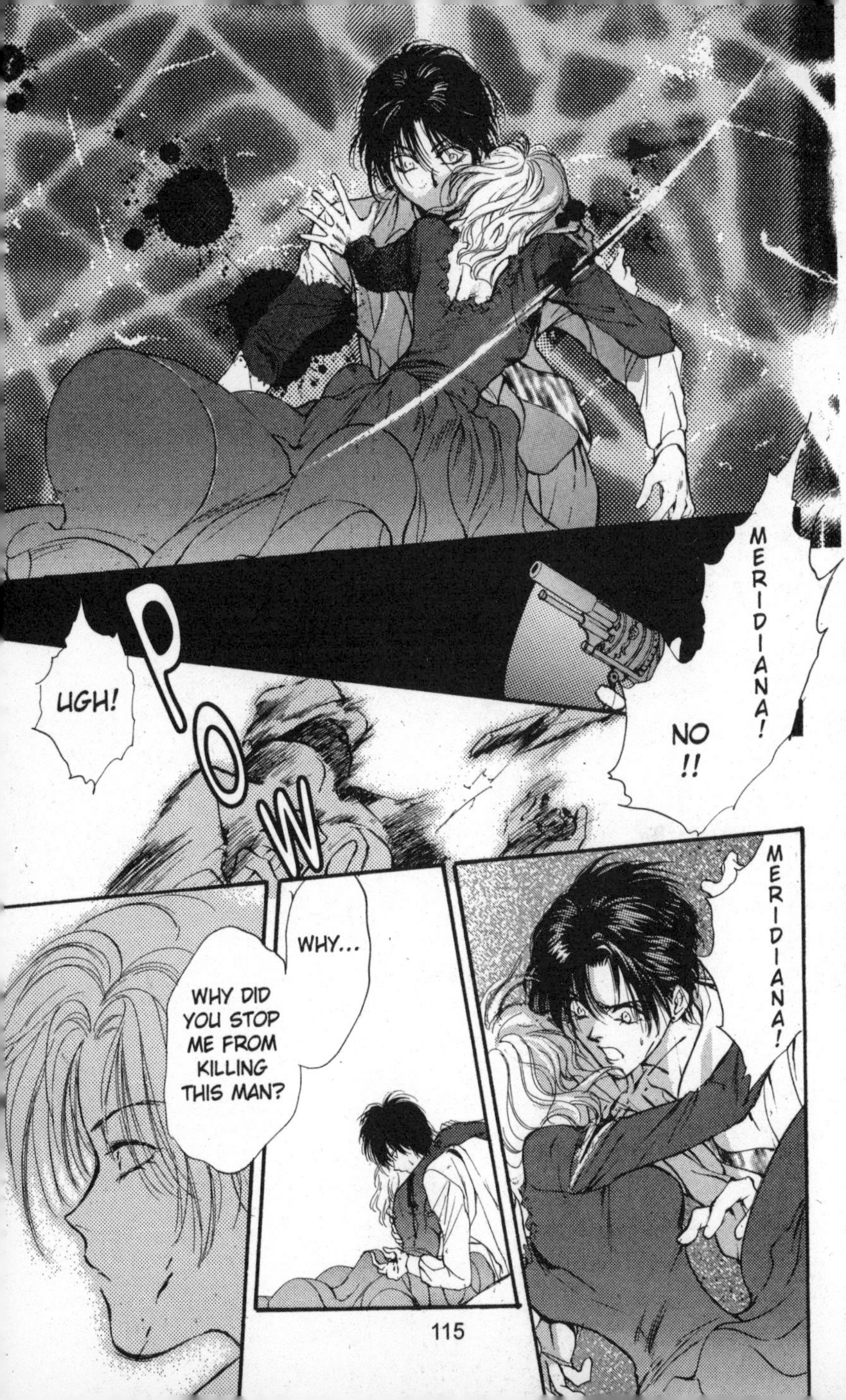
MERIDIANA!
NO !!
POW
UGH!
MERIDIANA!
WHY...
WHY DID YOU STOP ME FROM KILLING THIS MAN?

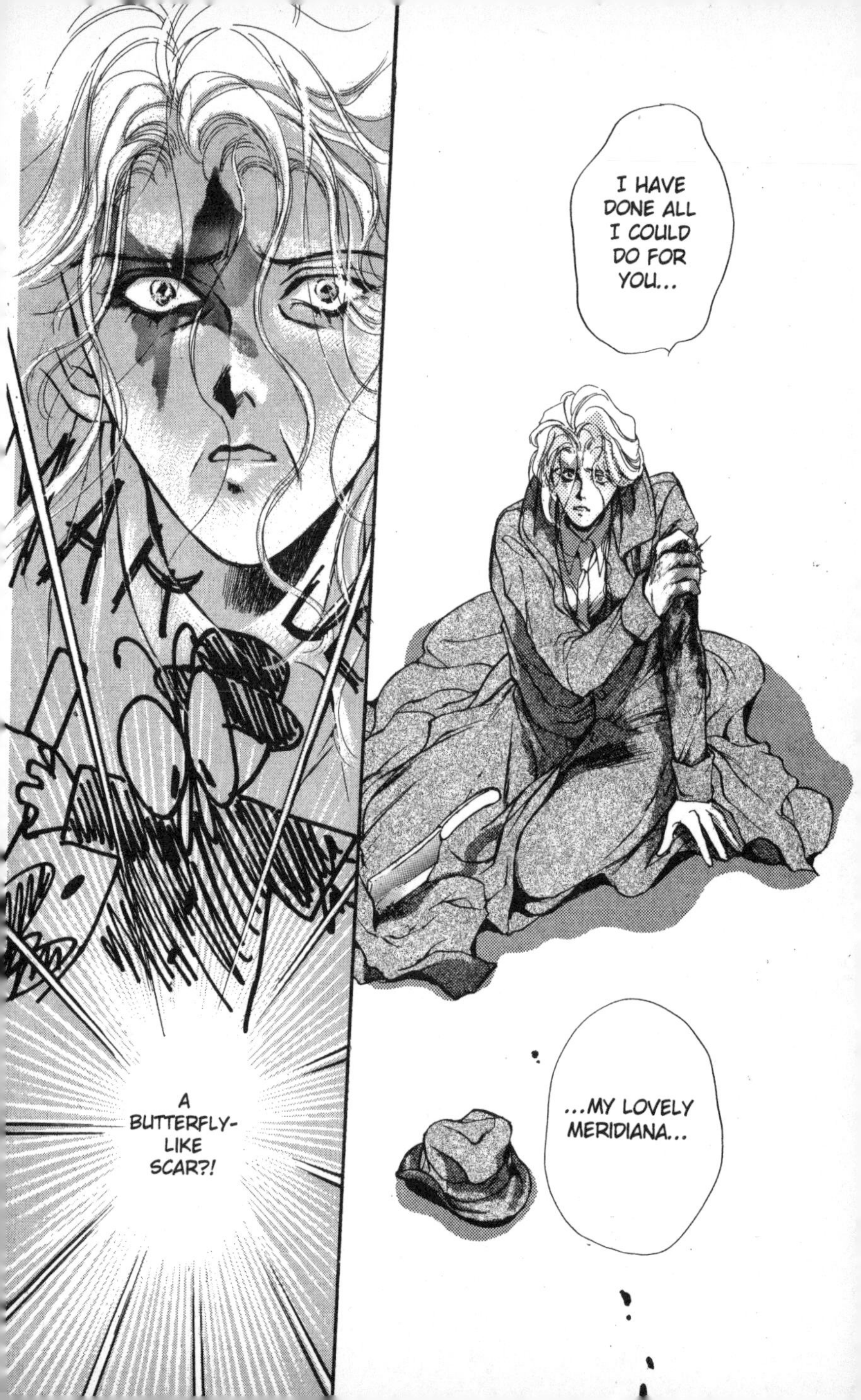
I HAVE DONE ALL I COULD DO FOR YOU...
...MY LOVELY MERIDIANA...
A BUTTERFLY-LIKE SCAR?!

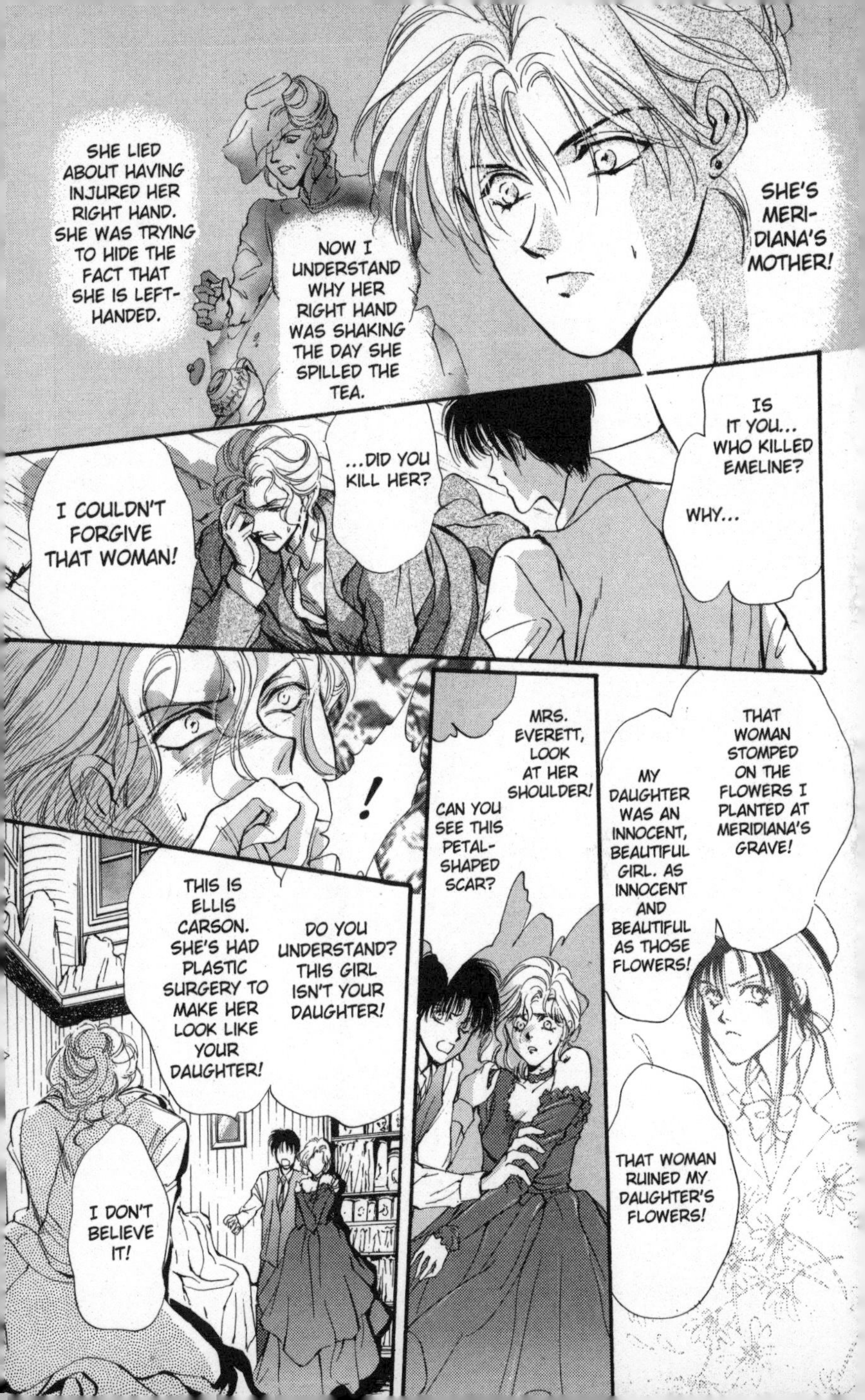
SHE'S MERI-DIANA'S MOTHER!
NOW I UNDERSTAND WHY HER RIGHT HAND WAS SHAKING THE DAY SHE SPILLED THE TEA.
SHE LIED ABOUT HAVING INJURED HER RIGHT HAND. SHE WAS TRYING TO HIDE THE FACT THAT SHE IS LEFT-HANDED.
IS IT YOU... WHO KILLED EMELINE?
WHY...
...DID YOU KILL HER?
I COULDN'T FORGIVE THAT WOMAN!
THAT WOMAN STOMPED ON THE FLOWERS I PLANTED AT MERIDIANA'S GRAVE!
MY DAUGHTER WAS AN INNOCENT, BEAUTIFUL GIRL. AS INNOCENT AND BEAUTIFUL AS THOSE FLOWERS!
THAT WOMAN RUINED MY DAUGHTER'S FLOWERS!
!
MRS. EVERETT, LOOK AT HER SHOULDER!
CAN YOU SEE THIS PETAL-SHAPED SCAR?
DO YOU UNDERSTAND? THIS GIRL ISN'T YOUR DAUGHTER!
THIS IS ELLIS CARSON. SHE'S HAD PLASTIC SURGERY TO MAKE HER LOOK LIKE YOUR DAUGHTER!
I DON'T BELIEVE IT!

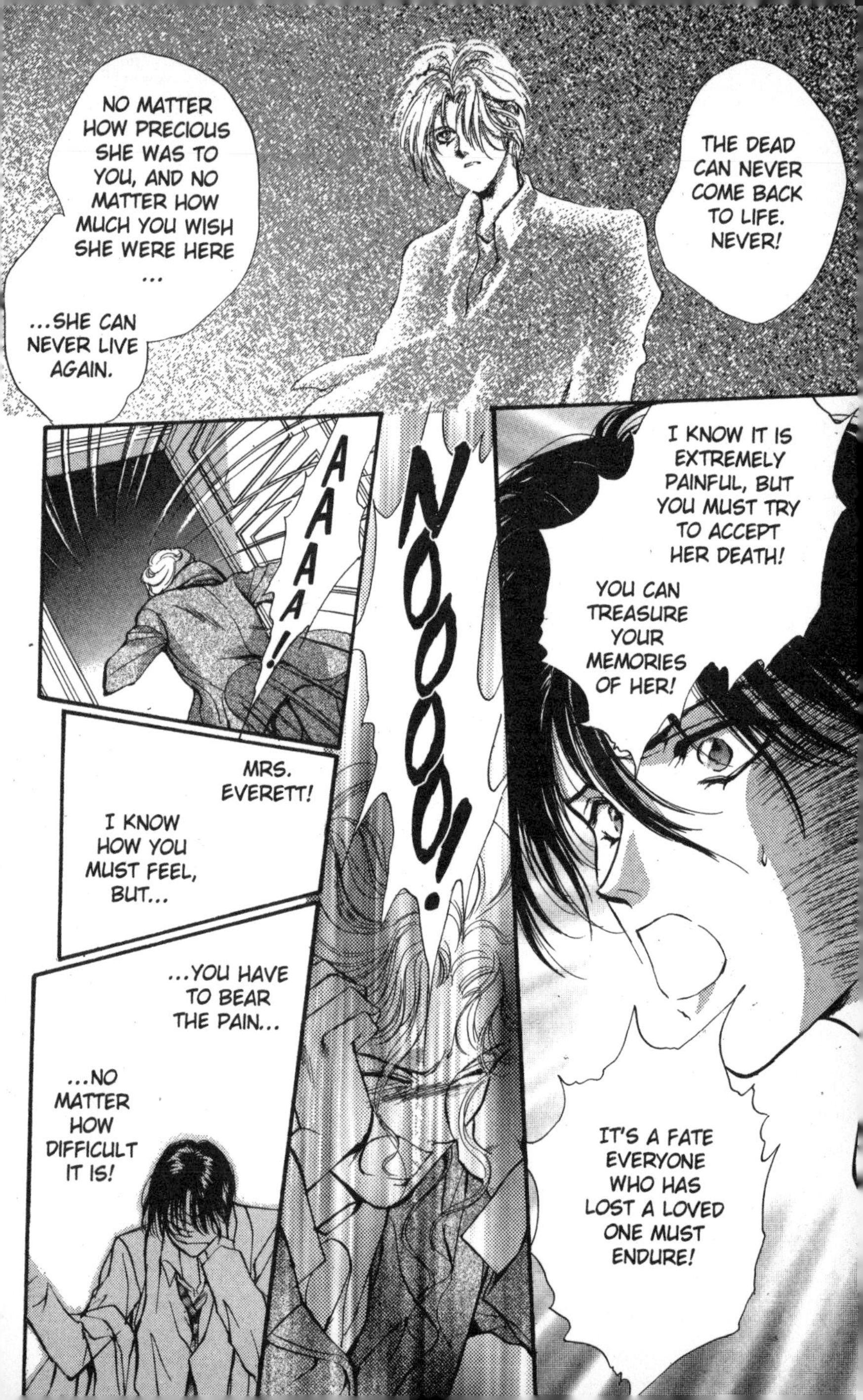
THE DEAD CAN NEVER COME BACK TO LIFE. NEVER!
NO MATTER HOW PRECIOUS SHE WAS TO YOU, AND NO MATTER HOW MUCH YOU WISH SHE WERE HERE ...
...SHE CAN NEVER LIVE AGAIN.
I KNOW IT IS EXTREMELY PAINFUL, BUT YOU MUST TRY TO ACCEPT HER DEATH!
YOU CAN TREASURE YOUR MEMORIES OF HER!
IT'S A FATE EVERYONE WHO HAS LOST A LOVED ONE MUST ENDURE!
NOOOOO!
AAAAA!
MRS. EVERETT!
I KNOW HOW YOU MUST FEEL, BUT...
...YOU HAVE TO BEAR THE PAIN...
...NO MATTER HOW DIFFICULT IT IS!

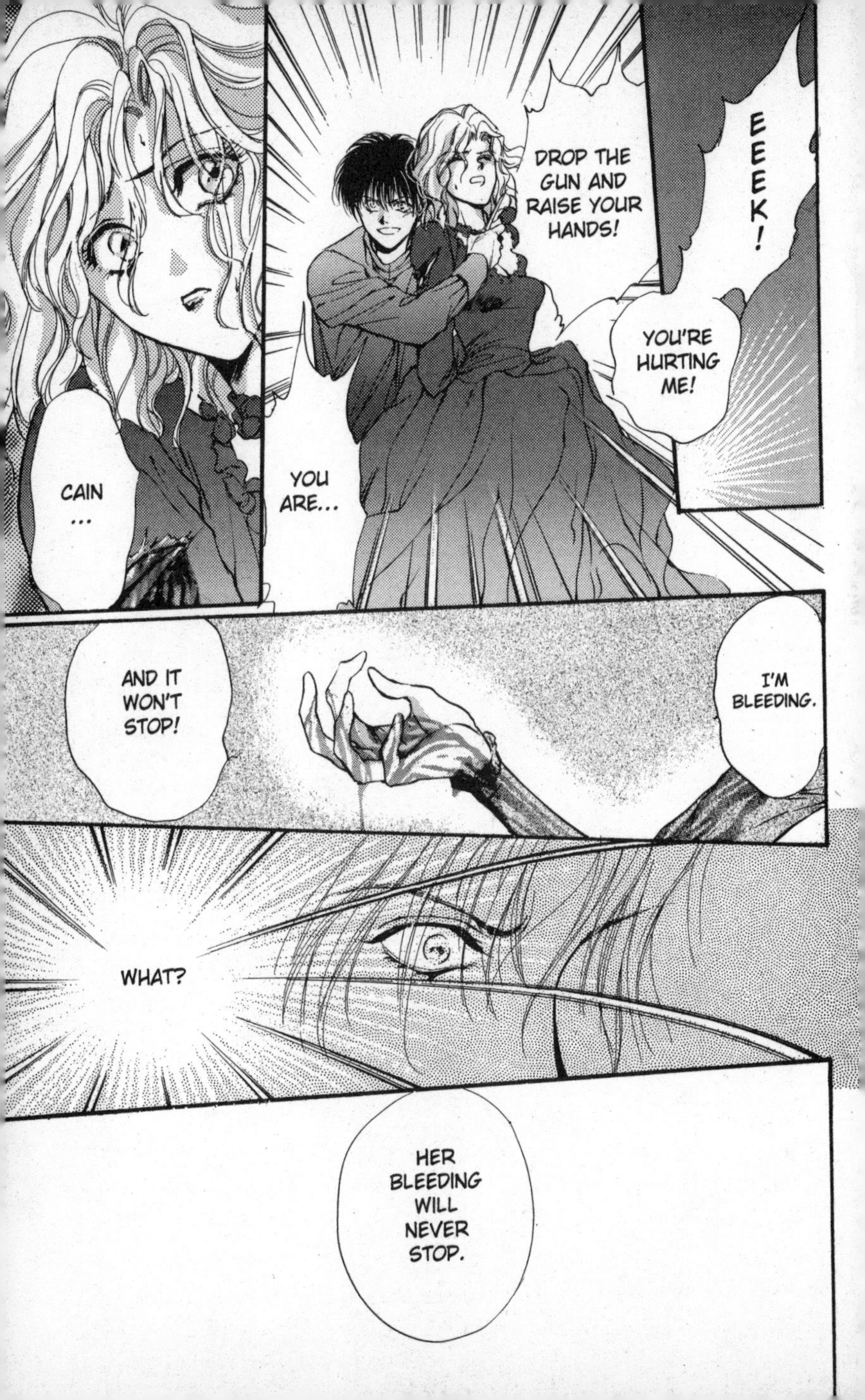
EEEK!
YOU'RE HURTING ME!
DROP THE GUN AND RAISE YOUR HANDS!
YOU ARE...
CAIN ...
I'M BLEEDING.
AND IT WON'T STOP!
WHAT?
HER BLEEDING WILL NEVER STOP.

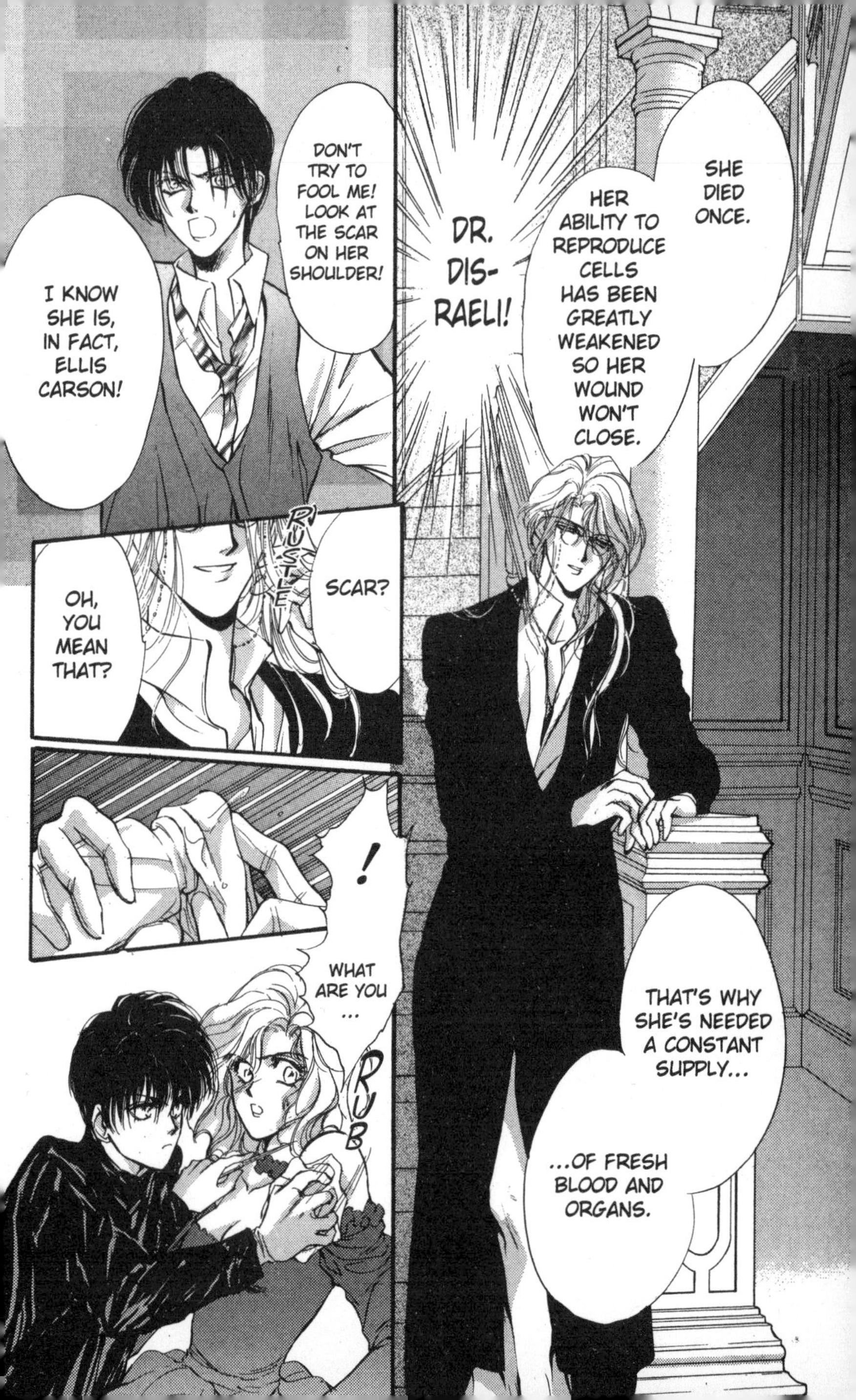
DON'T TRY TO FOOL ME! LOOK AT THE SCAR ON HER SHOULDER!
I KNOW SHE IS, IN FACT, ELLIS CARSON!
SCAR?
RUSTLE
OH, YOU MEAN THAT?
!
WHAT ARE YOU ...
RUB
DR. DIS-RAELI!
SHE DIED ONCE.
HER ABILITY TO REPRODUCE CELLS HAS BEEN GREATLY WEAKENED SO HER WOUND WON'T CLOSE.
THAT'S WHY SHE'S NEEDED A CONSTANT SUPPLY...
...OF FRESH BLOOD AND ORGANS.

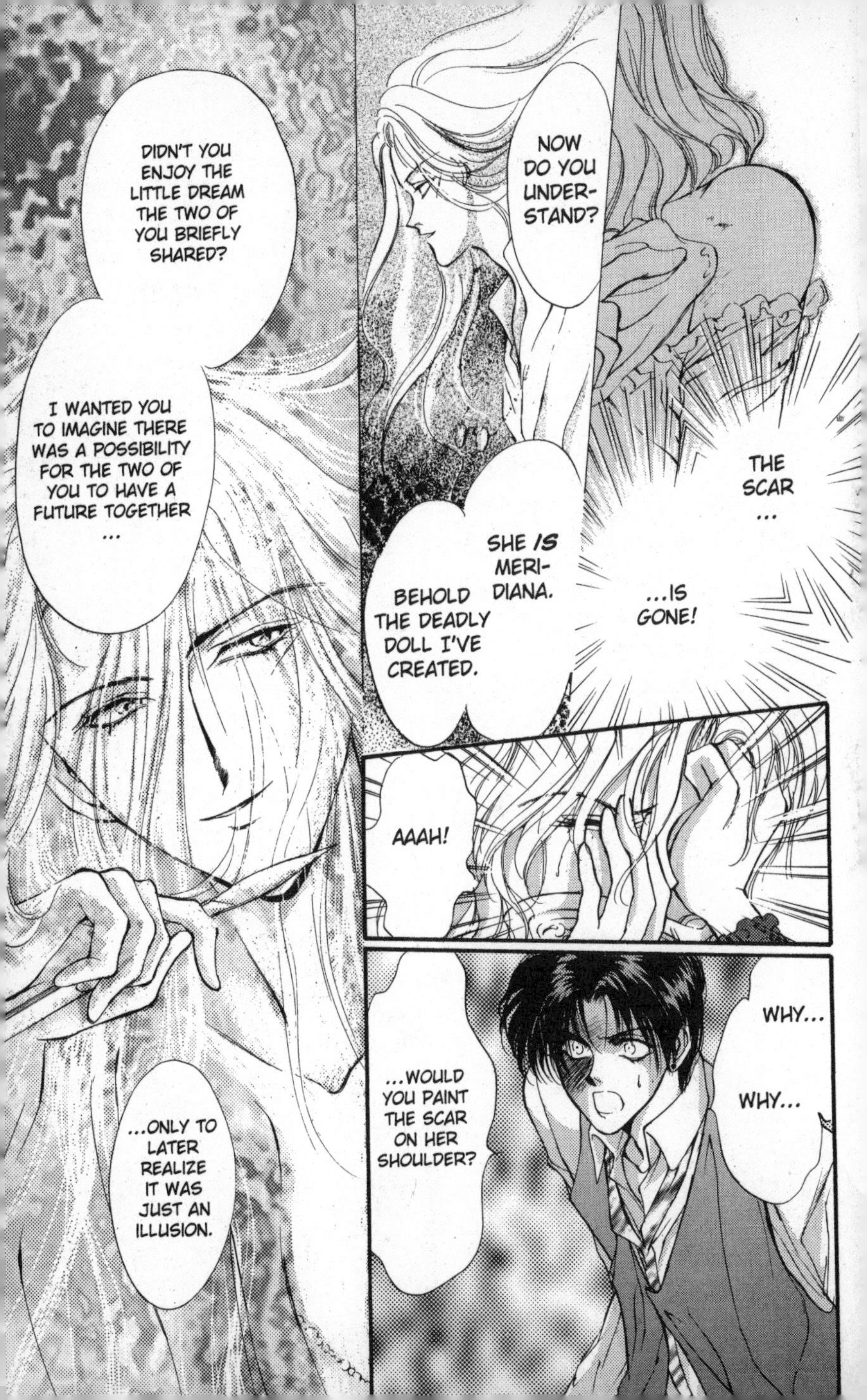
THE SCAR ...
...IS GONE!
NOW DO YOU UNDER-STAND?
SHE *IS* MERI-DIANA.
BEHOLD THE DEADLY DOLL I'VE CREATED.
AAAH!
WHY...
WHY...
...WOULD YOU PAINT THE SCAR ON HER SHOULDER?
DIDN'T YOU ENJOY THE LITTLE DREAM THE TWO OF YOU BRIEFLY SHARED?
I WANTED YOU TO IMAGINE THERE WAS A POSSIBILITY FOR THE TWO OF YOU TO HAVE A FUTURE TOGETHER ...
...ONLY TO LATER REALIZE IT WAS JUST AN ILLUSION.

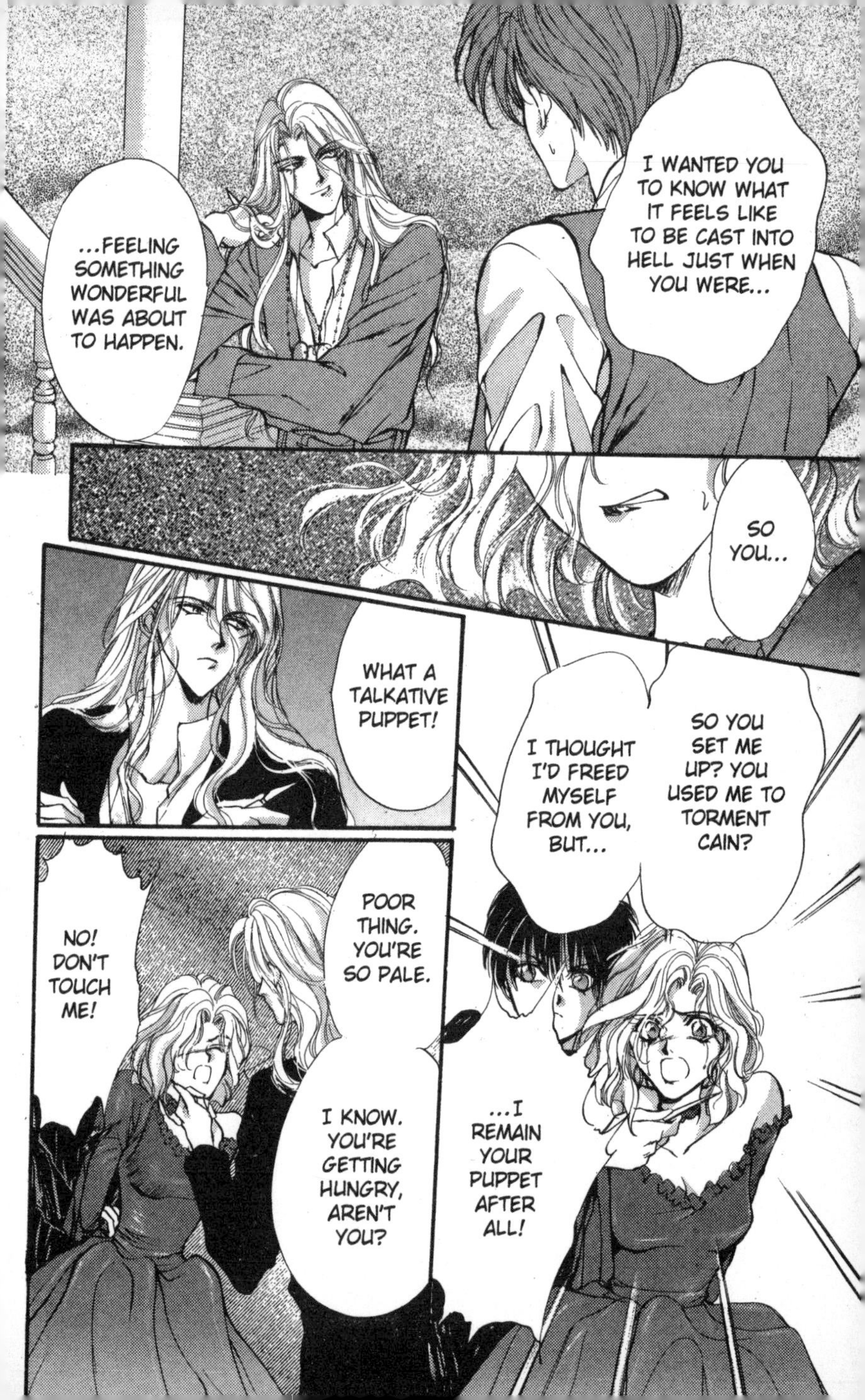
I WANTED YOU TO KNOW WHAT IT FEELS LIKE TO BE CAST INTO HELL JUST WHEN YOU WERE...
...FEELING SOMETHING WONDERFUL WAS ABOUT TO HAPPEN.
SO YOU...
WHAT A TALKATIVE PUPPET!
SO YOU SET ME UP? YOU USED ME TO TORMENT CAIN?
I THOUGHT I'D FREED MYSELF FROM YOU, BUT...
...I REMAIN YOUR PUPPET AFTER ALL!
POOR THING. YOU'RE SO PALE.
NO! DON'T TOUCH ME!
I KNOW. YOU'RE GETTING HUNGRY, AREN'T YOU?

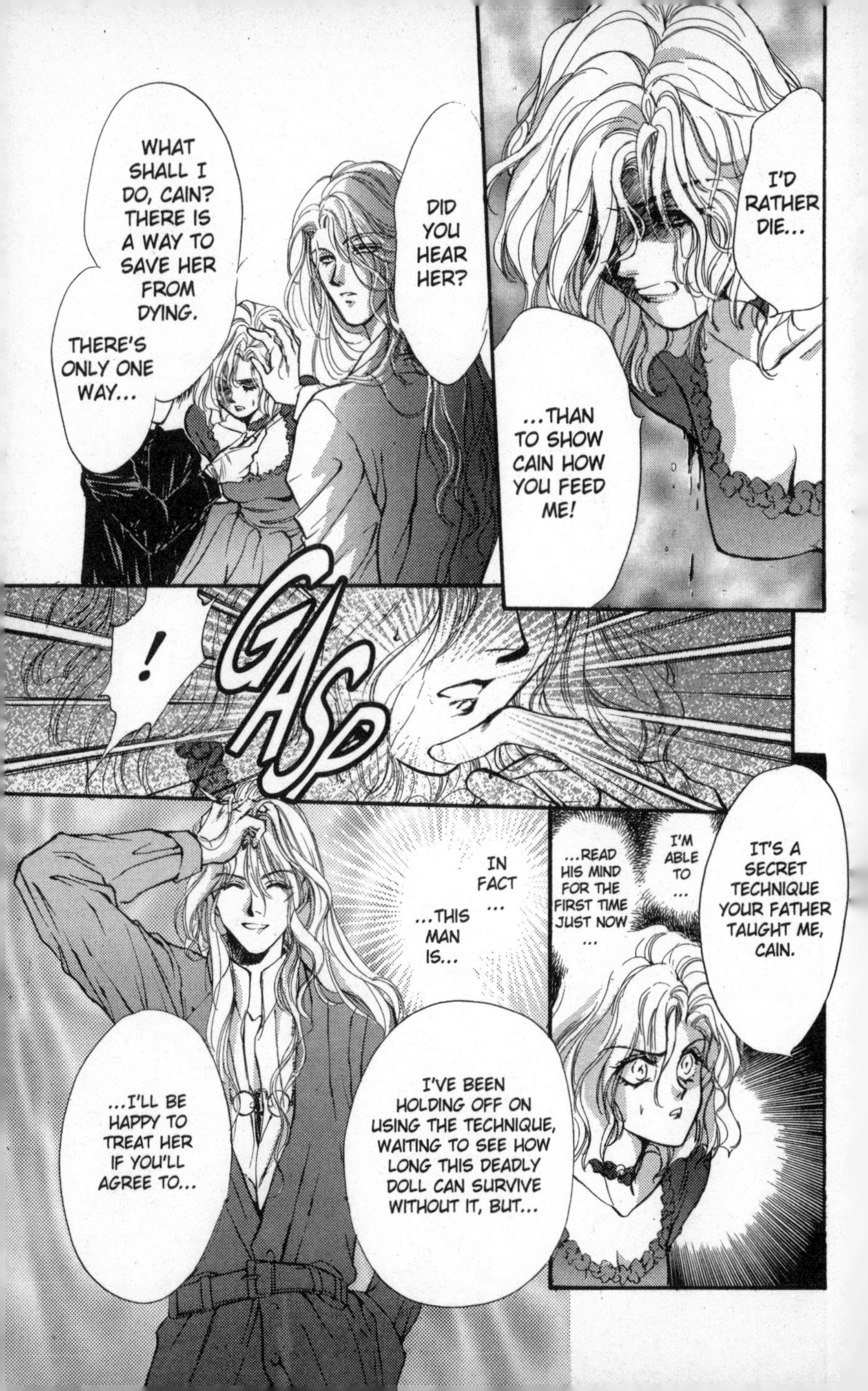
I'D RATHER DIE...
...THAN TO SHOW CAIN HOW YOU FEED ME!
DID YOU HEAR HER?
WHAT SHALL I DO, CAIN? THERE IS A WAY TO SAVE HER FROM DYING.
THERE'S ONLY ONE WAY...
GASP
!
IT'S A SECRET TECHNIQUE YOUR FATHER TAUGHT ME, CAIN.
I'M ABLE TO ...
...READ HIS MIND FOR THE FIRST TIME JUST NOW ...
IN FACT ...
...THIS MAN IS...
I'VE BEEN HOLDING OFF ON USING THE TECHNIQUE, WAITING TO SEE HOW LONG THIS DEADLY DOLL CAN SURVIVE WITHOUT IT, BUT...
...I'LL BE HAPPY TO TREAT HER IF YOU'LL AGREE TO...

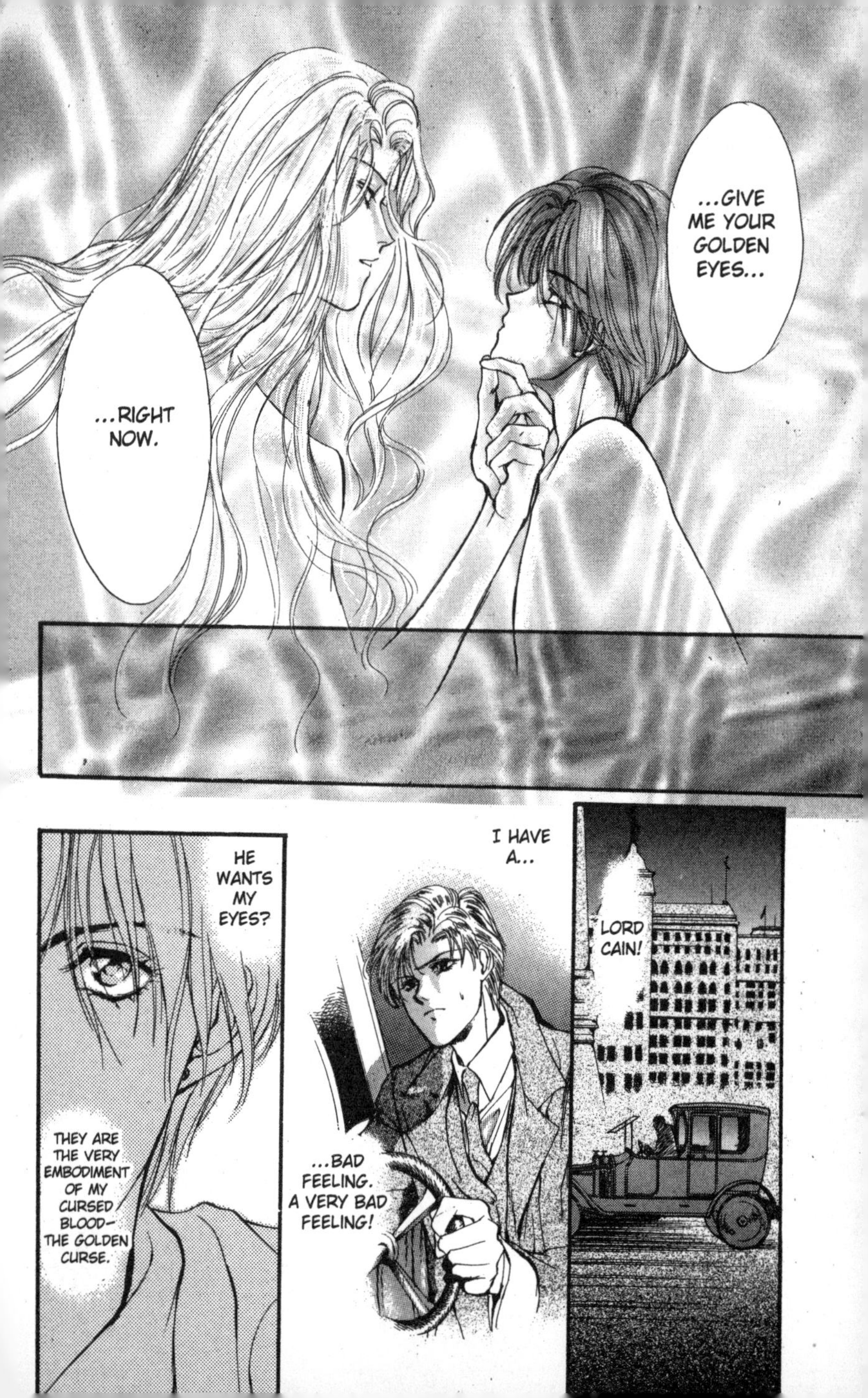
...GIVE ME YOUR GOLDEN EYES...
...RIGHT NOW.
LORD CAIN!
I HAVE A...
...BAD FEELING. A VERY BAD FEELING!
HE WANTS MY EYES?
THEY ARE THE VERY EMBODIMENT OF MY CURSED BLOOD—THE GOLDEN CURSE.

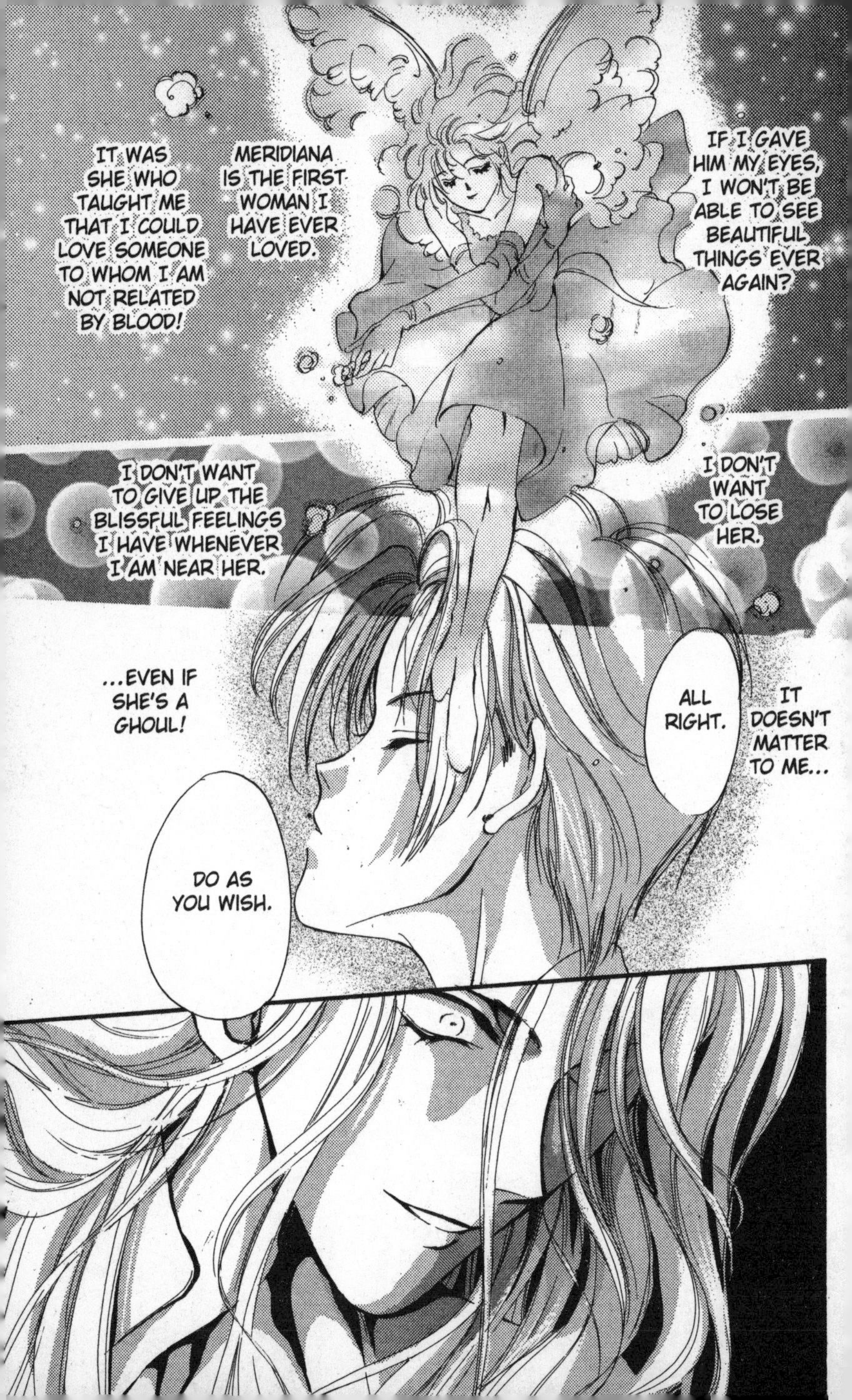
IF I GAVE HIM MY EYES, I WON'T BE ABLE TO SEE BEAUTIFUL THINGS EVER AGAIN?
MERIDIANA IS THE FIRST WOMAN I HAVE EVER LOVED.
IT WAS SHE WHO TAUGHT ME THAT I COULD LOVE SOMEONE TO WHOM I AM NOT RELATED BY BLOOD!
I DON'T WANT TO LOSE HER.
I DON'T WANT TO GIVE UP THE BLISSFUL FEELINGS I HAVE WHENEVER I AM NEAR HER.
IT DOESN'T MATTER TO ME...
ALL RIGHT.
...EVEN IF SHE'S A GHOUL!
DO AS YOU WISH.

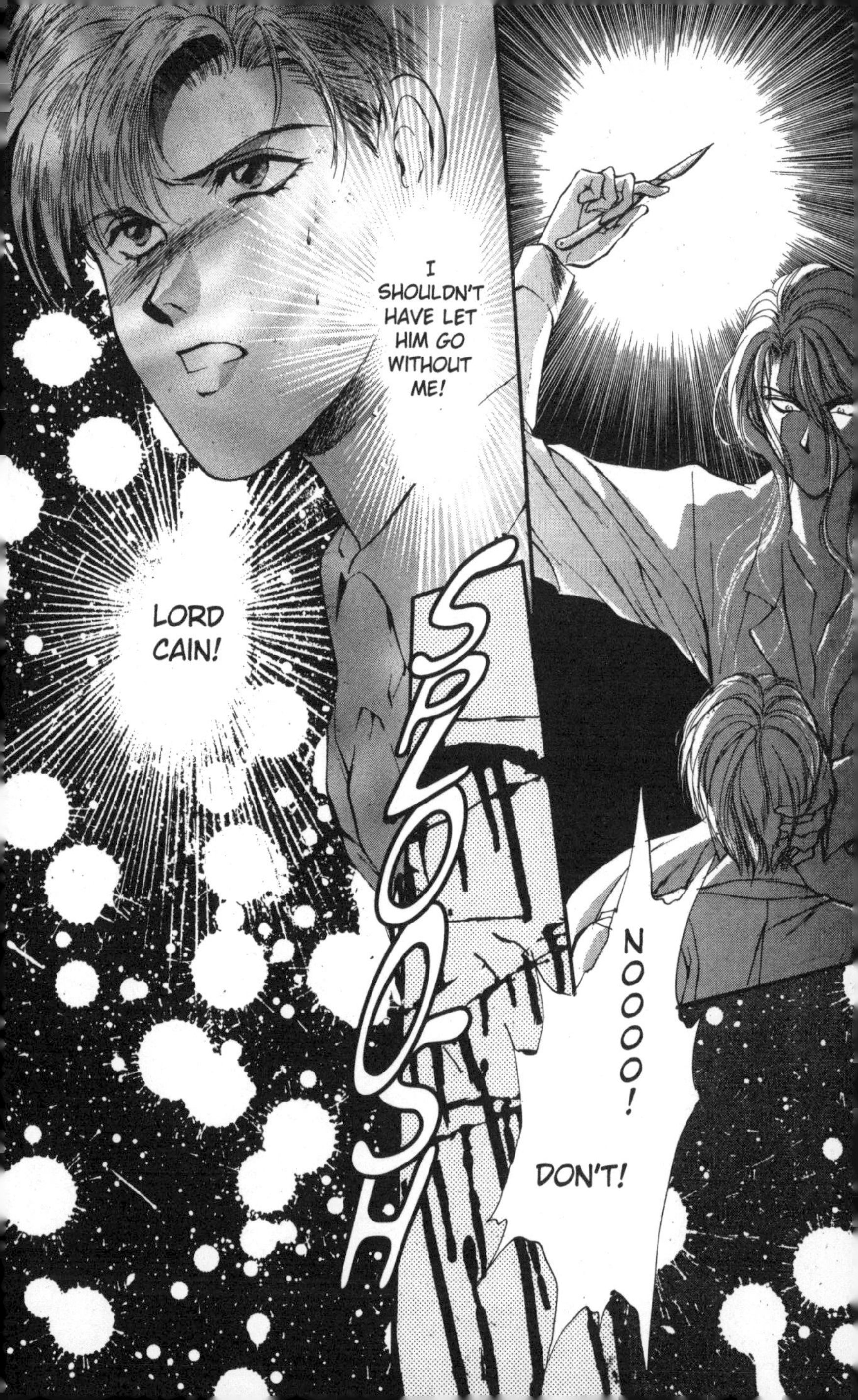
SPLOOSH
NOOOOO!
DON'T!
I SHOULDN'T HAVE LET HIM GO WITHOUT ME!
LORD CAIN!

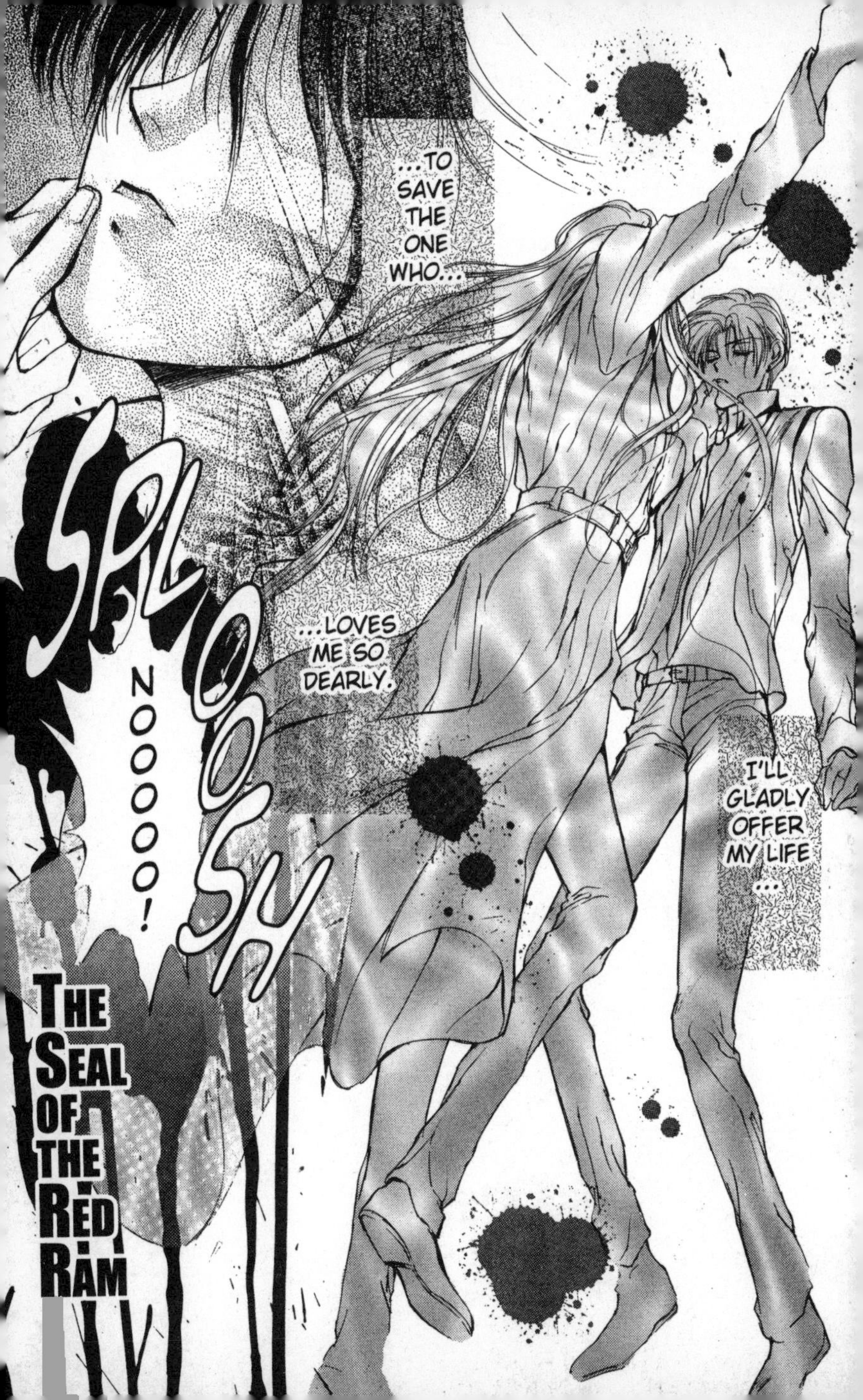
I'LL GLADLY OFFER MY LIFE ...
...TO SAVE THE ONE WHO...
...LOVES ME SO DEARLY.
SPLOOOSH
NOOOOOO!
THE SEAL OF THE RED RAM

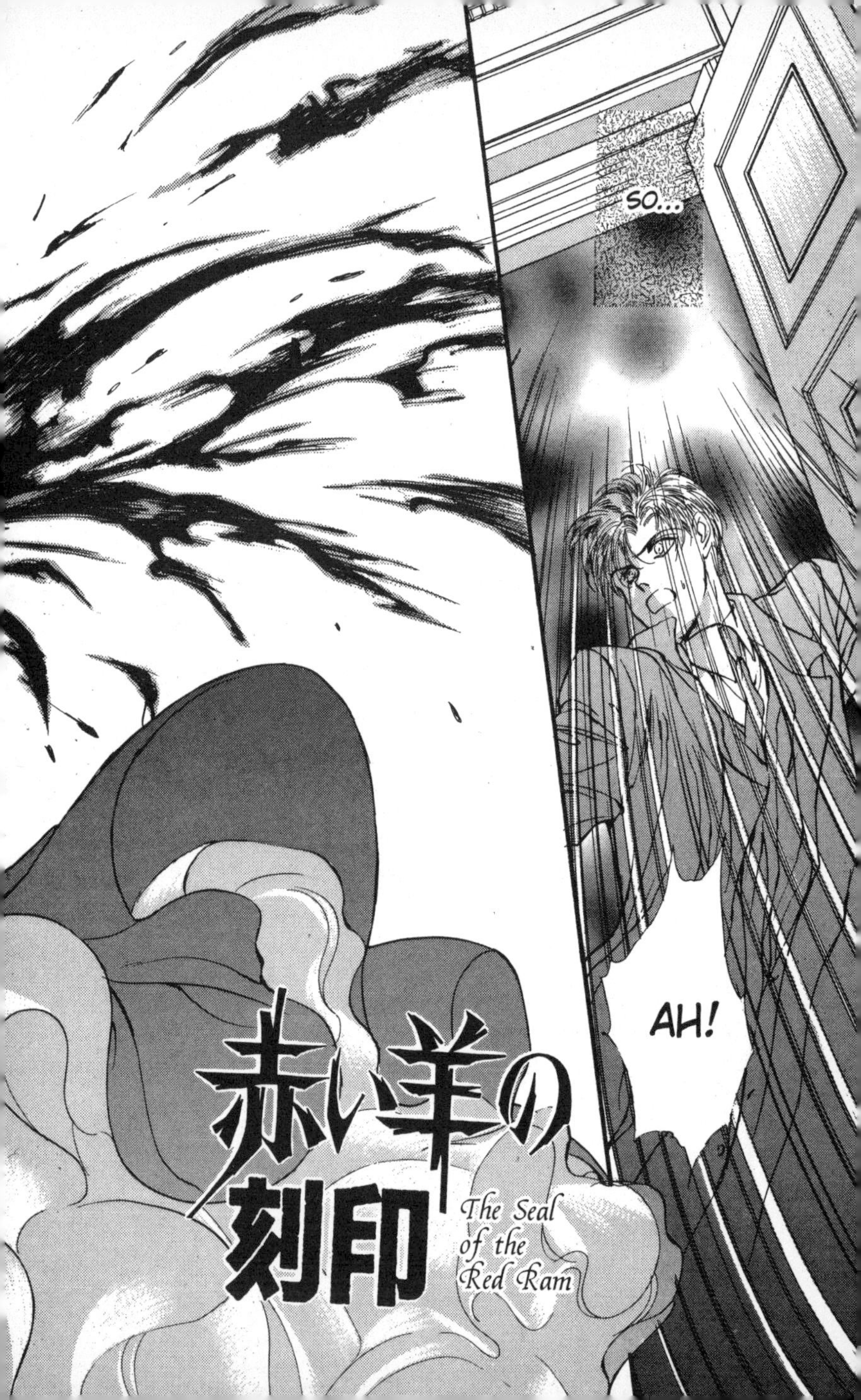
SO...
AH!
赤い羊の刻印
The Seal of the Red Ram

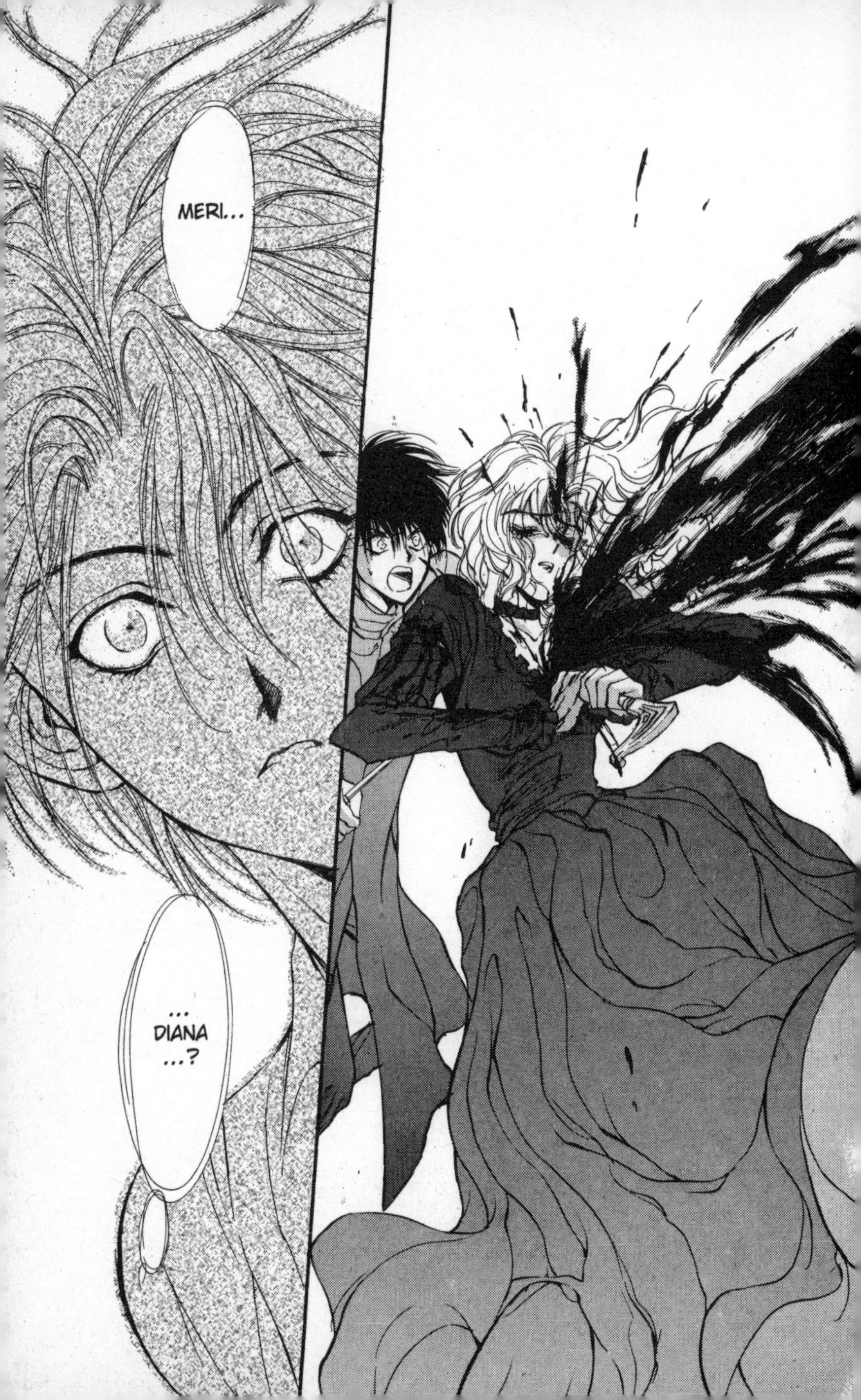
MERI...
...DIANA ...?

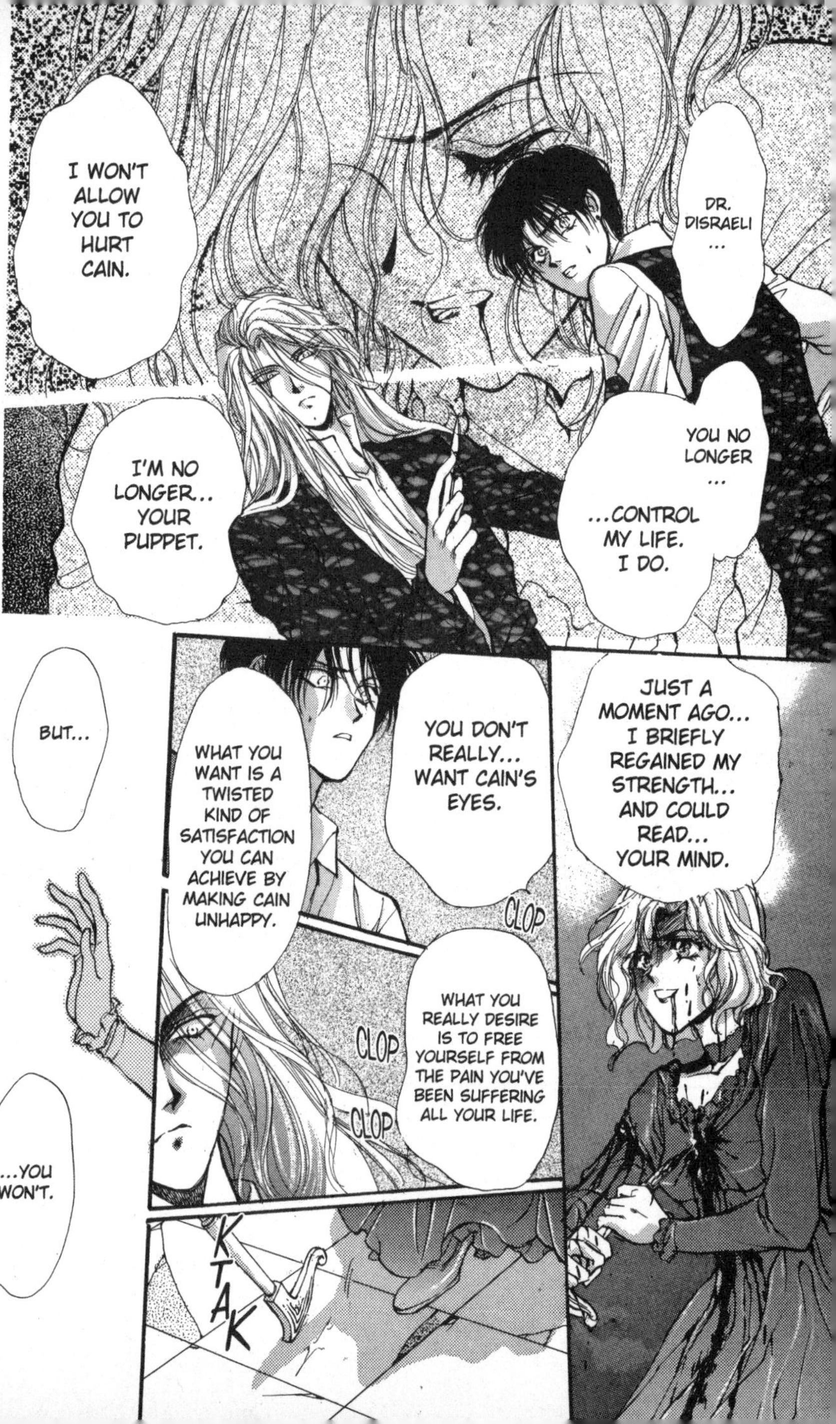
DR. DISRAELI ...
I WON'T ALLOW YOU TO HURT CAIN.
YOU NO LONGER ...
...CONTROL MY LIFE. I DO.
I'M NO LONGER... YOUR PUPPET.
JUST A MOMENT AGO... I BRIEFLY REGAINED MY STRENGTH... AND COULD READ... YOUR MIND.
YOU DON'T REALLY... WANT CAIN'S EYES.
WHAT YOU WANT IS A TWISTED KIND OF SATISFACTION YOU CAN ACHIEVE BY MAKING CAIN UNHAPPY.
CLOP
WHAT YOU REALLY DESIRE IS TO FREE YOURSELF FROM THE PAIN YOU'VE BEEN SUFFERING ALL YOUR LIFE.
CLOP
CLOP
BUT...
...YOU WON'T.
KTAK

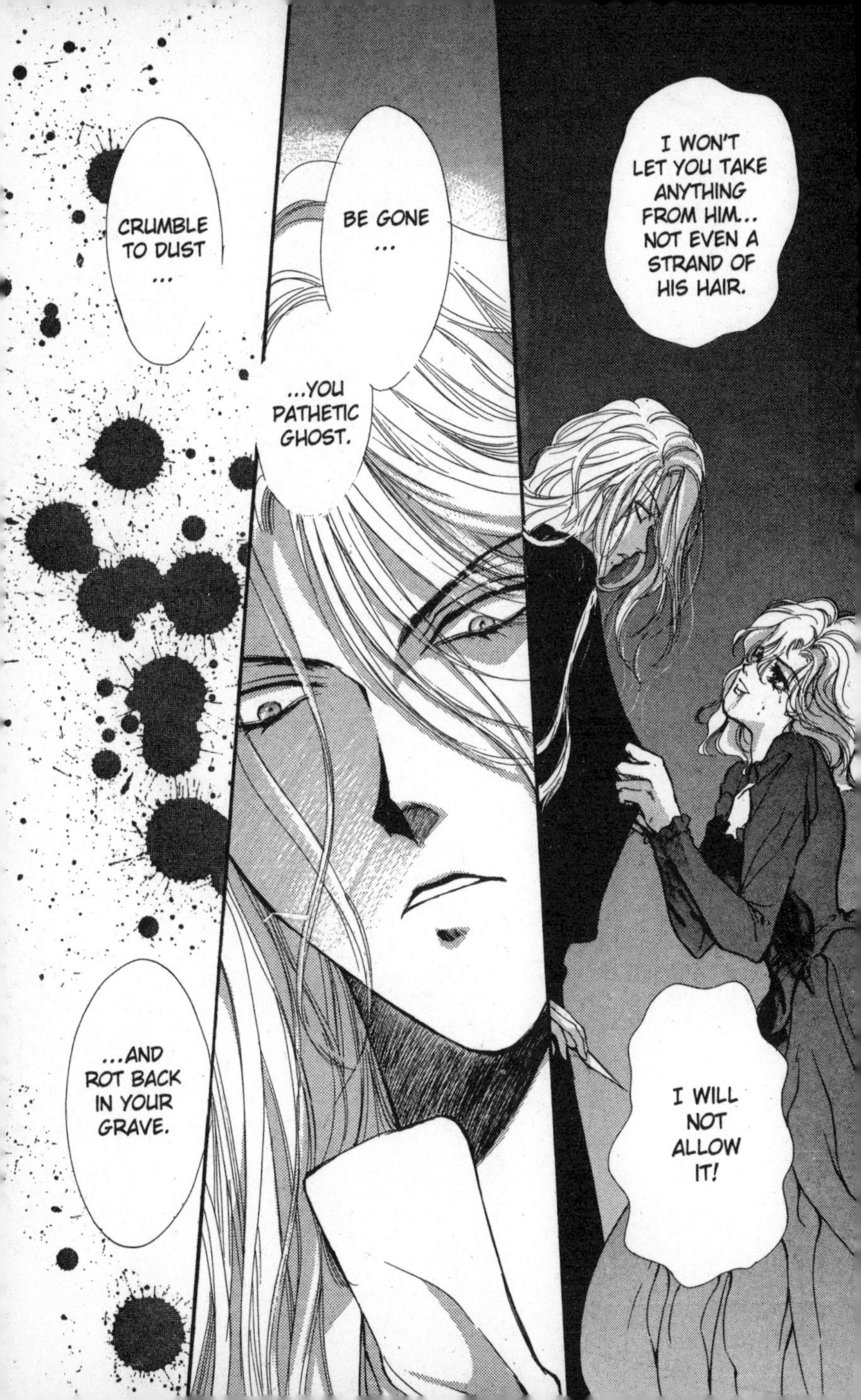
I WON'T LET YOU TAKE ANYTHING FROM HIM... NOT EVEN A STRAND OF HIS HAIR.
I WILL NOT ALLOW IT!
BE GONE ...
...YOU PATHETIC GHOST.
CRUMBLE TO DUST ...
...AND ROT BACK IN YOUR GRAVE.

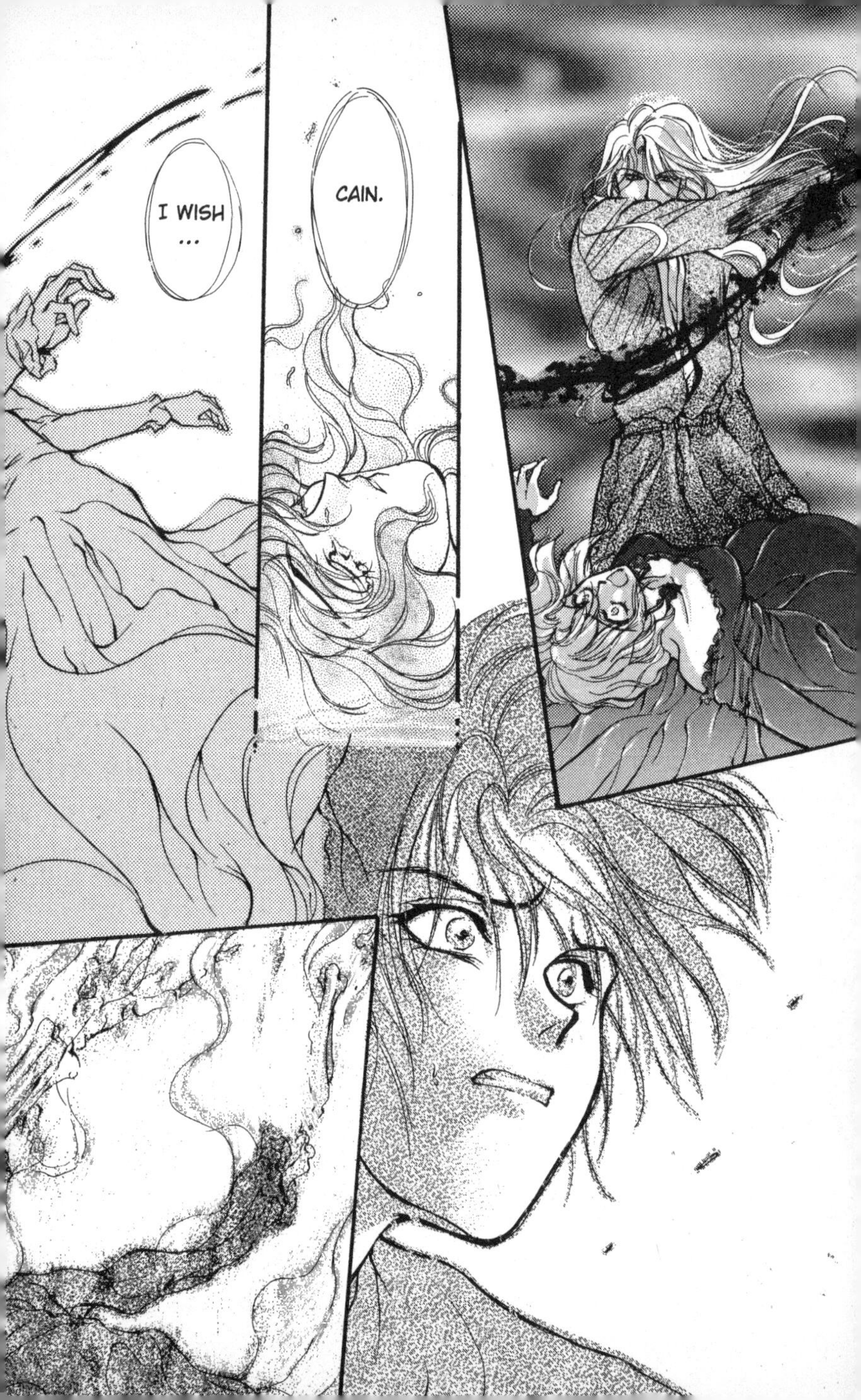
CAIN.
I WISH ...

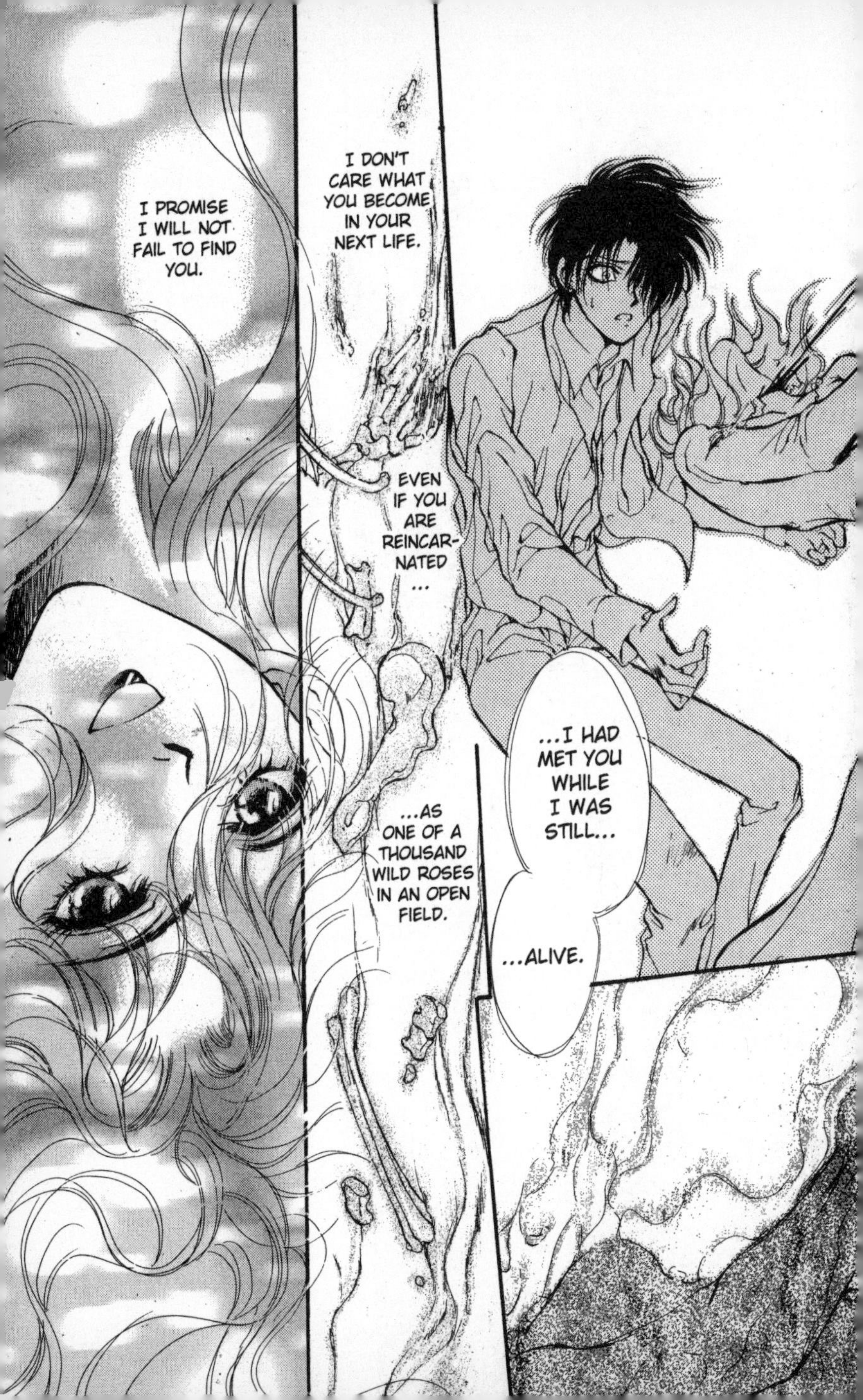
...I HAD MET YOU WHILE I WAS STILL...
...ALIVE.
I DON'T CARE WHAT YOU BECOME IN YOUR NEXT LIFE.
EVEN IF YOU ARE REINCAR-NATED...
...AS ONE OF A THOUSAND WILD ROSES IN AN OPEN FIELD.
I PROMISE I WILL NOT FAIL TO FIND YOU.

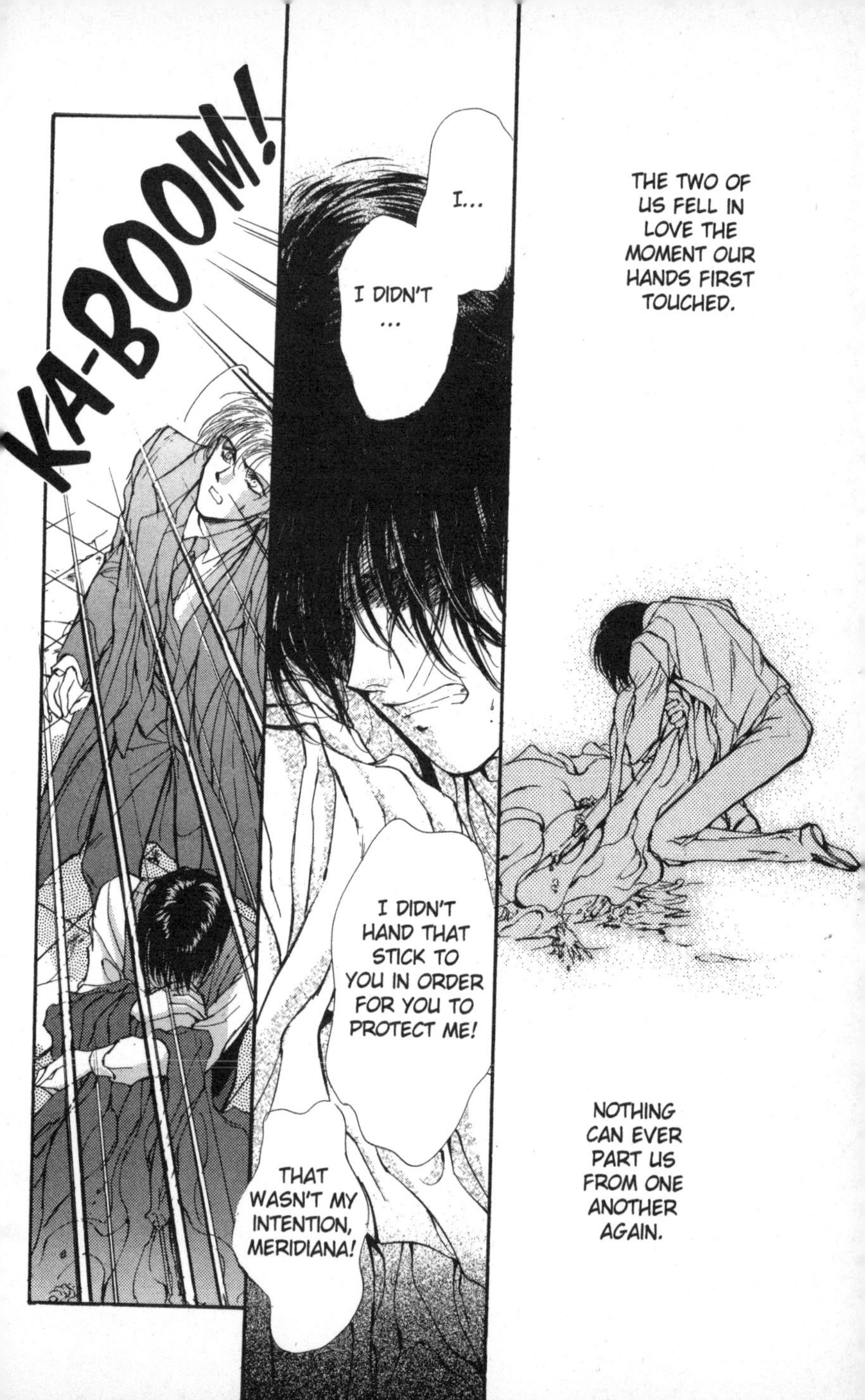
THE TWO OF US FELL IN LOVE THE MOMENT OUR HANDS FIRST TOUCHED.
NOTHING CAN EVER PART US FROM ONE ANOTHER AGAIN.
I...
I DIDN'T ...
I DIDN'T HAND THAT STICK TO YOU IN ORDER FOR YOU TO PROTECT ME!
THAT WASN'T MY INTENTION, MERIDIANA!
KA-BOOM!

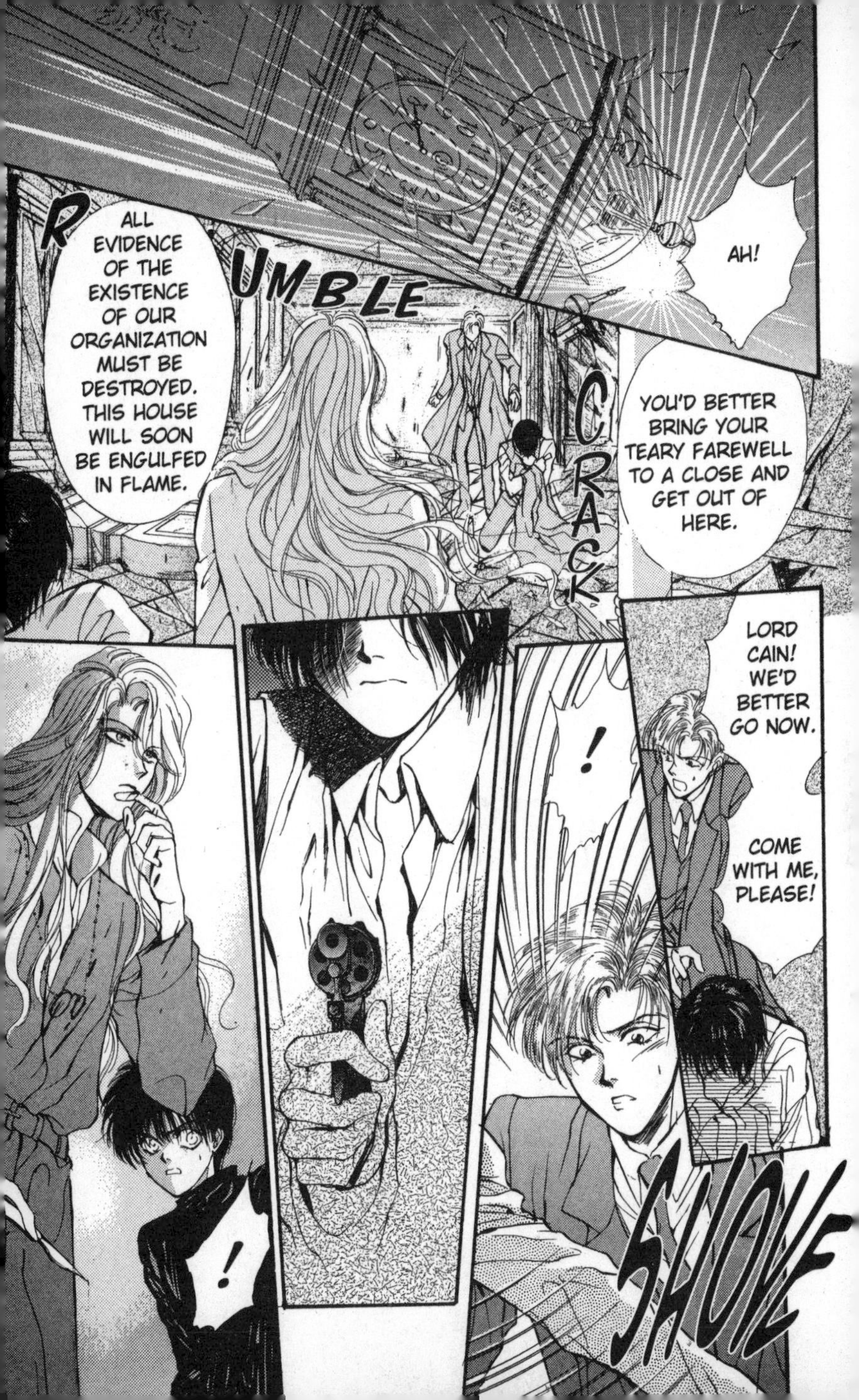

AH!
RUMBLE
ALL EVIDENCE OF THE EXISTENCE OF OUR ORGANIZATION MUST BE DESTROYED. THIS HOUSE WILL SOON BE ENGULFED IN FLAME.
CRACK
YOU'D BETTER BRING YOUR TEARY FAREWELL TO A CLOSE AND GET OUT OF HERE.
LORD CAIN! WE'D BETTER GO NOW.
COME WITH ME, PLEASE!
!
SHOVE
!

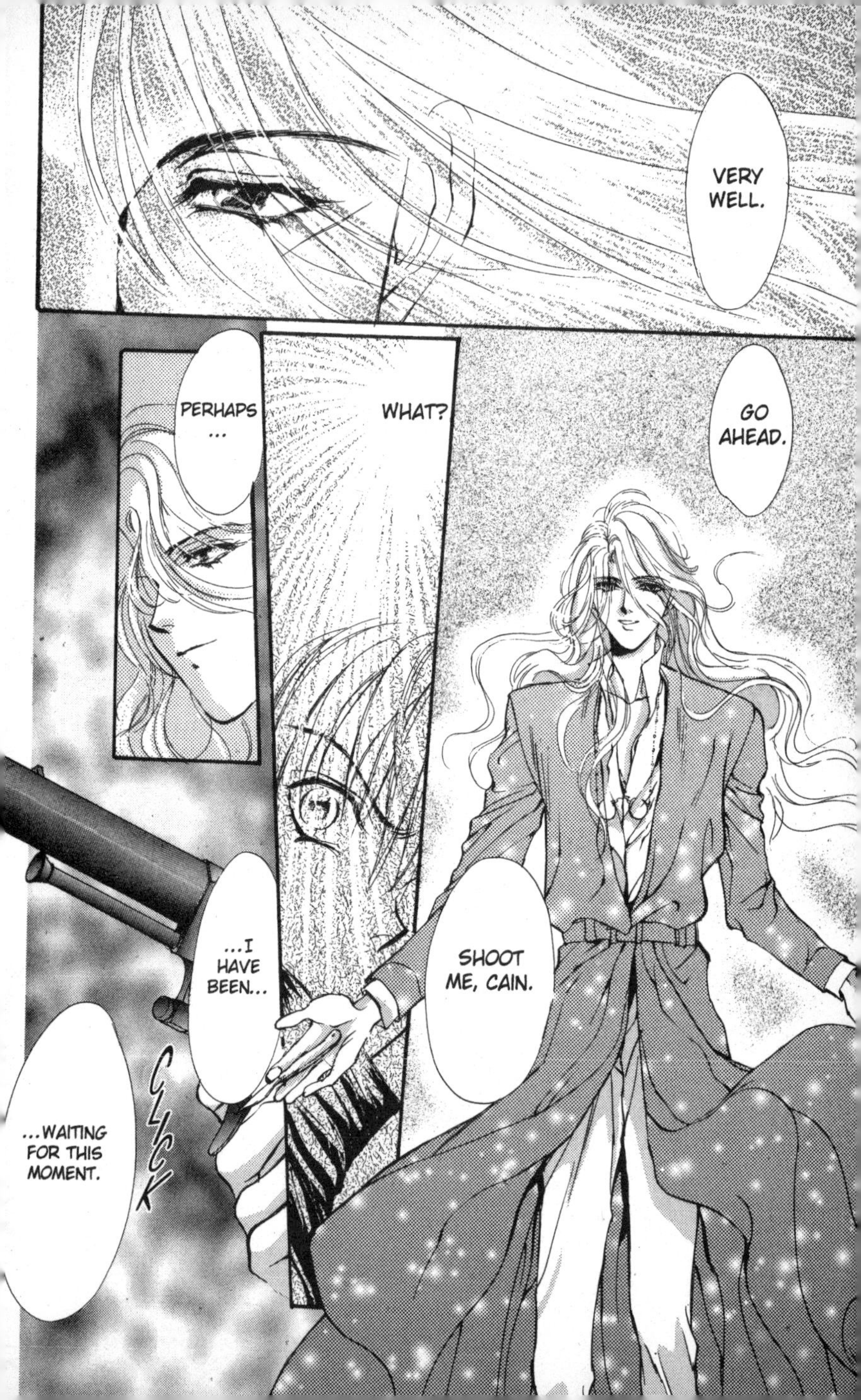
VERY WELL.
GO AHEAD.
SHOOT ME, CAIN.
WHAT?
PERHAPS ...
...I HAVE BEEN...
CLICK
...WAITING FOR THIS MOMENT.

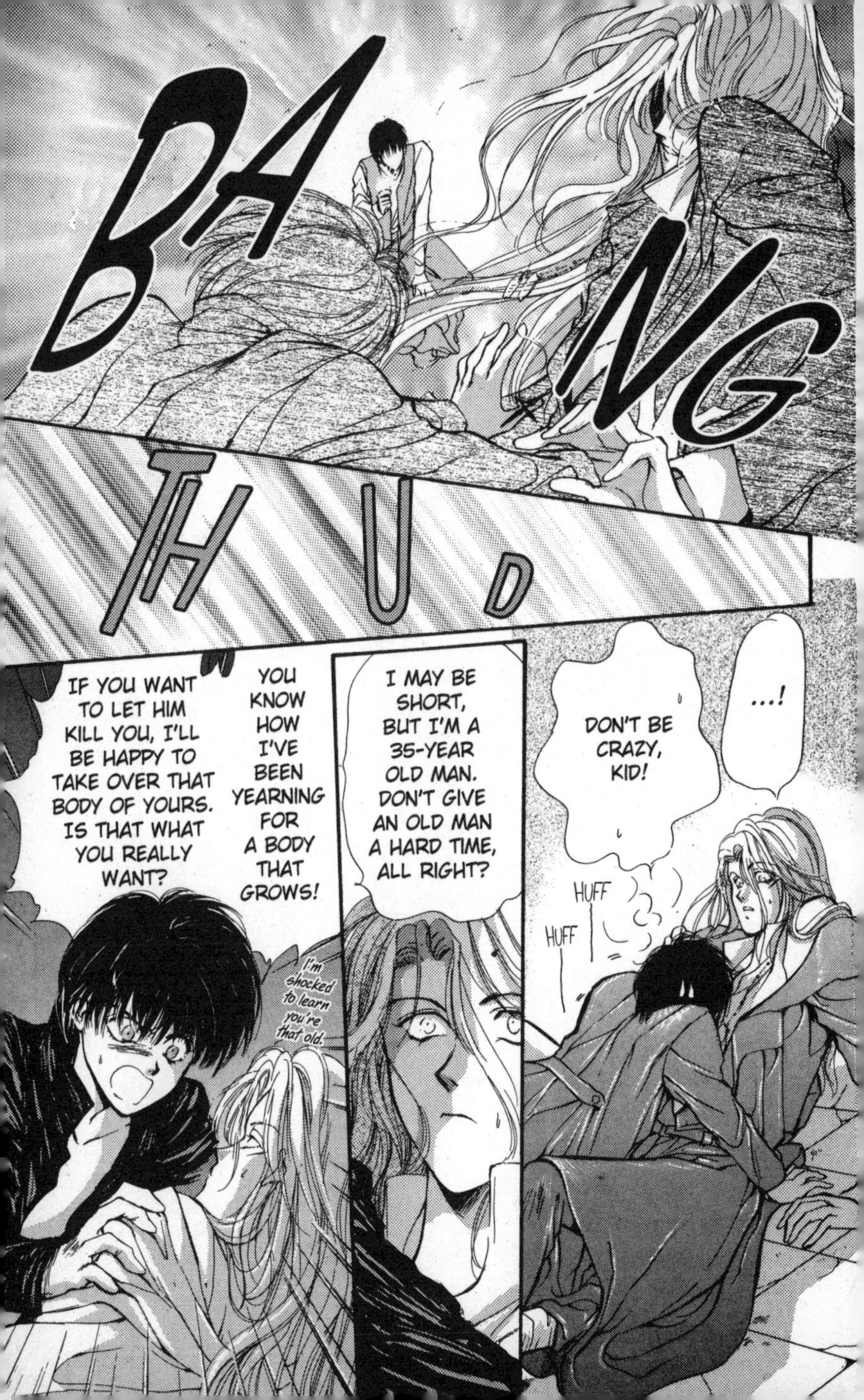
BANG
THUD
...!
DON'T BE CRAZY, KID!
HUFF
HUFF
I MAY BE SHORT, BUT I'M A 35-YEAR OLD MAN. DON'T GIVE AN OLD MAN A HARD TIME, ALL RIGHT?
YOU KNOW HOW I'VE BEEN YEARNING FOR A BODY THAT GROWS!
IF YOU WANT TO LET HIM KILL YOU, I'LL BE HAPPY TO TAKE OVER THAT BODY OF YOURS. IS THAT WHAT YOU REALLY WANT?
I'm shocked to learn you're that old.

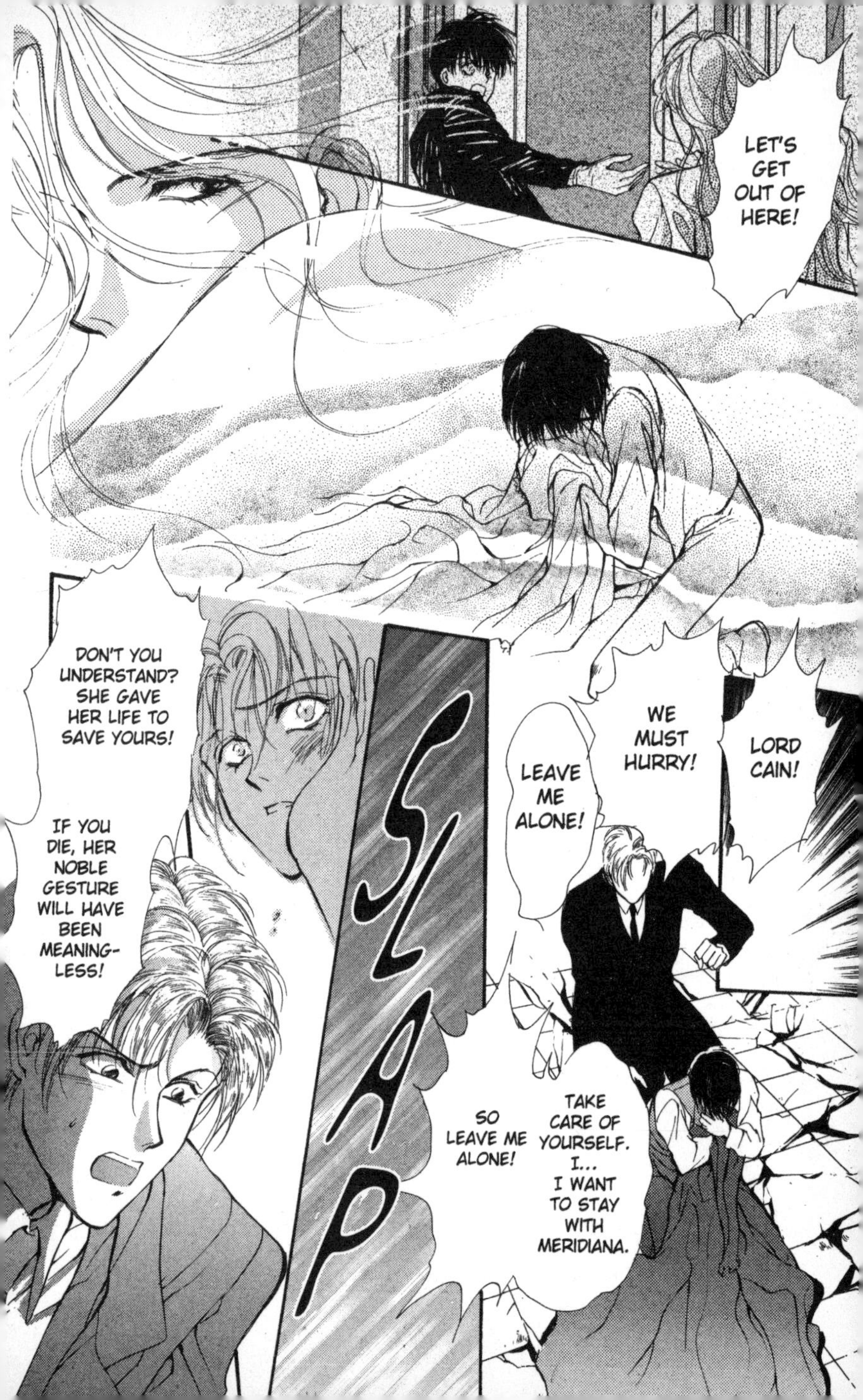
LET'S GET OUT OF HERE!
LORD CAIN!
WE MUST HURRY!
LEAVE ME ALONE!
TAKE CARE OF YOURSELF. I... I WANT TO STAY WITH MERIDIANA.
SO LEAVE ME ALONE!
SLAP
DON'T YOU UNDERSTAND? SHE GAVE HER LIFE TO SAVE YOURS!
IF YOU DIE, HER NOBLE GESTURE WILL HAVE BEEN MEANING-LESS!

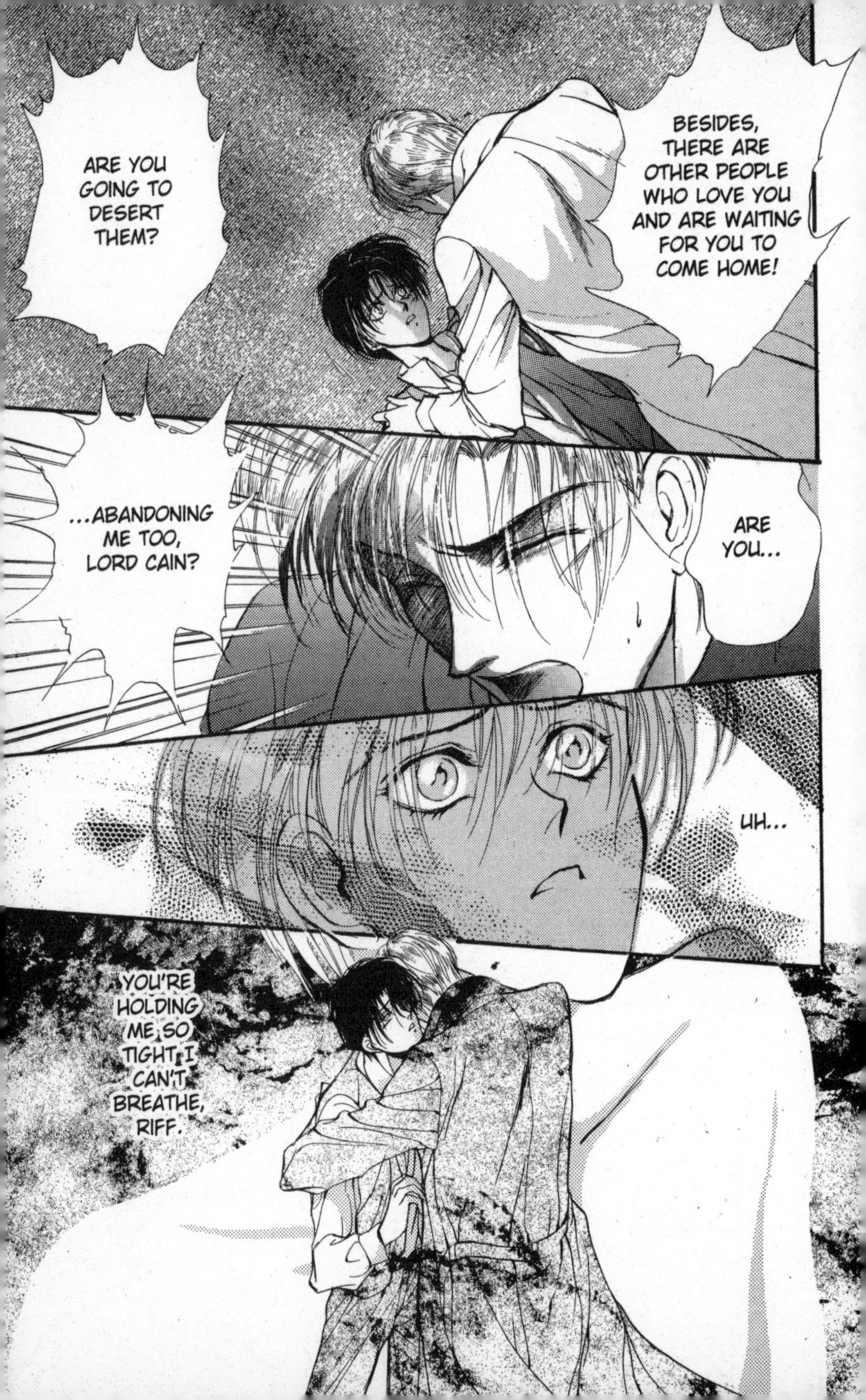
BESIDES, THERE ARE OTHER PEOPLE WHO LOVE YOU AND ARE WAITING FOR YOU TO COME HOME!
ARE YOU GOING TO DESERT THEM?
ARE YOU...
...ABANDONING ME TOO, LORD CAIN?
UH...
YOU'RE HOLDING ME SO TIGHT I CAN'T BREATHE, RIFF.

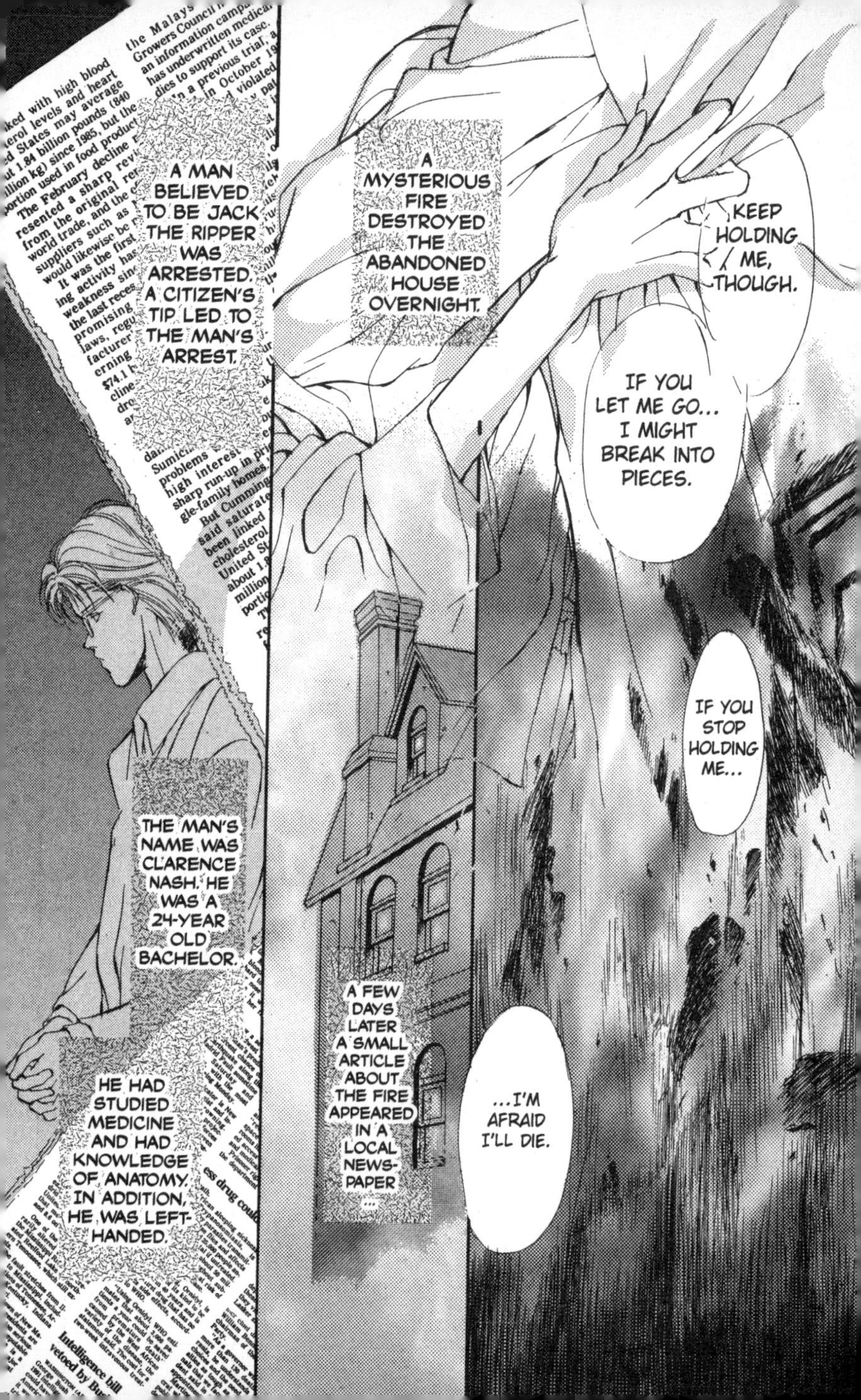
KEEP HOLDING ME, THOUGH.
IF YOU LET ME GO... I MIGHT BREAK INTO PIECES.
IF YOU STOP HOLDING ME...
...I'M AFRAID I'LL DIE.
A MYSTERIOUS FIRE DESTROYED THE ABANDONED HOUSE OVERNIGHT.
A FEW DAYS LATER A SMALL ARTICLE ABOUT THE FIRE APPEARED IN A LOCAL NEWSPAPER...
A MAN BELIEVED TO BE JACK THE RIPPER WAS ARRESTED. A CITIZEN'S TIP LED TO THE MAN'S ARREST.
THE MAN'S NAME WAS CLARENCE NASH. HE WAS A 24-YEAR OLD BACHELOR.
HE HAD STUDIED MEDICINE AND HAD KNOWLEDGE OF ANATOMY. IN ADDITION, HE WAS LEFT-HANDED.

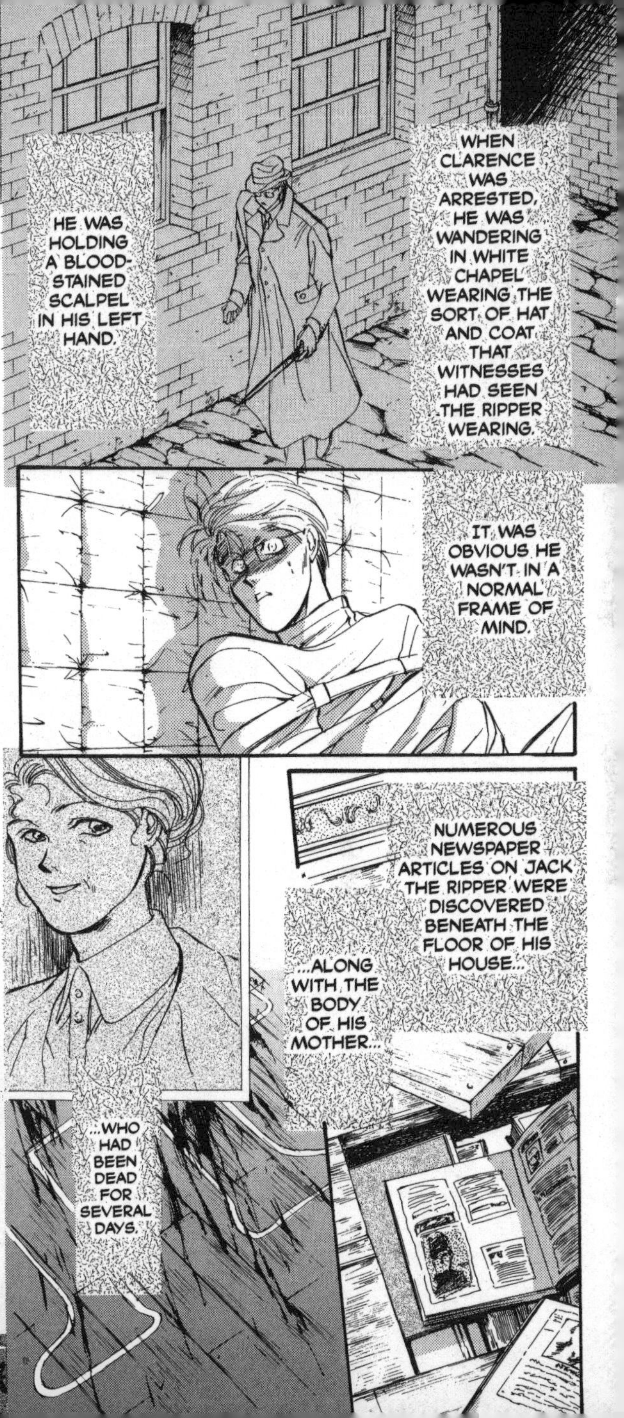
WHEN CLARENCE WAS ARRESTED, HE WAS WANDERING IN WHITE CHAPEL WEARING THE SORT OF HAT AND COAT THAT WITNESSES HAD SEEN THE RIPPER WEARING.
HE WAS HOLDING A BLOOD-STAINED SCALPEL IN HIS LEFT HAND.
IT WAS OBVIOUS HE WASN'T IN A NORMAL FRAME OF MIND.
NUMEROUS NEWSPAPER ARTICLES ON JACK THE RIPPER WERE DISCOVERED BENEATH THE FLOOR OF HIS HOUSE...
...ALONG WITH THE BODY OF HIS MOTHER...
...WHO HAD BEEN DEAD FOR SEVERAL DAYS.

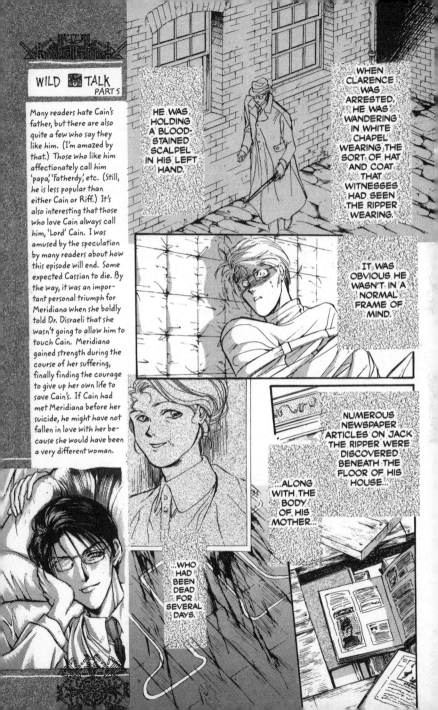

WILD TALK
PART 5

Many readers hate Cain's father, but there are also quite a few who say they like him. (I'm amazed by that.) Those who like him affectionately call him 'papa,' 'Fatherdy,' etc. (Still, he is less popular than either Cain or Riff.) It's also interesting that those who love Cain always call him, 'Lord' Cain. I was amused by the speculation by many readers about how this episode will end. Some expected Cassian to die. By the way, it was an important personal triumph for Meridiana when she boldly told Dr. Disraeli that she wasn't going to allow him to touch Cain. Meridiana gained strength during the course of her suffering, finally finding the courage to give up her own life to save Cain's. If Cain had met Meridiana before her suicide, he might have not fallen in love with her because she would have been a very different woman.

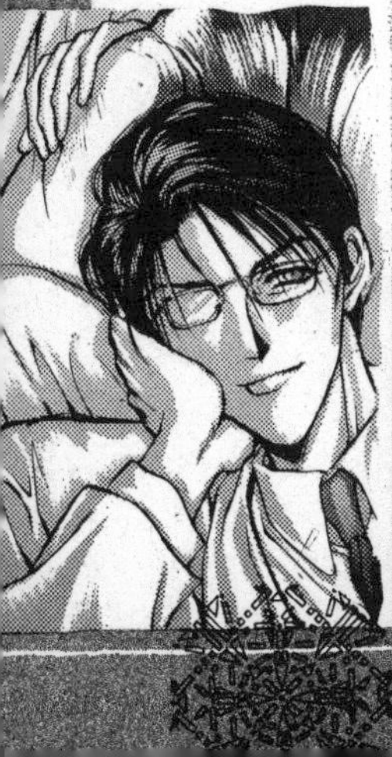

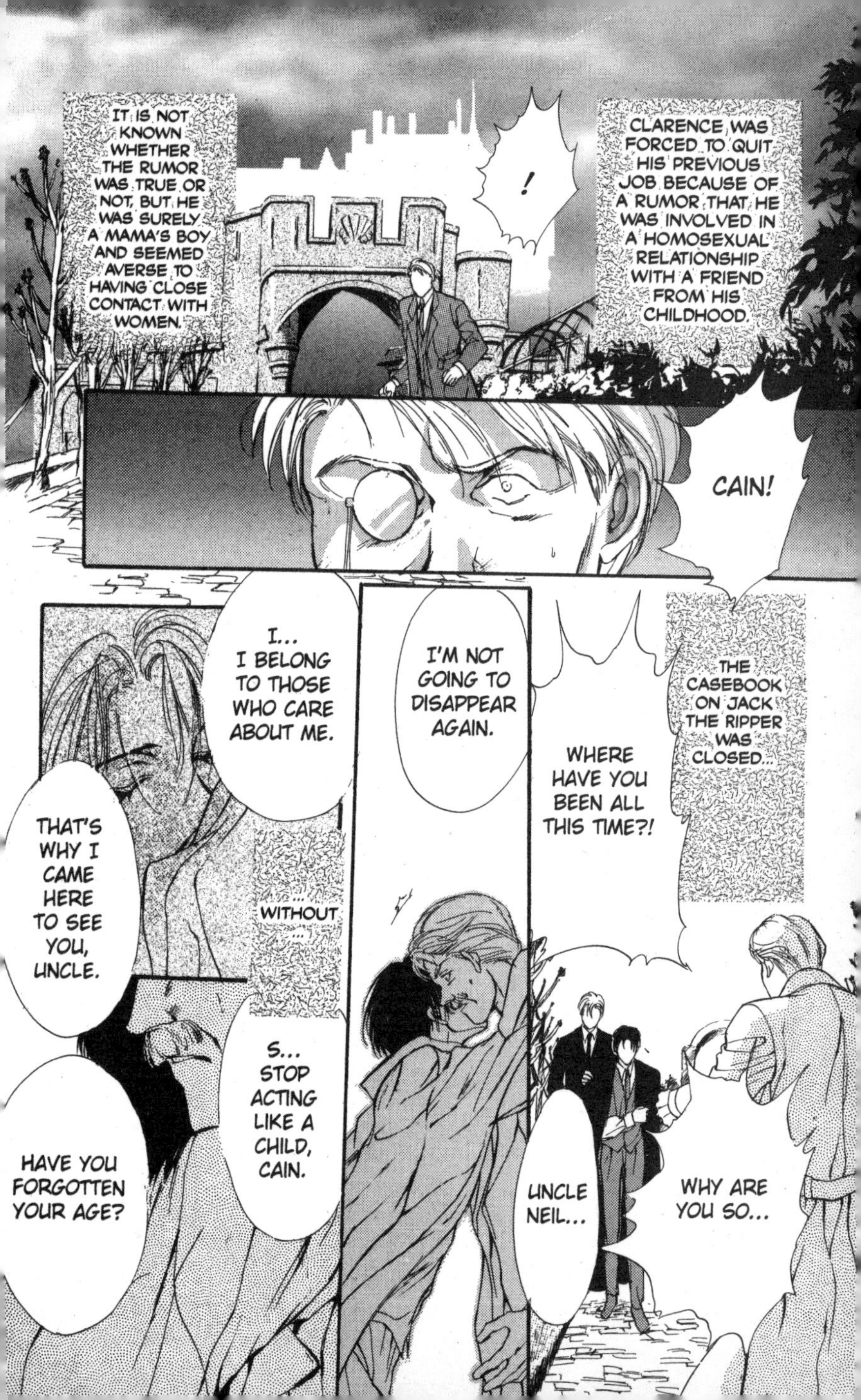
CLARENCE WAS FORCED TO QUIT HIS PREVIOUS JOB BECAUSE OF A RUMOR THAT HE WAS INVOLVED IN A HOMOSEXUAL RELATIONSHIP WITH A FRIEND FROM HIS CHILDHOOD.
!
IT IS NOT KNOWN WHETHER THE RUMOR WAS TRUE OR NOT, BUT HE WAS SURELY A MAMA'S BOY AND SEEMED AVERSE TO HAVING CLOSE CONTACT WITH WOMEN.
CAIN!
THE CASEBOOK ON JACK THE RIPPER WAS CLOSED...
WHERE HAVE YOU BEEN ALL THIS TIME?!
WHY ARE YOU SO...
UNCLE NEIL...
I'M NOT GOING TO DISAPPEAR AGAIN.
S... STOP ACTING LIKE A CHILD, CAIN.
I... I BELONG TO THOSE WHO CARE ABOUT ME.
...WITHOUT...
THAT'S WHY I CAME HERE TO SEE YOU, UNCLE.
HAVE YOU FORGOTTEN YOUR AGE?

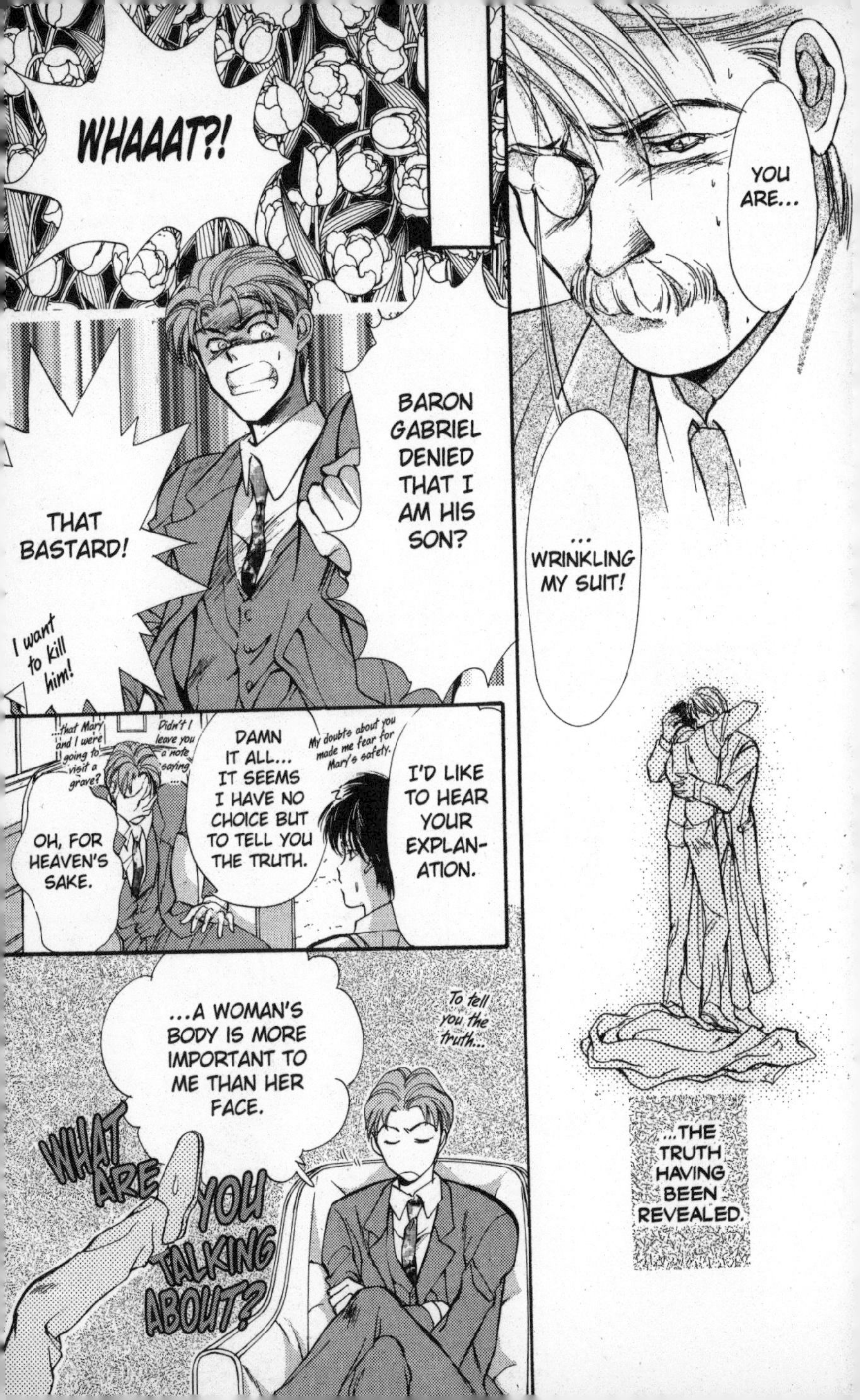
YOU ARE...
... WRINKLING MY SUIT!
...THE TRUTH HAVING BEEN REVEALED.
WHAAAT?!
BARON GABRIEL DENIED THAT I AM HIS SON?
THAT BASTARD!
I want to kill him!
I'D LIKE TO HEAR YOUR EXPLANATION.
My doubts about you made me fear for Mary's safety.
DAMN IT ALL... IT SEEMS I HAVE NO CHOICE BUT TO TELL YOU THE TRUTH.
Didn't I leave you a note saying...
...that Mary and I were going to visit a grave?
OH, FOR HEAVEN'S SAKE.
To tell you the truth...
...A WOMAN'S BODY IS MORE IMPORTANT TO ME THAN HER FACE.
WHAT ARE YOU TALKING ABOUT?

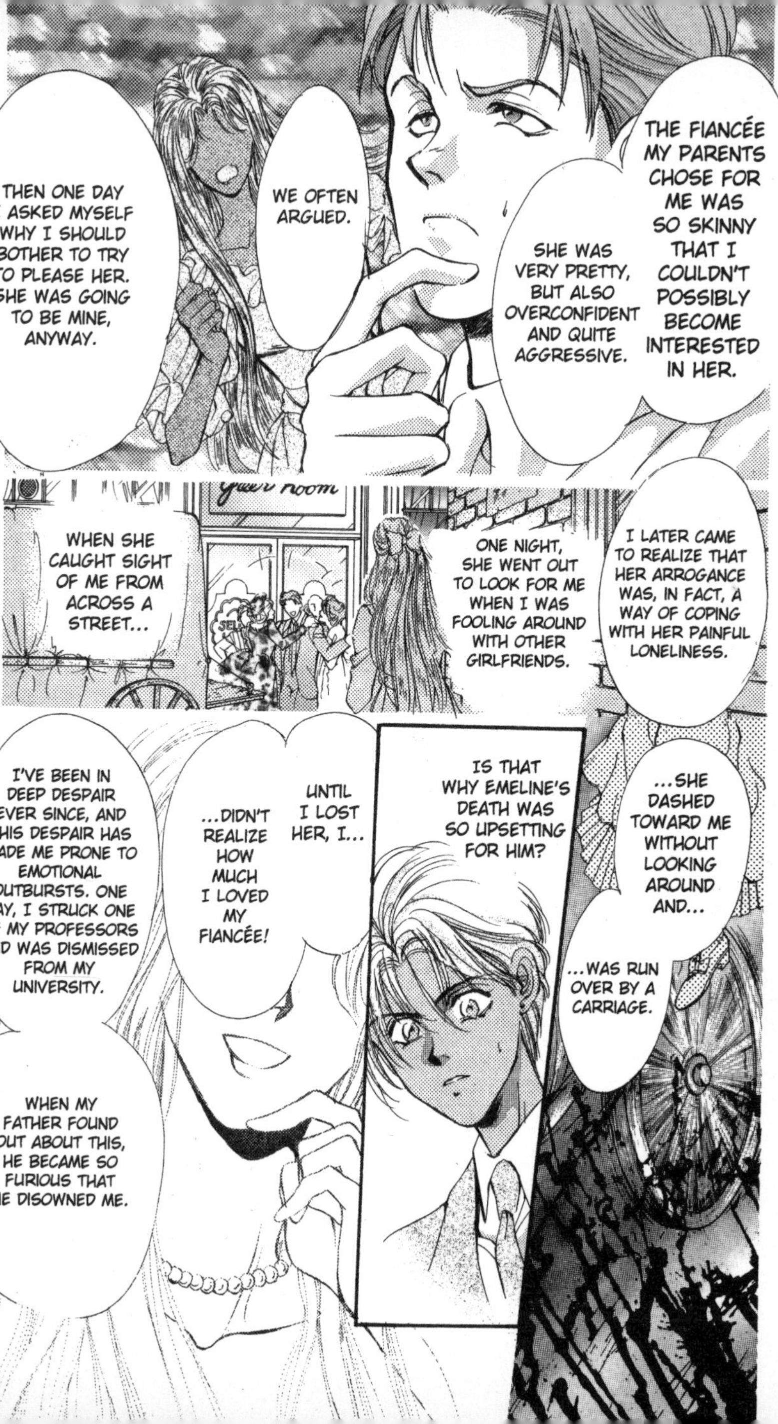
THE FIANCÉE MY PARENTS CHOSE FOR ME WAS SO SKINNY THAT I COULDN'T POSSIBLY BECOME INTERESTED IN HER.
SHE WAS VERY PRETTY, BUT ALSO OVERCONFIDENT AND QUITE AGGRESSIVE.
WE OFTEN ARGUED.
THEN ONE DAY I ASKED MYSELF WHY I SHOULD BOTHER TO TRY TO PLEASE HER. SHE WAS GOING TO BE MINE, ANYWAY.
I LATER CAME TO REALIZE THAT HER ARROGANCE WAS, IN FACT, A WAY OF COPING WITH HER PAINFUL LONELINESS.
ONE NIGHT, SHE WENT OUT TO LOOK FOR ME WHEN I WAS FOOLING AROUND WITH OTHER GIRLFRIENDS.
WHEN SHE CAUGHT SIGHT OF ME FROM ACROSS A STREET...
...SHE DASHED TOWARD ME WITHOUT LOOKING AROUND AND...
...WAS RUN OVER BY A CARRIAGE.
IS THAT WHY EMELINE'S DEATH WAS SO UPSETTING FOR HIM?
UNTIL I LOST HER, I...
...DIDN'T REALIZE HOW MUCH I LOVED MY FIANCÉE!
I'VE BEEN IN DEEP DESPAIR EVER SINCE, AND THIS DESPAIR HAS MADE ME PRONE TO EMOTIONAL OUTBURSTS. ONE DAY, I STRUCK ONE OF MY PROFESSORS AND WAS DISMISSED FROM MY UNIVERSITY.
WHEN MY FATHER FOUND OUT ABOUT THIS, HE BECAME SO FURIOUS THAT HE DISOWNED ME.

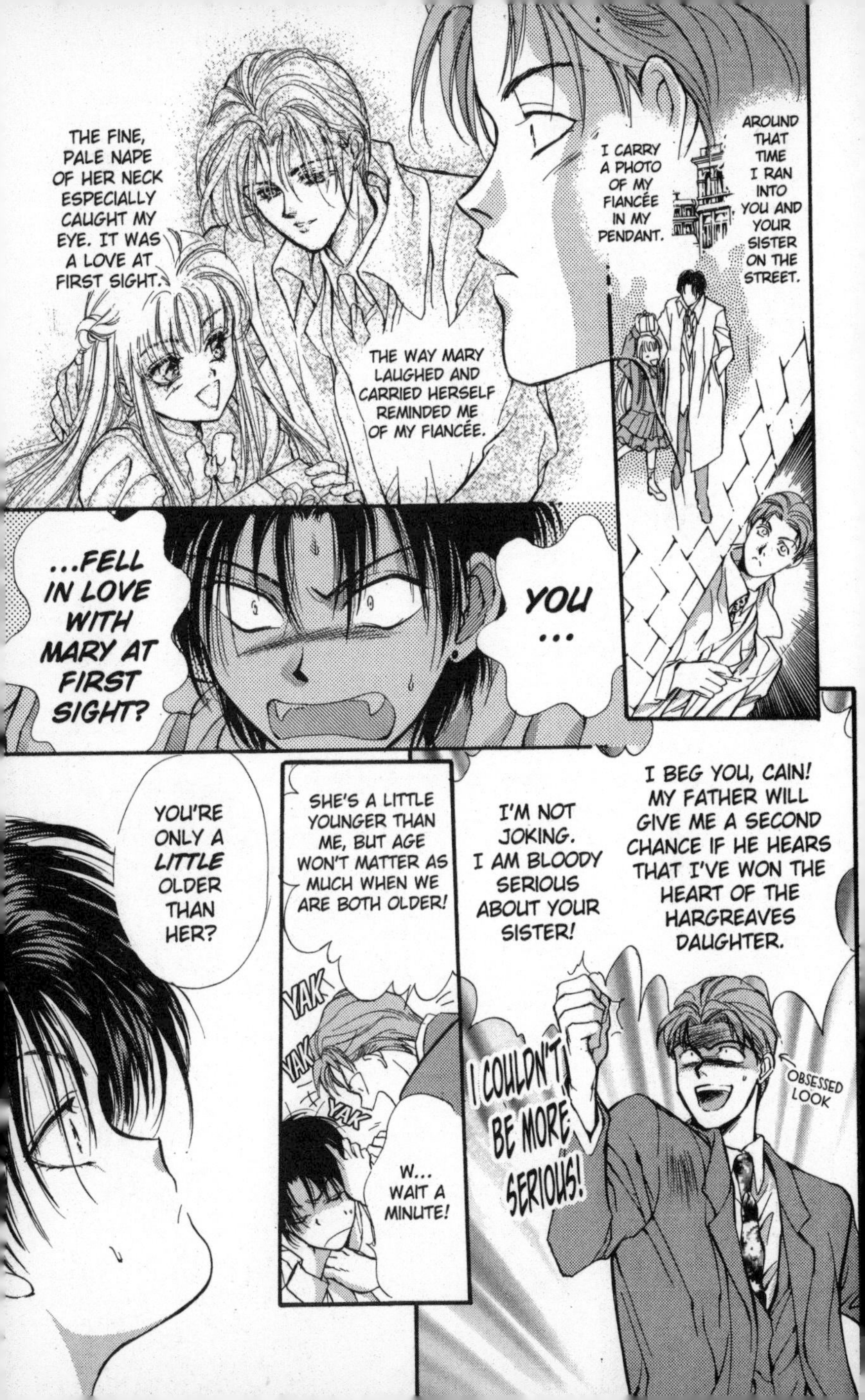
AROUND THAT TIME I RAN INTO YOU AND YOUR SISTER ON THE STREET.
I CARRY A PHOTO OF MY FIANCÉE IN MY PENDANT.
THE WAY MARY LAUGHED AND CARRIED HERSELF REMINDED ME OF MY FIANCÉE.
THE FINE, PALE NAPE OF HER NECK ESPECIALLY CAUGHT MY EYE. IT WAS A LOVE AT FIRST SIGHT.
YOU ...
...FELL IN LOVE WITH MARY AT FIRST SIGHT?
I BEG YOU, CAIN! MY FATHER WILL GIVE ME A SECOND CHANCE IF HE HEARS THAT I'VE WON THE HEART OF THE HARGREAVES DAUGHTER.
I'M NOT JOKING. I AM BLOODY SERIOUS ABOUT YOUR SISTER!
I COULDN'T BE MORE SERIOUS!
OBSESSED LOOK
SHE'S A LITTLE YOUNGER THAN ME, BUT AGE WON'T MATTER AS MUCH WHEN WE ARE BOTH OLDER!
YAK
YAK
YAK
W... WAIT A MINUTE!
YOU'RE ONLY A LITTLE OLDER THAN HER?

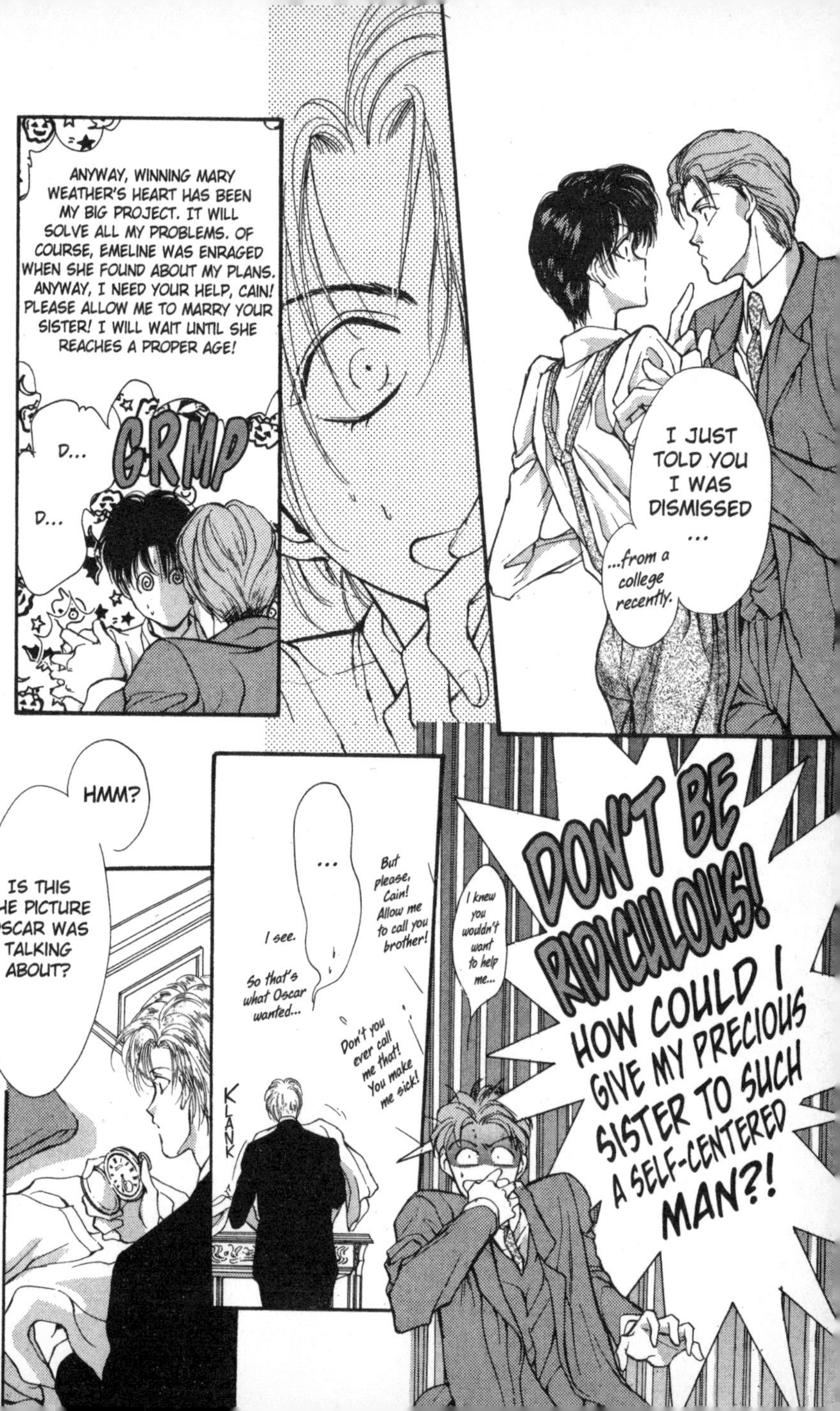
I JUST TOLD YOU I WAS DISMISSED ...
...from a college recently.
ANYWAY, WINNING MARY WEATHER'S HEART HAS BEEN MY BIG PROJECT. IT WILL SOLVE ALL MY PROBLEMS. OF COURSE, EMELINE WAS ENRAGED WHEN SHE FOUND ABOUT MY PLANS. ANYWAY, I NEED YOUR HELP, CAIN! PLEASE ALLOW ME TO MARRY YOUR SISTER! I WILL WAIT UNTIL SHE REACHES A PROPER AGE!
GRMP
D...
D...
DON'T BE RIDICULOUS!
HOW COULD I GIVE MY PRECIOUS SISTER TO SUCH A SELF-CENTERED MAN?!
I knew you wouldn't want to help me...
But please, Cain! Allow me to call you brother!
Don't you ever call me that! You make me sick!
KLANK
...
I see.
So that's what Oscar wanted...
HMM?
IS THIS THE PICTURE OSCAR WAS TALKING ABOUT?

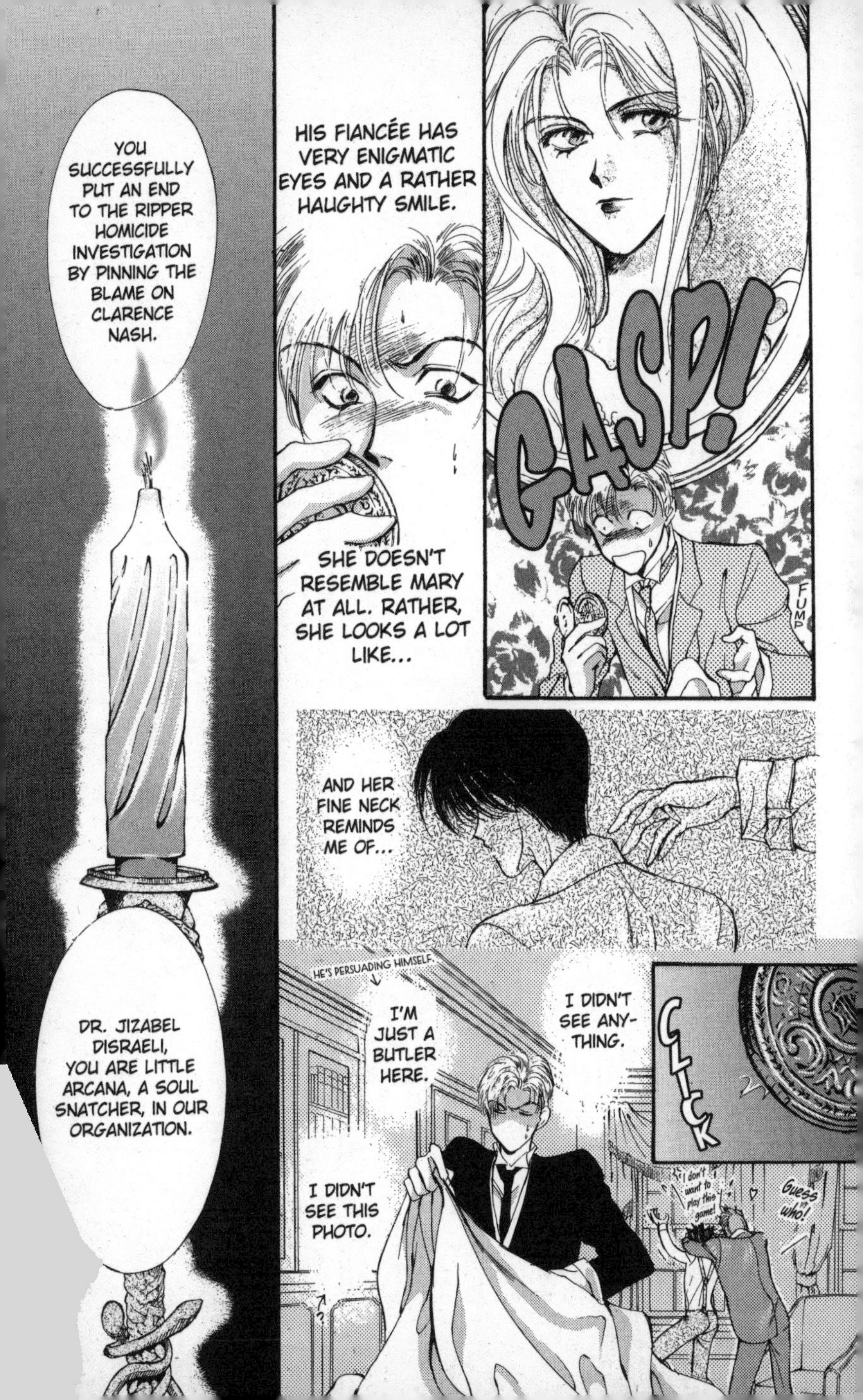
GASP!
FUMP
HIS FIANCÉE HAS VERY ENIGMATIC EYES AND A RATHER HAUGHTY SMILE.
SHE DOESN'T RESEMBLE MARY AT ALL. RATHER, SHE LOOKS A LOT LIKE...
AND HER FINE NECK REMINDS ME OF...
CLICK
I DIDN'T SEE ANYTHING.
I'M JUST A BUTLER HERE.
HE'S PERSUADING HIMSELF.
I DIDN'T SEE THIS PHOTO.
Guess who!
I don't want to play this game!
?
YOU SUCCESSFULLY PUT AN END TO THE RIPPER HOMICIDE INVESTIGATION BY PINNING THE BLAME ON CLARENCE NASH.
DR. JIZABEL DISRAELI, YOU ARE LITTLE ARCANA, A SOUL SNATCHER, IN OUR ORGANIZATION.

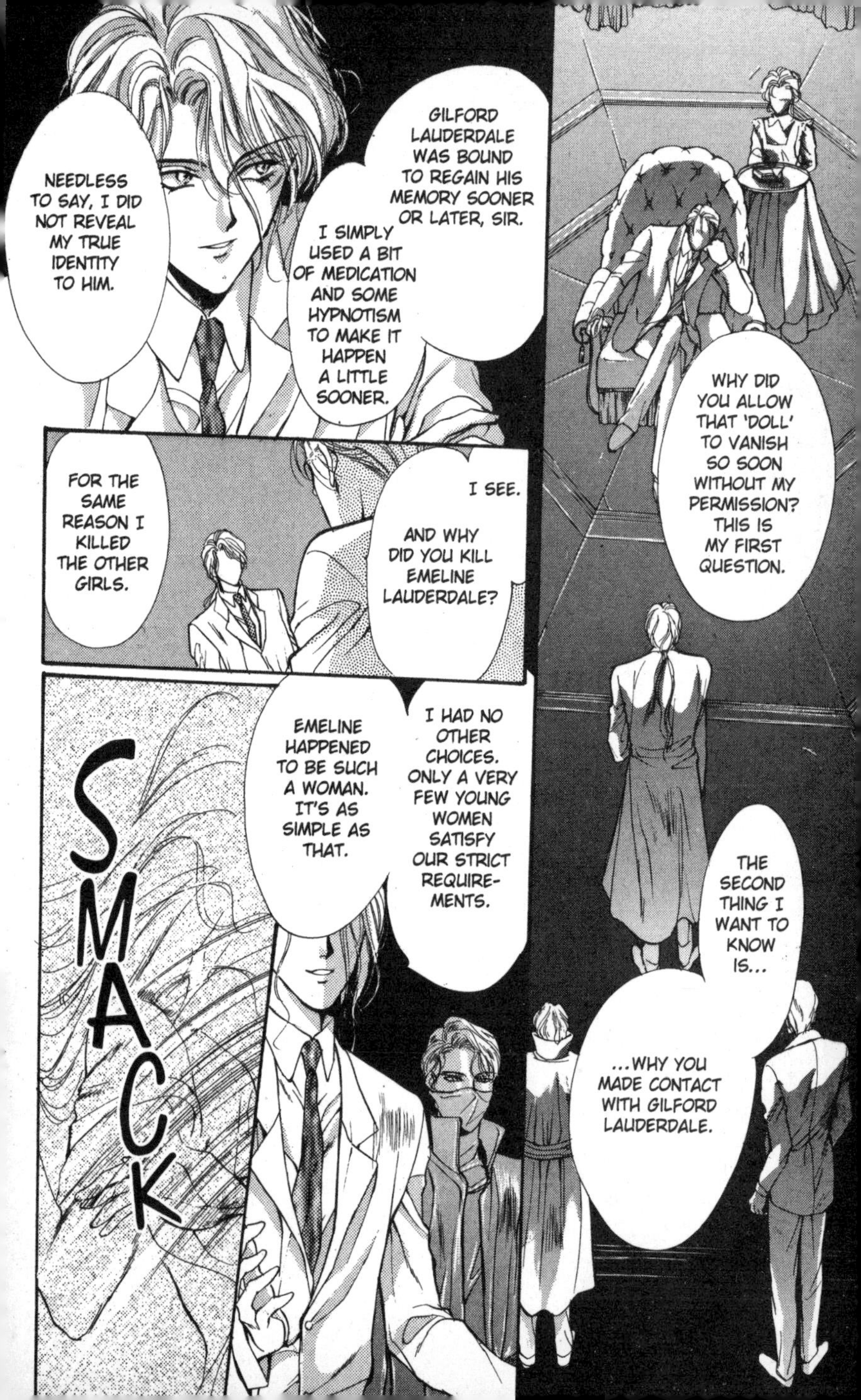
WHY DID YOU ALLOW THAT 'DOLL' TO VANISH SO SOON WITHOUT MY PERMISSION? THIS IS MY FIRST QUESTION.
THE SECOND THING I WANT TO KNOW IS...
...WHY YOU MADE CONTACT WITH GILFORD LAUDERDALE.
GILFORD LAUDERDALE WAS BOUND TO REGAIN HIS MEMORY SOONER OR LATER, SIR.
I SIMPLY USED A BIT OF MEDICATION AND SOME HYPNOTISM TO MAKE IT HAPPEN A LITTLE SOONER.
NEEDLESS TO SAY, I DID NOT REVEAL MY TRUE IDENTITY TO HIM.
I SEE.
AND WHY DID YOU KILL EMELINE LAUDERDALE?
FOR THE SAME REASON I KILLED THE OTHER GIRLS.
I HAD NO OTHER CHOICES. ONLY A VERY FEW YOUNG WOMEN SATISFY OUR STRICT REQUIRE-MENTS.
EMELINE HAPPENED TO BE SUCH A WOMAN. IT'S AS SIMPLE AS THAT.
SMACK

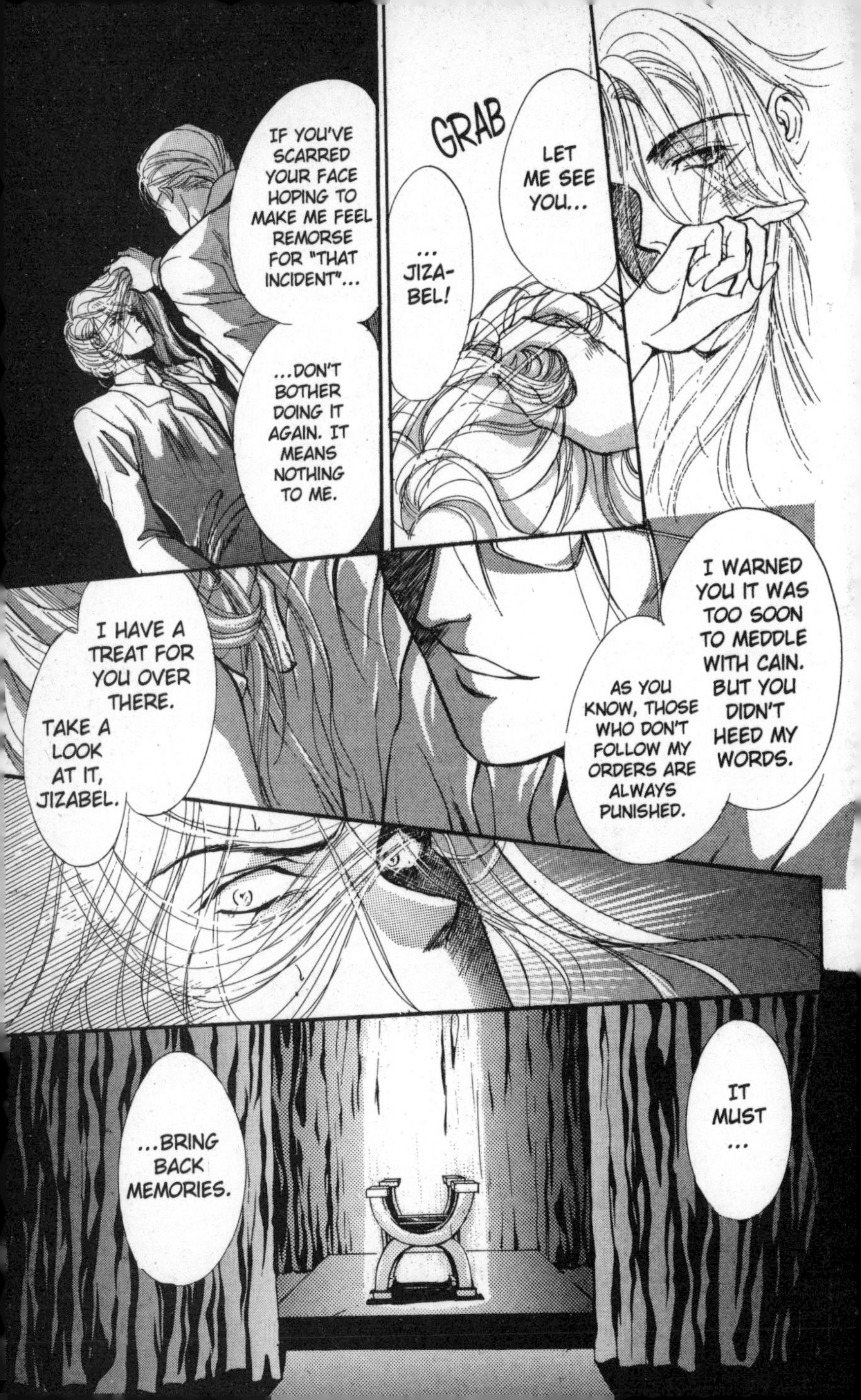
LET ME SEE YOU...
GRAB
... JIZA-BEL!
IF YOU'VE SCARRED YOUR FACE HOPING TO MAKE ME FEEL REMORSE FOR "THAT INCIDENT"...
...DON'T BOTHER DOING IT AGAIN. IT MEANS NOTHING TO ME.
I WARNED YOU IT WAS TOO SOON TO MEDDLE WITH CAIN. BUT YOU DIDN'T HEED MY WORDS.
AS YOU KNOW, THOSE WHO DON'T FOLLOW MY ORDERS ARE ALWAYS PUNISHED.
I HAVE A TREAT FOR YOU OVER THERE.
TAKE A LOOK AT IT, JIZABEL.
IT MUST ...
...BRING BACK MEMORIES.

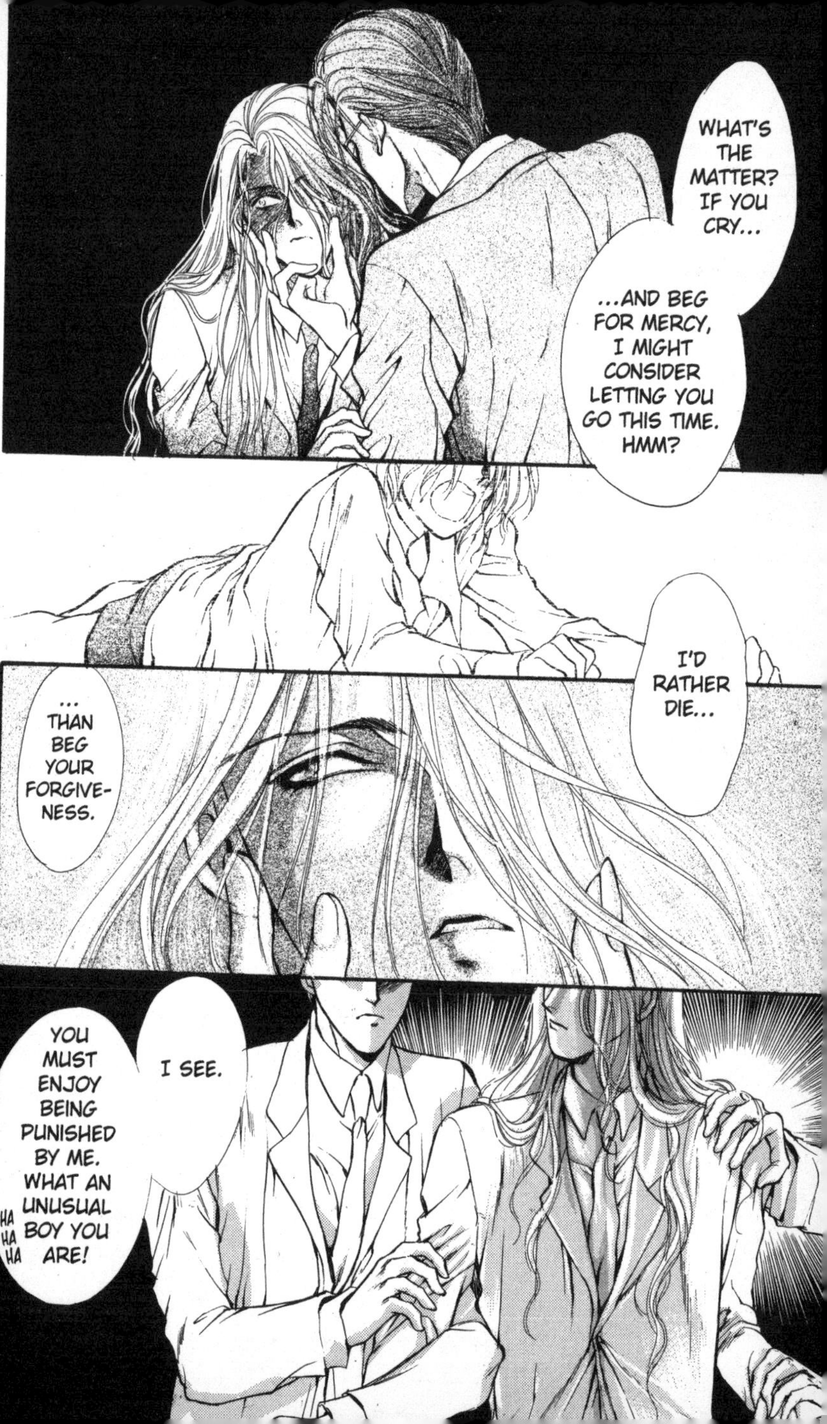
WHAT'S THE MATTER? IF YOU CRY...
...AND BEG FOR MERCY, I MIGHT CONSIDER LETTING YOU GO THIS TIME. HMM?
I'D RATHER DIE...
...THAN BEG YOUR FORGIVENESS.
I SEE.
YOU MUST ENJOY BEING PUNISHED BY ME. WHAT AN UNUSUAL BOY YOU ARE!
HA HA HA

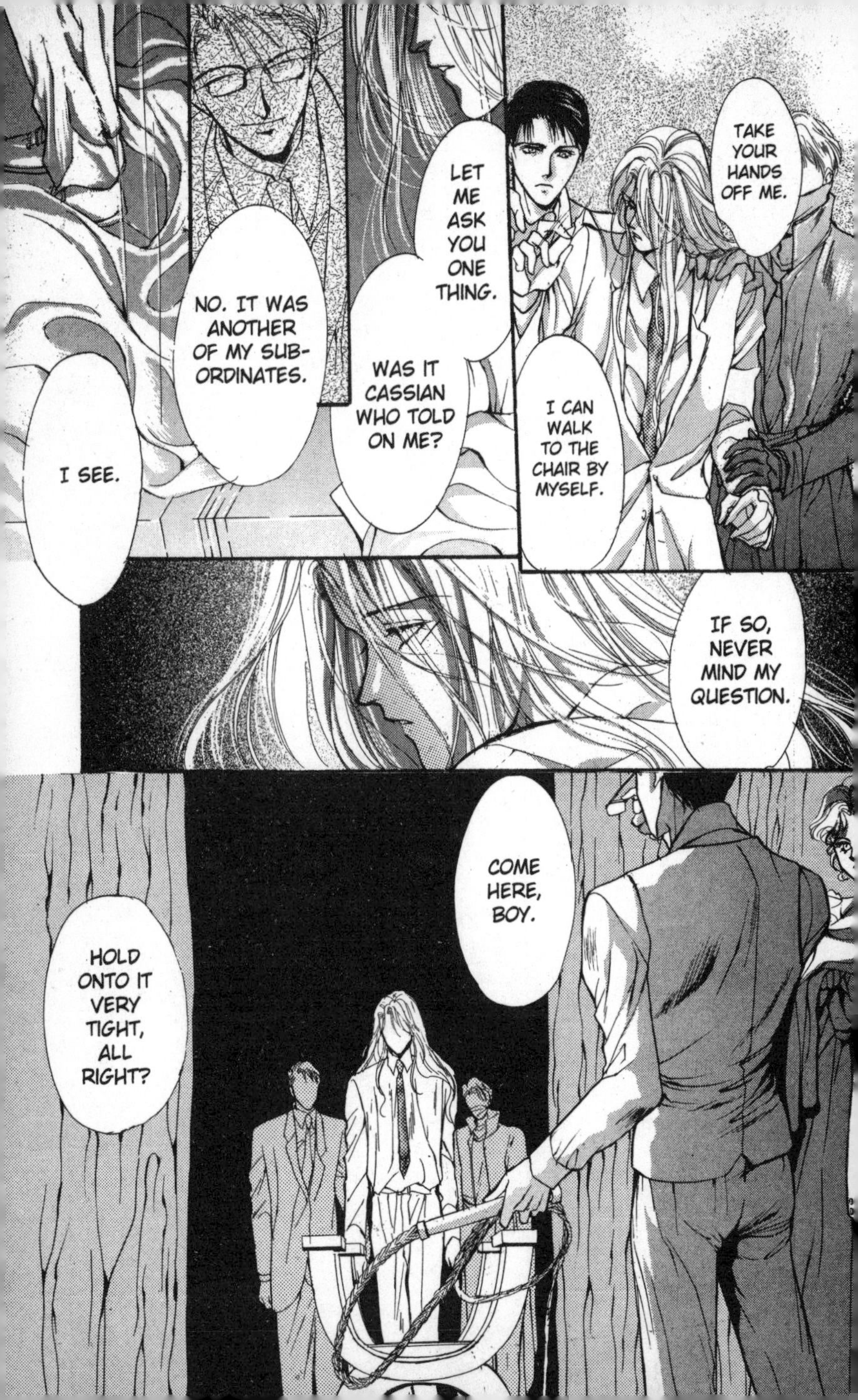
TAKE YOUR HANDS OFF ME.
I CAN WALK TO THE CHAIR BY MYSELF.
LET ME ASK YOU ONE THING.
WAS IT CASSIAN WHO TOLD ON ME?
NO. IT WAS ANOTHER OF MY SUB-ORDINATES.
I SEE.
IF SO, NEVER MIND MY QUESTION.
COME HERE, BOY.
HOLD ONTO IT VERY TIGHT, ALL RIGHT?

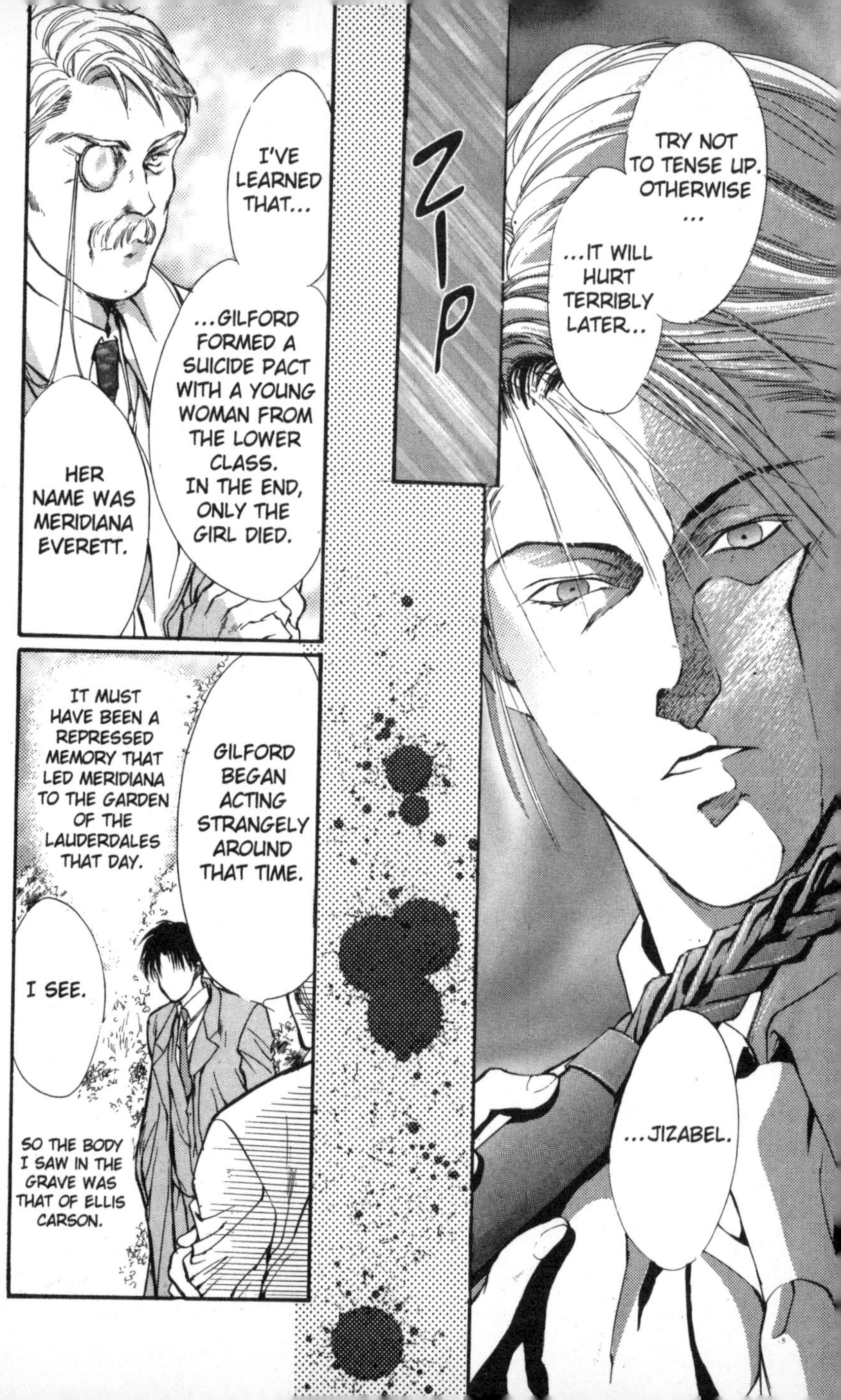
TRY NOT TO TENSE UP. OTHERWISE ...
...IT WILL HURT TERRIBLY LATER...
...JIZABEL.
ZIP
I'VE LEARNED THAT...
...GILFORD FORMED A SUICIDE PACT WITH A YOUNG WOMAN FROM THE LOWER CLASS. IN THE END, ONLY THE GIRL DIED.
HER NAME WAS MERIDIANA EVERETT.
GILFORD BEGAN ACTING STRANGELY AROUND THAT TIME.
IT MUST HAVE BEEN A REPRESSED MEMORY THAT LED MERIDIANA TO THE GARDEN OF THE LAUDERDALES THAT DAY.
I SEE.
SO THE BODY I SAW IN THE GRAVE WAS THAT OF ELLIS CARSON.

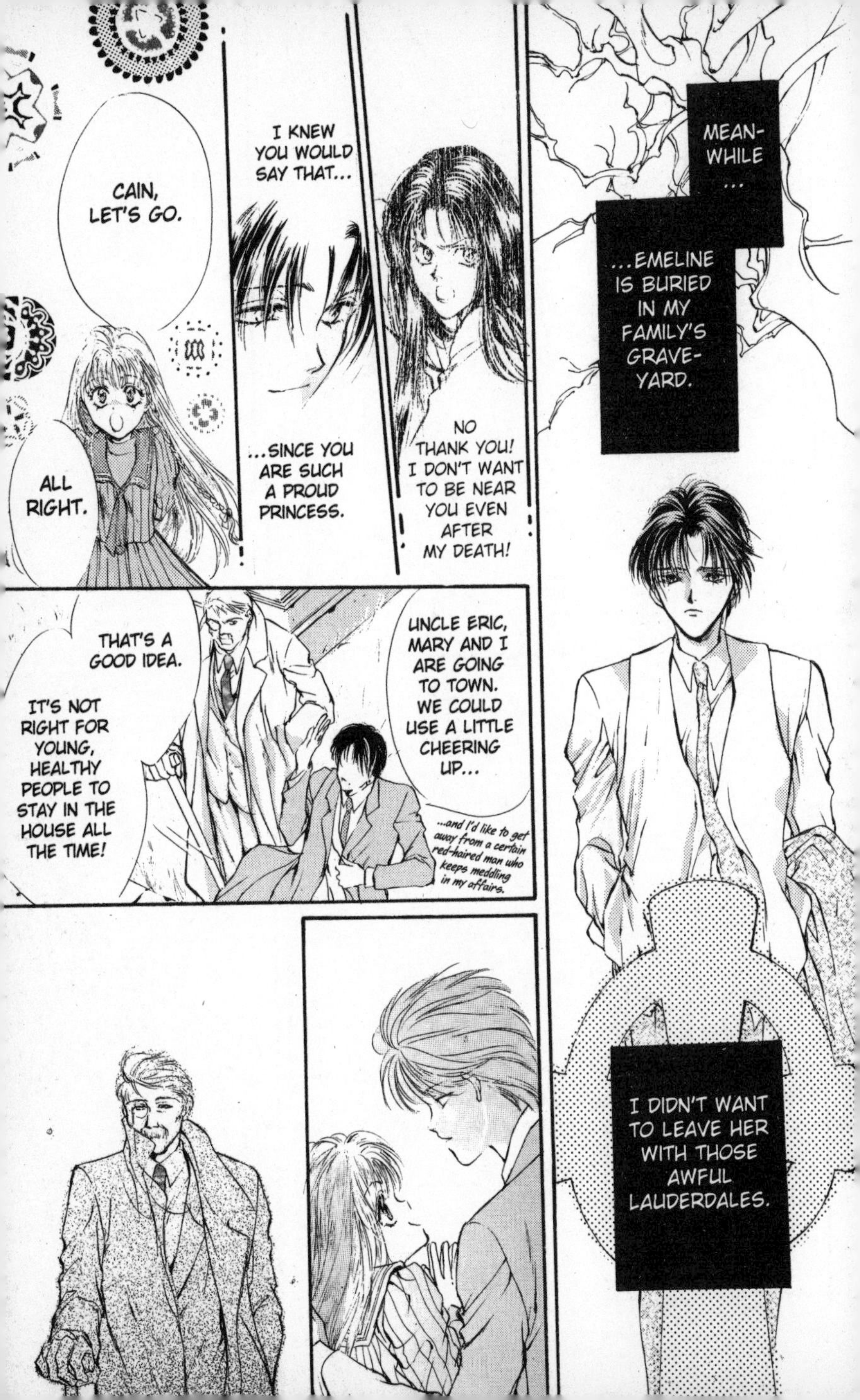
MEAN-WHILE...
...EMELINE IS BURIED IN MY FAMILY'S GRAVE-YARD.
I DIDN'T WANT TO LEAVE HER WITH THOSE AWFUL LAUDERDALES.
NO THANK YOU! I DON'T WANT TO BE NEAR YOU EVEN AFTER MY DEATH!
I KNEW YOU WOULD SAY THAT...
...SINCE YOU ARE SUCH A PROUD PRINCESS.
CAIN, LET'S GO.
ALL RIGHT.
UNCLE ERIC, MARY AND I ARE GOING TO TOWN. WE COULD USE A LITTLE CHEERING UP...
...and I'd like to get away from a certain red-haired man who keeps meddling in my affairs.
THAT'S A GOOD IDEA.
IT'S NOT RIGHT FOR YOUNG, HEALTHY PEOPLE TO STAY IN THE HOUSE ALL THE TIME!

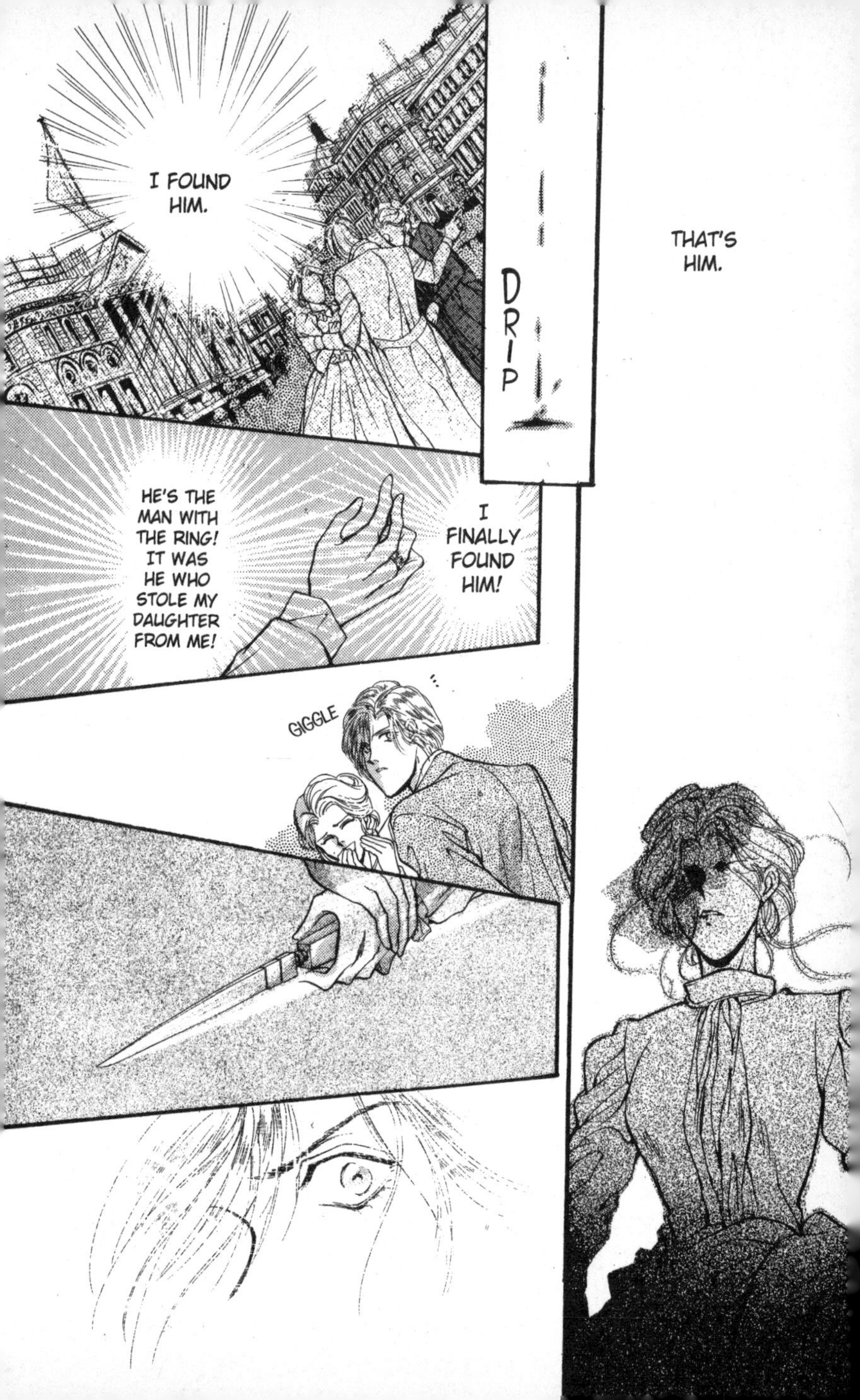
THAT'S HIM.
DRIP
I FOUND HIM.
I FINALLY FOUND HIM!
HE'S THE MAN WITH THE RING! IT WAS HE WHO STOLE MY DAUGHTER FROM ME!
GIGGLE

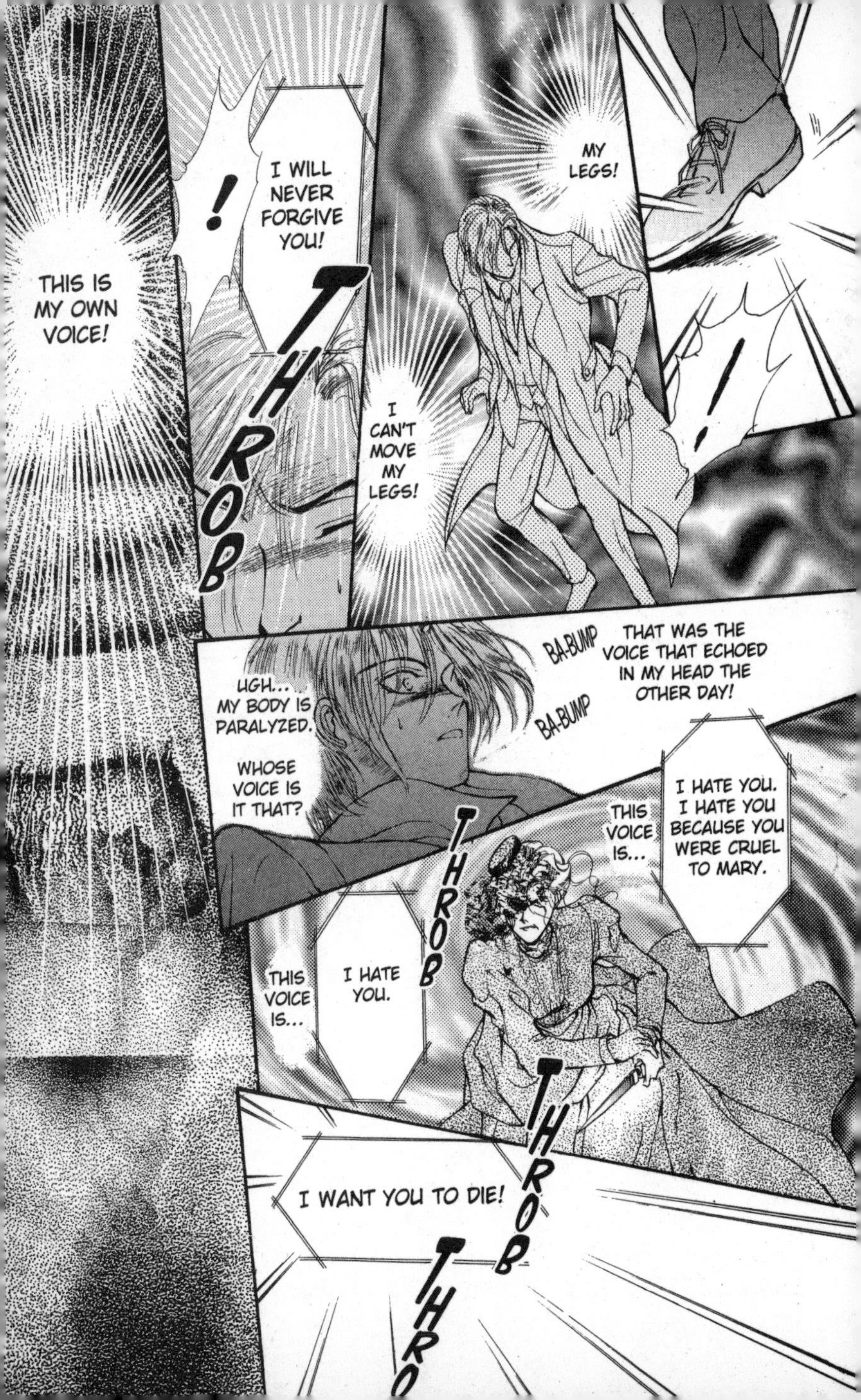

!
MY LEGS!
I CAN'T MOVE MY LEGS!
!
I WILL NEVER FORGIVE YOU!
THROB
BA-BUMP
THAT WAS THE VOICE THAT ECHOED IN MY HEAD THE OTHER DAY!
BA-BUMP
UGH... MY BODY IS PARALYZED.
WHOSE VOICE IS IT THAT?
I HATE YOU. I HATE YOU BECAUSE YOU WERE CRUEL TO MARY.
THIS VOICE IS...
THROB
I HATE YOU.
THIS VOICE IS...
THROB
I WANT YOU TO DIE!
THRO
THIS IS MY OWN VOICE!

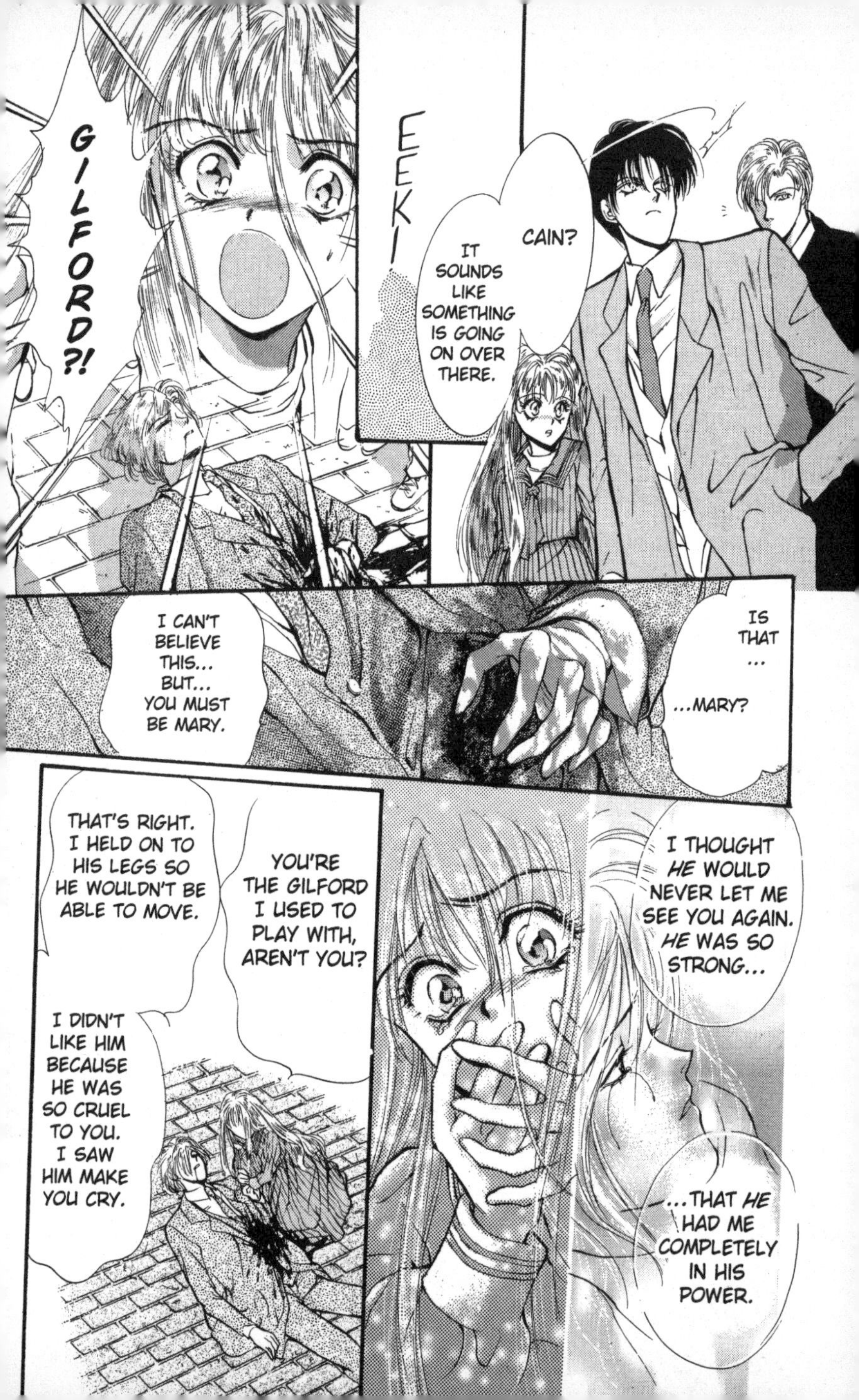
CAIN?
IT SOUNDS LIKE SOMETHING IS GOING ON OVER THERE.
EEK!
GILFORD?!
IS THAT ... ...MARY?
I CAN'T BELIEVE THIS... BUT... YOU MUST BE MARY.
I THOUGHT HE WOULD NEVER LET ME SEE YOU AGAIN. HE WAS SO STRONG...
...THAT HE HAD ME COMPLETELY IN HIS POWER.
YOU'RE THE GILFORD I USED TO PLAY WITH, AREN'T YOU?
THAT'S RIGHT. I HELD ON TO HIS LEGS SO HE WOULDN'T BE ABLE TO MOVE.
I DIDN'T LIKE HIM BECAUSE HE WAS SO CRUEL TO YOU. I SAW HIM MAKE YOU CRY.

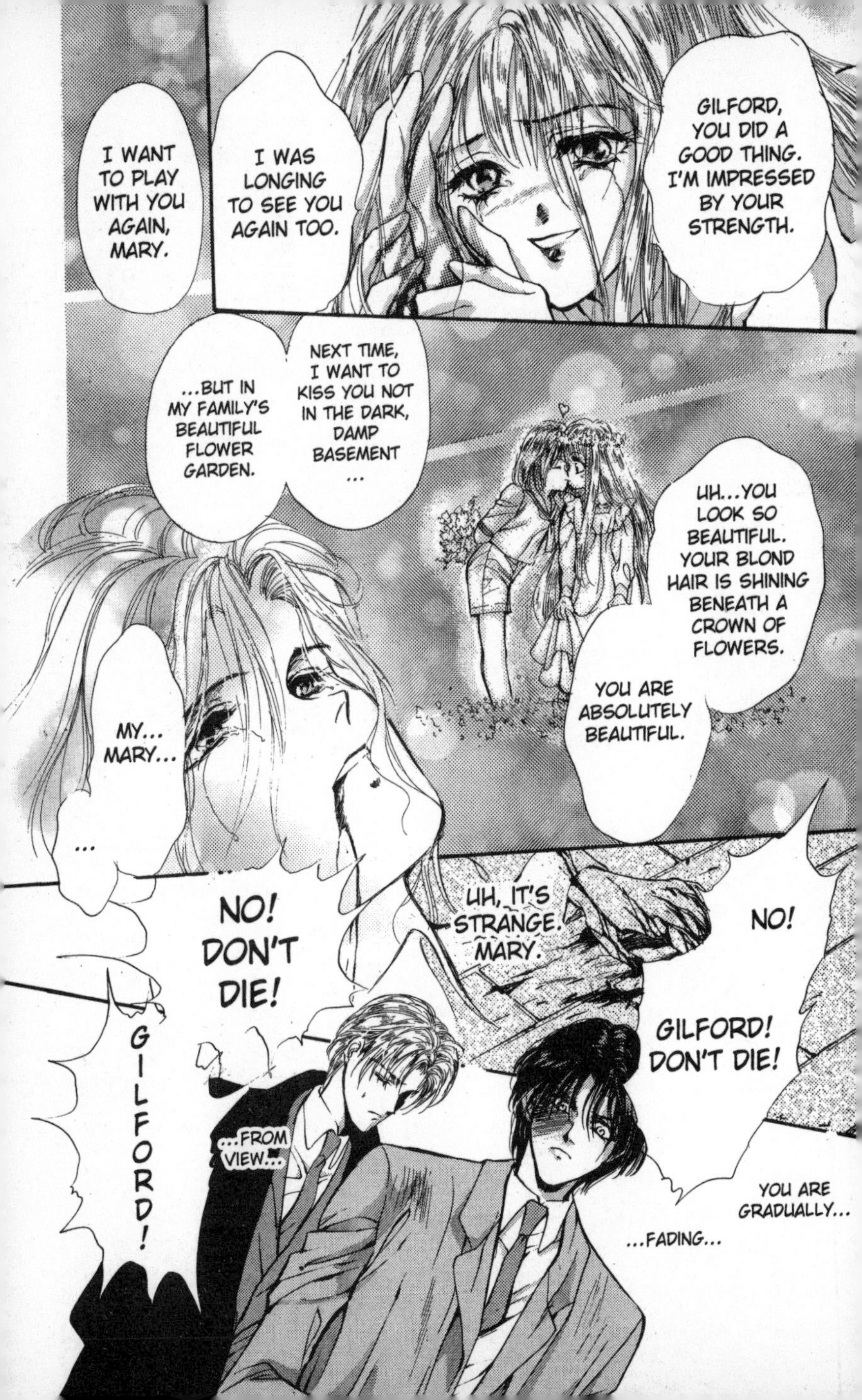
GILFORD, YOU DID A GOOD THING. I'M IMPRESSED BY YOUR STRENGTH.
I WAS LONGING TO SEE YOU AGAIN TOO.
I WANT TO PLAY WITH YOU AGAIN, MARY.
UH...YOU LOOK SO BEAUTIFUL. YOUR BLOND HAIR IS SHINING BENEATH A CROWN OF FLOWERS.
YOU ARE ABSOLUTELY BEAUTIFUL.
NEXT TIME, I WANT TO KISS YOU NOT IN THE DARK, DAMP BASEMENT ...
...BUT IN MY FAMILY'S BEAUTIFUL FLOWER GARDEN.
MY... MARY...
...
NO!
UH, IT'S STRANGE. MARY.
NO! DON'T DIE!
GILFORD! DON'T DIE!
YOU ARE GRADUALLY...
...FADING...
...FROM VIEW...
GILFORD!

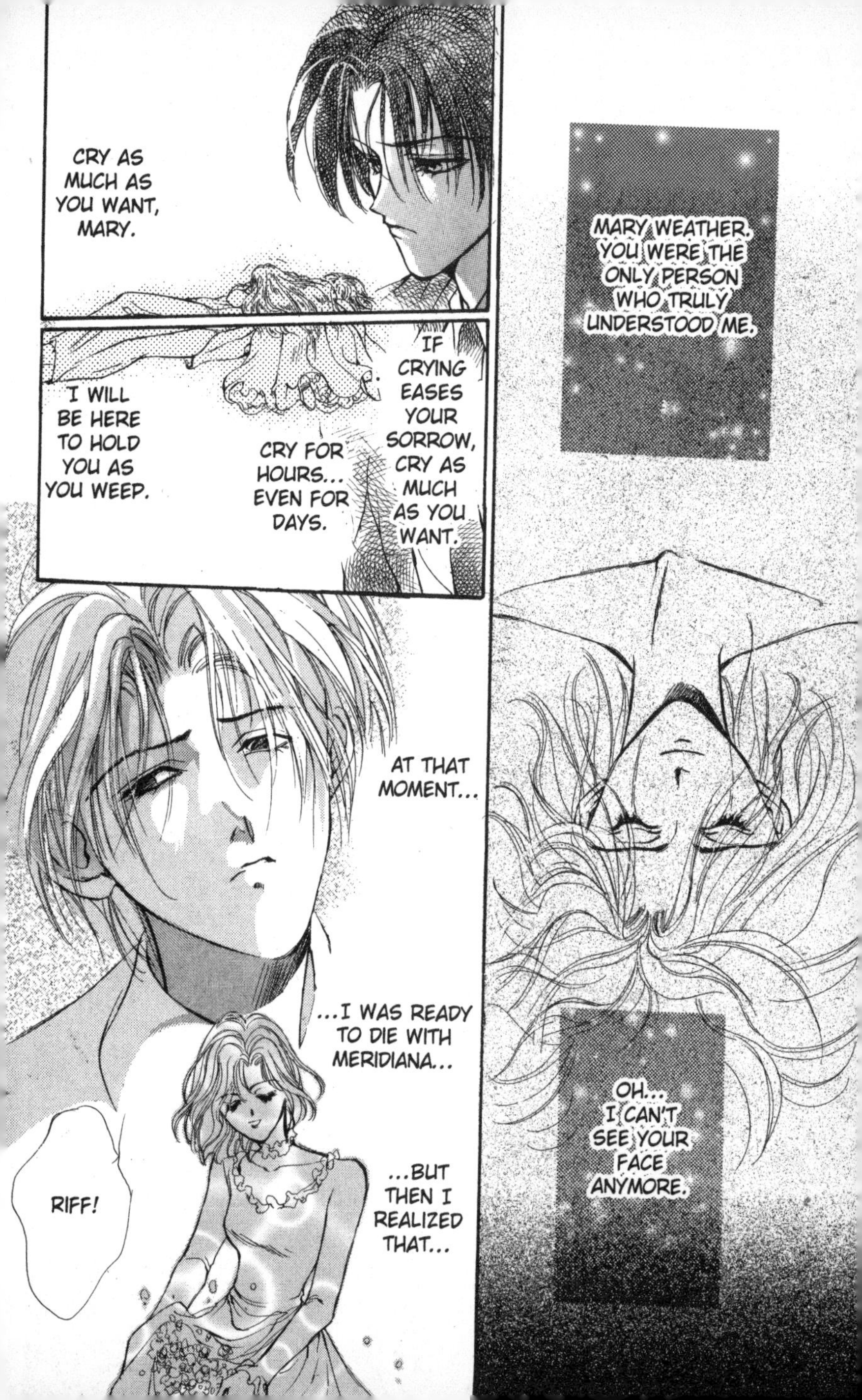
MARY WEATHER. YOU WERE THE ONLY PERSON WHO TRULY UNDERSTOOD ME.
OH... I CAN'T SEE YOUR FACE ANYMORE.
CRY AS MUCH AS YOU WANT, MARY.
IF CRYING EASES YOUR SORROW, CRY AS MUCH AS YOU WANT.
CRY FOR HOURS... EVEN FOR DAYS.
I WILL BE HERE TO HOLD YOU AS YOU WEEP.
AT THAT MOMENT...
...I WAS READY TO DIE WITH MERIDIANA...
...BUT THEN I REALIZED THAT...
RIFF!

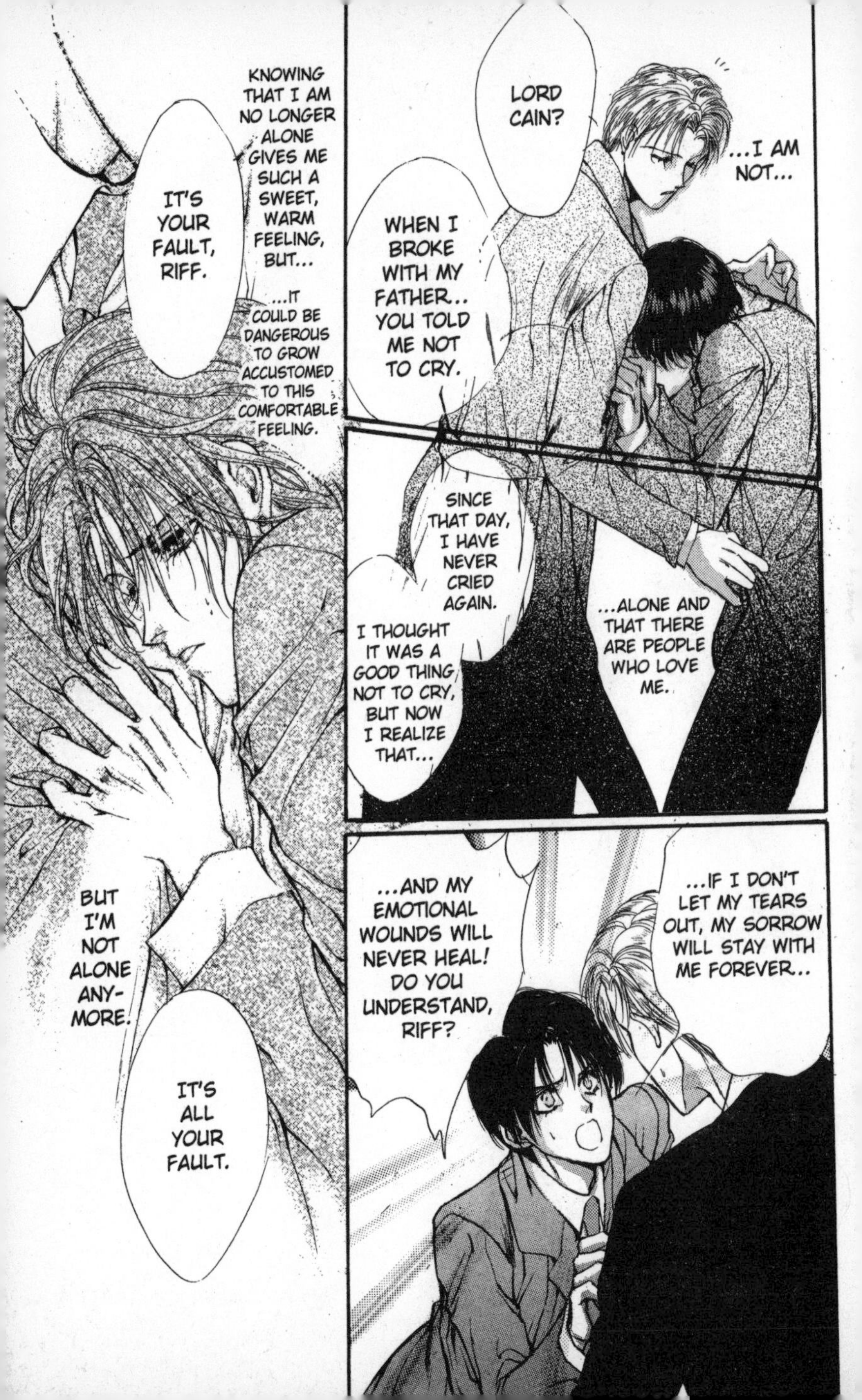
...I AM NOT...
LORD CAIN?
WHEN I BROKE WITH MY FATHER.. YOU TOLD ME NOT TO CRY.
...ALONE AND THAT THERE ARE PEOPLE WHO LOVE ME.
SINCE THAT DAY, I HAVE NEVER CRIED AGAIN.
I THOUGHT IT WAS A GOOD THING NOT TO CRY, BUT NOW I REALIZE THAT...
...IF I DON'T LET MY TEARS OUT, MY SORROW WILL STAY WITH ME FOREVER...
...AND MY EMOTIONAL WOUNDS WILL NEVER HEAL! DO YOU UNDERSTAND, RIFF?
KNOWING THAT I AM NO LONGER ALONE GIVES ME SUCH A SWEET, WARM FEELING, BUT...
IT'S YOUR FAULT, RIFF.
...IT COULD BE DANGEROUS TO GROW ACCUSTOMED TO THIS COMFORTABLE FEELING.
BUT I'M NOT ALONE ANY-MORE.
IT'S ALL YOUR FAULT.

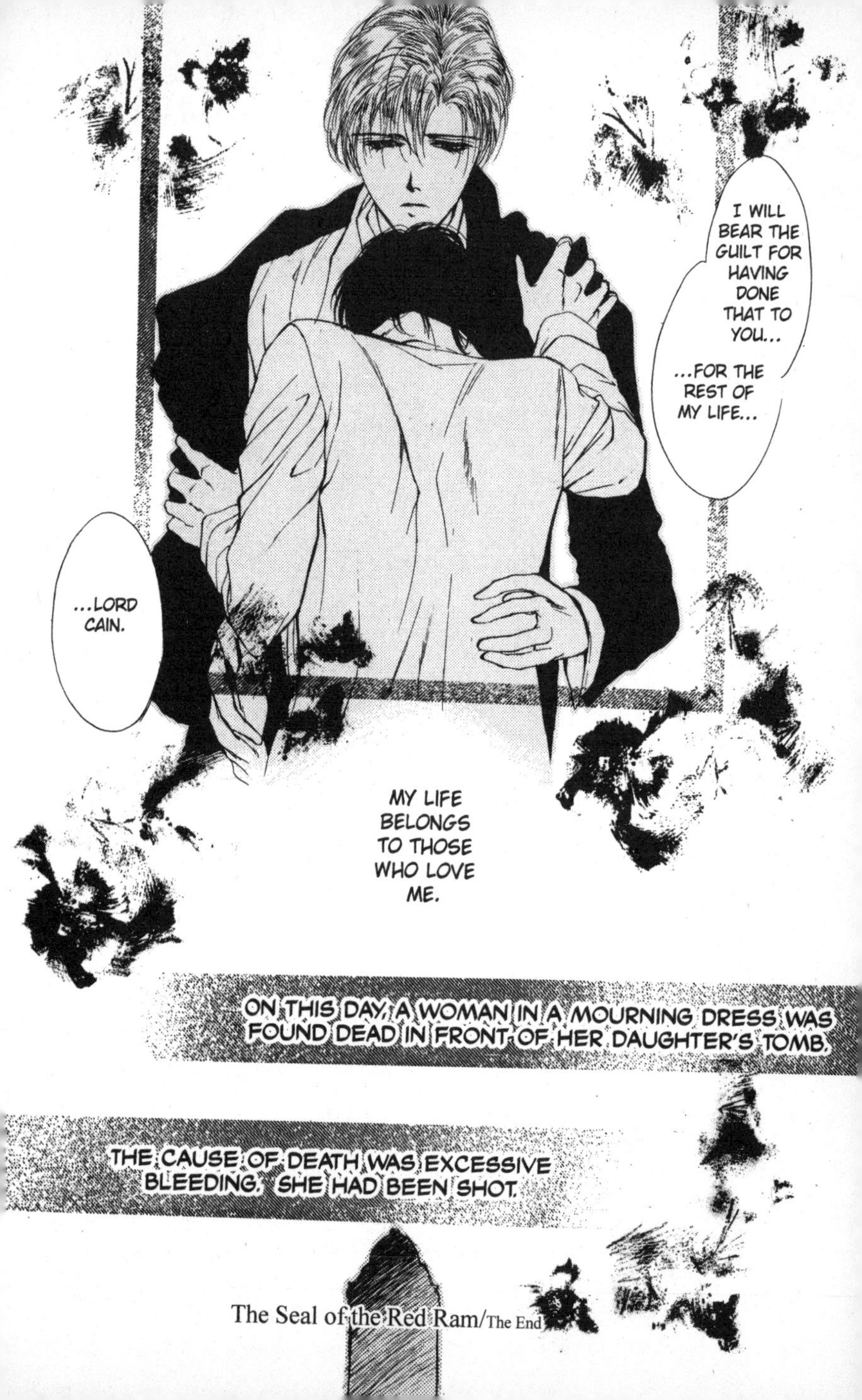
I WILL BEAR THE GUILT FOR HAVING DONE THAT TO YOU...
...FOR THE REST OF MY LIFE...
...LORD CAIN.
MY LIFE BELONGS TO THOSE WHO LOVE ME.
ON THIS DAY, A WOMAN IN A MOURNING DRESS WAS FOUND DEAD IN FRONT OF HER DAUGHTER'S TOMB.
THE CAUSE OF DEATH WAS EXCESSIVE BLEEDING. SHE HAD BEEN SHOT.
The Seal of the Red Ram/The End

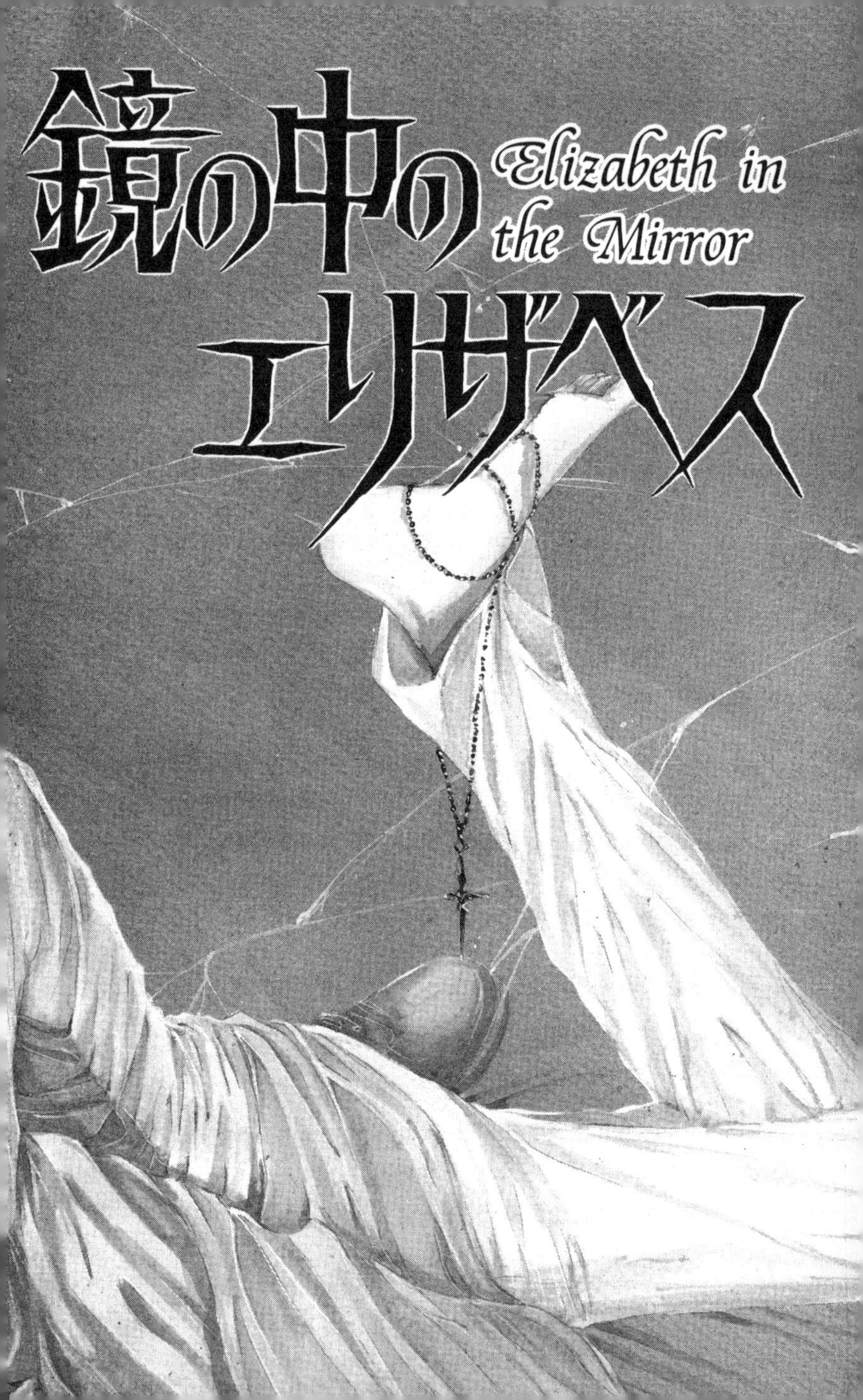
鏡の中のエリザベス
Elizabeth in the Mirror

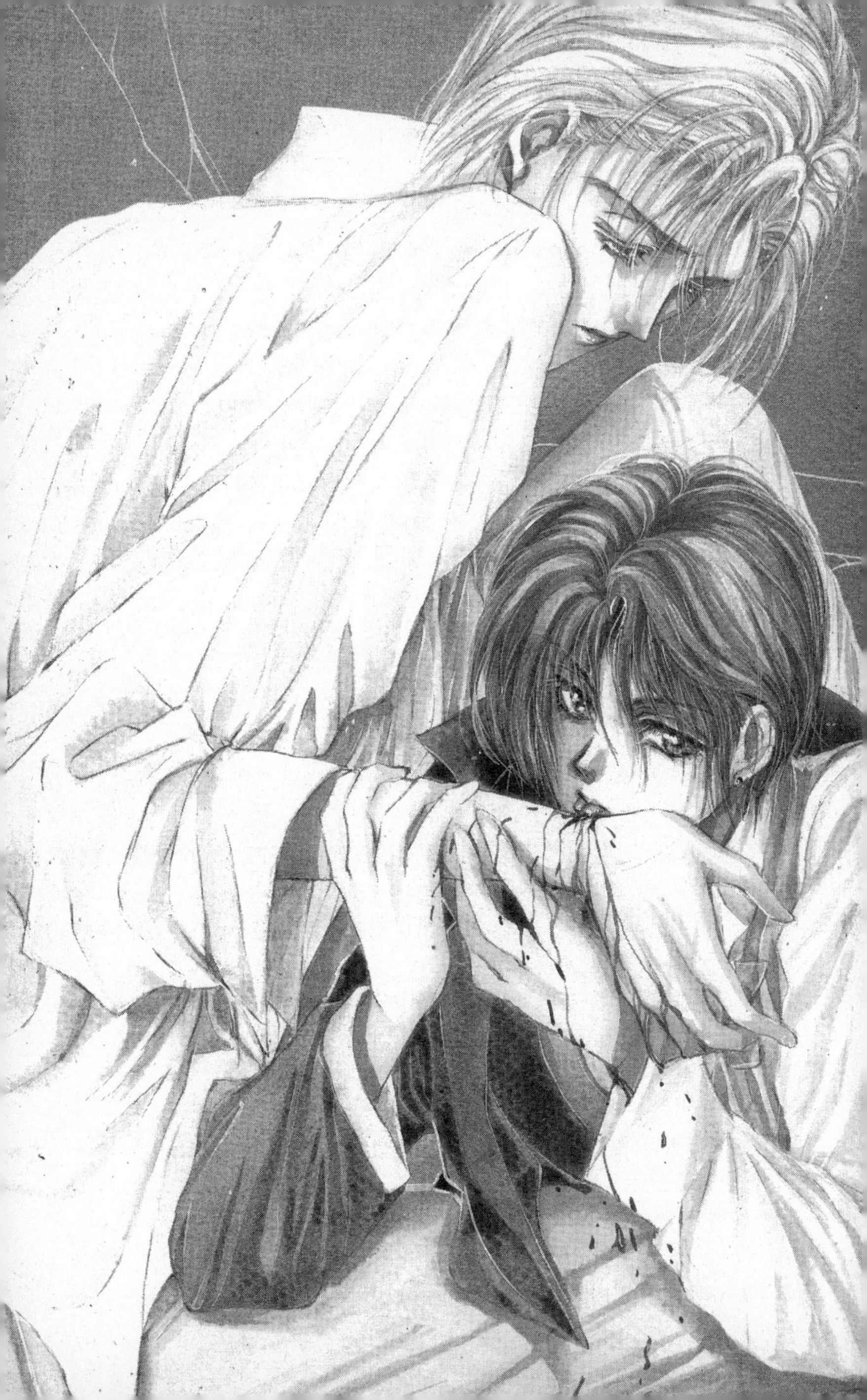

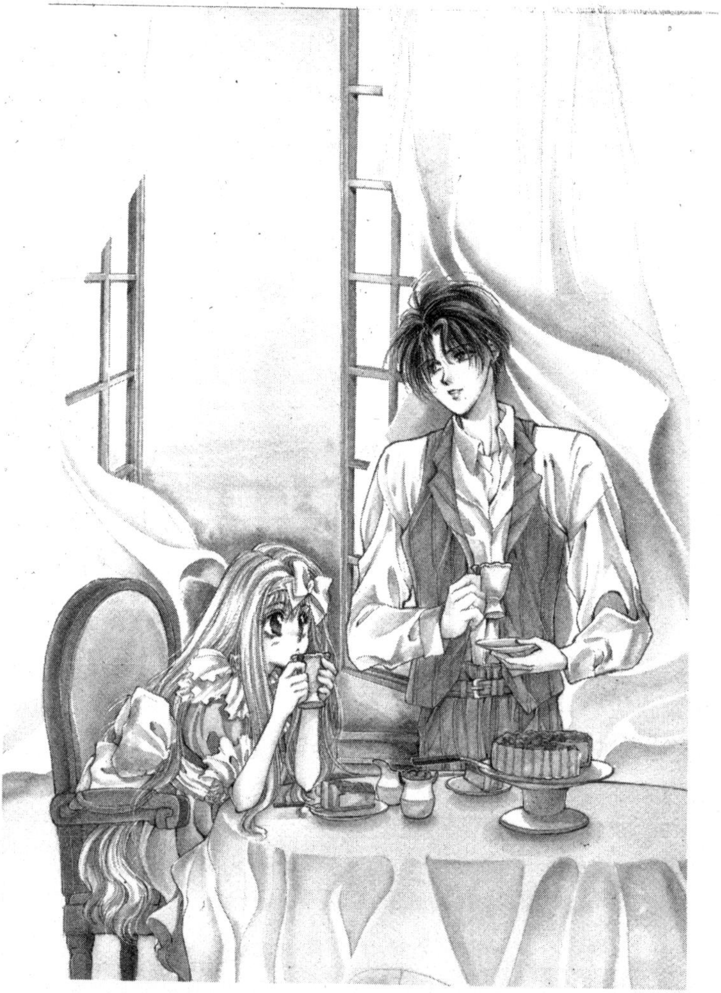

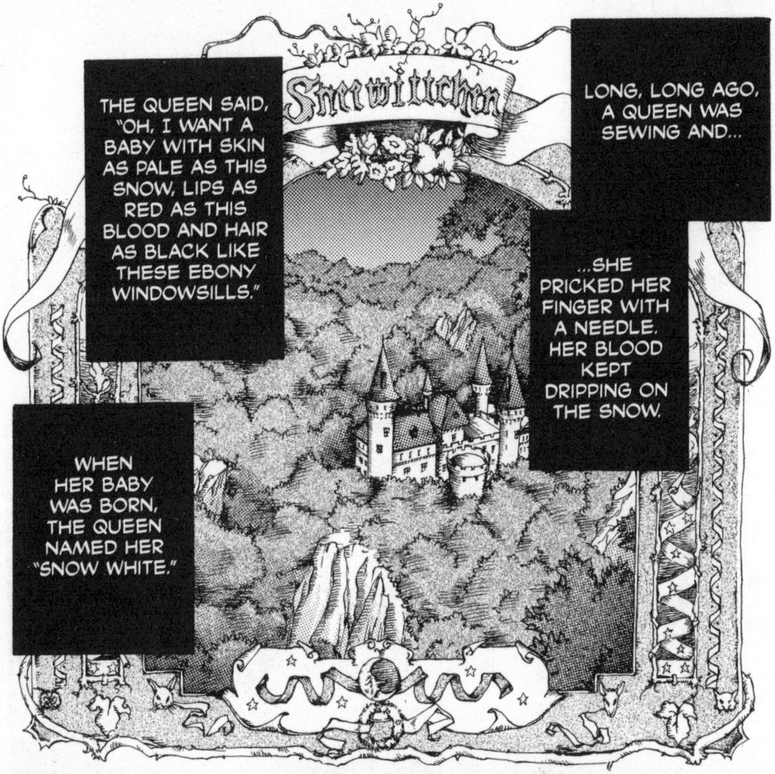
Sneewittchen
LONG, LONG AGO, A QUEEN WAS SEWING AND...
...SHE PRICKED HER FINGER WITH A NEEDLE. HER BLOOD KEPT DRIPPING ON THE SNOW.
THE QUEEN SAID, "OH, I WANT A BABY WITH SKIN AS PALE AS THIS SNOW, LIPS AS RED AS THIS BLOOD AND HAIR AS BLACK LIKE THESE EBONY WINDOWSILLS."
WHEN HER BABY WAS BORN, THE QUEEN NAMED HER "SNOW WHITE."

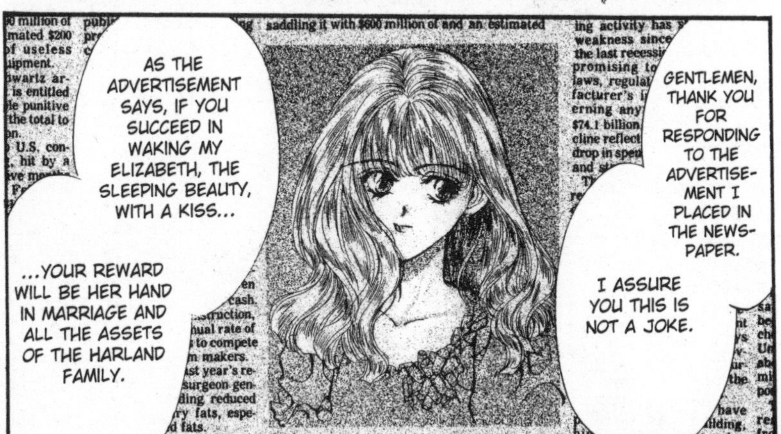
GENTLEMEN, THANK YOU FOR RESPONDING TO THE ADVERTISE-MENT I PLACED IN THE NEWS-PAPER.
I ASSURE YOU THIS IS NOT A JOKE.
AS THE ADVERTISEMENT SAYS, IF YOU SUCCEED IN WAKING MY ELIZABETH, THE SLEEPING BEAUTY, WITH A KISS...
...YOUR REWARD WILL BE HER HAND IN MARRIAGE AND ALL THE ASSETS OF THE HARLAND FAMILY.
saddling it with $600 million of and an estimated
Girl receives transplant

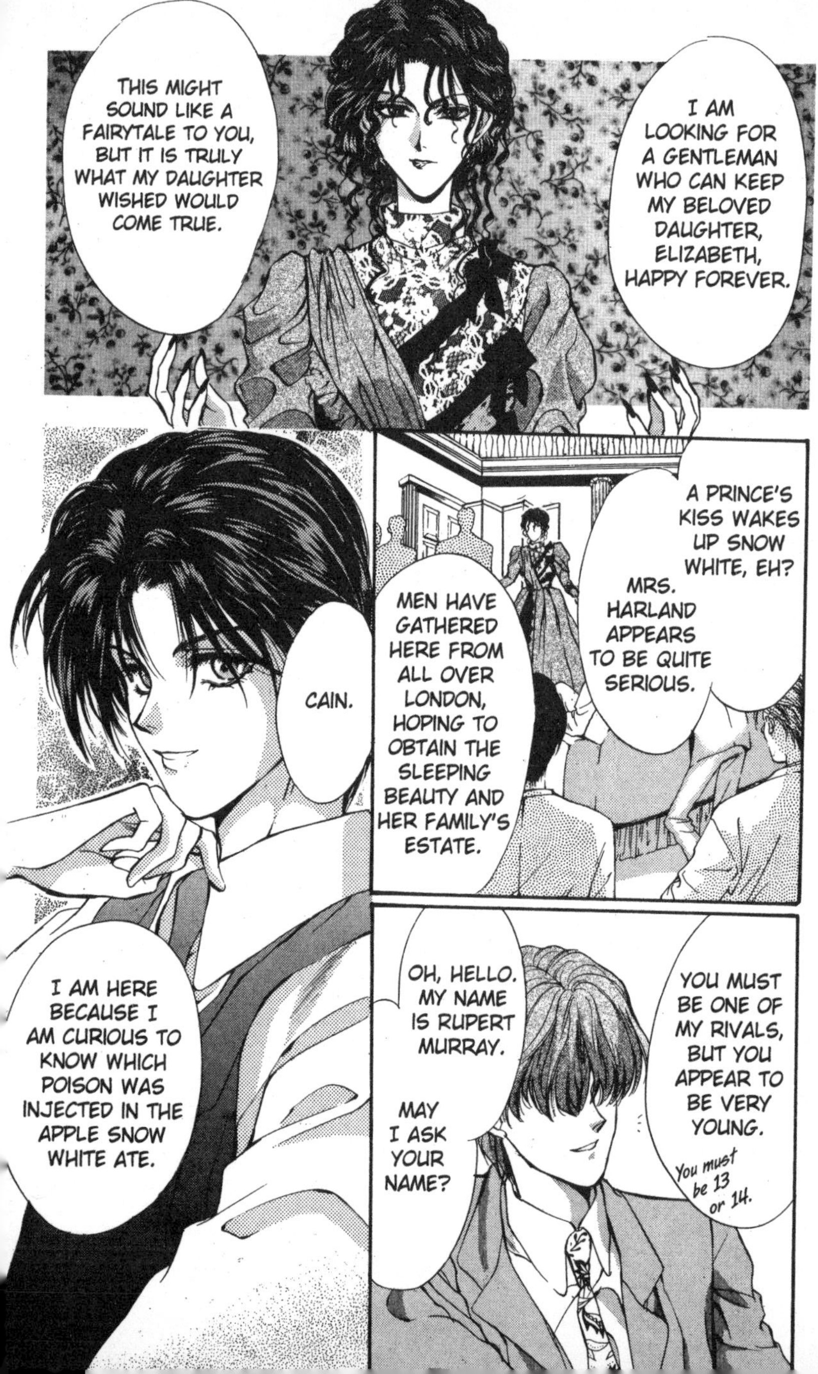
I AM LOOKING FOR A GENTLEMAN WHO CAN KEEP MY BELOVED DAUGHTER, ELIZABETH, HAPPY FOREVER.
THIS MIGHT SOUND LIKE A FAIRYTALE TO YOU, BUT IT IS TRULY WHAT MY DAUGHTER WISHED WOULD COME TRUE.
A PRINCE'S KISS WAKES UP SNOW WHITE, EH?
MRS. HARLAND APPEARS TO BE QUITE SERIOUS.
MEN HAVE GATHERED HERE FROM ALL OVER LONDON, HOPING TO OBTAIN THE SLEEPING BEAUTY AND HER FAMILY'S ESTATE.
YOU MUST BE ONE OF MY RIVALS, BUT YOU APPEAR TO BE VERY YOUNG.
You must be 13 or 14.
OH, HELLO. MY NAME IS RUPERT MURRAY.
MAY I ASK YOUR NAME?
CAIN.
I AM HERE BECAUSE I AM CURIOUS TO KNOW WHICH POISON WAS INJECTED IN THE APPLE SNOW WHITE ATE.

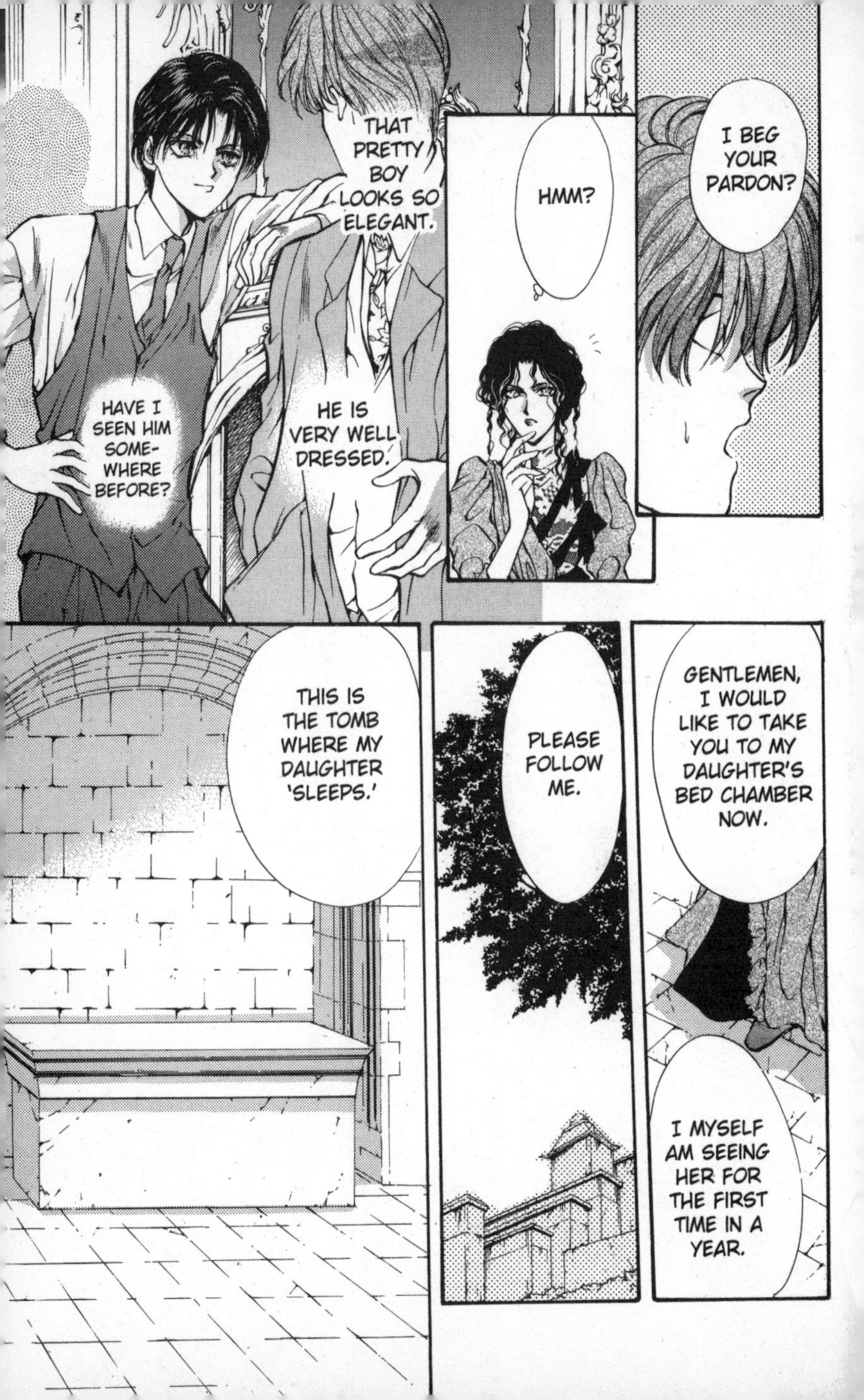
I BEG YOUR PARDON?
HMM?
THAT PRETTY BOY LOOKS SO ELEGANT.
HE IS VERY WELL DRESSED.
HAVE I SEEN HIM SOME-WHERE BEFORE?
GENTLEMEN, I WOULD LIKE TO TAKE YOU TO MY DAUGHTER'S BED CHAMBER NOW.
I MYSELF AM SEEING HER FOR THE FIRST TIME IN A YEAR.
PLEASE FOLLOW ME.
THIS IS THE TOMB WHERE MY DAUGHTER 'SLEEPS.'

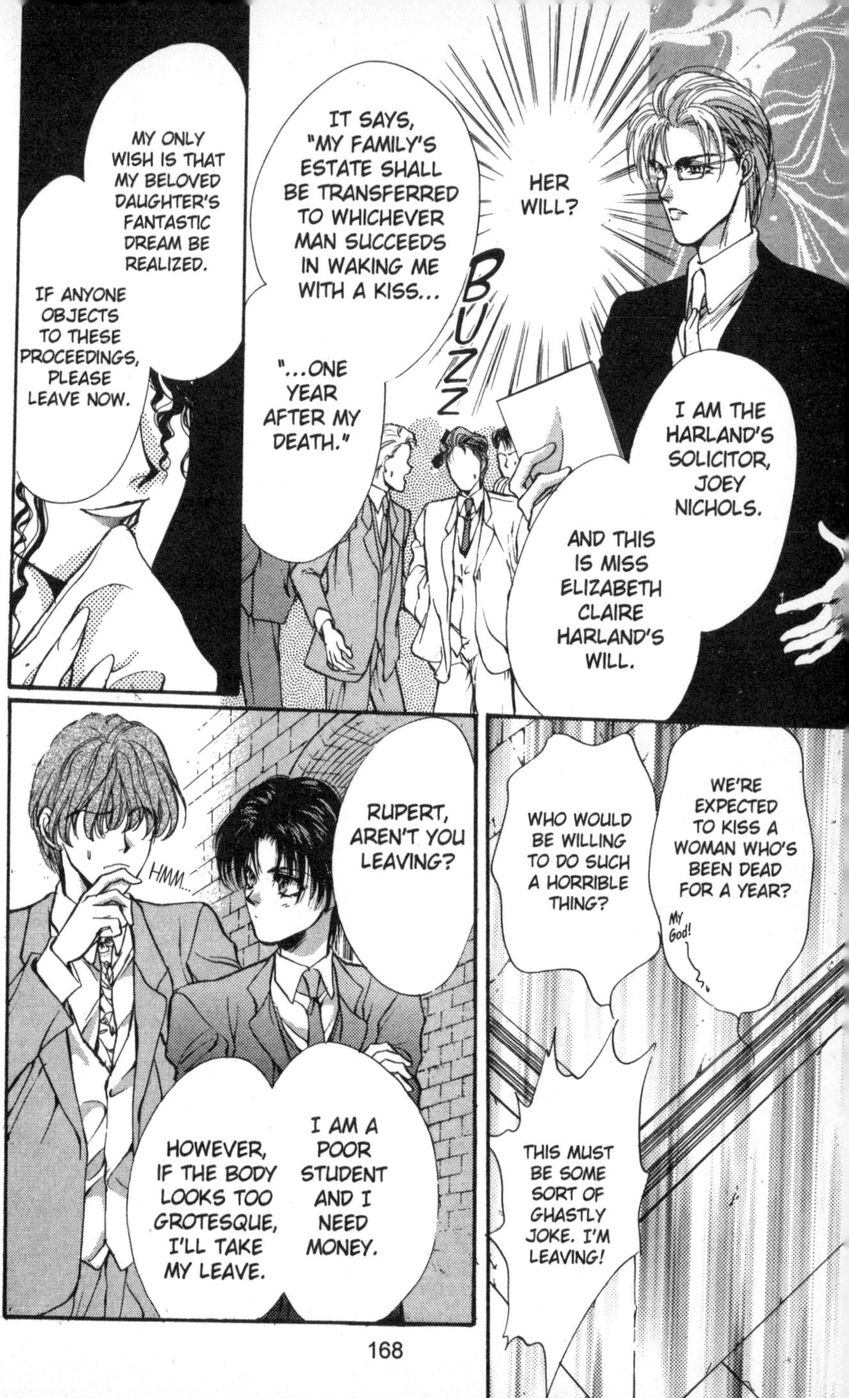
I AM THE HARLAND'S SOLICITOR, JOEY NICHOLS.
AND THIS IS MISS ELIZABETH CLAIRE HARLAND'S WILL.
HER WILL?
BUZZ
IT SAYS, "MY FAMILY'S ESTATE SHALL BE TRANSFERRED TO WHICHEVER MAN SUCCEEDS IN WAKING ME WITH A KISS...
"...ONE YEAR AFTER MY DEATH."
MY ONLY WISH IS THAT MY BELOVED DAUGHTER'S FANTASTIC DREAM BE REALIZED.
IF ANYONE OBJECTS TO THESE PROCEEDINGS, PLEASE LEAVE NOW.
WE'RE EXPECTED TO KISS A WOMAN WHO'S BEEN DEAD FOR A YEAR?
My God!
WHO WOULD BE WILLING TO DO SUCH A HORRIBLE THING?
THIS MUST BE SOME SORT OF GHASTLY JOKE. I'M LEAVING!
RUPERT, AREN'T YOU LEAVING?
HMM...
I AM A POOR STUDENT AND I NEED MONEY.
HOWEVER, IF THE BODY LOOKS TOO GROTESQUE, I'LL TAKE MY LEAVE.

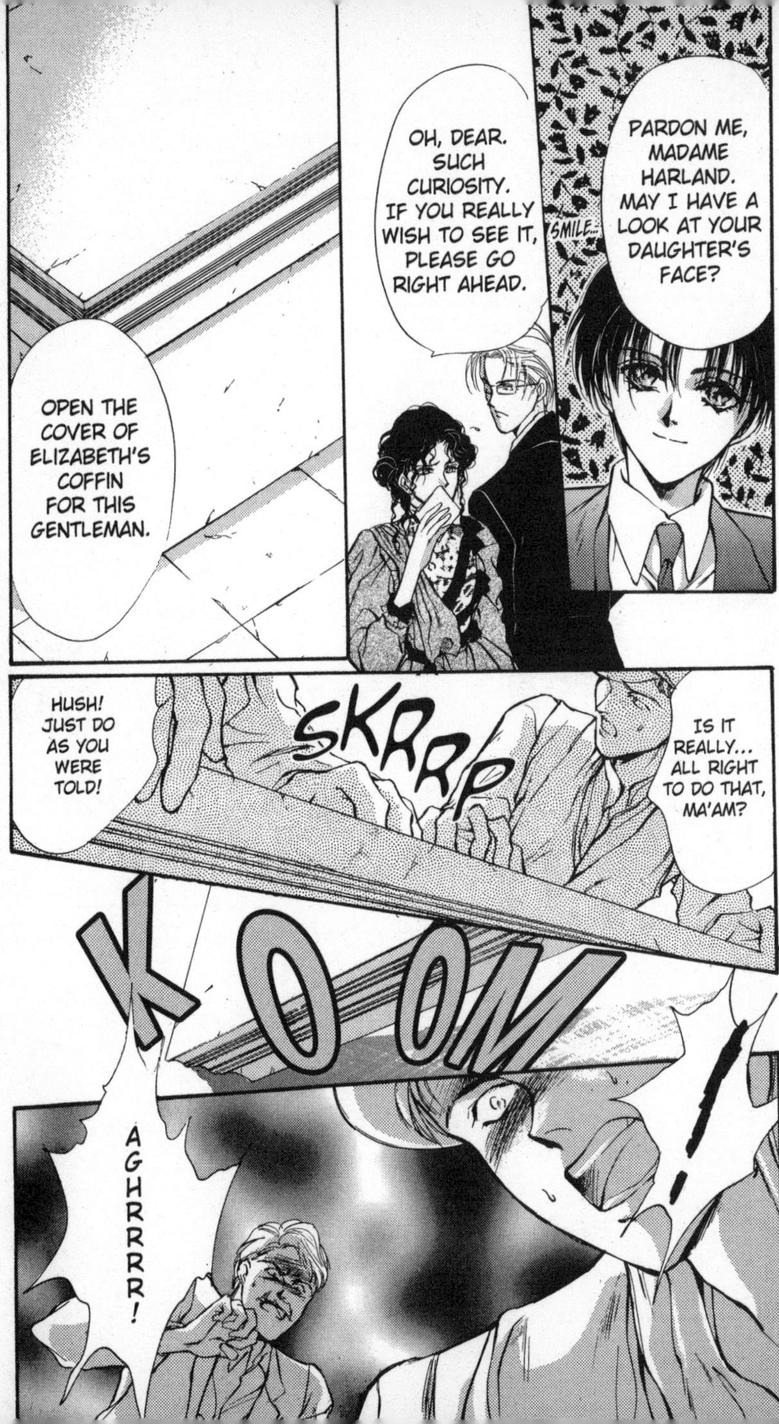
PARDON ME, MADAME HARLAND. MAY I HAVE A LOOK AT YOUR DAUGHTER'S FACE?
SMILE...
OH, DEAR. SUCH CURIOSITY. IF YOU REALLY WISH TO SEE IT, PLEASE GO RIGHT AHEAD.
OPEN THE COVER OF ELIZABETH'S COFFIN FOR THIS GENTLEMAN.
IS IT REALLY... ALL RIGHT TO DO THAT, MA'AM?
HUSH! JUST DO AS YOU WERE TOLD!
SKRRP
KOOM
!
AGHRRRR!

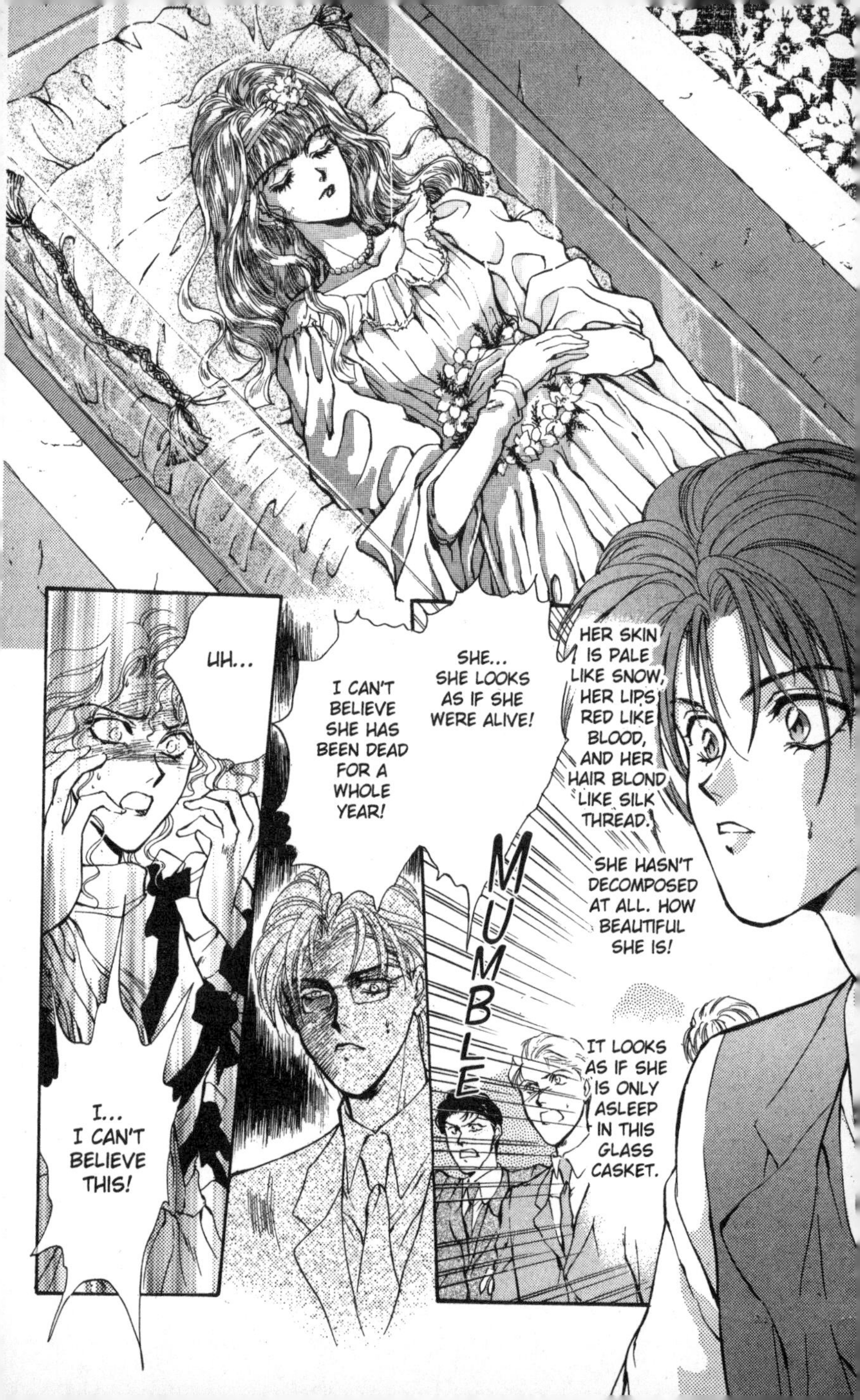
HER SKIN IS PALE LIKE SNOW, HER LIPS RED LIKE BLOOD, AND HER HAIR BLOND LIKE SILK THREAD.
SHE HASN'T DECOMPOSED AT ALL. HOW BEAUTIFUL SHE IS!
IT LOOKS AS IF SHE IS ONLY ASLEEP IN THIS GLASS CASKET.
SHE... SHE LOOKS AS IF SHE WERE ALIVE!
I CAN'T BELIEVE SHE HAS BEEN DEAD FOR A WHOLE YEAR!
MUMBLE
UH...
I... I CAN'T BELIEVE THIS!

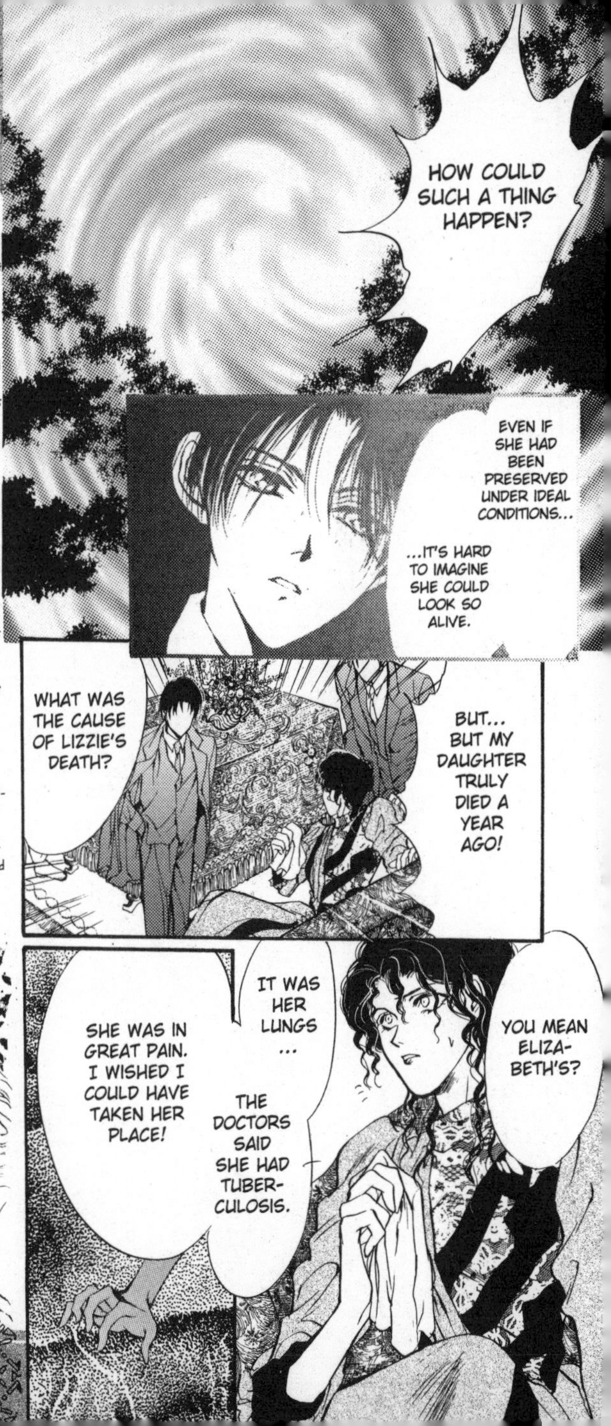
HOW COULD SUCH A THING HAPPEN?
EVEN IF SHE HAD BEEN PRESERVED UNDER IDEAL CONDITIONS...
...IT'S HARD TO IMAGINE SHE COULD LOOK SO ALIVE.
BUT... BUT MY DAUGHTER TRULY DIED A YEAR AGO!
WHAT WAS THE CAUSE OF LIZZIE'S DEATH?
YOU MEAN ELIZA-BETH'S?
IT WAS HER LUNGS...
THE DOCTORS SAID SHE HAD TUBER-CULOSIS.
SHE WAS IN GREAT PAIN. I WISHED I COULD HAVE TAKEN HER PLACE!

THE LAST OF

WILD TALK

"Elizabeth in the Mirror" is an unforgettable piece for me because...it required such tremendous effort to produce TWO different stories for one volume! In particular, telling a complete story in just thirty pages was a huge challenge for me. (Therefore, please be kind and ignore any flaws you might have noticed in this story.)

During the research on fairy tales I did before creating the "Elizabeth" piece, I couldn't help wondering if Snow White wasn't a rather stupid girl. She keeps making the same mistakes, nearly dying again and again. She is extraordinarily lucky to keep surviving all the calamities she encounters. Being pretty certainly helped her too. What Cain says about cruelty in fairy tales in the last part of "Elizabeth" is true. While studying the Grimm's Fairy Tales, I came across quite a few terrifying stories. By the way, the man who appears on the cover page of this piece is Riff, not Joey. (I agree he looks like Joey, though.) This story takes place at a time just after Cain met Riff.

The book I looked up was entitled, 'White Snow.'

Here are some examples of cruelty in the Grimm's: In "Rapunzel," the heroine becomes pregnant and the prince who fathered her baby loses his eyes. In "Little Red Hood," the grandmother dies. "Hansel and Gretel" is not an exception either...

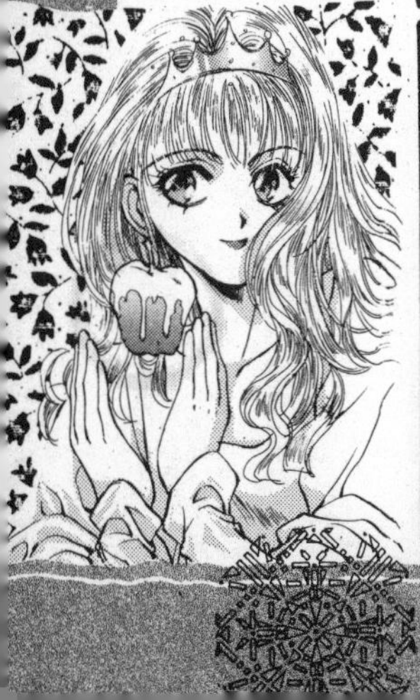

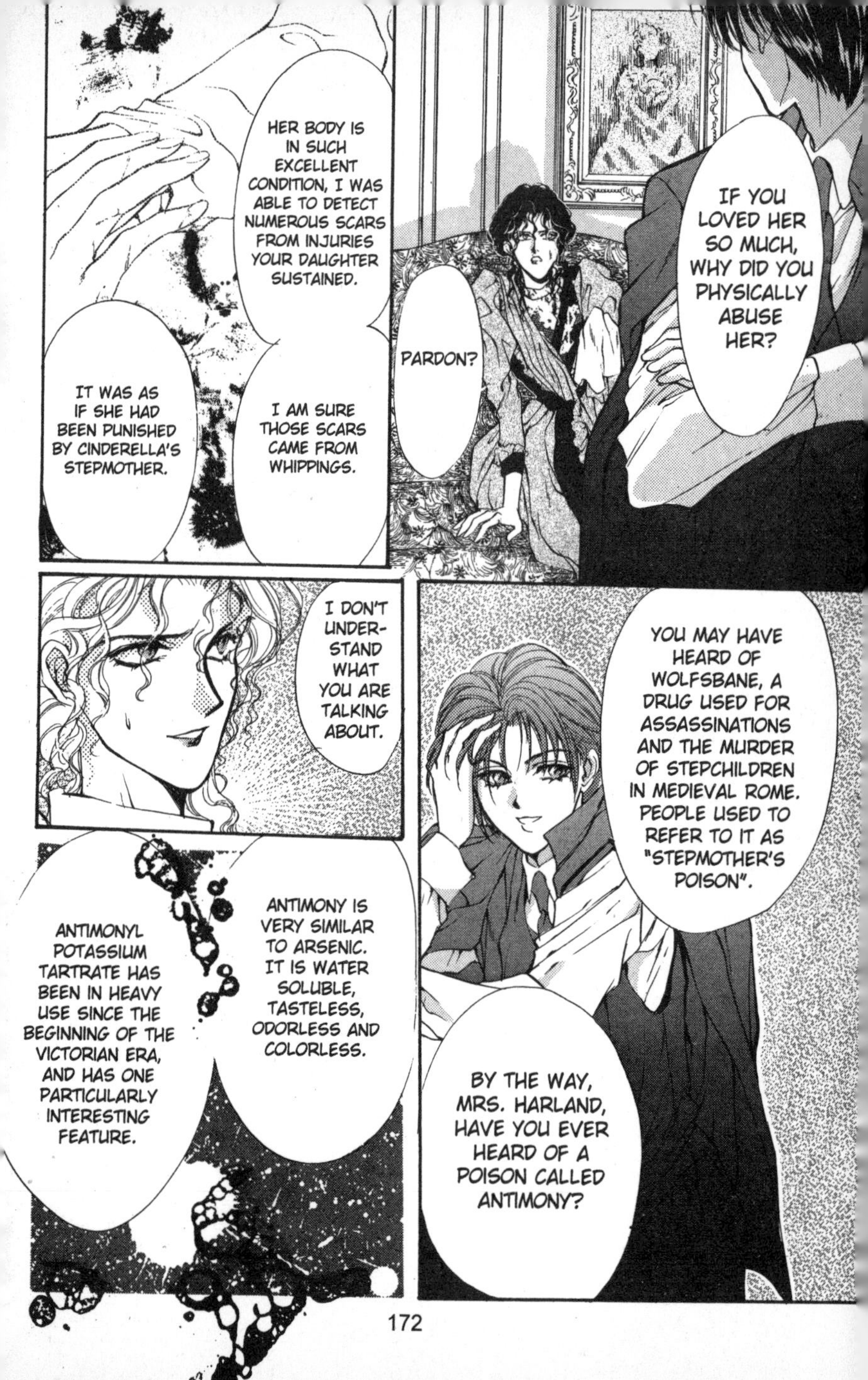
IF YOU LOVED HER SO MUCH, WHY DID YOU PHYSICALLY ABUSE HER?
PARDON?
HER BODY IS IN SUCH EXCELLENT CONDITION, I WAS ABLE TO DETECT NUMEROUS SCARS FROM INJURIES YOUR DAUGHTER SUSTAINED.
I AM SURE THOSE SCARS CAME FROM WHIPPINGS.
IT WAS AS IF SHE HAD BEEN PUNISHED BY CINDERELLA'S STEPMOTHER.
YOU MAY HAVE HEARD OF WOLFSBANE, A DRUG USED FOR ASSASSINATIONS AND THE MURDER OF STEPCHILDREN IN MEDIEVAL ROME. PEOPLE USED TO REFER TO IT AS "STEPMOTHER'S POISON".
BY THE WAY, MRS. HARLAND, HAVE YOU EVER HEARD OF A POISON CALLED ANTIMONY?
I DON'T UNDER-STAND WHAT YOU ARE TALKING ABOUT.
ANTIMONY IS VERY SIMILAR TO ARSENIC. IT IS WATER SOLUBLE, TASTELESS, ODORLESS AND COLORLESS.
ANTIMONYL POTASSIUM TARTRATE HAS BEEN IN HEAVY USE SINCE THE BEGINNING OF THE VICTORIAN ERA, AND HAS ONE PARTICULARLY INTERESTING FEATURE.

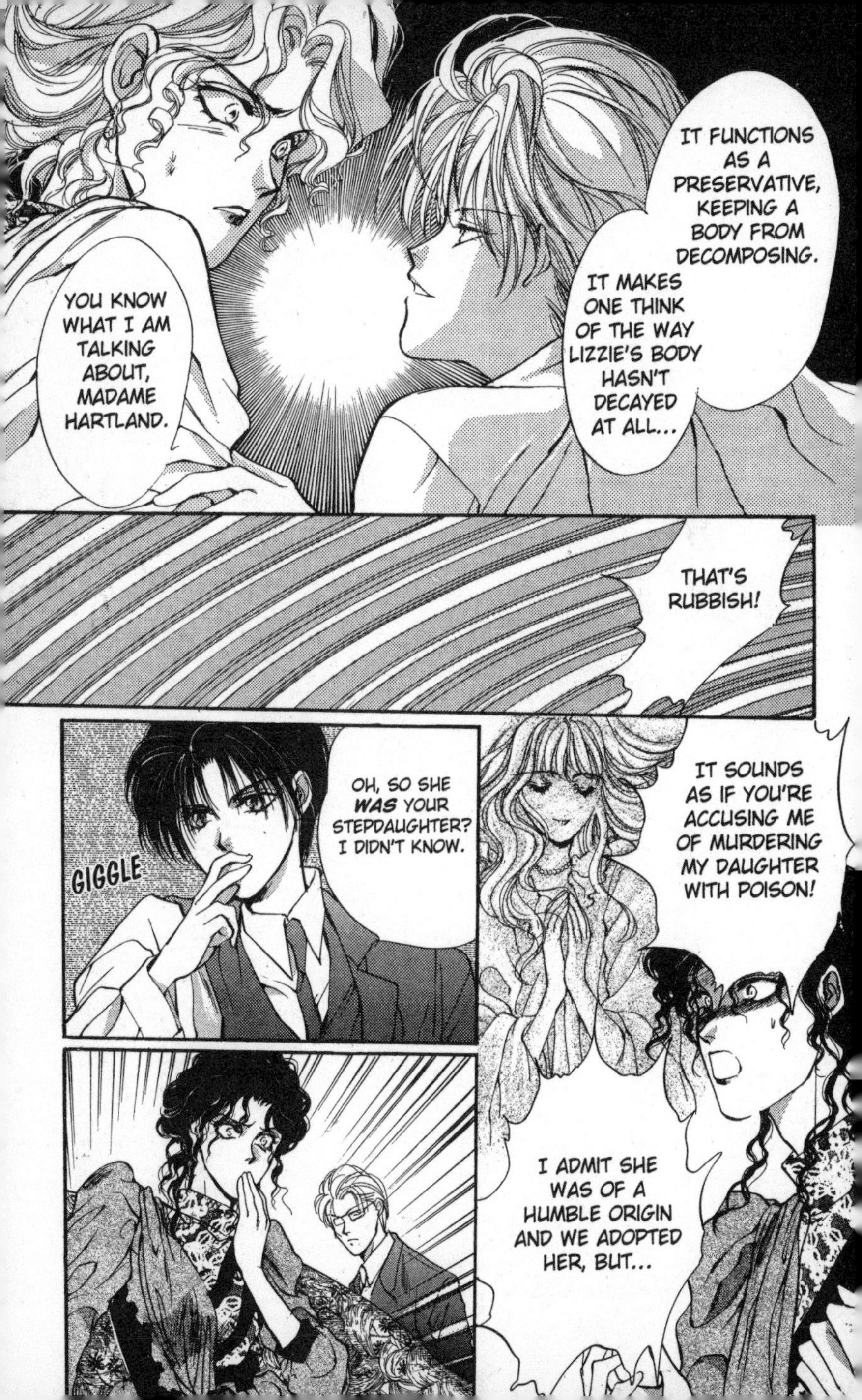
IT FUNCTIONS AS A PRESERVATIVE, KEEPING A BODY FROM DECOMPOSING.
IT MAKES ONE THINK OF THE WAY LIZZIE'S BODY HASN'T DECAYED AT ALL...
YOU KNOW WHAT I AM TALKING ABOUT, MADAME HARTLAND.
THAT'S RUBBISH!
IT SOUNDS AS IF YOU'RE ACCUSING ME OF MURDERING MY DAUGHTER WITH POISON!
I ADMIT SHE WAS OF A HUMBLE ORIGIN AND WE ADOPTED HER, BUT...
OH, SO SHE ***WAS*** YOUR STEPDAUGHTER? I DIDN'T KNOW.
GIGGLE

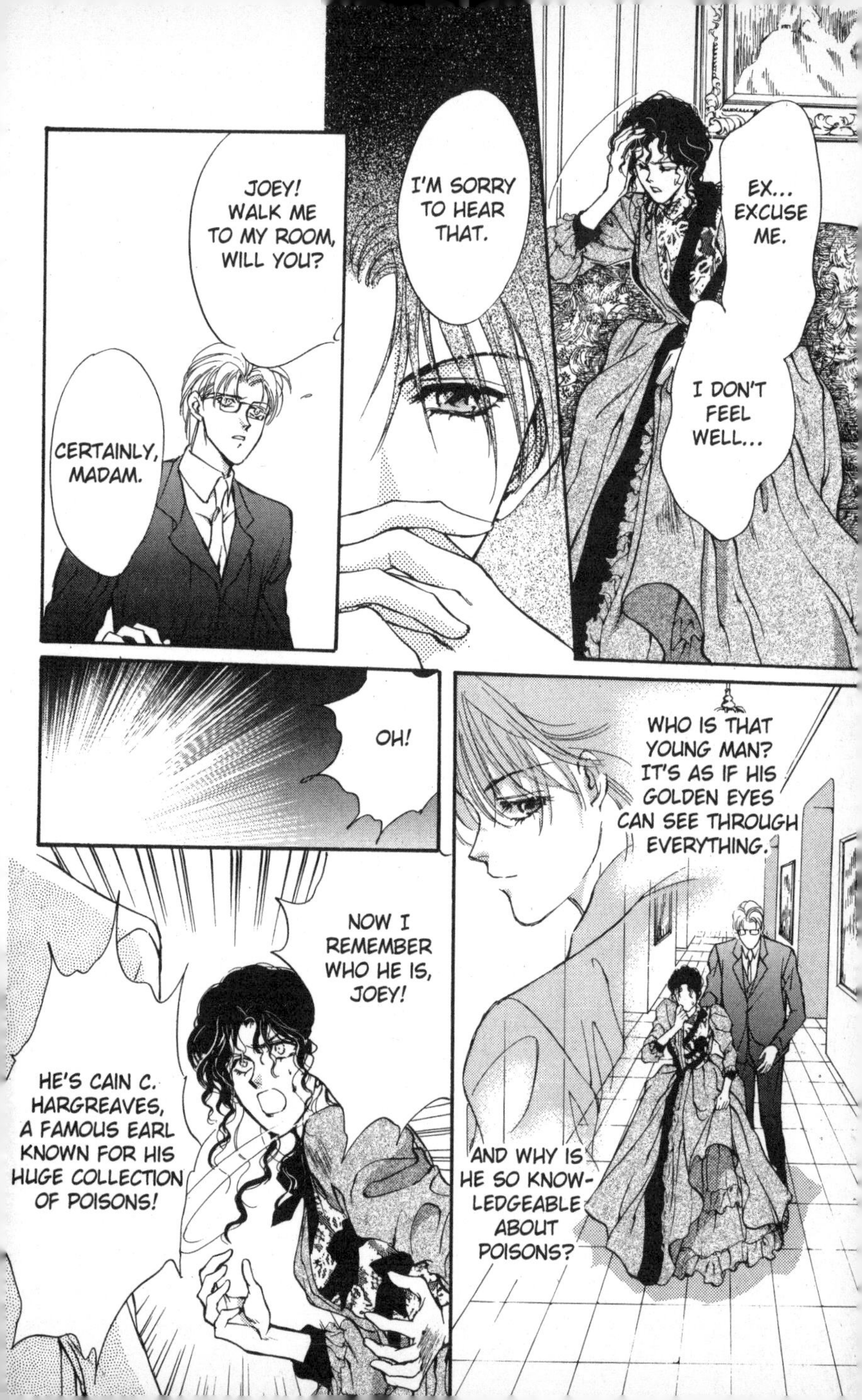
EX... EXCUSE ME.
I DON'T FEEL WELL...
I'M SORRY TO HEAR THAT.
JOEY! WALK ME TO MY ROOM, WILL YOU?
CERTAINLY, MADAM.
WHO IS THAT YOUNG MAN? IT'S AS IF HIS GOLDEN EYES CAN SEE THROUGH EVERYTHING.
AND WHY IS HE SO KNOW-LEDGEABLE ABOUT POISONS?
OH!
NOW I REMEMBER WHO HE IS, JOEY!
HE'S CAIN C. HARGREAVES, A FAMOUS EARL KNOWN FOR HIS HUGE COLLECTION OF POISONS!

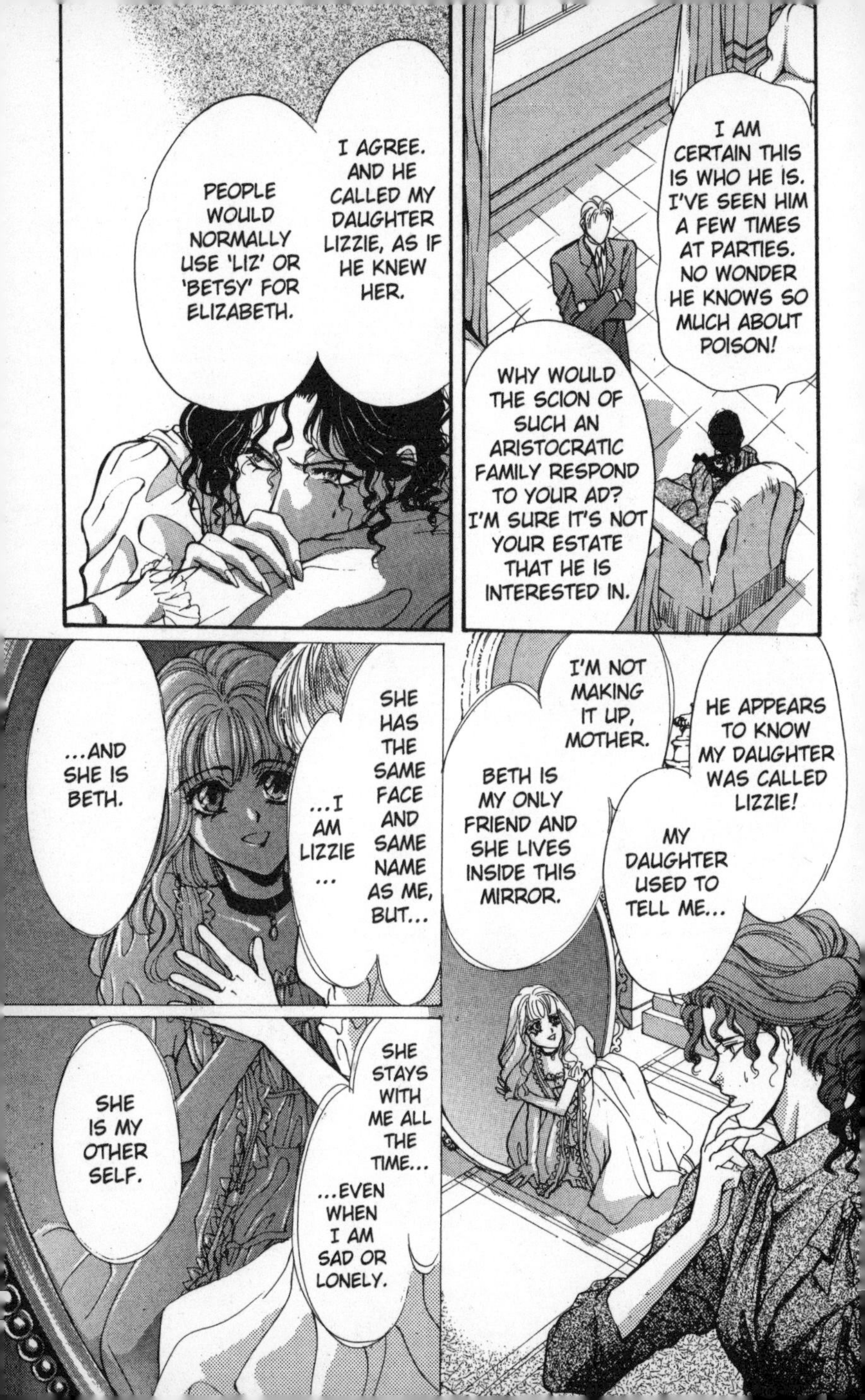
I AM CERTAIN THIS IS WHO HE IS. I'VE SEEN HIM A FEW TIMES AT PARTIES. NO WONDER HE KNOWS SO MUCH ABOUT POISON!
WHY WOULD THE SCION OF SUCH AN ARISTOCRATIC FAMILY RESPOND TO YOUR AD? I'M SURE IT'S NOT YOUR ESTATE THAT HE IS INTERESTED IN.
I AGREE. AND HE CALLED MY DAUGHTER LIZZIE, AS IF HE KNEW HER.
PEOPLE WOULD NORMALLY USE 'LIZ' OR 'BETSY' FOR ELIZABETH.
HE APPEARS TO KNOW MY DAUGHTER WAS CALLED LIZZIE!
MY DAUGHTER USED TO TELL ME...
I'M NOT MAKING IT UP, MOTHER.
BETH IS MY ONLY FRIEND AND SHE LIVES INSIDE THIS MIRROR.
SHE HAS THE SAME FACE AND SAME NAME AS ME, BUT...
...I AM LIZZIE...
...AND SHE IS BETH.
SHE STAYS WITH ME ALL THE TIME...
...EVEN WHEN I AM SAD OR LONELY.
SHE IS MY OTHER SELF.

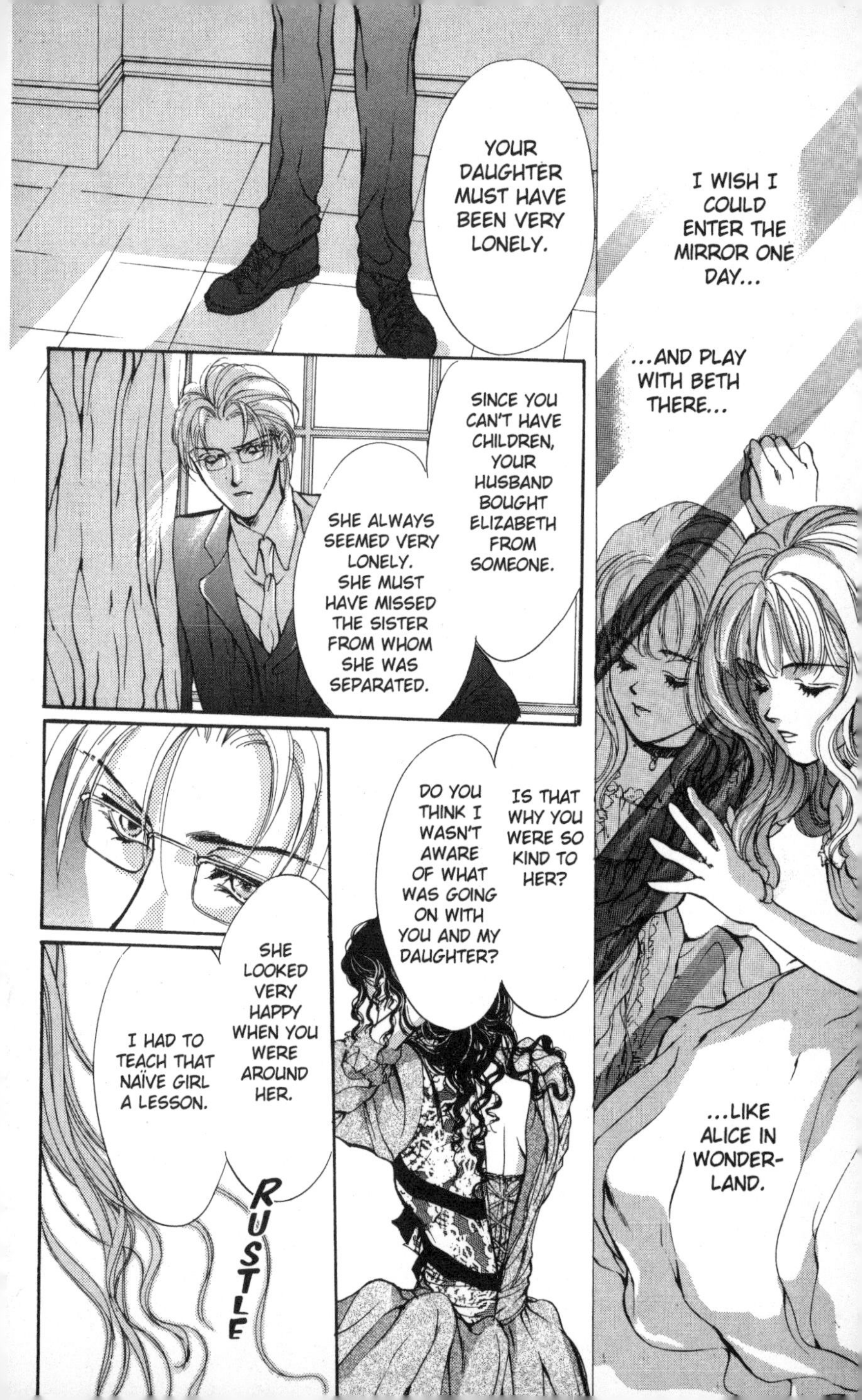
I WISH I COULD ENTER THE MIRROR ONE DAY...
...AND PLAY WITH BETH THERE...
...LIKE ALICE IN WONDER-LAND.
YOUR DAUGHTER MUST HAVE BEEN VERY LONELY.
SINCE YOU CAN'T HAVE CHILDREN, YOUR HUSBAND BOUGHT ELIZABETH FROM SOMEONE.
SHE ALWAYS SEEMED VERY LONELY. SHE MUST HAVE MISSED THE SISTER FROM WHOM SHE WAS SEPARATED.
IS THAT WHY YOU WERE SO KIND TO HER?
DO YOU THINK I WASN'T AWARE OF WHAT WAS GOING ON WITH YOU AND MY DAUGHTER?
SHE LOOKED VERY HAPPY WHEN YOU WERE AROUND HER.
I HAD TO TEACH THAT NAÏVE GIRL A LESSON.
RUSTLE

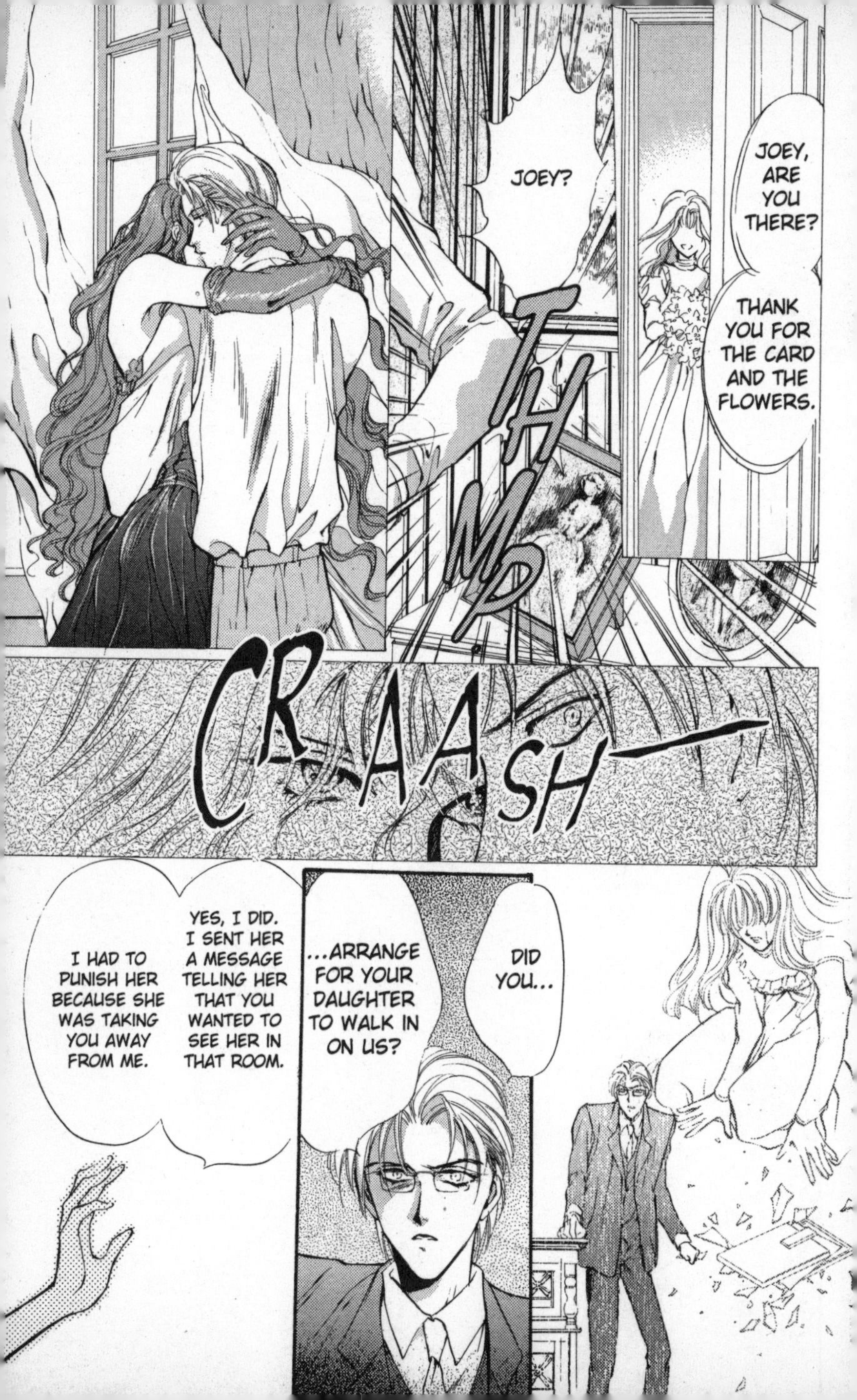
JOEY, ARE YOU THERE?
THANK YOU FOR THE CARD AND THE FLOWERS.
JOEY?
THMP
CRAASH
DID YOU...
...ARRANGE FOR YOUR DAUGHTER TO WALK IN ON US?
YES, I DID. I SENT HER A MESSAGE TELLING HER THAT YOU WANTED TO SEE HER IN THAT ROOM.
I HAD TO PUNISH HER BECAUSE SHE WAS TAKING YOU AWAY FROM ME.

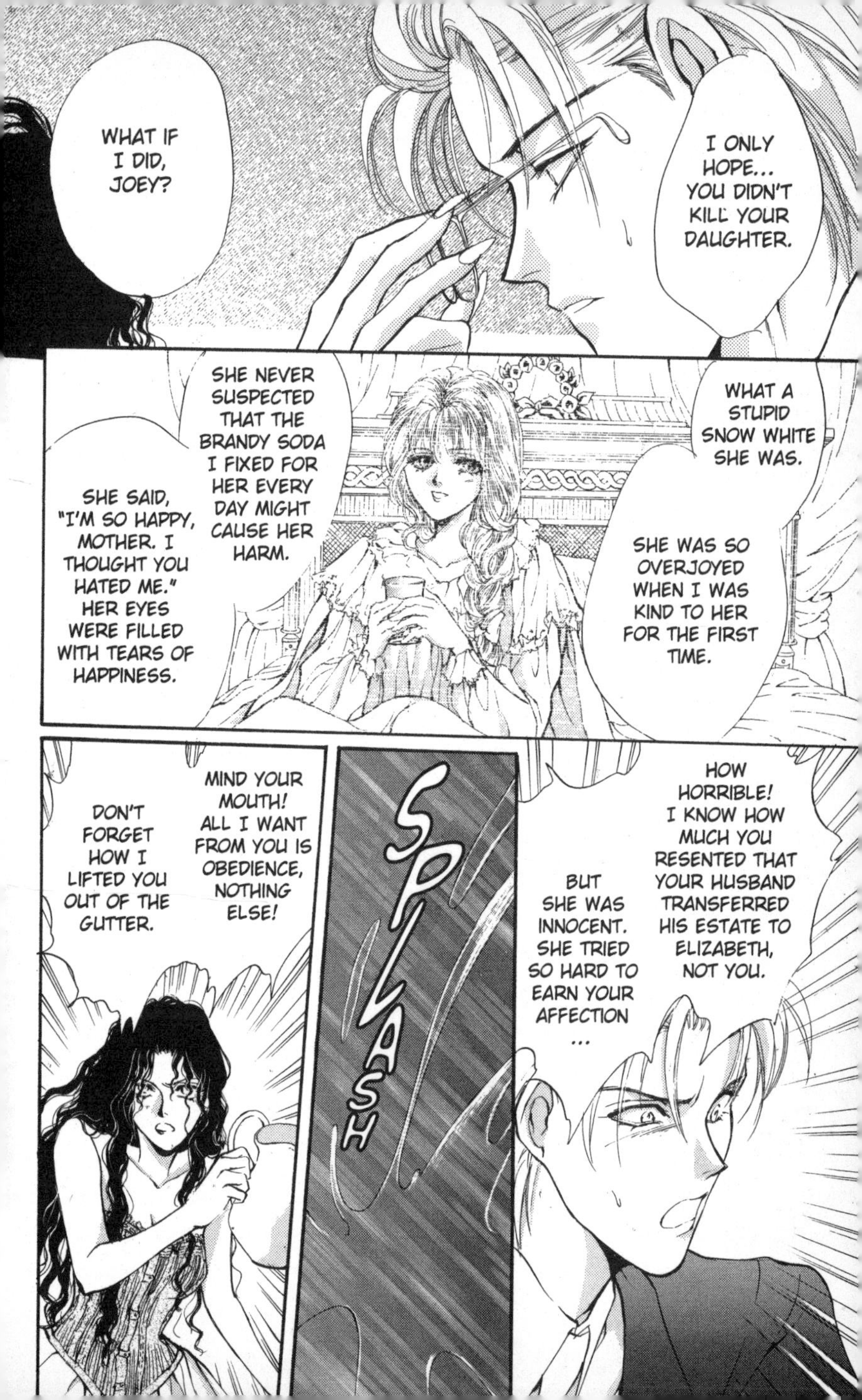
I ONLY HOPE... YOU DIDN'T KILL YOUR DAUGHTER.
WHAT IF I DID, JOEY?
WHAT A STUPID SNOW WHITE SHE WAS.
SHE WAS SO OVERJOYED WHEN I WAS KIND TO HER FOR THE FIRST TIME.
SHE NEVER SUSPECTED THAT THE BRANDY SODA I FIXED FOR HER EVERY DAY MIGHT CAUSE HER HARM.
SHE SAID, "I'M SO HAPPY, MOTHER. I THOUGHT YOU HATED ME." HER EYES WERE FILLED WITH TEARS OF HAPPINESS.
HOW HORRIBLE! I KNOW HOW MUCH YOU RESENTED THAT YOUR HUSBAND TRANSFERRED HIS ESTATE TO ELIZABETH, NOT YOU.
BUT SHE WAS INNOCENT. SHE TRIED SO HARD TO EARN YOUR AFFECTION...
SPLASH
MIND YOUR MOUTH! ALL I WANT FROM YOU IS OBEDIENCE, NOTHING ELSE!
DON'T FORGET HOW I LIFTED YOU OUT OF THE GUTTER.

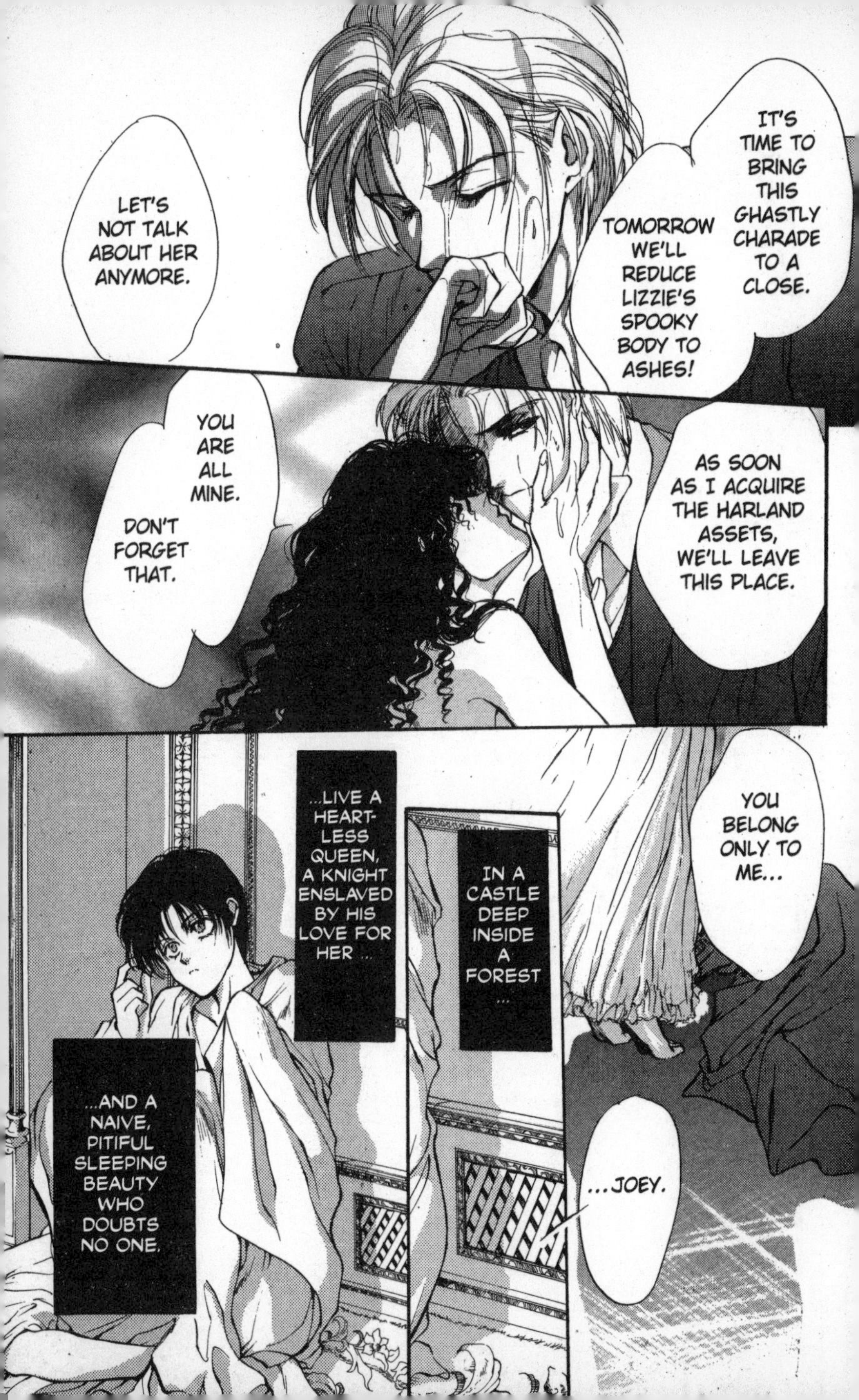

IT'S TIME TO BRING THIS GHASTLY CHARADE TO A CLOSE.
TOMORROW WE'LL REDUCE LIZZIE'S SPOOKY BODY TO ASHES!
LET'S NOT TALK ABOUT HER ANYMORE.
AS SOON AS I ACQUIRE THE HARLAND ASSETS, WE'LL LEAVE THIS PLACE.
YOU ARE ALL MINE.
DON'T FORGET THAT.
YOU BELONG ONLY TO ME...
...JOEY.
IN A CASTLE DEEP INSIDE A FOREST...
...LIVE A HEART-LESS QUEEN, A KNIGHT ENSLAVED BY HIS LOVE FOR HER...
...AND A NAIVE, PITIFUL SLEEPING BEAUTY WHO DOUBTS NO ONE.

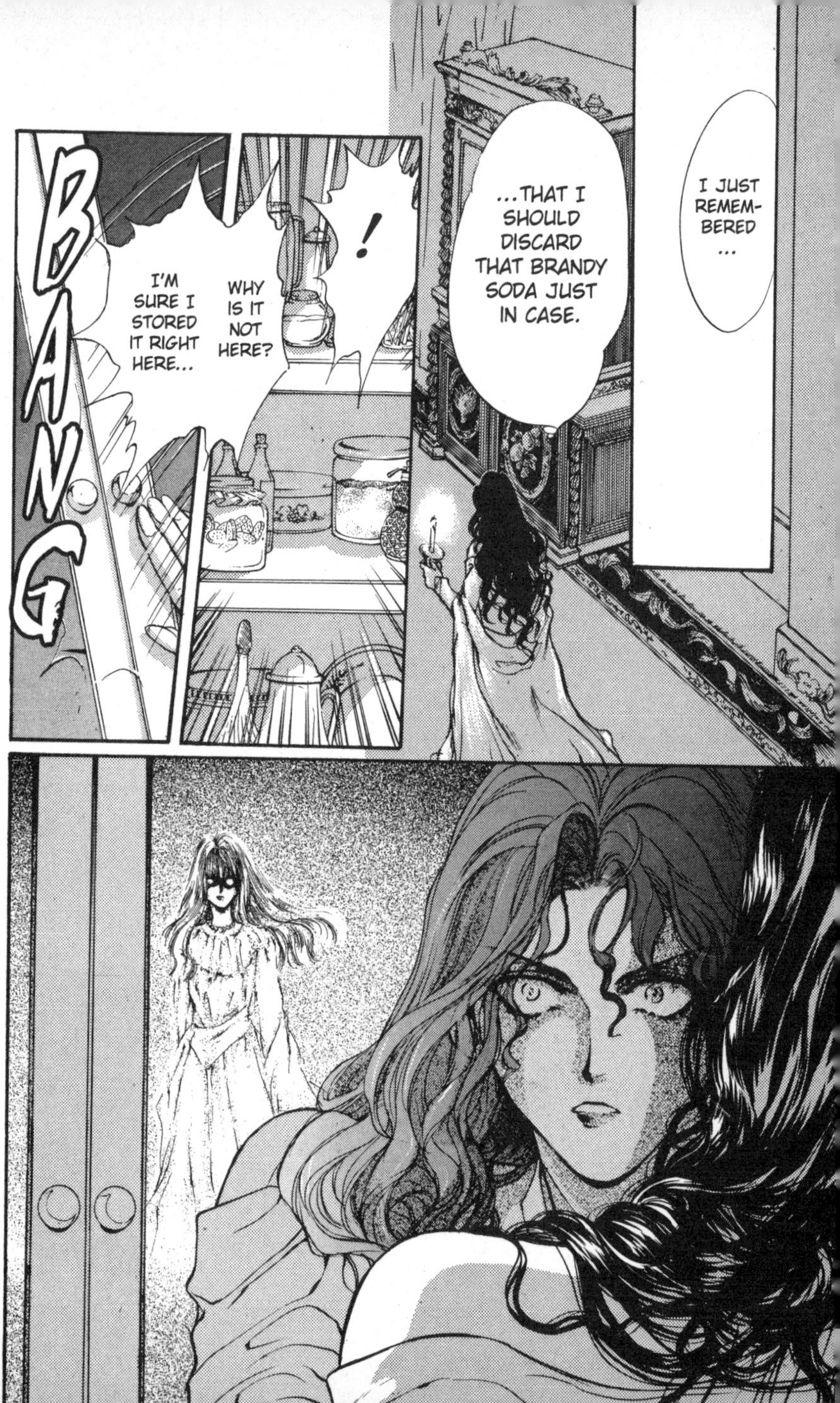
I JUST REMEMBERED...
...THAT I SHOULD DISCARD THAT BRANDY SODA JUST IN CASE.
!
WHY IS IT NOT HERE?
I'M SURE I STORED IT RIGHT HERE...
BANG

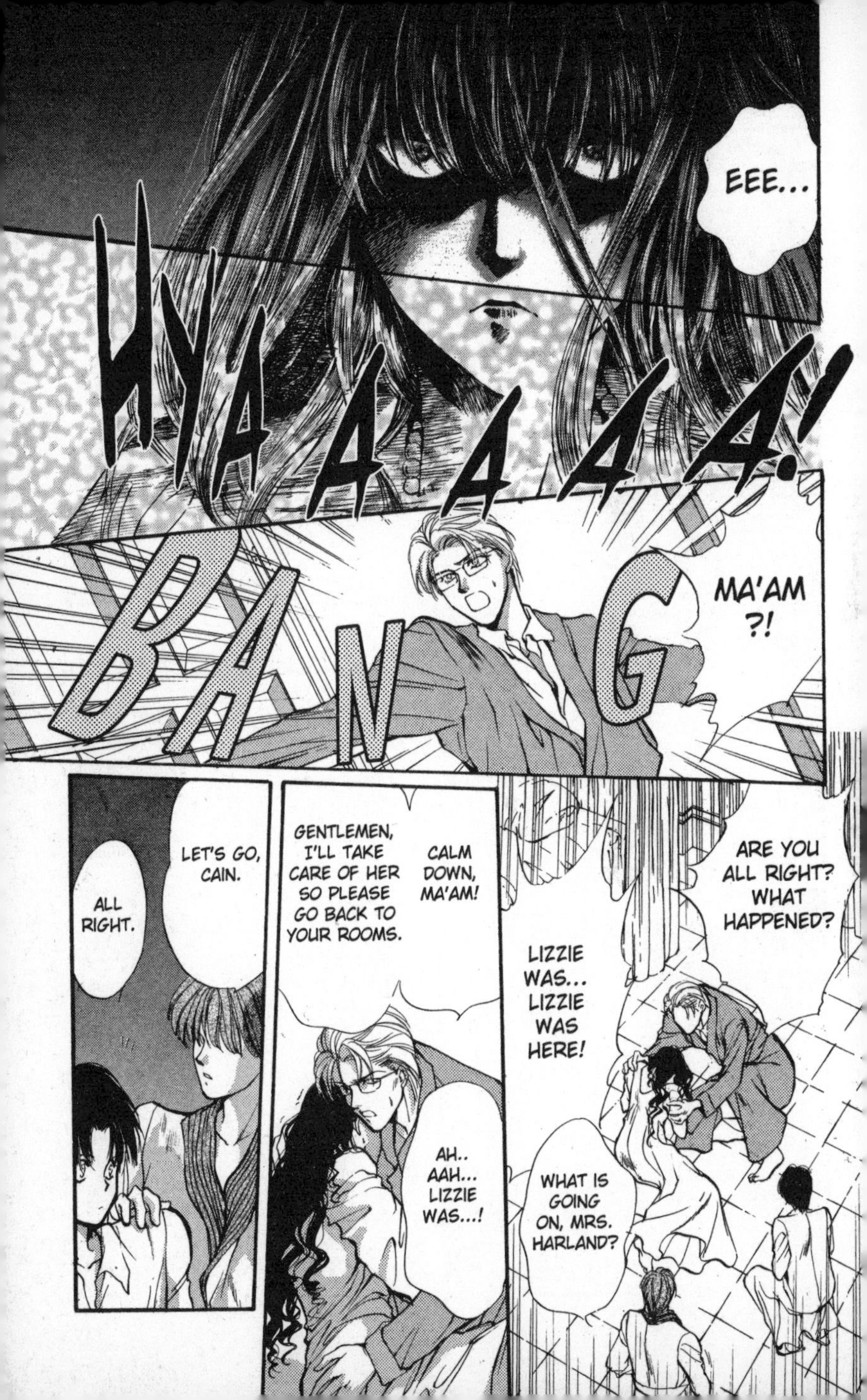
EEE...
HYAAAAA!
BANG
MA'AM ?!
ARE YOU ALL RIGHT? WHAT HAPPENED?
LIZZIE WAS... LIZZIE WAS HERE!
WHAT IS GOING ON, MRS. HARLAND?
CALM DOWN, MA'AM!
GENTLEMEN, I'LL TAKE CARE OF HER SO PLEASE GO BACK TO YOUR ROOMS.
AH.. AAH... LIZZIE WAS...!
LET'S GO, CAIN.
ALL RIGHT.

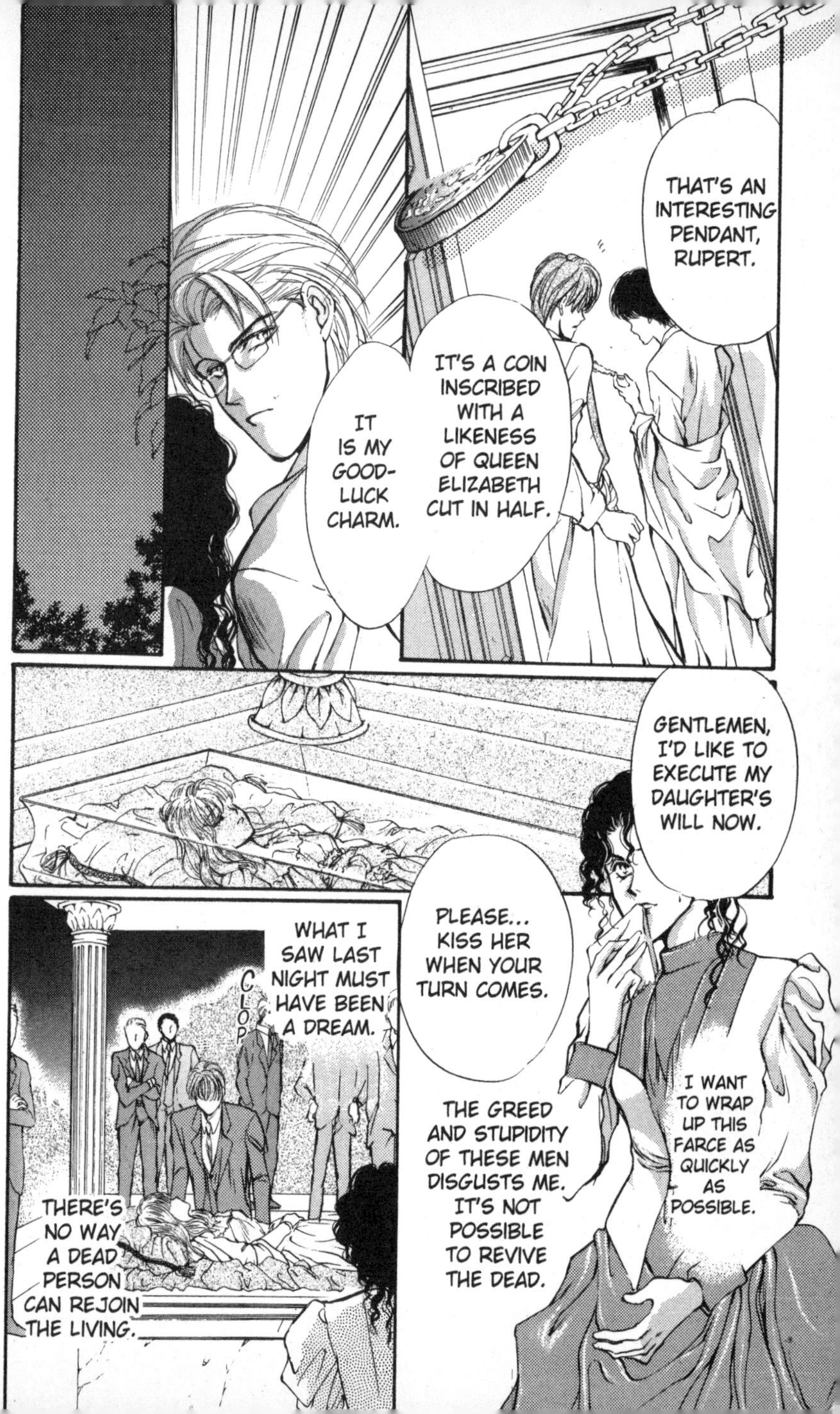
THAT'S AN INTERESTING PENDANT, RUPERT.
IT'S A COIN INSCRIBED WITH A LIKENESS OF QUEEN ELIZABETH CUT IN HALF.
IT IS MY GOOD-LUCK CHARM.
GENTLEMEN, I'D LIKE TO EXECUTE MY DAUGHTER'S WILL NOW.
PLEASE... KISS HER WHEN YOUR TURN COMES.
I WANT TO WRAP UP THIS FARCE AS QUICKLY AS POSSIBLE.
THE GREED AND STUPIDITY OF THESE MEN DISGUSTS ME. IT'S NOT POSSIBLE TO REVIVE THE DEAD.
WHAT I SAW LAST NIGHT MUST HAVE BEEN A DREAM.
CLOP
THERE'S NO WAY A DEAD PERSON CAN REJOIN THE LIVING.

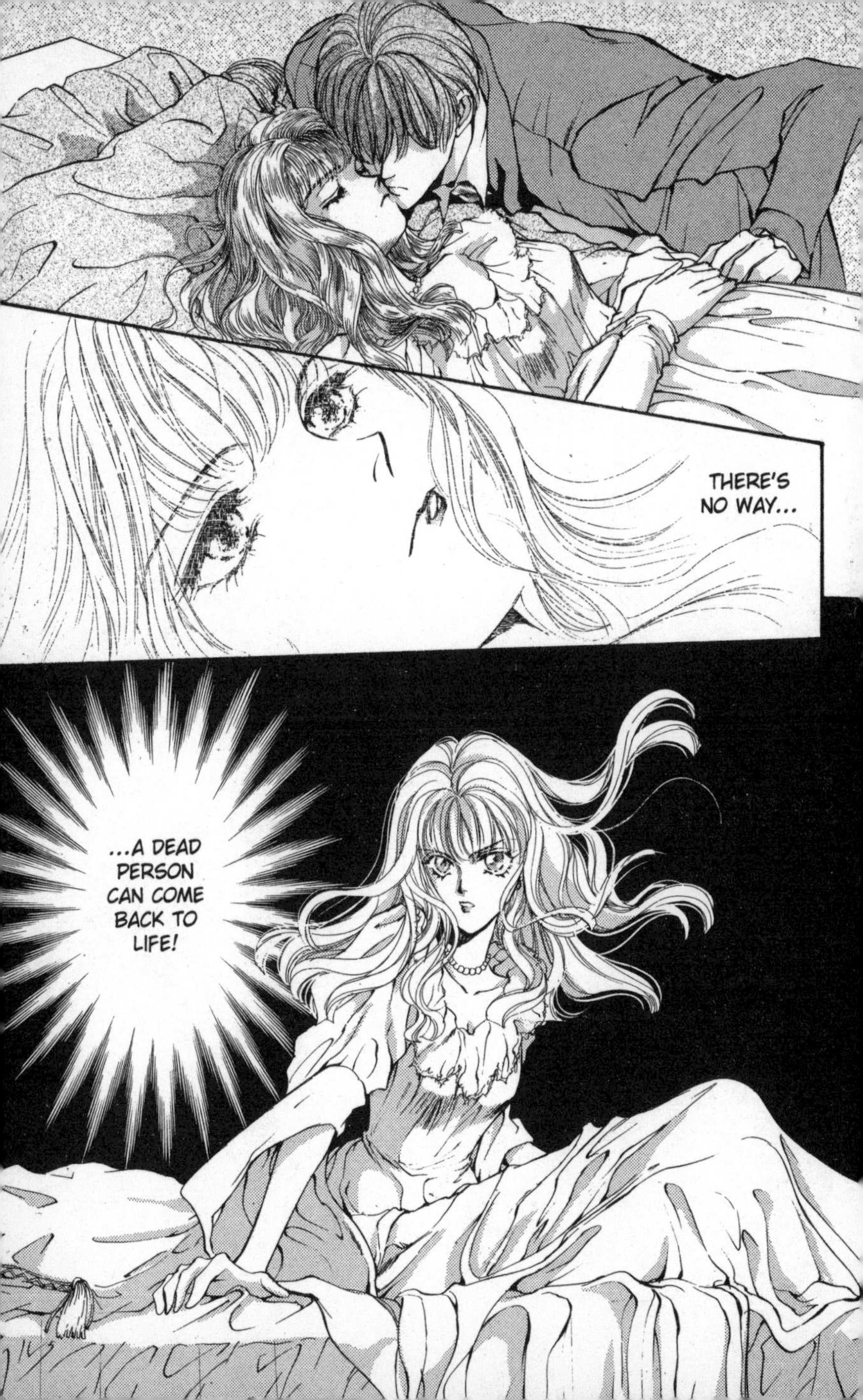
THERE'S NO WAY...
...A DEAD PERSON CAN COME BACK TO LIFE!

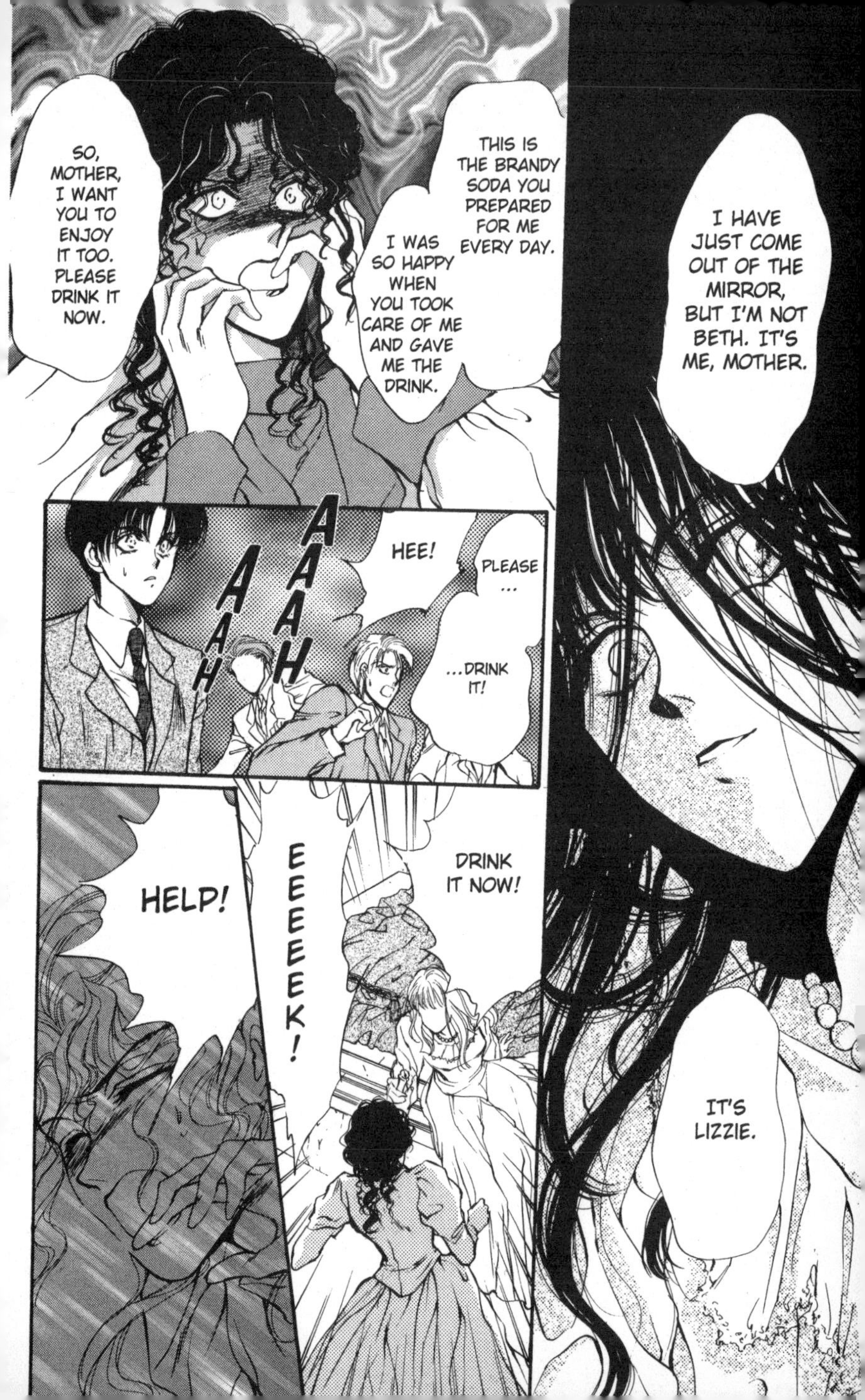

I HAVE JUST COME OUT OF THE MIRROR, BUT I'M NOT BETH. IT'S ME, MOTHER.
IT'S LIZZIE.
THIS IS THE BRANDY SODA YOU PREPARED FOR ME EVERY DAY.
I WAS SO HAPPY WHEN YOU TOOK CARE OF ME AND GAVE ME THE DRINK.
SO, MOTHER, I WANT YOU TO ENJOY IT TOO. PLEASE DRINK IT NOW.
PLEASE ...
...DRINK IT!
HEE!
AAAAH
AAAH
DRINK IT NOW!
EEEEEEK!
HELP!

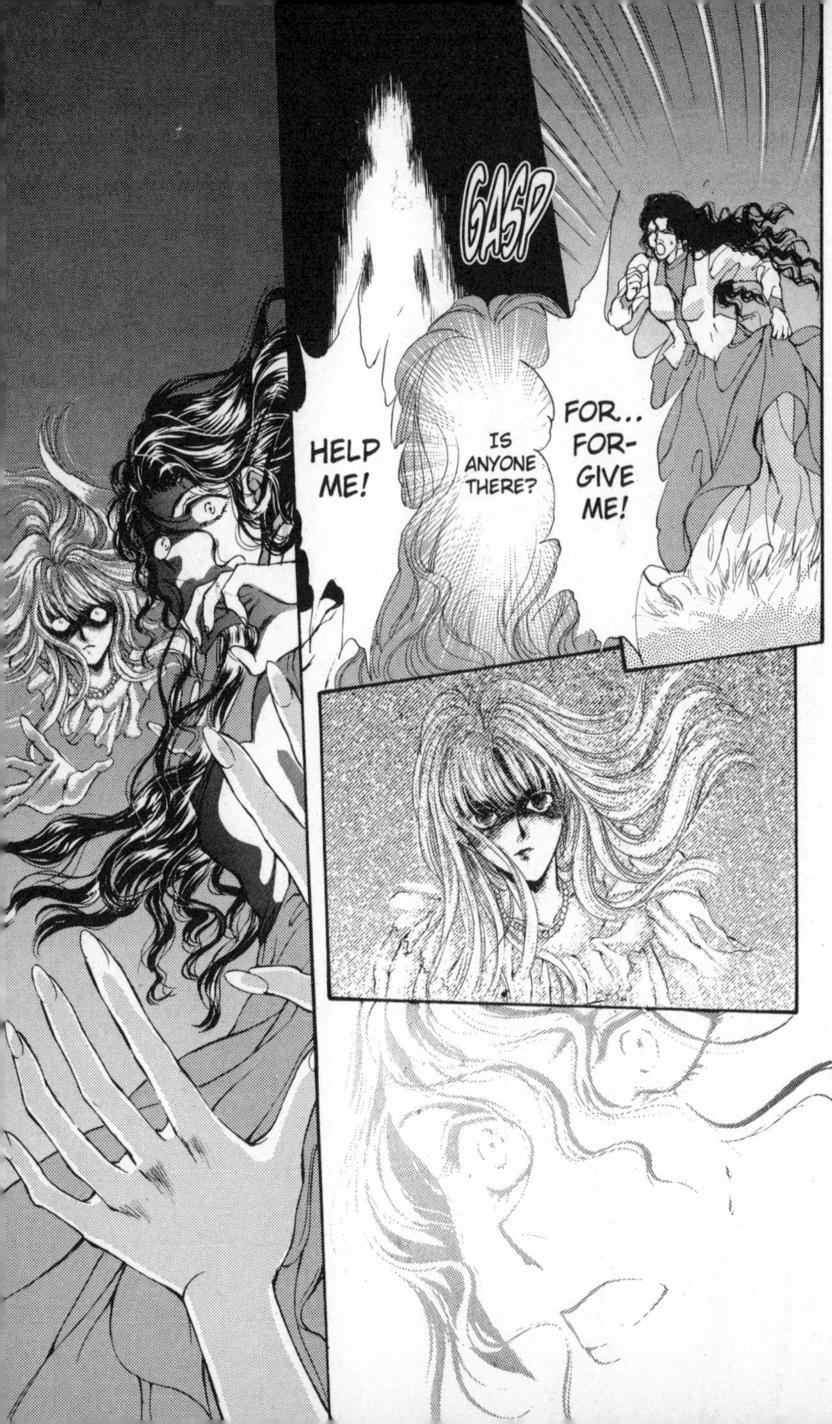
GASP
FOR... FOR-GIVE ME!
IS ANYONE THERE?
HELP ME!

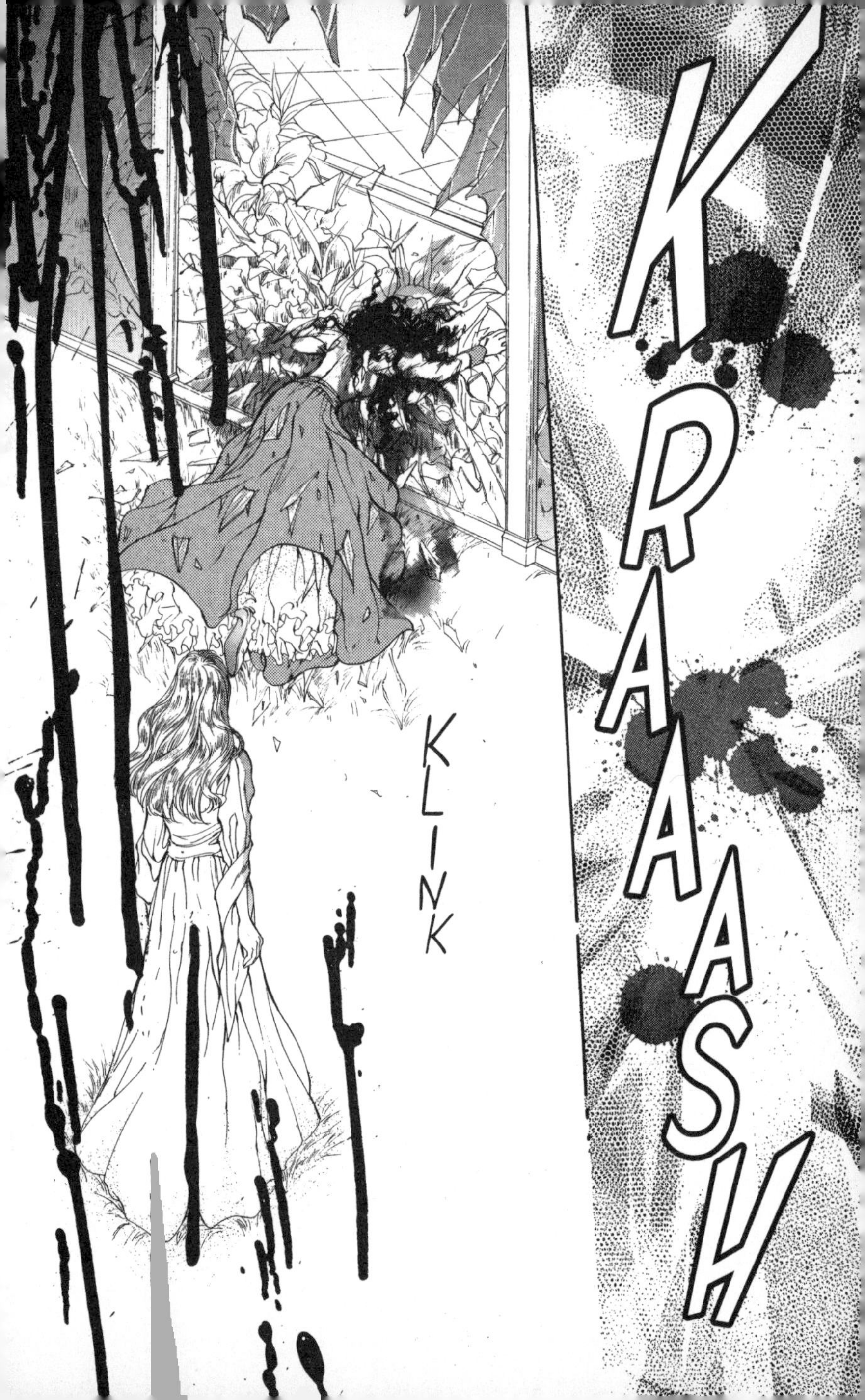
KRAAAASH
KLINK

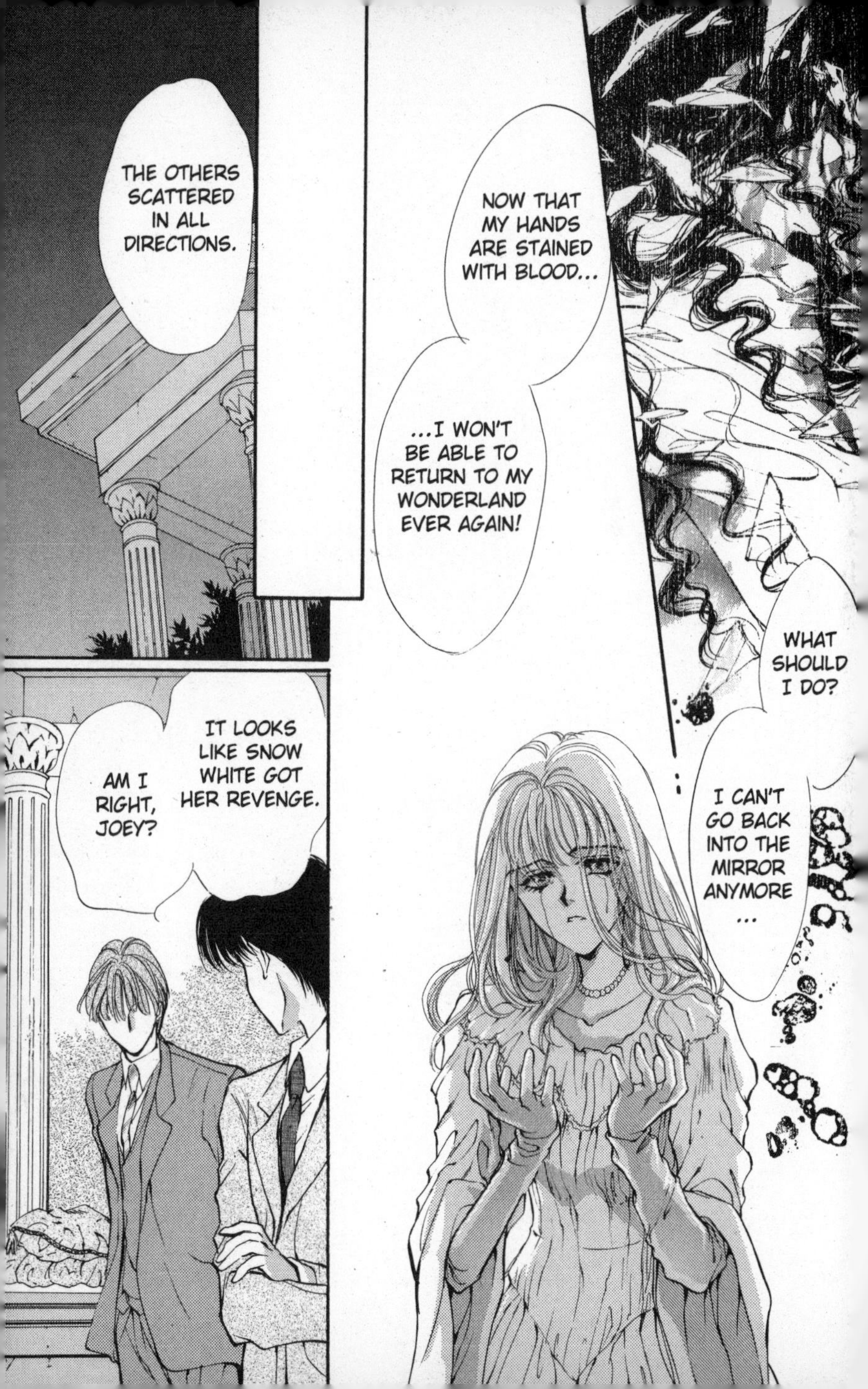
NOW THAT MY HANDS ARE STAINED WITH BLOOD...
...I WON'T BE ABLE TO RETURN TO MY WONDERLAND EVER AGAIN!
WHAT SHOULD I DO?
I CAN'T GO BACK INTO THE MIRROR ANYMORE...
THE OTHERS SCATTERED IN ALL DIRECTIONS.
IT LOOKS LIKE SNOW WHITE GOT HER REVENGE.
AM I RIGHT, JOEY?

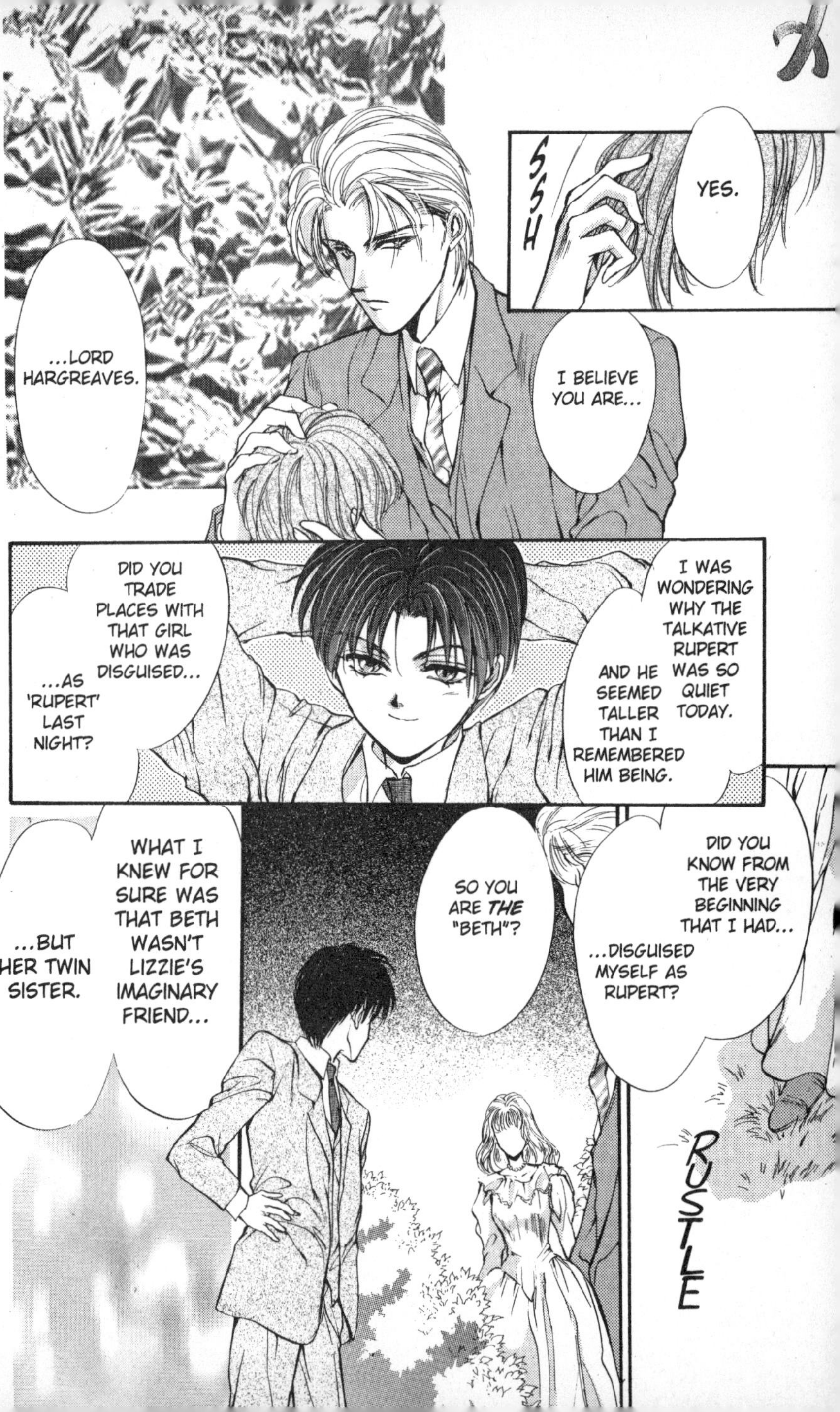
SSH
YES.
I BELIEVE YOU ARE...
...LORD HARGREAVES.
I WAS WONDERING WHY THE TALKATIVE RUPERT WAS SO QUIET TODAY.
AND HE SEEMED TALLER THAN I REMEMBERED HIM BEING.
DID YOU TRADE PLACES WITH THAT GIRL WHO WAS DISGUISED...
...AS 'RUPERT' LAST NIGHT?
DID YOU KNOW FROM THE VERY BEGINNING THAT I HAD...
...DISGUISED MYSELF AS RUPERT?
RUSTLE
SO YOU ARE *THE* "BETH"?
WHAT I KNEW FOR SURE WAS THAT BETH WASN'T LIZZIE'S IMAGINARY FRIEND...
...BUT HER TWIN SISTER.

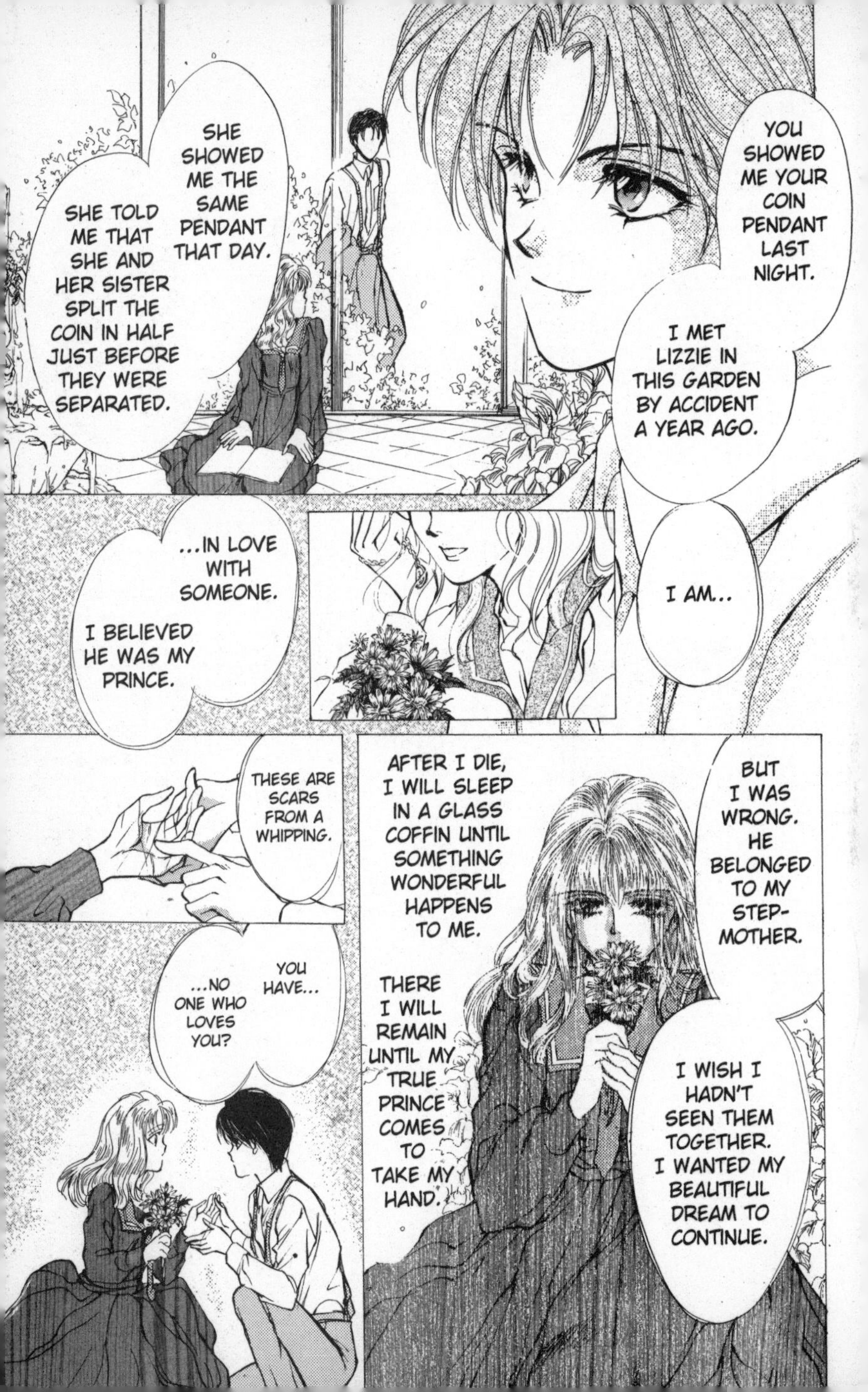
YOU SHOWED ME YOUR COIN PENDANT LAST NIGHT.
I MET LIZZIE IN THIS GARDEN BY ACCIDENT A YEAR AGO.
SHE SHOWED ME THE SAME PENDANT THAT DAY.
SHE TOLD ME THAT SHE AND HER SISTER SPLIT THE COIN IN HALF JUST BEFORE THEY WERE SEPARATED.
I AM...
...IN LOVE WITH SOMEONE.
I BELIEVED HE WAS MY PRINCE.
BUT I WAS WRONG. HE BELONGED TO MY STEP-MOTHER.
I WISH I HADN'T SEEN THEM TOGETHER. I WANTED MY BEAUTIFUL DREAM TO CONTINUE.
AFTER I DIE, I WILL SLEEP IN A GLASS COFFIN UNTIL SOMETHING WONDERFUL HAPPENS TO ME.
THERE I WILL REMAIN UNTIL MY TRUE PRINCE COMES TO TAKE MY HAND.
THESE ARE SCARS FROM A WHIPPING.
YOU HAVE...
...NO ONE WHO LOVES YOU?

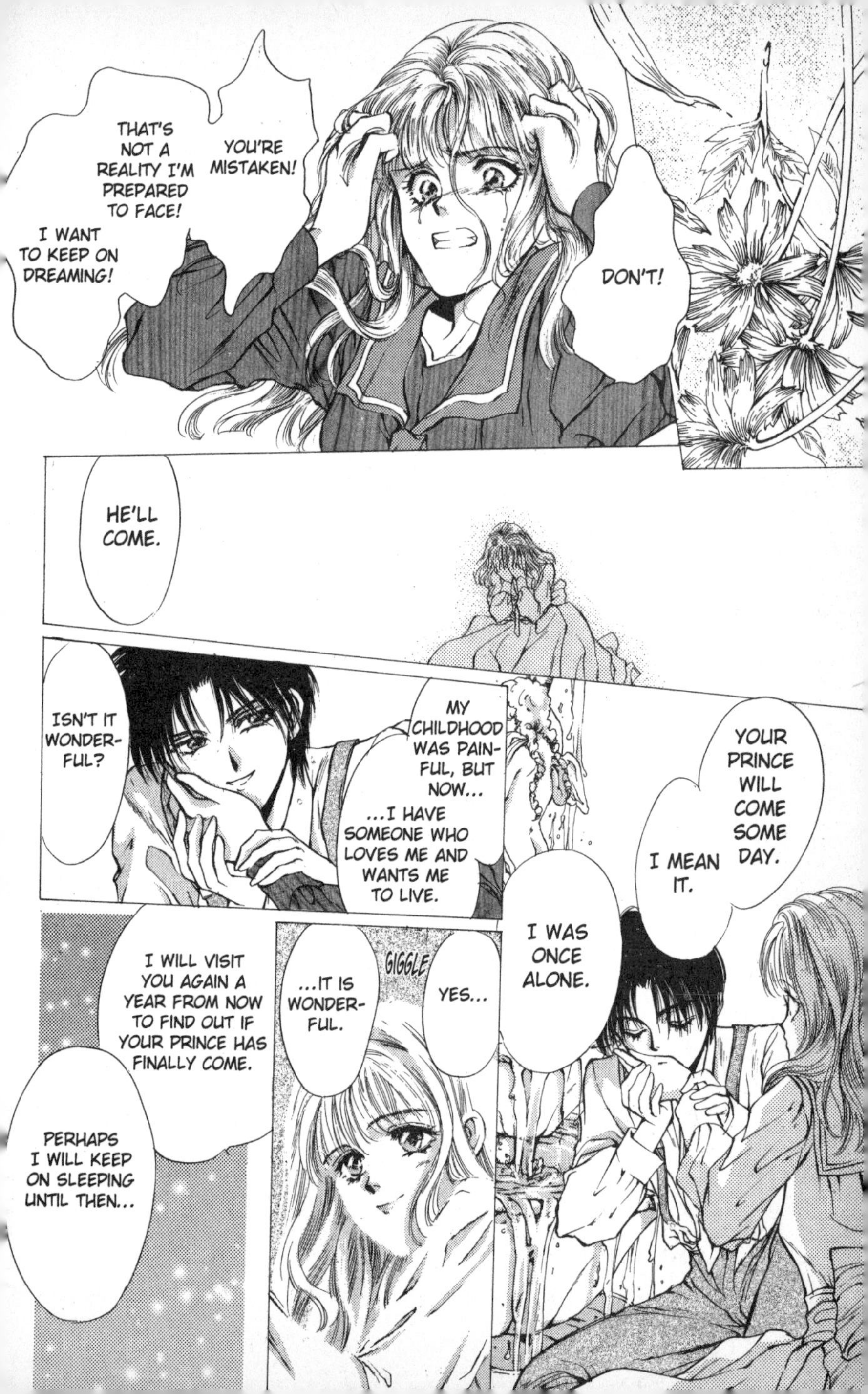
DON'T!
YOU'RE MISTAKEN!
THAT'S NOT A REALITY I'M PREPARED TO FACE!
I WANT TO KEEP ON DREAMING!
HE'LL COME.
YOUR PRINCE WILL COME SOME DAY.
I MEAN IT.
I WAS ONCE ALONE.
MY CHILDHOOD WAS PAIN-FUL, BUT NOW...
...I HAVE SOMEONE WHO LOVES ME AND WANTS ME TO LIVE.
ISN'T IT WONDER-FUL?
YES...
GIGGLE
...IT IS WONDER-FUL.
I WILL VISIT YOU AGAIN A YEAR FROM NOW TO FIND OUT IF YOUR PRINCE HAS FINALLY COME.
PERHAPS I WILL KEEP ON SLEEPING UNTIL THEN...

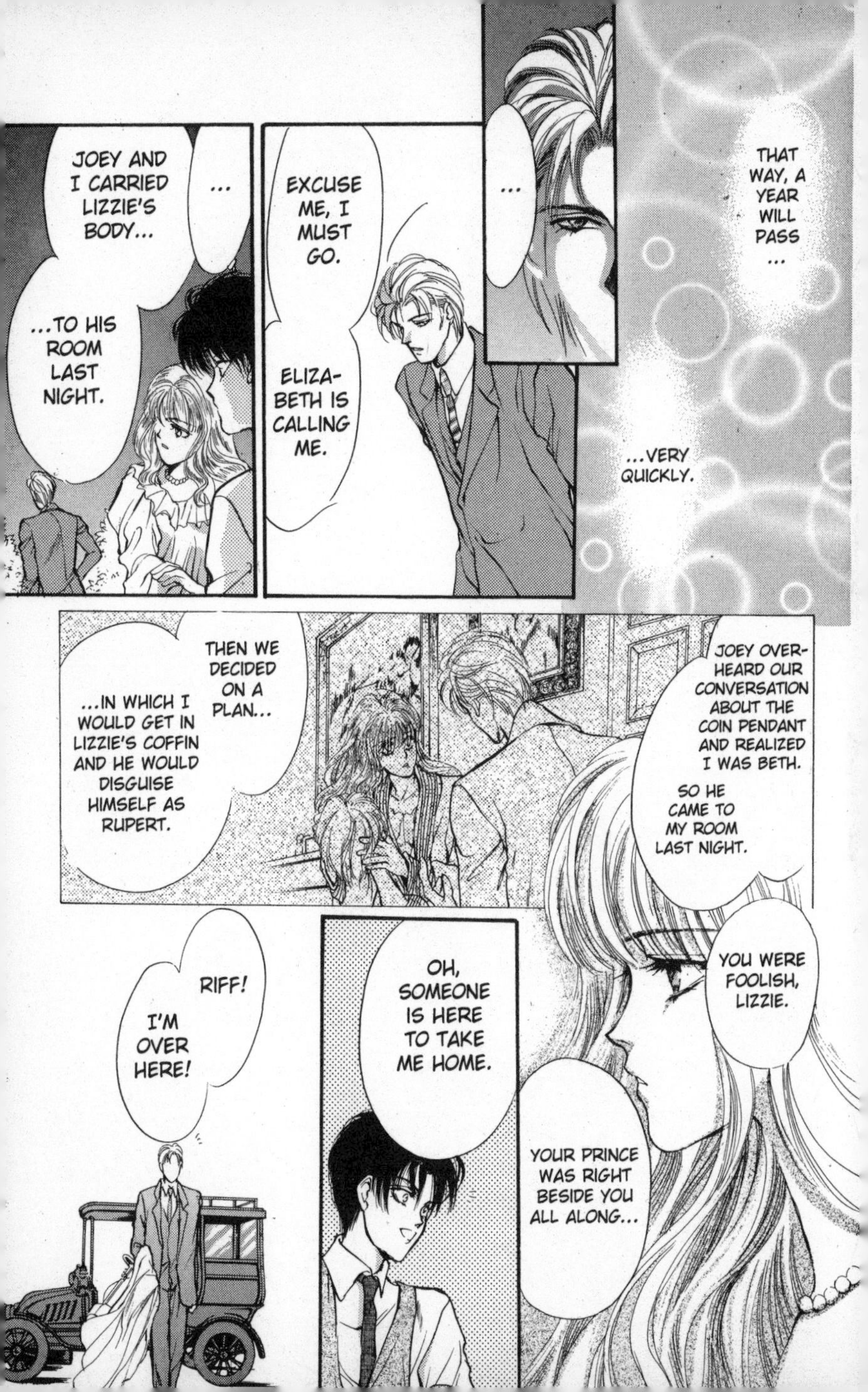
THAT WAY, A YEAR WILL PASS ...
...
...VERY QUICKLY.
EXCUSE ME, I MUST GO.
ELIZA-BETH IS CALLING ME.
...
JOEY AND I CARRIED LIZZIE'S BODY...
...TO HIS ROOM LAST NIGHT.
JOEY OVER-HEARD OUR CONVERSATION ABOUT THE COIN PENDANT AND REALIZED I WAS BETH.
SO HE CAME TO MY ROOM LAST NIGHT.
THEN WE DECIDED ON A PLAN...
...IN WHICH I WOULD GET IN LIZZIE'S COFFIN AND HE WOULD DISGUISE HIMSELF AS RUPERT.
YOU WERE FOOLISH, LIZZIE.
YOUR PRINCE WAS RIGHT BESIDE YOU ALL ALONG...
OH, SOMEONE IS HERE TO TAKE ME HOME.
RIFF!
I'M OVER HERE!

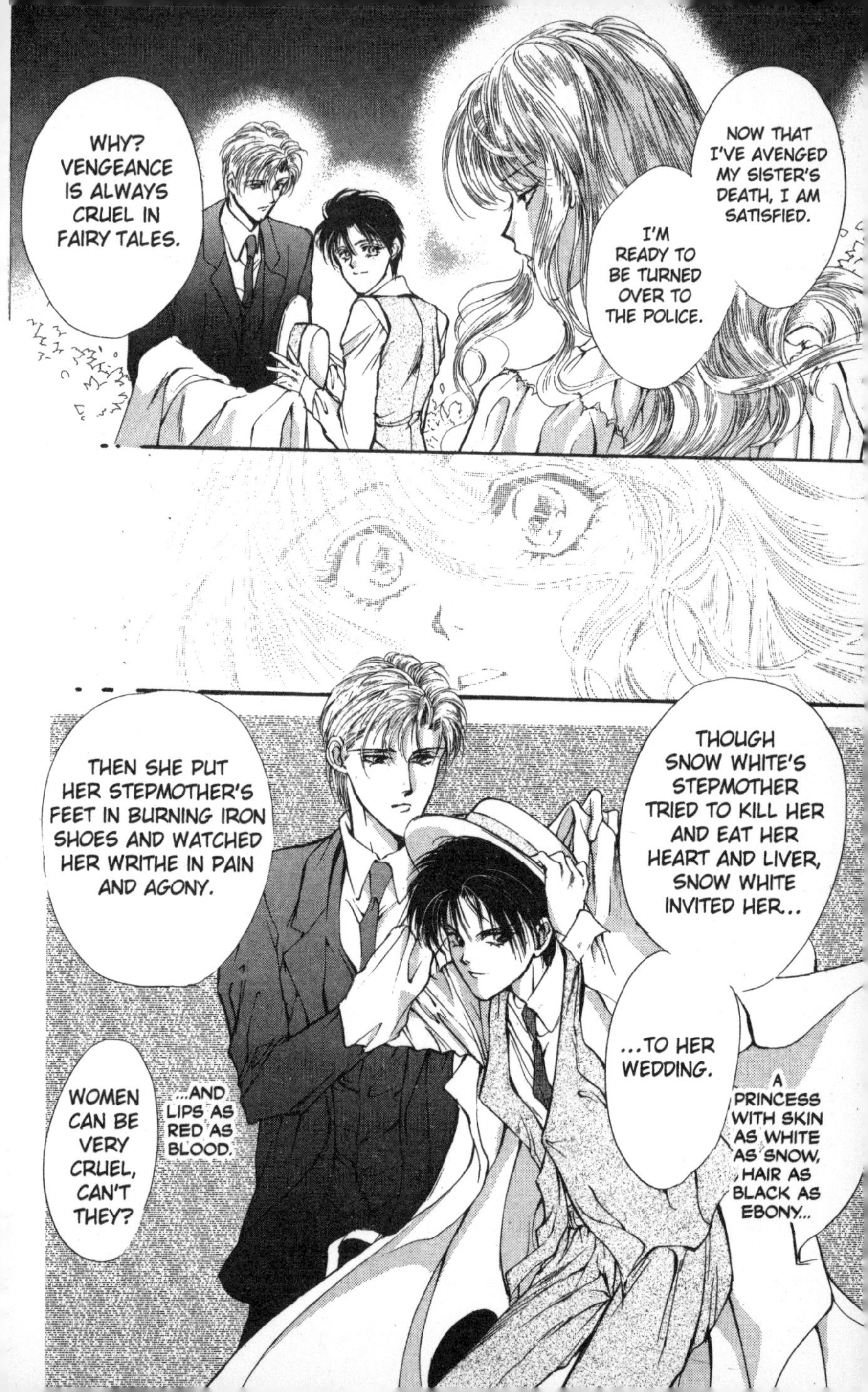
NOW THAT I'VE AVENGED MY SISTER'S DEATH, I AM SATISFIED.
I'M READY TO BE TURNED OVER TO THE POLICE.
WHY? VENGEANCE IS ALWAYS CRUEL IN FAIRY TALES.
THOUGH SNOW WHITE'S STEPMOTHER TRIED TO KILL HER AND EAT HER HEART AND LIVER, SNOW WHITE INVITED HER...
...TO HER WEDDING.
THEN SHE PUT HER STEPMOTHER'S FEET IN BURNING IRON SHOES AND WATCHED HER WRITHE IN PAIN AND AGONY.
A PRINCESS WITH SKIN AS WHITE AS SNOW, HAIR AS BLACK AS EBONY...
...AND LIPS AS RED AS BLOOD.
WOMEN CAN BE VERY CRUEL, CAN'T THEY?

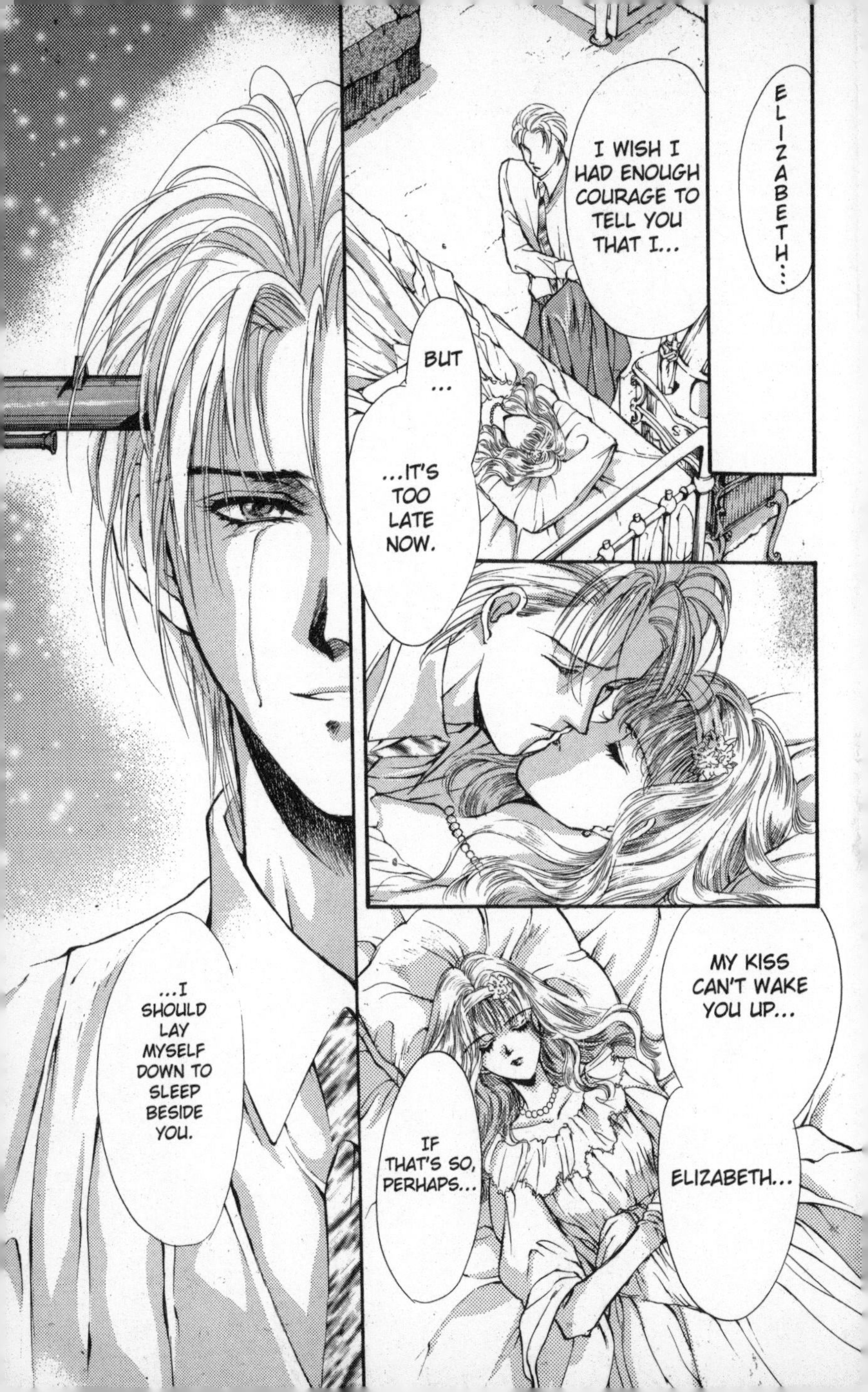
ELIZABETH...
I WISH I HAD ENOUGH COURAGE TO TELL YOU THAT I...
BUT ...
...IT'S TOO LATE NOW.
MY KISS CAN'T WAKE YOU UP...
ELIZABETH...
IF THAT'S SO, PERHAPS...
...I SHOULD LAY MYSELF DOWN TO SLEEP BESIDE YOU.

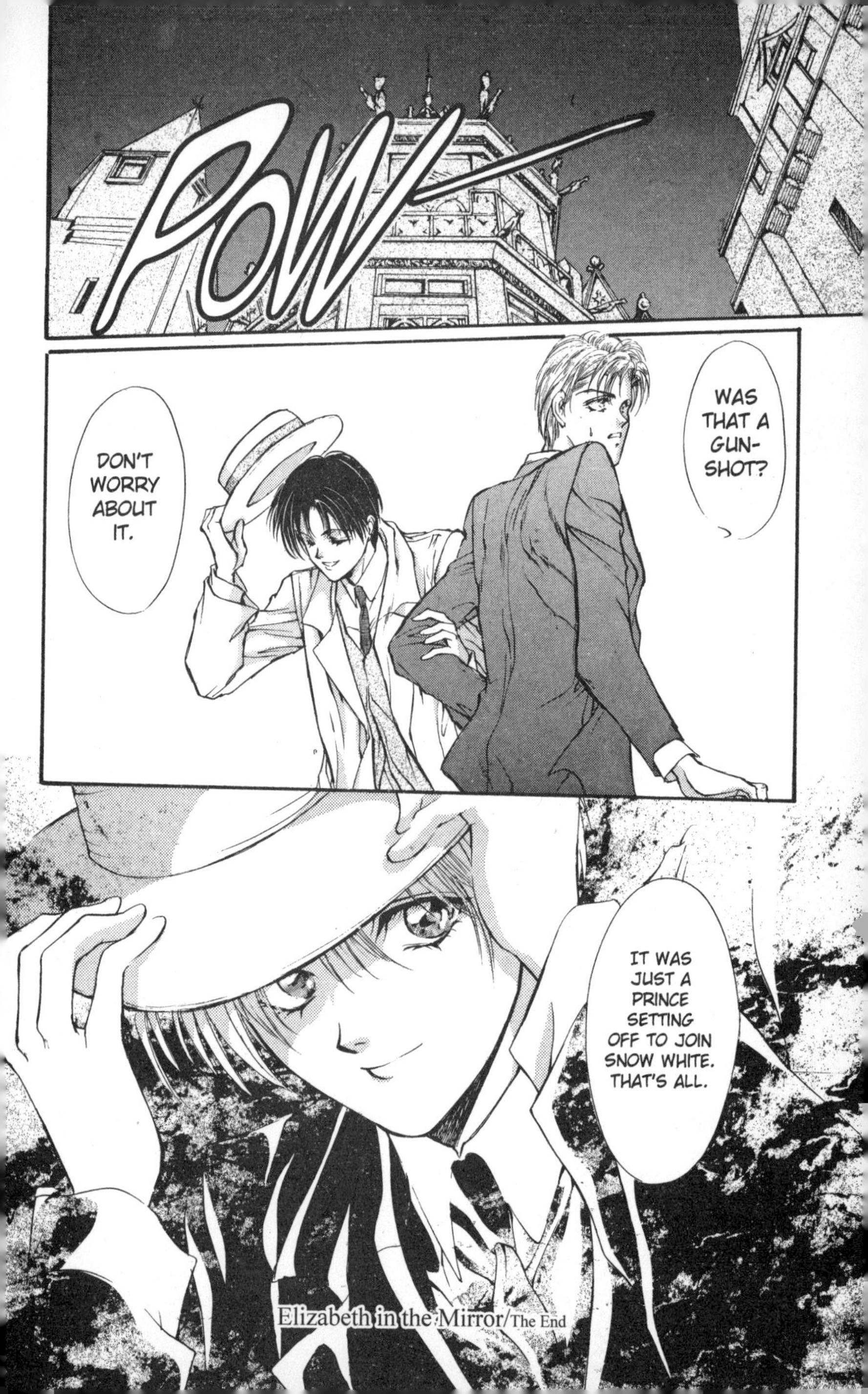
POW
WAS THAT A GUN-SHOT?
DON'T WORRY ABOUT IT.
IT WAS JUST A PRINCE SETTING OFF TO JOIN SNOW WHITE. THAT'S ALL.
Elizabeth in the Mirror/The End

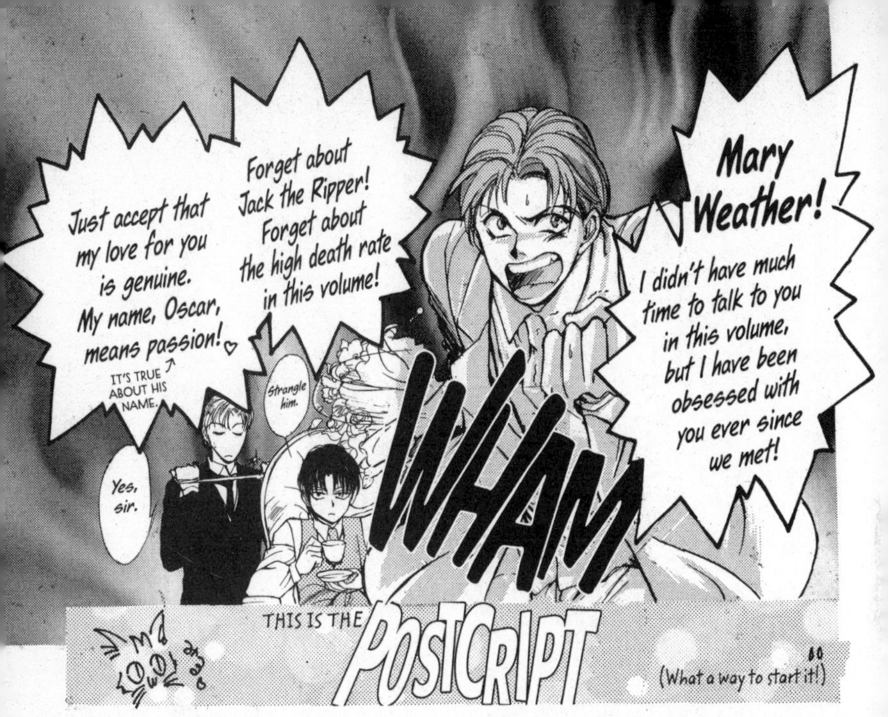
Mary Weather!
I didn't have much time to talk to you in this volume, but I have been obsessed with you ever since we met!
Forget about Jack the Ripper! Forget about the high death rate in this volume!
Just accept that my love for you is genuine. My name, Oscar, means passion! ♡
IT'S TRUE ABOUT HIS NAME.
Strangle him.
Yes, sir.
WHAM

THIS IS THE POSTCRIPT

(What a way to start it!)

Yes, Oscar is right. I killed so many characters in this volume. (Some characters narrowly escaped death only because I ran out of space.) Also, I wasn't sure if I should reveal Oscar's past or not, but I did it anyway. I know I have a penchant for depicting tragic love affairs. In any case, Oscar, 20, is highly likely to keep appearing at the Hargreaves as a cheerful but mysterious guy. Oh, by the way, some readers thought the Earl Cain series had ended because I have begun publishing another story. They are wrong. The Earl Cain series will continue. I'm not sure when exactly, but I would love to release a sequel to Earl Cain sometime in the future. I have many episodes in mind. For the time being, however, I'd appreciate it if you check out my "Angel Sanctuary (Tenshi Kinryouku)" since I have been putting a lot of effort into it. My thanks to those who sent me their fan publications! They're all very well done and filled with love for my work. I treasure all those magazines! ♡ (Some had interesting questionnaires. Each one has different information about my characters. Surprisingly, none of them were too outrageous. Or, perhaps, the really weird ones simply weren't sent to me.)

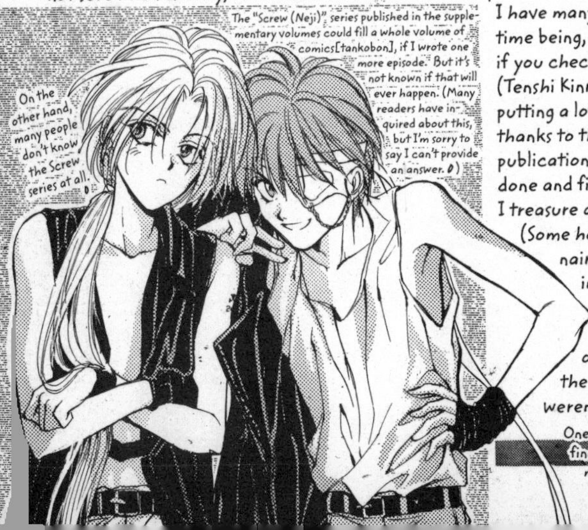
The "Screw (Neji)" series published in the supplementary volumes could fill a whole volume of comics[tankobon], if I wrote one more episode. But it's not known if that will ever happen. (Many readers have inquired about this, but I'm sorry to say I can't provide an answer.)
On the other hand, many people don't know the Screw series at all.

One last thing: Emeline's death was finally avenged when Meridiana's mother, who killed Emeline, died.

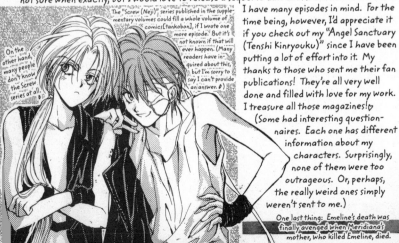

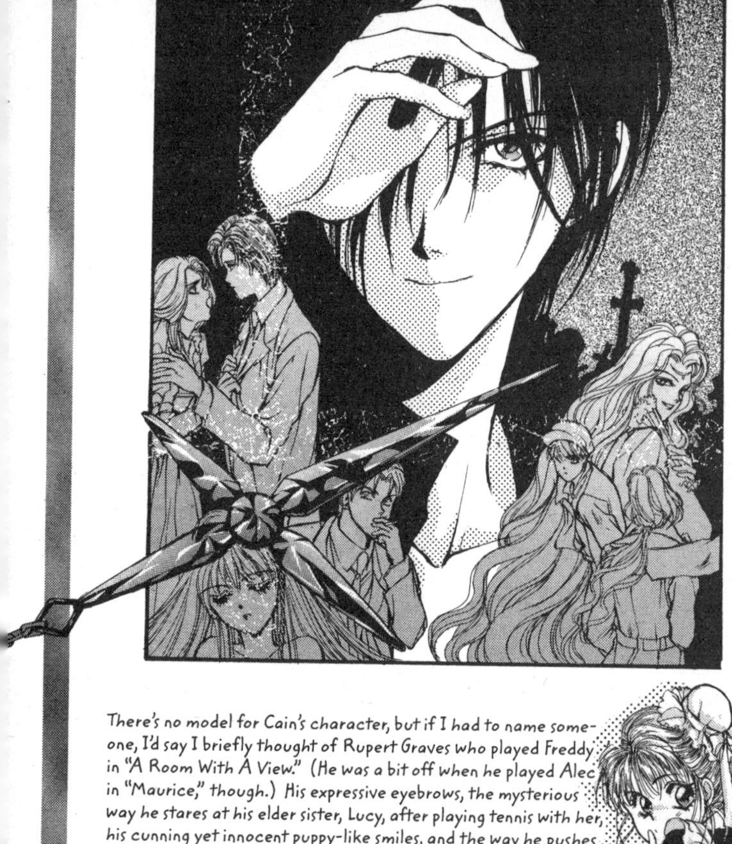

There's no model for Cain's character, but if I had to name someone, I'd say I briefly thought of Rupert Graves who played Freddy in "A Room With A View." (He was a bit off when he played Alec in "Maurice," though.) His expressive eyebrows, the mysterious way he stares at his elder sister, Lucy, after playing tennis with her, his cunning yet innocent puppy-like smiles, and the way he pushes his hair back with his fingers left a strong impression on me. ♡ I'm sure the director of that film adored Rupert because he was so lovingly filmed in so many long scenes. (His swimming scenes were especially drawn out.)

My readers often write me about Cain's voice, suggesting someone as a possible voice-over actor. Unfortunately, I don't know much about voiceover actors and I have no idea how Cain's voice might sound. (But I agree that Dr. Jizabel might sound like Shaa in Gundam.) Some readers sent me music tapes with songs based on the Earl Cain series. ♡ I enjoy them very much. Thank you! ♡ I am also thankful to those who sent me videotapes and presents. I hope to present the next episode of Earl Cain in the near future. Until then, please remember Cain and the other characters. See you again!

Please wait patiently until the key to the secret room... ...opens the door.

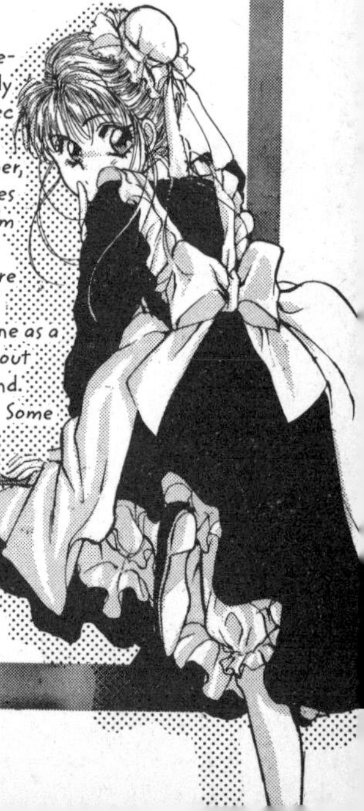

Postscript/The End

Creator: Kaori Yuki

Date of Birth: December 18

Blood Type: B

Major Works: *Angel Sanctuary* and *Godchild*

K aori Yuki was born in Tokyo and started drawing at a very early age. Following her debut work *Natsufuku no Erie* (Ellie in Summer Clothes) in the Japanese magazine *Bessatsu Hana to Yume* (1987), she wrote a compelling series of short stories: *Zankoku na Douwatachi* (Cruel Fairy Tales), *Neji* (Screw), and *Sareki Ōkoku* (Gravel Kingdom).

As proven by her best-selling series *Angel Sanctuary* and *Godchild*, her celebrated body of work has etched an indelible mark on the gothic comics genre. She likes mysteries and British films, and is a fan of the movie *Dead Poets Society* and the show *Twin Peaks*.

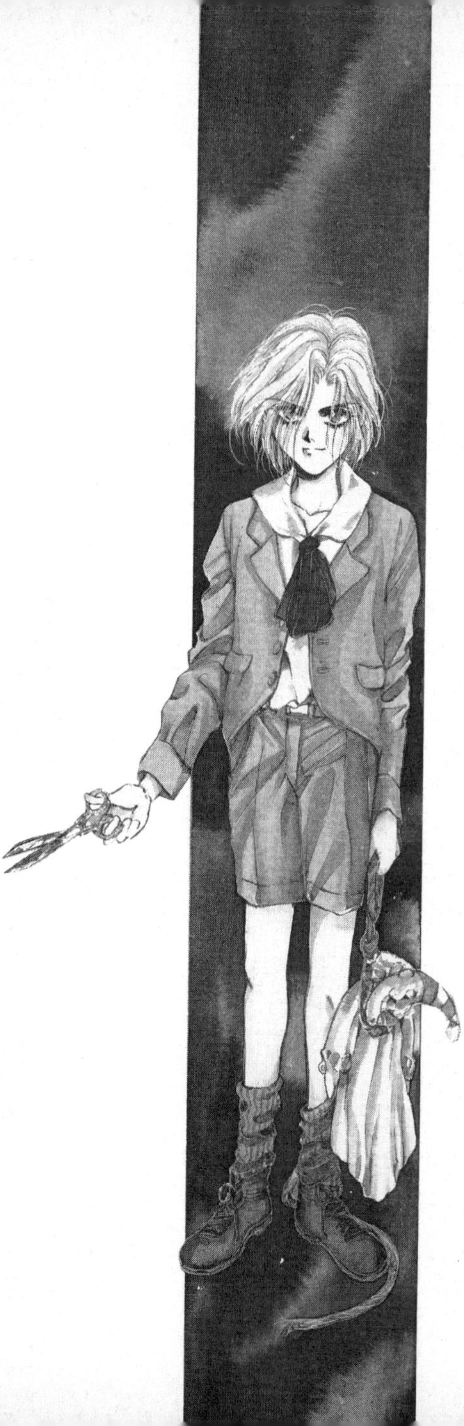

THE CAIN SAGA, vol. 4
The Seal of the Red Ram, part 2
The Shojo Beat Manga Edition

STORY & ART BY KAORI YUKI

Translation/Yuko Sawada
Touch-up Art & Lettering/James Gaubatz
Design/Izumi Evers
Editor/Joel Enos

Managing Editor/Megan Bates
Editorial Director/Elizabeth Kawasaki
Editor in Chief, Books/Alvin Lu
Editor in Chief, Magazines/Marc Weidenbaum
Sr. Director of Acquisitions/Rika Inouye
Sr. VP of Marketing/Liza Coppola
Exec. VP of Sales & Marketing/John Easum
Publisher/Hyoe Narita

Printed in Canada

Published by VIZ Media, LLC
P.O. Box 77010
San Francisco, CA 94107

Shojo Beat Manga Edition
10 9 8 7 6 5 4 3 2 1
First printing, June 2007

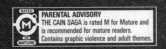

store.viz.com

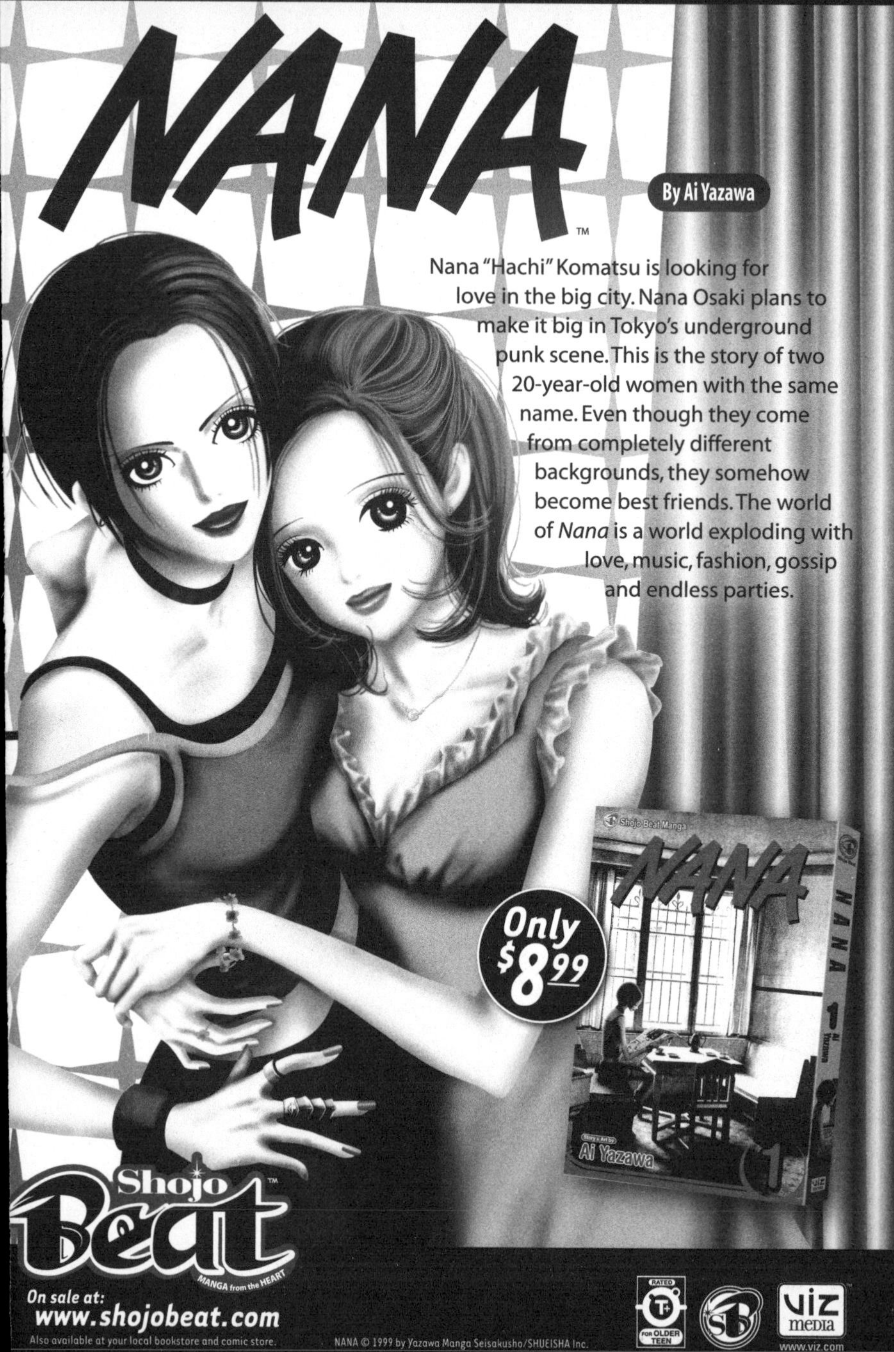
NANA™
By Ai Yazawa
Nana "Hachi" Komatsu is looking for love in the big city. Nana Osaki plans to make it big in Tokyo's underground punk scene. This is the story of two 20-year-old women with the same name. Even though they come from completely different backgrounds, they somehow become best friends. The world of *Nana* is a world exploding with love, music, fashion, gossip and endless parties.
Only $8.99
Shojo Beat Manga
NANA
Story & Art by
Ai Yazawa
Shojo Beat™
MANGA from the HEART
On sale at:
www.shojobeat.com
Also available at your local bookstore and comic store.
NANA © 1999 by Yazawa Manga Seisakusho/SHUEISHA Inc.
RATED T+ FOR OLDER TEEN
viz media
www.viz.com

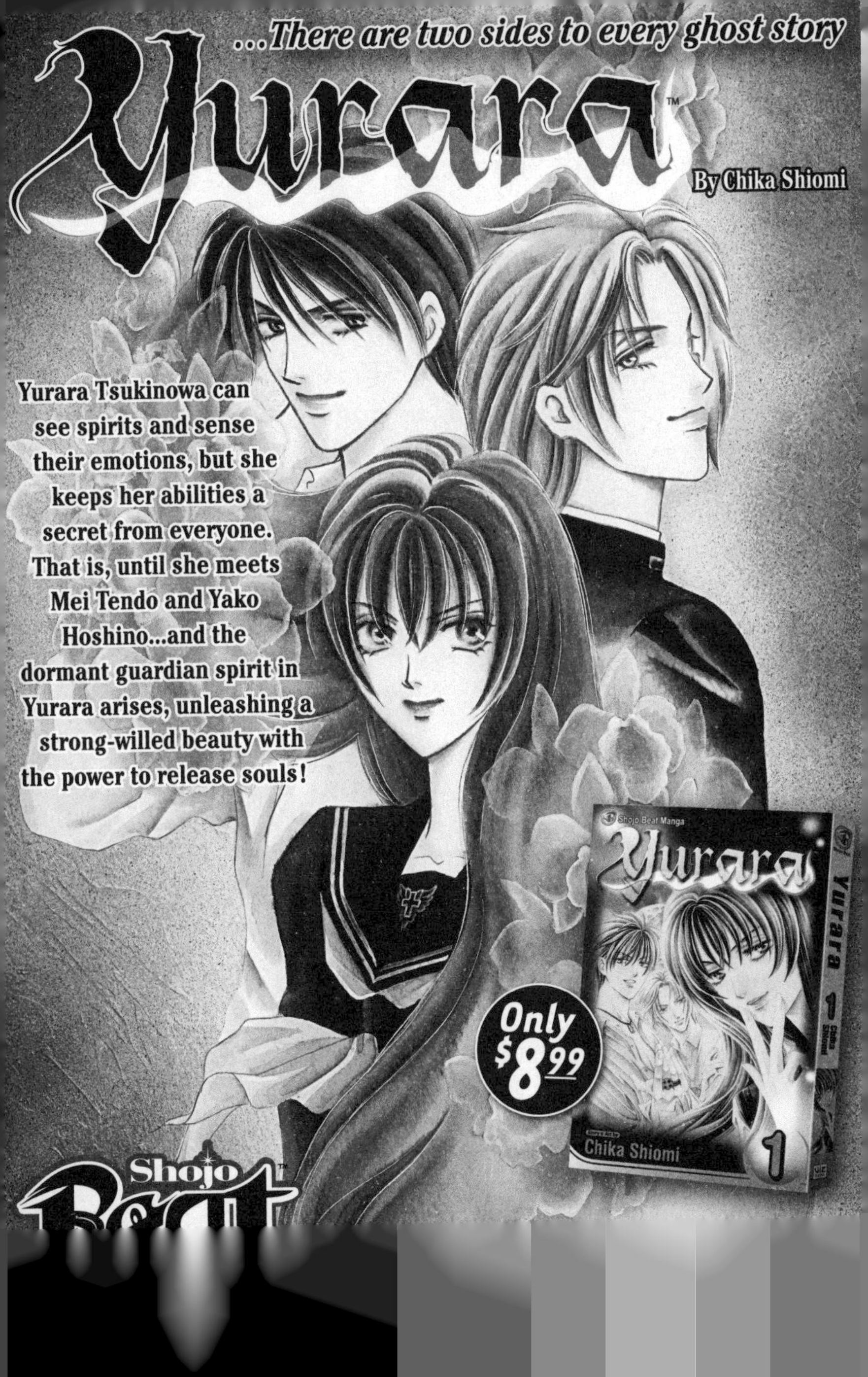

...There are two sides to every ghost story
Yurara™
By Chika Shiomi
Yurara Tsukinowa can see spirits and sense their emotions, but she keeps her abilities a secret from everyone. That is, until she meets Mei Tendo and Yako Hoshino...and the dormant guardian spirit in Yurara arises, unleashing a strong-willed beauty with the power to release souls!
Shojo Beat Manga
Yurara
Yurara 1
Chika Shiomi
1
Only $8.99
Shojo Beat™

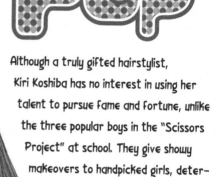

Tell us what you think about Shojo Beat Manga!

Our survey is now available online. Go to:

shojobeat.com/mangasurvey

Help us make our product offerings better!

THE REAL DRAMA BEGINS IN...